AF876234

The Global Financial Crisis and Housing

KDI SERIES IN ECONOMIC POLICY AND DEVELOPMENT

Series Editor: Korea Development Institute

KDI was established in 1971 as an independent, non-profit research institute. It supports high profile research in all fields of economics and related areas through conferences, seminars, workshops and monograph publication. The main objective of KDI is to foster interactions among academics, policy makers and business practitioners with a view to finding solutions to socio-economic problems in Korea and the wider world.

The KDI Series in Economic Policy and Development publishes state of the art research findings in all aspects of economics and related areas. This series will be essential reading for academics, policy makers and business practitioners.

The Global Financial Crisis and Housing

A New Policy Paradigm

Edited by

Susan Wachter

Professor, Real Estate and Finance, University of Pennsylvania, USA

Man Cho

Professor, Public Policy and Management, KDI School, Korea

Moon Joong Tcha

Senior Fellow, Center for International Development, Korea Development Institute, Korea

A JOINT PUBLICATION OF THE KOREA DEVELOPMENT INSTITUTE AND EDWARD ELGAR PUBLISHING LTD

Edward Elgar

Cheltenham, UK • Northampton, MA, USA

KDI

© Korea Development Institute 2014

All rights reserved. No part of this publication may be reproduced, stored in a retrieval system or transmitted in any form or by any means, electronic, mechanical or photocopying, recording, or otherwise without the prior permission of the publisher.

Published by
Edward Elgar Publishing Limited
The Lypiatts
15 Lansdown Road
Cheltenham
Glos GL50 2JA
UK

Edward Elgar Publishing, Inc.
William Pratt House
9 Dewey Court
Northampton
Massachusetts 01060
USA

A catalogue record for this book
is available from the British Library

Library of Congress Control Number: 2013949877

This book is available electronically in the ElgarOnline.com
Economics Subject Collection, E-ISBN 978 1 78347 288 8

FSC www.fsc.org MIX Paper from responsible sources FSC® C013056

ISBN 978 1 78347 287 1

Typeset by Servis Filmsetting Ltd, Stockport, Cheshire
Printed and bound in Great Britain by T.J. International Ltd, Padstow

Contents

Contributors

Chin-Oh Chang, Distinguished Professor, Department of Land Economics, National Chengchi University, Taiwan

Ming-Chi Chen, Professor, Department of Finance, National Sun Yat-sen University, Taiwan

Man Cho, Professor, Public Policy and Management, KDI School, South Korea

Giovanni Dell'Ariccia, Advisor, International Monetary Fund (IMF), USA

Hans-Joachim Dübel, Finpolconsult.de, Germany

Min Hwang, Professor, Finance Department, The George Washington University, USA

Matteo Iacoviello, Division of International Finance, Federal Reserve Board, USA

Deniz Igan, Economist, International Monetary Fund (IMF), USA

Kabsung Kim, Professor, Department of Urban Planning and Engineering, Yonsei University, South Korea

Kyung-Hwan Kim, Professor, School of Economics, Sogang University and President, Korea Research Institute For Human Settlements (KRIHS), South Korea

Young Il Kim, Fellow, Department of Macroeconomic and Financial Policy, Korea Development Institute (KDI), South Korea

Chang-Moo Lee, Professor, Urban Planning and Engineering, Hanyang University, South Korea

Young-Man Lee, Professor, Department of Real Estate, Hansung University, South Korea

Jae-young Son, Professor, Department of Real Estate Studies, Konkuk University, South Korea

Inho Song, Fellow, Department of Macroeconomic Policy, Korea Development Institute (KDI), South Korea

Seoung Hwan Suh, Professor, Department of Economics, Yonsei University, South Korea

Moon Joong Tcha, Senior Fellow, Center for International Development, Korea Development Institute (KDI), South Korea

Susan Wachter, Professor, Real Estate and Finance, University of Pennsylvania, USA

Tyler T. Yang, Integrated Financial Engineering, USA

Jessie Y. Zhang, Integrated Financial Engineering, USA

PART I

Introduction and summary

1. The global financial crisis and housing: a new policy paradigm

Susan Wachter, Man Cho and Moon Joong Tcha

1. MOTIVATION

It is at our peril that we ignore the role played by real estate markets in global financial stability. In the U.S., this should have been clear after such disasters as the commercial real estate crash in the late 1970s and the savings and loan crisis in the early 1990s, for with these downturns came the seizure of financial markets and the hurried response of policymakers to assuage the panic before it triggered a national meltdown. Elsewhere too, national economies were threatened with real estate booms and banking busts, including Norway, the UK, and most prominently Japan, in the early 1990s. But these abbreviated fears were quickly forgotten, exposing the Asian markets to an even more severe real estate crash in 1997. This shockwave really did go global, but only momentarily – and like the others, its passing was treated as cause for renewed faith in the system, rather than much-needed inquiry into the vulnerability that seems to continually plague the housing market. Thus did we invite rampant excess to run roughshod over this vulnerable market. Thus did the Great (global) Financial Crisis (GFC) strike exactly one decade later.[1]

This continuity is key, for it underscores an important fact: What we are dealing with here is a repeated cycle, an interdependent yet fragile link between real estate markets and the global economy. In East Asia, the GFC was in many ways a no-show, in part because of the macroprudential policies put in place following the 1997 crisis. There are important lessons to be mined from these repeated blows, and it is for this reason that we have assembled this book: To compare and contrast, and thereby to extract policy lessons from, the interaction of real estate dynamics with macro-stability as this has played out in various countries across the globe, especially on both sides of the Pacific.

Real estate is not like other assets. There is, for example, a much greater time lag in matching demand and supply in real estate than in, say, the extraction of natural resources or the manufacturing of other commodities. The quantity of housing desired when a construction project begins may differ significantly from the quantity needed by the time the structure has been built. Real estate supply, which depends on land supply and land use controls, is inelastic in the short run and sometimes in the long run. Short run lags in construction can cause price spikes and excess construction. This is how, during an epic over-building episode in the 1980s, the construction industry built over half of the commercial real estate that has been built in the history of the United States. Builders and investors learned the painful truth of Niels Bohr's observation that "Prediction is very difficult, especially about the future."

Another failure in the real estate market is the inability to short sell the underlying asset due to the illiquidity, complexity, and heterogeneity of land and structures. As a result, the market is lacking a critical feedback mechanism to signal overpricing. Instead, the price is set by optimists at the margin. In the U.S., even when credit default swaps were introduced as a proxy for "betting against" price appreciation, they traded in opaque, dealer-centered markets rife with information asymmetry. They served as a signal to no one. In the end, they proved to be worse than useless, as they were backed by insufficient capital, calling into question not only their solvency but also their long-term credibility as a solution for this market failure.

While it is extremely difficult to short the underlying real estate asset, it is possible to transact, buy and sell securities related to real estate, thus otentially completing the real estate market. But in the GFC, securitization, because it was opaque, created an information failure and acted as an accelerant to the problem of limited arbitrage. At the heart of this information failure is the debt vehicle that finances the asset. Unlike many other types of loans, mortgages are non-recourse, meaning the borrower can walk away with zero liability if they default. As a result, mortgages work like a put option in that the borrower can "put" the asset back to the lender. In pricing put options, it is essential to correctly assess the risk of default, which translates into the interest rate that the borrower pays to the lender. When the supply of risky products increases, the mortgage rate should diverge from the "riskless" Treasury rate, signaling a higher "risk premium" for mortgage lending. During credit bubbles, however, the opposite occurs: the mortgage rate tends to decline relative to Treasury bonds, underpricing risk. Cheap credit encourages excessive borrowing, enabling lenders to expand market share by lowering lending standards and attracting borrowers with higher likelihood of defaulting. This is precisely the dynamic that occurred in the U.S. during the housing bubble that preceded the GFC.[2]

This dynamic also played a critical role in the East Asian Financial Crisis. While the exchange rate crisis was apparent from the start, many observers failed to appreciate the real estate crash that preceded – and probably precipitated – it. In fact, most foreign exchange crises have followed closely on the heels of a sharp decline in domestic asset prices. This pattern is a clue to the transmission mechanism for the GFC: the financial system. Real estate crashes almost always lead to financial crises because banks (and shadow banking) intermediate real estate financing and therefore are vulnerable to credit crunches and asset price spirals. During the boom, they tend to increase leverage and reduce capital cushions. When the bubble pops, it takes only a small price decline to threaten their solvency and endanger lending apparatus on which the rest of the economy depends. If credit seizes up, the "real" economy grinds to a halt.[3]

After such crises, it is common to blame speculators. What is less commonly understood is the relation between speculation and the inherent failures in the real estate market. Speculation in itself is merely an amplifier. In an informed market, it is the engine of efficiency, arbitraging away mispricing. In an imperfect market such as real estate, information asymmetry profits insiders who are interested in short term fee generation at the expense of long term performance, generating excess volatility. Sophisticated securitizers push down the price of risk to sell riskier products, leaving homeowners and taxpayers to bear the burden of the bust when income growth can no longer keep up with and sustain accelerating asset appreciation.[4]

Magnifying these idiosyncrasies in the real estate market is its unmatched influence on the larger economy. No other consumer purchase comprises such a large percentage of household assets. No other fixed investment requires so much debt – and therefore so much risk of default. No other commodity has been so manipulated by financial institutions to build layers of trades in capital markets on its success or failure. No other financial asset is so complex and so heterogeneous, allowing originators and securitizers to underprice risk so egregiously because investors and insurers have so little information about the underlying asset. Seen through this lens, for the sake of the stability of the overall economy, real estate markets should be at the center of macroprudential policy efforts.

Global policymakers now face the challenge of addressing these market failures and moderating the volatile cycle they generate. Unfortunately, they lack the necessary information and tools to craft the proper solutions. Previous research, for example, did not combine financial and macroeconomic models to explain the dynamic of cyclical fluctuations, particularly with contagion effects and liquidity traps. The preceding literature is also lacking an empirical quantification of the effect of real estate price changes on different economies with different financial structures and regulatory frameworks.

This book begins to fill those gaps. By treating the housing market as part of a broader dynamic that periodically pushes the economy into extreme states, we can better understand how the housing bubble in the U.S. and the Great Recession that ensued had differing effects on various countries – and therefore what those countries can do to prevent a repeat of such a swift and significant negative shock. It is especially important that we study how these assets were (and are) financed and how this credit buildup motivates the system to abandon the boundaries of behavior that usually exist as a means of self-preservation. One of the great tragedies of modern capitalism is its tendency to sabotage the very operations that make it so productive. The authors in this volume are committed to re-wiring this feedback loop for sustainable growth.

Such an enterprise must begin with a candid acknowledgement of the sanctified role that housing plays in modern (and especially Western) society. In the United States, we refer to homeownership as "the American dream," but of course this aspiration is not unique to Americans. The United States has merely been one of the leaders in a global movement to promote homeownership through tax deductions, government-sponsored liquidity support, and when necessary, equity infusions to the financial intermediaries that finance the housing market. Whether these are the proper means to such an end, however, remains up for debate, and it is a debate that the chapters in this book do not shy away from. The challenge before us is not only to make housing safe for the global economy but also to make the global economy supportive of an affordable and yet efficient housing market for billions of households. It will not be easy in an environment where interest rates have nowhere to go but up and the "middle class" – traditionally the greatest source of housing demand – is shrinking in the Western world, but the proposals in this book outline several possible ways to revive – and restore faith in – this vision. Thus shall we create a new policy paradigm.

2. HOUSING AND MACROECONOMY: KEY LINKAGES

A large and contagious shock in housing price impacts the macroeconomy through various transmission channels, and can eventually pose a system-wide tail-risk event. This shock-wave generally follows a sequence of several steps: first, housing (or other real estate) prices deviate from their fundamental levels for a long and sustained time period, which we conventionally refer to as a housing bubble; second, the deviation is corrected through a multi-year downturn in housing market outcomes, in particular, in price, residential mortgage lending, and new construction; third, the downturn contracts macroeconomic activities through three main transmission channels of private consumption, investment, and the financial service sector; and finally, the contracted aggregate demand in the broad economy inflicts a secondary effect on the housing market through depressed household income and labor markets (Figure 1.1). Capturing all these inter-linked dynamics in one conceptually-sound and analytically-tractable model is close to impossible. For one thing, detecting a housing price bubble, whatever geographical aggregation is adopted, always takes the nature of a joint test for model specification and existence of the bubble. Furthermore, one also has to factor in various micro features of the housing sector, such as the interaction between the housing stock and the flow of new construction, submarket dynamics between owner-occupied vs. renter-occupied segments, and pro-cyclical home mortgage lending.[5] Hence, our approach in this volume is to examine the linkages, and relevant policy issues by each of four inter-related analytical topics in an international comparative perspective: (1) macroeconomic transmission channels of the housing cycle; (2) the role of the housing finance system; (3) construction financing as a cycle amplifier; and, (4) the rental housing market and public policy.

As to the macroeconomic transmission channels, the wealth effect is the subject of various recent studies. For example, Catte et al. (2004) report that the long-term (short-term) elasticity of private consumption in response to a change in housing prices is 0.06–0.15 (0.04–0.26) for OECD countries, and fairly similar ranges of elasticities are documented by Kim (2010) for Korea. Furthermore, the housing wealth effect is generally shown to be larger than the stock wealth effect (Case, Quigley, and Shiller 2005, 2011), and expansion of the home mortgage lending sector caused by financial liberalization tends to increase the elasticity (Aron and Muellbauer 2006; Lustig, Van Nieuwerberg and Verdelhan 2008). On the investment channel, Leamer (2006) empirically demonstrates that, in eight out of ten post-World War II recessions in the U.S., the housing investment is the most pronounced early indicator. With these and other prior studies as backdrop, the following research questions are examined in Chapters 2 to 4 of Part II:[6]

- What do we know about the housing price-consumption channel in different countries, and what role did the GFC and other major economic shocks (the Asian Financial Crisis, AFC, in particular) play in terms of the wealth and collateral effects in the U.S., Europe, and emerging market countries?

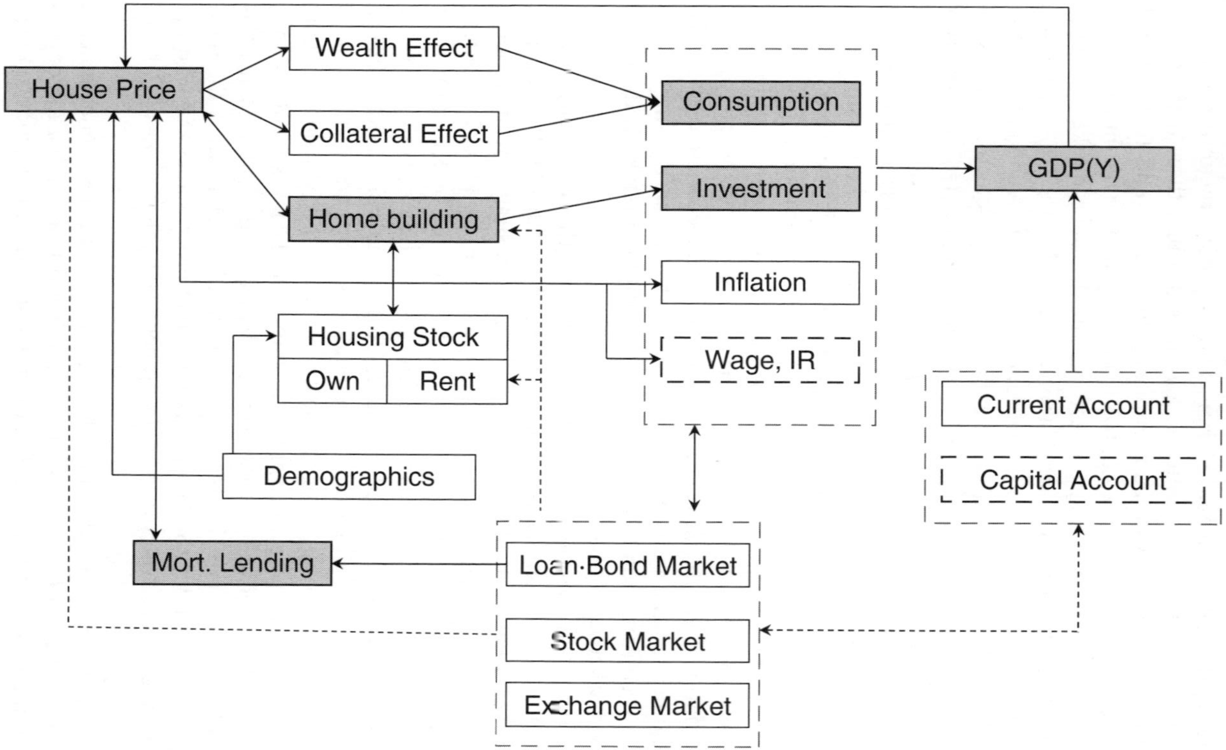

Figure 1.1 *Endogenous interactions of housing with the macroeconomy*

- Is Leamer's finding consistent in Korea and other emerging market countries? If not, what are the underlying reasons for that?
- Given what we already know, what policy implications can we extract with regard to micro- and macro-prudential regulations, and what are common and idiosyncratic factors to be considered in different countries?
- What are appropriate data and monitoring mechanisms to be used, such as an Early Warning System, to assess long-term and short-term anomalies in the housing market?

Pro-cyclical home mortgage lending and its interaction with speculative housing demand has been the subject of various recent studies. That is, during an upturn, mortgage lenders tend to relax the loan-to-value (LTV) ratio and other non-price terms in lending (e.g., debt-to-income (DTI) ratio, consumer credit ratings, repayment conditions, and so on), which, in turn, raises the proportion of natural (or optimistic) buyers in the real estate market and bids up the marginal price of housing assets. However, when facing bad news in the market-place (e.g., declining housing prices, rising mortgage delinquencies, and ramping-up mortgage interest rates), lenders constrain the lending conditions, which often leads to a credit crunch and deep downturn in the real estate market (Herring and Wachter 1999; Fostel and Geanakoplos 2008; Geanakoplos 2010). In the case of subprime mortgage lending in the U.S., a number of empirical studies document this cyclical lending pattern and its effect on the cycle amplification (Gorton 2009; Mian and Sufi 2009; Pavlov and Wachter 2011; Crowe et al. 2011). The following research questions are examined in Chapters 5 and 6 of Part II:

- What patterns of home mortgage lending do we see before and after the GFC in the U.S. and European countries? What similarities and dissimilarities do we see from them compared to prior lending cycles?
- What post-GFC policy responses do we observe from the advanced economies, and what policy implications do they offer to emerging market countries?
- What role do various institutional factors in mortgage lending, e.g., lending products, underwriting criteria, funding methods, play in terms of market stability and housing affordability?
- What do we know about designing a proper regulatory design (e.g., appropriate LTV and DTI levels, dynamic provision and other prudential controls), and what future research issues do we have to pursue further?

Construction and development (C&D) financing – in particular, its role in the real estate cycle – is the next topic. It has long been argued that the construction lag is an important source of the real estate cycle (Grenadier 1996; Wheaton 1999), and that an "unholy alliance" of developers with C&D lenders works as a volatility-enhancer (Litan 1992). That is, being influenced by a rising price trend, developers initiate more and more new projects during the upturn, which increases volume of newly-constructed unsold housing units and, hence, deepens the downturn. During the GFC, it is documented that such cyclical home building and the resulting excess supply were more severe in the U.S. than in European countries (Ellis 2008). With this backdrop, some of the key research questions posed in Chapters 7–9 of Part III are as follows:

- What cyclical patterns are observed in the C&D lending sector before and after the GFC in the U.S. and other advanced economies?
- In the viewpoint of emerging market countries, Korea and Taiwan in particular, what experience do they have in the C&D lending sector?
- What role do various institutional factors such as the presale of residential property play in raising real estate market volatility?
- What policy responses can we consider for counter-cyclical C&D lending, in terms of product design, underwriting, risk management, and funding?

Last but not least, Chapters 10 to 12 of Part IV discuss recent research findings as to the effectiveness of different policy regimes, including monetary policy, fiscal policy, and macro-prudential policy, to combat a real estate bubble.

3. SUMMARY OF FINDINGS

Housing and Mortgage Markets

As to the first channel, Matteo Iacoviello elaborates on the collateral effects of housing prices on borrowing, which allows credit-constrained households to increase their spending with appreciated collateral values, and vice versa. However, rising home values can force more savings by renters for their future acquisition, reducing their current consumption expenditure. Iacoviello demonstrates empirically that, as in other countries, the collateral effect dominates the forced saving effect in the U.S.: the elasticity of consumption to housing wealth is shown to be 0.14, which is larger than the elasticity of consumption to non-housing wealth (which is 0.06).

The reported elasticity is in line with the estimates documented for other countries. For example, the estimates are 0.06–0.15 in the long-term and 0.04–0.26 in the short-term for OECD countries, and similar ranges are reported for Korea as well.[7] Quoting his prior research,[8] he elaborates how wage rigidity in the housing sector plays a crucial role in explaining the large sensitivity of residential investment to changes in short-term interest rates.

Iacoviello also discusses the strength and weakness of the Dynamic, Stochastic, General Equilibrium (DSGE) models, the popularized measurement framework that explicitly deals with the endogenous nature of housing-macro linkages. He emphasizes that the next generation DSGE models should devote increasing attention to modeling important, but omitted, features of the housing market such as mortgage intermediation and the role of non-performing loans. In so doing, he stresses, modelers should improve, rather than extend, existing models: namely, improving means that an unappealing feature of the model should be removed, discarded, or abandoned as an uninteresting special case of a better model, whereas extending means in most cases just adding a layer over another, without questioning the existing framework. In that juncture, taking one country's model to another country would make the model outcome spurious.

As to the investment channel, Young Il Kim investigates the role of housing volume cycles in macroeconomic fluctuations in Korea, by following the analytical framework put forth by Leamer in his famous 2006 paper. His finding is that, as in the U.S., housing volume cycles in Korea exhibited a pronounced co-movement with GDP cycles before the 1997 Asian financial crisis (AFC), serving as an early warning indicator of the incoming recessions. However, after the AFC, housing volume cycles are shown to be neither co-moving with GDP cycles nor having the same predictability for the incoming recessions, while contributing to boosting the economy out of recessions after the crisis. He ascribes the post-AFC results to the opening up of the Korean economy, for both real sector and financial sector, after the crisis, but calls for further research as to why the role of housing volume cycles in the macroeconomy differs across countries and may change over time.

Due to difficulty in forecasting housing prices, Seoung Hwan Suh and Kabsung Kim advocate the use of an Early Warning System (EWS) for perceiving a contagious housing cycle, and demonstrate how an EWS developed in their prior research works in detecting future housing market crisis in Korea. Specifically, characteristics and determinants of Korean housing price movements have been empirically analyzed, by putting special attention on the post-GFC changes in home price dynamics in Korea. They also point out that the effect of the GFC upon the Korean housing market is smaller than that of the AFC, although an international synchronization of housing prices, which is rather pronounced, is observed after the GFC.

One of the sources of the amplified real estate cycles in the U.S. and Europe was the residential mortgage lending sector. It is well-documented by now that the pro-cyclical mortgage lending, (i.e., excessive liquidity supply during the boom followed by a credit crunch during the bust), was the source of increased volatility in the home price movements in those countries.[9] Even before the GFC, the long-term cointegrated relationships between private credit and housing prices for OECD countries were documented in the literature.[10] In the seminar, specifics of what happened before and after the GFC in different countries in terms of the correlation, and what policy measures were employed in consequence, are explored.

By comparing the U.S. and Korea, Man Cho reports a regime-shifting nature of causal relationships between housing price and mortgage credit cycles in the U.S.: that is, the mortgage credit and housing price cycles exhibit statistically significant co-movement in the most recent one (1997–2010) but not in the prior two cycles since the 1970s. His result implies that the incidence of the subprime mortgage debacle in the U.S. is unique to the market environments in the U.S. at that time, and has limited policy implications for other countries where mortgage markets and institutions are very different. He also documents the rapid expansion of the residential mortgage market in Korea, due to financial liberalization after the AFC in the late 1990s, and the effects of the mortgage lending restrictions employed in the country. In particular, he simulates the effects of the maximum loan-to-value (LTV) ratios adopted from the early 2000s based on a general equilibrium macroeconomic model, and reports that the control does contribute to stabilizing private consumption and housing price movement.

In comparing mortgage market outcomes in the U.S. and Europe, Hans-Joachim Dübel claims that the GFC was truly a Transatlantic crisis. Quite comparable to the U.S. where funding for mortgage lending surged via securitization during the boom, covered bond issuance activity in Europe also financed huge housing booms in some countries. For example, the Spanish case highlights the pre-GFC wholesale funding pattern: with the deposit base being depleted by high credit growth in the early 2000s, heavy issuance of both covered bonds and securitizations extended the boom until 2007. He estimates that Spain sold some 60% of covered bonds issued in the mid-2000s to foreign investors. Yet, the opposite observation is made for Hungary: here, liquidity for the housing finance boom was created via interbank and customer deposits in foreign currency, predominantly Swiss Franc, and foreign banks were willing to aggressively price cross-border funding. During the downturn after 2007, almost all European covered bond markets were temporarily de-facto nationalized via guarantee commitments or ECB intervention. For the European case, he also reports similar micro features of mortgage products and underwriting as observed in the U.S. before the GFC, including maturity extension, negative amortization, cyclical change in leverage ratio, increase in interest-only loans, appraisal bias, among others. He stresses that the central focus of regulatory reform should be to promote the shock absorption capacity of the system against a given liquidity shock, domestic or cross-border, and proposes two versions of the Volcker rule in his conclusion. He also claims that the housing price and credit booms were not as severe in those countries where rental housing markets are large and active, e.g., Germany, France, Netherlands, and Denmark in particular.

Construction and Development Financing

Another source of volatility is the construction financing sector. Long before the GFC, an "unholy alliance" between lenders and real estate developers during the upturn of the real estate market was quoted as a crucial factor in amplifying the real estate cycle, such as the commercial real estate boom-bust in the U.S. in the 1980s. More recently, the real estate project financing (PF) lending in Korea, which rapidly grew from the mid-2000s and served as the predominant source of liquidity for land development and construction, became a sore spot in the financial system of the country after the GFC. In the seminar, the ADC (acquisition, development and construction) lending sectors of three countries are compared, in terms of post-GFC outcomes: the U.S., Korea, and Taiwan.

For the U.S. case, Min Hwang investigates why the ADC loans show substantially worse performance compared to other bank loans after the GFC. After an extensive survey of the ADC sector in the U.S. and some relevant literature, he performs empirical analysis by using the Federal Reserve's Senior Loan Officer Opinion Survey data. Out of his analysis, he reports that the current magnitude of the deterioration in performance of ADC loans, with delinquency rate of 16% or higher, is reminiscent of their similar performance during the previous financial crisis, the S&L crisis in the 1980s. He claims that the poor performance is mainly due to weakened underwriting standards during the boom period and a collapse in the commercial real estate market. He also claims that these two factors are closely related to inherent risks of real estate development, market risk and idiosyncratic project risk, and the current performance is a combined outcome of these two risks. Given the fact that loan terms and covenants for ADC loans are very diverse and contain various idiosyncratic factors, making it highly costly and impractical to monitor all those terms, he proposes to create an index based on actual loan terms and include it as a part of macroprudential regulations. If it is carefully created so as to encompass diverse loan terms, as he argues, it can be aggregated by region and by industry to the national level and can be further used for dynamic provisioning or capital requirement for lenders.

For the Korean case, Jae-Young Son examines the boom-bust in the real estate PF lending in Korea, based on his recent survey of 300 or so market participants (including developers, lenders, and construction company employees). From his analysis, some specific recommendations to make the sector more efficient and stable include: employing a strong internal project evaluation and risk management procedure by lenders and construction companies; providing government assistance in developing standard evaluation tools and necessary data to participants of development projects; imposing minimum capital requirements for developers along with appropriate supervision of financial institutions; and, exploring new sources of construction financing such as REITs, land trusts, and third party insurance.

For the Taiwan case, Chin-Oh Chang and Ming-Chi Chen report that, over time, large quantities of resources and capital were attracted into the construction industry in Taiwan, and that the sector was developed under a conservative financial system. Project financing and informal measures, such as the pre-sale system, were utilized to acquire sufficient funds to complete development. When housing prices soared, the government rarely took action to control housing prices because most political parties and elected representatives had support from construction companies. After housing prices soared excessively, the government was forced to employ certain measures to suppress prices, resulting in bankruptcies of construction companies with overinvestment.

The most special characteristic for Taiwanese construction financing is the pre-sale system. Although the pre-sale system caused some problems in the early years, Taiwan has developed an escrow scheme and other regulations as preventive measures. There is also similar real estate project financing in Taiwan, as the main financing method for Taiwanese housing development. The authors claim that the PF lending sector has contributed significantly to that development without producing a housing shortage problem for the past forty years. Project financing appears to be more effective for construction development, despite its inherently higher credit risk, in Taiwan.

Policy Reform to Deal with Housing Boom-bust

Tyler T. Yang and Jessie Zhang present four important lessons of the GFC for the mortgage lending sector: (1) responsible underwriting standards focusing on borrowers' ability to sustain mortgage repayments through an uncertain future economy; (2) the ability to accurately measure mortgage credit risks embedded in various mortgage product types, structured securities, and derivatives; (3) integrated capital rules that can stabilize housing markets; and (4) a clear definition of the government's roles by balancing the goals of affordable housing and the soundness of the national financial system. They also summarize, and assess, various new policies and regulations introduced and implemented by the U.S. government in response to the GFC, in particular, the Qualified Residential Mortgage (QRM) and the alternative capital requirement rules.

Regarding effects of mortgage lending restrictions, Inho Song tests the economy-wide impact of housing loan-to-value (LTV) ratio control in Korea on housing prices and consumption. Using a Dynamic Stochastic General Equilibrium (DSGE) model, the chapter provides results of impulse-response analyses to gauge effects of different levels of LTV restriction on private consumption and housing price change. The results of DSGE simulations present an overview that LTV control does contribute to stabilizing private consumption and housing price movements. In particular, the responsiveness of both housing prices and constrained households' consumption are more sensitive to the higher LTV ratio. The lower LTV ratio, however, sacrifices housing affordability for housing market stability, another dimension that a design of macro-prudential regulation such as LTV control should consider.

A well-functioning private rental housing sector is appreciated more than ever in recent years, given the recognition that pushing home ownership too far in the U.S. was a contributor to the subprime mortgage crisis. Kyung-Hwan Kim, Chang-Moo Lee and Young-Man Lee investigate the role of private rental sector in promoting financial stability by conducting an international comparison of the pattern of the volatility of housing price and rents paying attention to the differences in institutions and policies. They also present the case of Chonsei, an asset-based rental system that has dominated the Korean rental sector for many years. The authors report that private rental housing sector tends to be responsive to the institutional arrangements and government policies on financing, taxation and regulations that affect the profitability of rental housing business. As to the specific policy implication to Korea, there is a strong case for increasing the supply of rental housing, given that the country is experiencing a decrease in demand for home ownership in recent years, partly driven by the negative prospects for capital gains. However, institutional investors are not likely to put their money in the Korean rental market because the private rental housing business does not generate a competitive return, and the asset-based Chonsei system fails to generate a steady cash flow. They discuss how to overcome this hurdle via real estate taxes and other policy initiatives.

As the keynote speaker and the panel session presenters, Giovanni Dell'Ariccia and Deniz Igan summarize their ongoing research on policy responses to deal with the housing boom-bust. They argue that, until the Global Financial Crisis, the widespread consensus was that it was better to wait for the bust and pick up the pieces than to attempt to prevent the boom. The crisis has challenged this view: that is, post-bust policy intervention was of limited effectiveness, and, thus, the costs associated with this particular bust were daunting. While early intervention may engender its own distortions, it may be best to undertake policy action on the basis of a judgment call (as with inflation) if there is a real risk that inaction could result in catastrophe.

The chapter explores various policy options by taking the characteristics of housing cycles and the linkages between housing and mortgage markets and business cycles into consideration. A more proactive policy stance can help reduce the risks associated with real estate booms, but will inevitably entail costs and distortions, and its effectiveness will be limited by loopholes and implementation problems. With this in mind, they reach the following conclusions: Policy efforts should focus on booms that are financed through credit and when leveraged institutions are directly involved, as the following busts tend to be more costly. They argue that monetary policy is too blunt and costly a tool to deal with the vulnerabilities associated with increased leverage, unless the boom occurs as a result of or at the same time as broader economic overheating; fiscal tools may be effective in principle, but, in practice, they would likely create distortions and are difficult to use in a counter-cyclical fashion; and, macroprudential measures seem to be the best option to achieve the objective of curbing real estate prices and leverage because they attack the problem at its source, adapt to specific circumstances in different locations at different times, and give the added benefit of increasing the resilience of the banking system. Nonetheless, the correct policy response to real estate booms is, like many other policymaking decisions, an art more than a science.

Looking ahead, as they argue, should a more proactive use of macroprudential tools become the norm, the question arises of who should be in control of these levers. In particular, the close interaction with monetary policy raises the question of whether the central bank should be charged with both price and financial stability. In that context, a trade-off emerges between policy credibility/accountability and the efficiencies stemming from coordination. When the former is paramount, separate agencies are preferable, while, when the latter prevails, a centralized solution would dominate.

NOTES

1. The very causes of the GFC are now fairly well-documented. Among others, they include: the speculative home buyers, many of whom leveraged 20 times (of their own equity) or higher; the originate-to-distribute mortgage lenders, who maximized business volume without proper due diligence on lending risks; the yield-curve playing investors, who enjoyed steep yield spreads thanks to the historically low interest rate environment in the early to mid 2000s; the oligopolistic rating agencies, who stamped top-quality ratings on the arcane and exotic mortgage securities; the fragmented banking supervisors, who were ill-equipped to assess embedded risks in mortgage and MBS products. See Ashcraft and Schuermann (2008), Levitin and Wachter (2010) among others.
2. This dynamic was first identified by Pavlov and Wachter (2004). It was later applied to the U.S. market by Pavlov and Wachter (2006).
3. Shortly after the East Asian Financial Crisis, this link was identified by Herring and Wachter (1999).
4. Malpezzi and Wachter (2005).
5. Nonetheless, our understanding of these linkages is being advanced with recent path-breaking studies, such as Iacoviello (2005) and Iacoviello and Neri (2010) among others.
6. This volume contains the papers presented at the international conference, entitled "A New Paradigm in Housing Policy After Global Financial Crisis," which was sponsored by Korea Development Institute (KDI) in December 2011. The conference was an inter-sectoral and inter-disciplinary forum in that we invited experts in different fields of economics, including macroeconomists, housing and real estate economists, as well as financial market specialists. The sessions were organized around the four themes: (1) macroeconomic linkages of housing, (2) residential mortgage lending, (3) construction and development financing, and (4) rental housing market and policy.
7. See Catte et al. (2004) for OECD countries and Young Il Kim (2010) for Korea.
8. Iacoviello and Neri (2010).
9. See Pavlov and Wachter (2011), Mian and Sufi (2009), Gorton (2008) among others.
10. Goodhart and Hofmann (2007).

REFERENCES

Aron, Janine, and John Muellbauer, 2006, "Estimates Of Household Sector Wealth For South Africa, 1970–2003," Review of Income and Wealth, International Association for Research in Income and Wealth, vol. 52(2), pages 285–307, 06.

Ashcraft, Adam, and Til Schuermann, 2008, "Understanding the Securitization of Subprime Mortgage Credit," Federal Reserve Bank of New York Staff Report 318.

Case, Karl E., John M. Quigley, and Robert J. Shiller, 2005, "Comparing Wealth Effects: the Stock Market versus the Housing Market," Advances in Microeconomics, 5(1), 2005: 1–32.

Case, Karl E., John M. Quigley, Robert J. Shiller, 2011, "Wealth Effects Revisited 1978–2009," NBER Working Paper No. 16848.

Catte, Pietro, N. Girouard, R. Price, and C. Andre, 2004, "Housing Markets, Wealth and the business Cycle," Economic Department Working Papers No. 394.

Crowe, Christopher, Giovanni Dell'Ariccia, Deniz Igan, and Pau Rabanal, 2011, "Policies for Macrofinancial Stability: Options to Deal with Real Estate Booms," IMF Staff Discussion Note SDN/11/02.

Ellis, L., 2008, "The Housing Meltdown: Why did it happen in the United States?," BIS Working Papers no.259.

Fostel, Ana, and John Geanakoplos, 2008, "Leverage Cycles and the Anxious Economy," American Economic Review 98:4, 1211–1244.

Geanakoplos, John, 2010, "Solving the Present Crisis and Managing the Leverage Cycle," FRBNY Economic Policy Review 16:1, 101–131.

Goodhart, Charles, and Boris Hofmann, 2007, House Prices and the Macroeconomy: Implications for Banking and Price Stability, Oxford: Oxford University Press.

Gorton, Gary, 2008, "The Panic of 2007," In Maintaining Stability in a Changing Financial System, Presented at the 2008 Jackson Hole Conference, Federal Reserve Bank of Kansas City.

Gorton, Gary, 2009, "Securitized Banking and Run on Repo," NBER Working Paper 15223.

Grenadier, S., 1996, "The Strategic Exercise of Options: Development Cascades and Overbuilding in Real Estate Markets," Journal of Finance, 51(5) 1220–1338.

Iacoviello, Matteo, (2005), "House Prices, Borrowing Constraints, and Monetary Policy in the Business Cycle," American Economic Review, 95, 739–764.

Iacoviello, Matteo, and Stefano Neri, 2010, "Housing Market Spillovers: Evidence from an Estimated DSGE Model," AEJ Macro, April.

Herring, Richard J., and Susan M. Wachter, 1999, "Real Estate Booms and Banking Busts: An International Perspective," Wharton School Center for Financial Institutions Working Paper 99–27, University of Pennsylvania.

Leamer, Edward E., 2006, "Homes and Jobs and Bonds," UCLA Anderson Forecast, June.

Kim, Young Il, "Asset Prices and Consumption Dynamics in Korea", Korea Development Institute, KDI Journal of Economic Policy Vol. 32, 2010.

Levitin, Adam, and Susan Wachter, 2010, "Explaining the Housing Bubble," Georgetown Law Journal, Vol. 100, No. 4, pp. 1177–1258.

Litan, Robert E., 1992, "Banks and real estate: regulating the unholy alliance," Conference Series; [Proceedings], Federal Reserve Bank of Boston, pages 187–229.

Lustig, Hanno, Stijn Van Nieuwerburgh and Adrien Verdelhan, 2008, "The Wealth-Consumption Ratio," NBER Working Papers 13896, National Bureau of Economic Research, Inc.

Malpezzi, Stephen, and Susan M. Wachter, (2005), "The Role of Speculation in Real Estate Cycles," *Journal of Real Estate Literature* 13(2).

Mian, Atif R., and Amir Sufi, 2009, "The Consequence of Mortgage Credit Expansion: Evidence from the U.S. Mortgage Default Crisis," Quarterly Journal of Economics 124:4, 1449–1496.

Pavlov, Andrey, and Susan M. Wachter, (2004), "Robbing the Bank: Non-recourse Lending and Asset Prices," *Journal of Real Estate Finance and Economics* 28(2–3): 147–160

Pavlov, Andrey, and Susan M. Wachter, (2006), "The Inevitability of Marketwide Underpricing of Mortgage Default Risk," *Real Estate Economics* 34(4): 479–496.

Pavlov, Andrey, and Susan Wachter, 2011, "Subprime Lending and Real Estate Prices," Real Estate Economics, Volume 39, Issue 1.

William C. Wheaton, 1999, "Real Estate "Cycles": Some Fundamentals," Real Estate Economics, Volume 27, Issue 2.

PART II

Housing and mortgage markets

2. Macroeconomics of housing

Matteo Iacoviello*

1. INTRODUCTION

The global recession of 2008 and 2009 has served as a dramatic reminder to economists, policymakers and ordinary citizens of the importance of developments in the housing market for the broader economy. While cause and effect are difficult to establish, it is obvious that what has happened in the housing sector has mattered for the health of the financial sector, of businesses and consumers alike. The assets of many financial institutions have suffered precipitous declines in value when concerns about the quality of their mortgage portfolios have become widespread. Small businesses that depended on the weakened financial sector (for their financing) or on the weakened housing sector have sharply contracted during the recession. Consumers whose houses have dropped in value have experienced massive declines in their net worth.

For macroeconomists, one of the unintended consequences of the recession has been that research on the housing market and the macroeconomy has finally become mainstream. And it has become mainstream, I believe, because economists have understood that the importance of housing for the broader economy reaches beyond the small share of housing in aggregate Gross Domestic Product (GDP). Only ten years ago "housing" was not part of mainstream economic research, and was confined to a subfield of economics named "real estate economics." Today, things have changed. Many popular undergraduate and graduate textbooks still devote little space to housing, but economists have finally begun to restore the imbalance between the practical and empirical relevance of housing for macroeconomics on the one hand, and the treatment that macroeconomic models devote to housing on the other.

In this chapter, I will offer some reflections on the role of housing within the class of macroeconomic models that have become known as dynamic, stochastic, general equilibrium (DSGE) models (see Woodford, 2009, and Fernández-Villaverde, 2009, for recent surveys). The cost of confining my attention to DSGE models is that the chapter will not cover the growing literature that links housing with search models, with models of urban economics, or with asset pricing models, unless this research has used elements of DSGE models. The benefit is that a large portion of modern macro research – especially in central banks and international financial institutions uses DSGE models for forecasting and for policy advice, as an alternative or as a complement to large scale non-structural macroeconomic models. My hope is that users of DSGE models who are not familiar with housing research will find this review useful.

2. FACTS ABOUT HOUSING AND THE MACROECONOMY

There are several interesting dimensions that matter as far as housing prices, housing investment and housing wealth are concerned. To illustrate their importance, I will focus on some interesting facts about housing. These facts are not new, and have been noted by other authors – including myself – before. I just want to arrange them together in order to organize my discussion.

1. Housing wealth (the market value of all residential capital stock, whether rented or owned) is an important component of national wealth. In fact, it accounts for almost half of household wealth in most developed economies. Figure 2.1 illustrates this case for the United States, using data (in billions of 2005$) from 1952 to 2008.[1]
2. Housing wealth is larger than GDP, and fluctuates considerably over time. Figure 2.2 plots the ratio of nominal housing wealth to nominal GDP for the United States.[2] The ratio of housing wealth to GDP has averaged around 1.5 between 1952 and 2008. However, it has moved dramatically throughout this period: it was equal to 1.27 at the beginning of the sample period; it was as low as 1.20 in 1962; and reached a value of 2.26 at the end of 2005, at the peak of the recent housing boom. (Figure 2.3 shows the correlation of housing wealth and aggregate consumption expenditures, explored further below.)
3. Movements in housing wealth are typically accompanied by large movements in housing investment in the same direction.[3] These movements in housing investment, in turn, substantially affect aggregate GDP and employment, even if the share of housing investment in GDP is relatively small.[4] For instance, since its 2005 peak, the share of housing investment in GDP fell by half, from about 6 percent to 3 percent in about three years (see Figure 2.4): simple back-of-the-envelope economics suggests that this reduction has subtracted several percentage points from GDP growth throughout the same period.

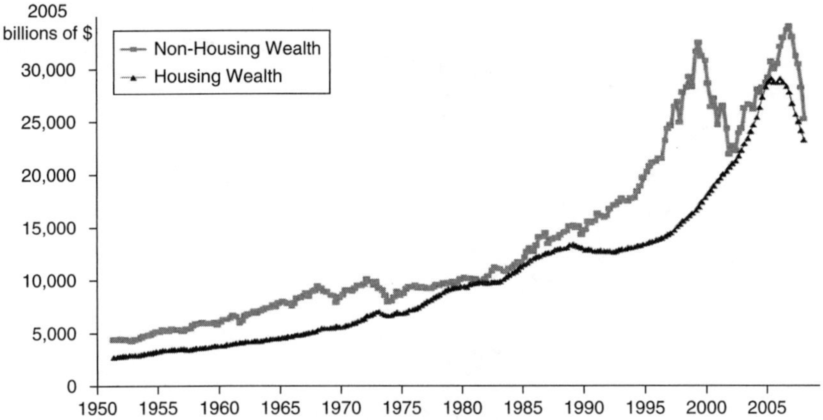

Note: Both variables have been deflated with the deflator for Personal Consumption Expenditures.

Figure 2.1 Housing wealth and non-housing wealth in the United States

Note: Both numerator and denominator are expressed in dollar terms.

Figure 2.2 Ratio of housing wealth to GDP

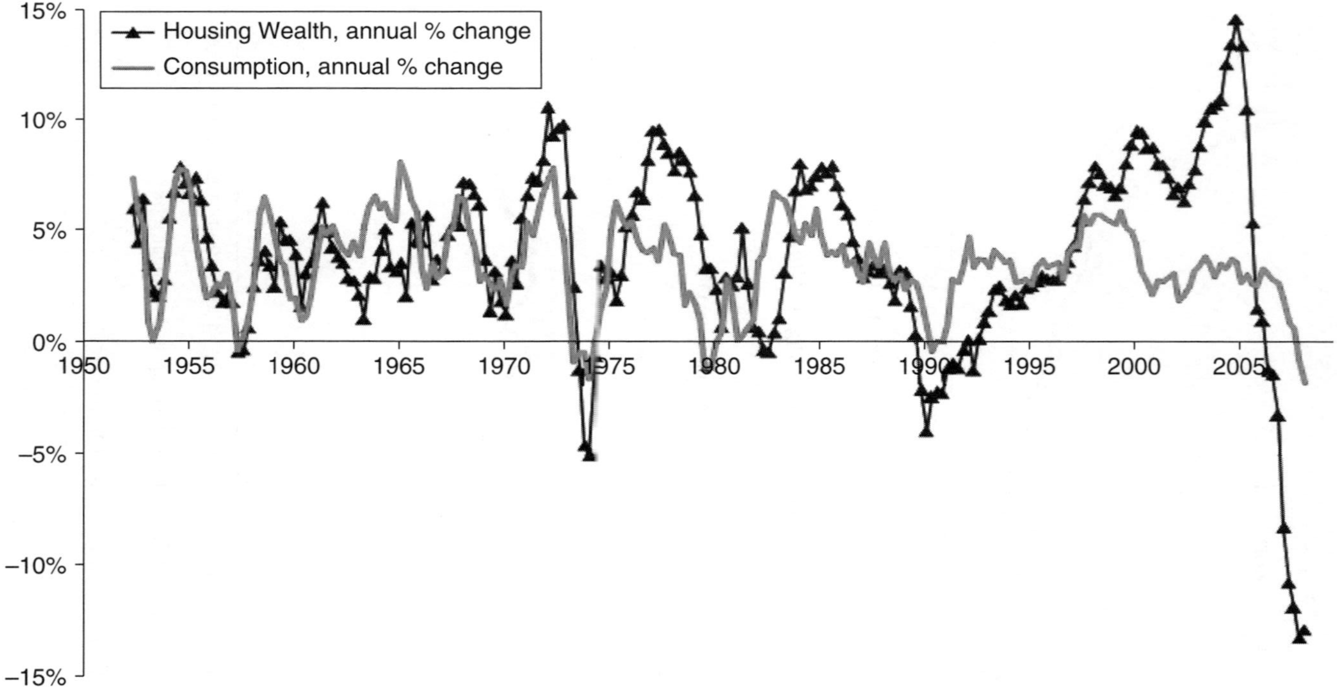

Note: Both variables are expressed in year-on-year growth rates and have been deflated with the deflator for Personal Consumption Expenditures.

Figure 2.3 Changes in housing wealth and changes in consumption expenditures

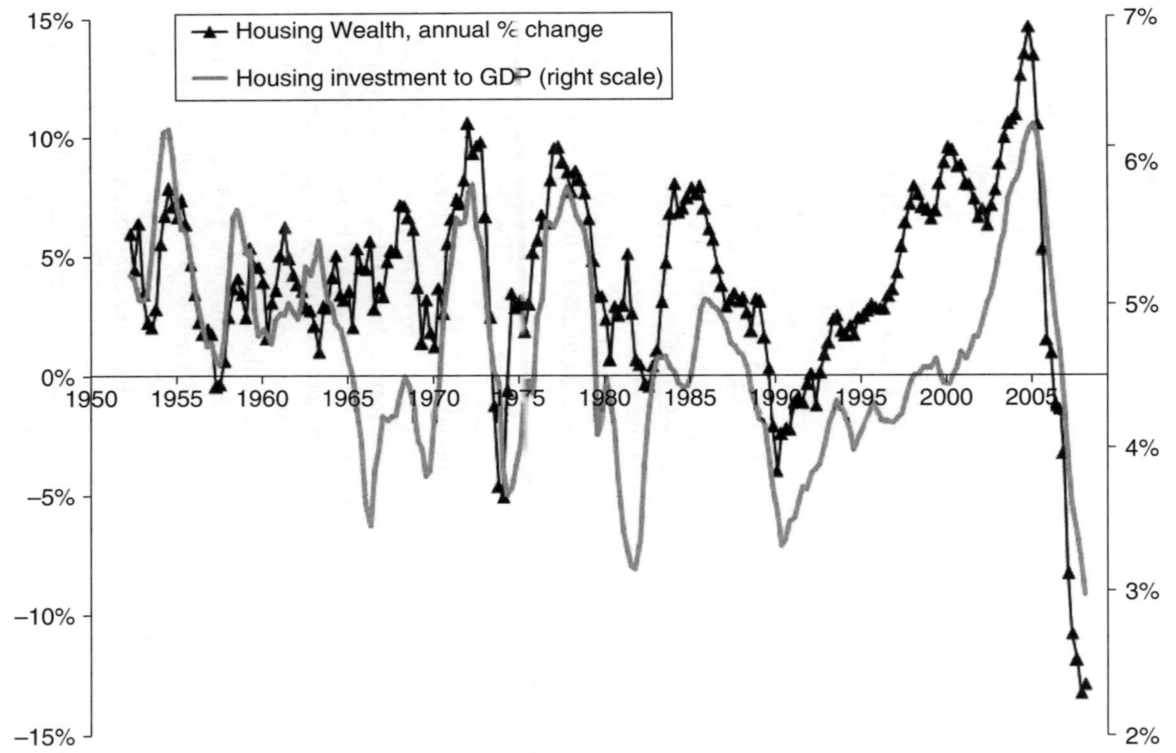

Note: Housing wealth has been deflated with the deflator for Personal Consumption Expenditures and is expressed in year-on-year growth rate. The Housing Investment to GDP ratio is the ratio of the two variables, both expressed in dollar terms.

Figure 2.4 Changes in housing wealth and ratio of housing investment to GDP

4. Movements in the price of housing are only loosely connected to movements in other prices.[5] Figure 2.5 plots consumer price inflation alongside two measures of house price inflation, the Census Price Index of new homes sold and the Freddie Mac Conventional Mortgage House Price Index.[6] The contemporaneous correlation between quarter-on-quarter changes in consumer prices and house prices is in the 0.3–0.4 range, depending on the time period and the house price measure used. If anything, housing price inflation leads consumer price inflation by approximately two to three quarters, and this tendency is more pronounced in the last decades. In addition, house price inflation is more volatile than consumer price inflation: for instance, the standard deviation of quarter-on-quarter house price inflation (using the Freddie Mac Conventional Mortgage House Price index) from 1970 to 2008 is 1.19%. The corresponding number for consumer price inflation is 0.67%. This result also holds if one uses less noisy measures (such as year-on-year growth rates) of inflation.
5. Housing (Residential Fixed) investment leads nonhousing (Nonresidential Fixed) investment, and is more volatile. This pattern can be seen in Figure 2.6.[7] Peaks and troughs in housing investment generally precede peaks and troughs in business investment.
6. In U.S. data over the last 45 years, inflation-adjusted house prices display an upward trend, even after controlling for the boom and bust in prices of the last decade. Figure 2.7 illustrates this pattern. See Davis and Heathcote (2005) and Iacoviello and Neri (2010) for additional discussion on these issues.
7. If one looks at the U.S. National Income and Product Accounts (NIPA), the direct contribution of housing to GDP is rather small, and boils down to two components: rents and housing investment. Rents are the largest of the two, and include actual rents paid by tenants, as well as the imputed value of housing services received by homeowners who live in their houses: rents account for approximately one tenth of total GDP; and have a slight upward trend in the last fifty years, having risen somewhat steadily from 10 to 13 percent. Housing investment (the official name is residential fixed investment) includes the value of additions and renovations to the existing housing stock, as well as the value of new residential homes that are put in place: this component accounts in 2011 for slightly more than 2 percent of total GDP; has a slight downward trend in the last fifty years, having fallen from a share of 5 percent in the 1960s; and is very volatile: to give an idea, it rose to 6 percent of total GDP at the peak of the housing boom of the early 2000s, before falling sharply beginning in 2006 (see Figure 2.4 for housing investment; rents are just too boring to deserve a plot of their own).[8]

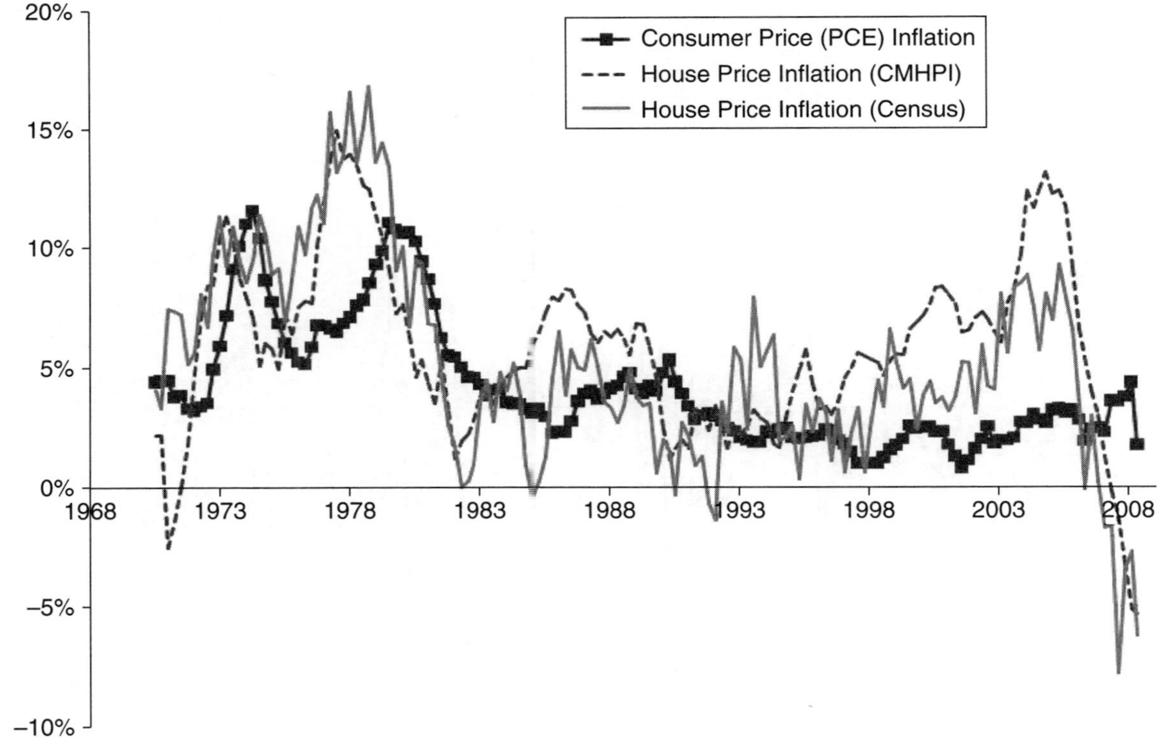

Note: All variables are expressed in year-on-year growth rates.

Figure 2.5 House price inflation and consumer price inflation

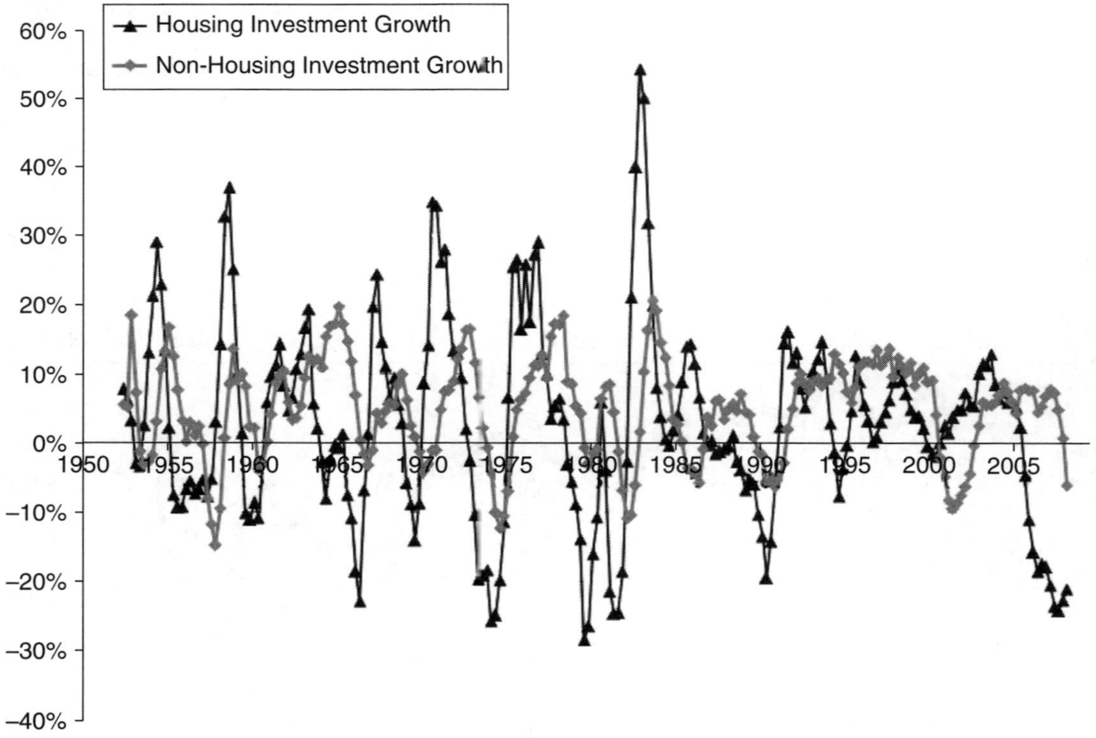

Note: Both variables are chain-weighted and expressed in year-on-year growth rates.

Figure 2.6 Housing investment and nonhousing investment

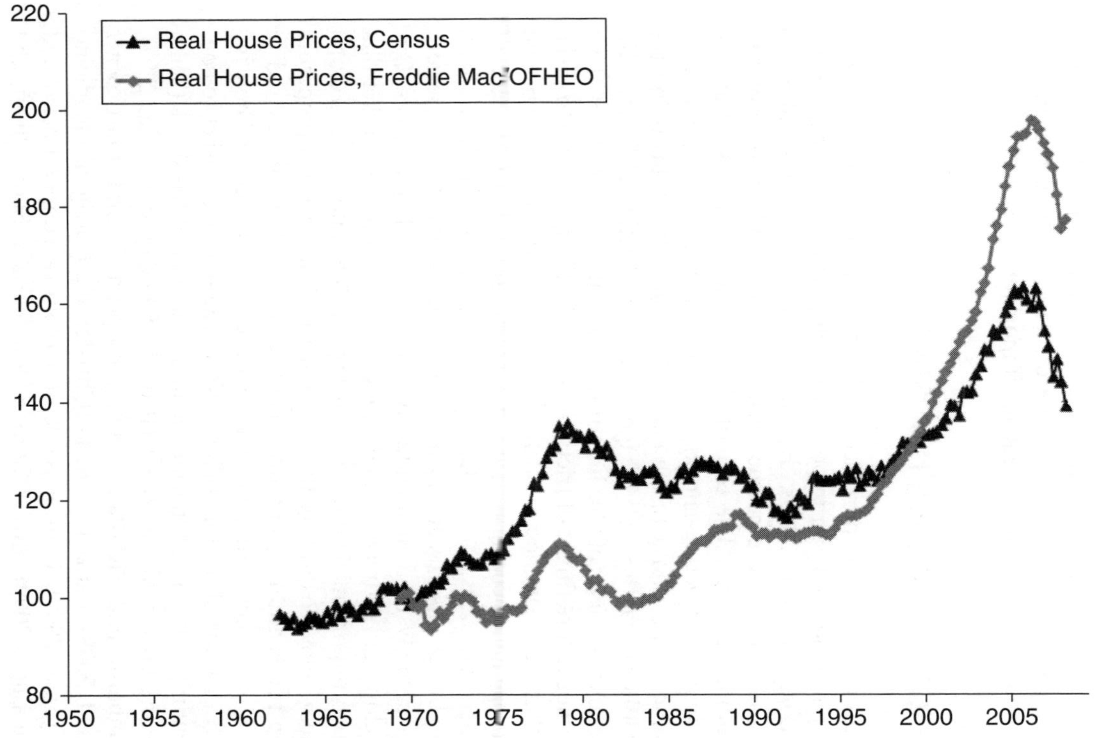

Note: Both indices have been normalized to 100 in 1970Q1. Both series have been deflated with the deflator for Personal Consumption Expenditures.

Figure 2.7 Real house price indices

These facts should be considered as an important yardstick to measure the success of macro-economic models of housing. My experience with referees, discussants and colleagues tells me that, depending on tastes (as well as intellectual capital previously spent on each particular question), everyone has his own ranking of these facts. I do not want to take a stance here, and might have omitted other interesting facts about housing that some economists might regard as equally important.[9]

3. A DSGE MODEL OF HOUSING

The recognition of the importance of housing for the macroeconomy has taken place alongside an important development in macroeconomic research. Since the early 2000s, dynamic stochastic general equilibrium (DSGE) models have become the cornerstone of modern, quantitative macroeconomic research. The core of these models, as the word attests, features a dynamic structure, shocks, and an attempt to be consistent with equilibrium concepts and with the national accounts.[10] At this point, the usual rant follows that these models ignore financial frictions, but, as a contributor to and as a user of this literature, I can attest that many of these models do not ignore financial frictions, so I will skip this rant. However, it is true that many of these models ignore the importance of debt and housing altogether, focusing mostly on financial frictions on the side of firms, rather than consumers. The paper by Iacoviello and Neri (2010) attempts to bridge this gap, adding a rich housing sector to this framework that is increasingly used in quantitative monetary policy analysis. Our paper develops and estimates a DSGE model of the housing market that captures two important features of housing: on the supply side, sectoral heterogeneity allows capturing the different trend and cyclical properties of housing prices and housing investment relative to other prices and to other forms of demand; on the demand side, collateral effects of housing prices on borrowing allow for spillovers from the housing market to consumer spending. Versions of this model have been used at Riksbank (Sellin and Walentin, 2010), Norges Bank (Brubak, Elekdag and Maih, 2007), ECB (Lombardo and McAdam, 2008), European Commission (Roeger and in't Veld, 2009), Bank of Canada (Christensen, Corrigan, Mendicino and Nishiyama, 2009), Central Bank of Colombia (López Enciso and Salamanca Lugo, 2009), IMF (Kannan, Rabanal and Scott, 2009), and elsewhere.

In this section, I will briefly review the main elements of the Iacoviello and Neri model.

Let me start with the production side of the economy. Iacoviello and

Neri assume that the economy is best approximated by multiple sectors with different rates of technological progress. The non-housing sector produces consumption, business investment, intermediate goods (using capital and labor). The housing sector produces new homes, which add to the existing stock, using capital, labor, land, and intermediate goods. Following the lead of most of the DSGE literature, Iacoviello and Neri allow for nominal wage rigidity in both the non-housing and housing sector and allow for price rigidity in the non-housing sector. The multi-sector structure is meant to capture two important observations about the housing market: first, there is a long-run upward trend in the relative price of housing in post-World War II U.S. data, which is – at least in part – due to heterogeneous trends in technological progress between housing and other sectors of the economy. Second, the production of housing is land intensive: hence, the assumption that the same production mix is used to produce houses and other goods is too restrictive. It is important to bear in mind that the two sector structure nests the traditional one-sector business cycle model as a special case. But it is necessary to have this structure if one wants to model prices and quantities in the housing market with some basic amount of realism.

On the demand side, Iacoviello and Neri split households into two types: patient (lenders) and impatient (borrowers). Patient households work, consume and accumulate housing: they own the productive capital of the economy, and supply funds to firms on the one hand, and to impatient households on the other. Impatient households work, consume and accumulate housing: because of their high impatience, they accumulate only the required net worth to finance the down payment on their home and are up against their housing collateral constraint in equilibrium. Along the equilibrium path, in turn, fluctuations in housing values affect borrowing and spending capacity of constrained households. Again, the split nests the representative agent model as a special case, to the extent that the wage share of impatient households becomes arbitrarily small.

Iacoviello and Neri use U.S. time series to estimate the model's structural parameters and to ask a series of questions concerning the macroeconomic importance of housing market spillovers.

Their main findings are:

- The slow rate of technological progress in housing construction explains the upward trend in real housing prices of the last decades. Part of the trend growth reflects supply constraints from land, but their contribution is small (10% of the total trend increase in house prices). The remainder reflects different rates of technological progress.

- The wage share of credit constrained households is estimated at around 20 percent. The credit constrained households are those who suffer (benefit) the most from drops (increases) in housing values. At the aggregate level, this fraction is large enough to amplify effects on consumption from fluctuations in housing values (especially for high values of the loan-to-value ratio). The presence of credit constrained households also reinforces the correlation between movements in consumption and movements in housing wealth.[11]
- Wage rigidity in the housing sector is crucial to explain important features of the data, in particular the large sensitivity of residential investment to changes in short-term interest rates: with flexible house prices, wage rigidity is important in making housing investment very sensitive to monetary shocks, something that is apparent in the data.
- The Iacoviello and Neri model can be used to assess sources of fluctuations in housing prices and quantities, can be used to quantify macroeconomic consequences of housing market shocks, and can be used to think about optimal responses to asset prices. In what follows, however, I will mainly indicate some directions in which I think and hope this setup can be extended to address topical questions in macroeconomics.

4. HOUSING AND CONSUMPTION

Housing wealth and aggregate consumption expenditures tend to move together in post-World War II U.S. history. Over the 1952–2008 period, their contemporaneous correlation is 0.47 (using year-on-year real growth rates). Figure 2.3 illustrates the joint co-movement between the two variables. This correlation is larger than the correlation between consumption and the residual components of household wealth: for instance, the contemporaneous correlation between changes in inflation-adjusted financial wealth and changes in consumption equals 0.38. It is this observation that had led many to study the so-called housing wealth effect: see Iacoviello and Neri (2010) and Iacoviello (2012) for further discussion of this topic and for additional references. Iacoviello (2012) summarizes the key findings of various empirical research that connects movements in housing prices with movements in aggregate consumption expenditures. Consider the simple linear regression on quarterly United States data for the period 1952.I–2008.IV of:

$$\Delta(\log C) = a + \text{ß}HW\, \Delta\log(HW-1) + \text{ß}N\, W\, \Delta\log(NW-1)$$

where C, HW and NW measure respectively consumption, housing wealth and non-housing wealth, and Δ is the first difference operator.

Such regression yields the following coefficients (standard errors are reported below):

$$\Delta (\log C) = \underset{0.0006}{0.007} + \underset{0.035}{0.136}\Delta (\log HW-1) + \underset{0.013}{0.056.6} (\log N\ W-1).$$

More sophisticated regressions yield similar results. This simple regression has the virtue of being simple, easy to estimate, replicable and straightforward to interpret. According to this regression, the elasticity of consumption to housing wealth is 0.14, after controlling for movements in non-housing wealth (the elasticity of consumption to non-housing wealth is lower, at 0.06). These estimates are more often converted into dollar-to-dollar estimates using the fact that, in the sample in question, the average ratio of housing wealth to annual consumption is about 2.3, and the average ratio of non-housing wealth to annual consumption is about 2.75. A one dollar increase in housing wealth then generates an increase in annualized consumption of about 6 cents, and one dollar increase in non-housing wealth generates an increase in consumption of about 2 cents.

5. THE ROLE OF FINANCIAL INTERMEDIATION

The Iacoviello and Neri model is silent about the role of financial intermediation. In the model, financial intermediation occurs without frictions, since patient households can costlessly transform savings into loans using a constant returns to scale technology. This assumption, which is implicit in the neoclassical growth model, is equivalent to treating the financial sector as a veil. When thinking about the 2008 financial crisis, however, it is hard not to notice that one important effect of fluctuations in housing prices is linked to the potential effect of house price movements on the balance sheets of financial intermediaries. In the Iacoviello and Neri model, it is only the borrowers who are hurt from declines in housing values: the model's implicit assumption, in fact, is that borrowers will always honor their debts. As a consequence, lenders are virtually insulated from movements in housing wealth. Consider, instead, a financial crisis episode: reductions in house prices may lead to smaller repayments on part of the borrowers (some borrowers walk away from their obligations when the collateral is worth less than the face value of debt). The smaller repayments, in turn, may lead to reductions in the net worth of financial intermediaries.

If financial intermediaries are able to absorb these losses raising capital elsewhere, the lack of repayment should be equivalent to a redistributive shock that should not generate large aggregate effects. Suppose, instead, that financial intermediaries themselves face credit constraints. In other words, assume that patient households lend resources to bankers, and that bankers lend resources to impatient households. If bankers face credit constraints (for instance, they need to satisfy some minimum capital requirement), a negative repayment shock can cause a loss for the lenders which, in turn, may cause an aggregate credit crunch.

In ongoing work (Iacoviello, 2011), I develop a model along the lines developed above in order to study the role of banks in the transmission of financial shocks. This work complements the excellent work of many others who have developed models of banking and credit frictions in a general equilibrium context. A non-exhaustive list includes Gertler and Karadi (2009), Gerali, Neri, Sessa and Signoretti (2009), Angeloni and Faia (2009), Gertler and Kiyotaki (2009), Meh and Moran (2004), and Dib (2009).

The main finding of my paper can be summarized as follows: a realistically calibrated financial shock can induce a cumulated GDP loss of nearly 8 percent after 3 years, which would correspond to the 2008–10 period for which we have available data to compare with the model. The data counterpart, depending on the method that one uses to detrend GDP, ranges from 11 percent (for HP-filter) to 14 percent (using the CBO estimates of potential output) to 18 percent (detrending GDP using a quadratic trend).[12] Hence the model can account for values between 40 and 75 percent of the entire decline in output during the Great Recession. A somewhat larger labor supply elasticity, higher intensity of financial frictions, and smaller capital adjustment costs could explain a larger fraction of the decline in output in the data. In this sense, to the extent that one believes that the losses to the banking sector were caused by the decline in house prices, house price movements are one of the main drivers of the last recession.

6. HOW TO STABILIZE HOUSING MARKETS

In earlier work (Iacoviello, 2005), I have found that monetary policy shocks affect house prices more than consumer prices: this result would suggest that, at least in principle, monetary authorities have the tools to mitigate fluctuations in housing prices. However, given the large fluctuations in house prices that are observed in the data, it is not clear whether interest rate policies alone can successfully stabilize house prices, or, provided that they can do so, that they can stabilize house prices without causing excessive volatility in other macroeconomic variables.

The above observation leads to an obvious question: are there policy instruments that can be quantitatively successful in stabilizing house prices? Can tax credits (such as, for instance, the Worker, Homeownership, and Business Assistance Act of 2009) significantly affect housing demand and prices? Do "macroprudential" supervisory tools – such as those used by the Hong Kong Monetary Authority imposing caps on maximum loan-to-value ratios – work? Digging more into these issues – using DSGE models – seems to me a sensible way to address these questions.

One proposal that I have found quite intriguing involves direct purchases of housing assets by the government in times when the housing market is depressed. One such example comes from South Korea. In 2008, the South Korean government promised to spend US$4 billion to save the construction industry, by promising to buy unsold homes and land from domestic builders who want to pay off debt. In a similar vein, recent proposals to create a government-controlled bad bank (The Project Financing Stabilization Bank (PFSB)), which takes off bad loans (owed by builders and property developers) from banks' balance sheets, could also restore the more efficient functioning of the financial system.

To a large extent, many of the proposals and policy initiatives that have been undertaken in Korea are similar to those that have been discussed or adopted in the United States. My sense (or my bias, for that matter) is that understanding the relative merits of each of them will require a fully-fledged quantitative model that can assess costs and benefits of alternative policies.

7. CONCLUSIONS

As the recent housing turmoil has shown, a better understanding of the workings of the housing market holds the key to a better understanding of macroeconomic fluctuations in general. My hope is that the next generation of DSGE models will devote increasing attention to modeling the housing market. Housing, for better or worse, is no small niche anymore.

Several commentators have expressed concerns on the usefulness of DSGE models of the housing sector, claiming that these models are bad at explaining house prices, that they omit important features of the reality, and that they miss important nonlinearities that are important in understanding housing markets. I think that these concerns are a symptom that many people write (and blog) too much and read too little. It is true, however, that the entire research field (of DSGE macro) features some strange herd behavior: people will ignore a topic unless some big guy writes a paper on it, taking a shortcut or two to get the model going. At that point, the shortcut becomes mainstream, many of those who have followed the shortcut do not know or understand why the shortcut was taken, and a literature proceeds slowly or in the wrong direction for several years. To avoid this, it is fundamental that the new generations (aka, graduate students) who embark on the research topic of DSGE macro acknowledge virtues and defects of all models, and try to improve them, not to extend them. The difference between improvement and extension is fundamental. Improving means that an unappealing feature of the model should be removed, discarded, or abandoned as an uninteresting special case of a better model. Extending means in most cases just adding a layer over another, without questioning the existing framework: for instance, taking the one-country model and making it two-country. In most cases, improvements yield far better payoffs than extensions.

I hope that in the next five to ten years we will have models with learning, with nonlinearities, with occasionally binding constraints, which will drastically improve upon the existing generation of models of housing in the context of DSGE models. I do not see in any way how often-heard rants against DSGE models will become mainstream economics. It takes a model to beat a model, after all.

NOTES

* The material in this chapter is the topic of a presentation at the KDI in Seoul, December 2011. Most of the material draws heavily on earlier work of mine on the topics that are covered in this chapter.

1. The data source for housing wealth is the Flow of Funds Accounts of the United States. The details of data construction can be found in Iacoviello (2012).
2. Most of the fluctuations in nominal housing wealth reflect movements in the price of housing, rather than movements in the stock.
3. Part of this comovement reflects the simple fact that, by adding to the stock, an increase in housing investment will necessarily lead to an increase in housing wealth, holding prices constant. However, a larger fraction of this comovement might reflect the endogenous response of housing investment to exogenous changes in housing demand that jointly affect both the price and the quantity of housing: Iacoviello and Neri (2010) present a DSGE model that captures this mechanism.
4. The share of housing investment in GDP ranged between 3 and 6 percent throughout the 1952–2008 period. It has fallen below 3 percent of GDP since the end of 2008, and is 2.2 percent of GDP at the end of 2011.
5. My emphasis here is on unconditional correlations. It is possible that, once some other variables or exogenous shocks are factored in, conditional correlations might be larger.
6. The Census series starts in 1963. The Freddie Mac series starts in 1970. For this reason, I restrict my attention to observations from 1970 onwards only. See Rappaport (2007) for a survey of the differences between different house price measures for the U.S.
7. Fisher (2007) documents this result in detail and offers a DSGE model of housing that can explain this result. See also Davis and Heathcote (2005) for a related model.
8. As a matter of fact, the role and contribution of rents to macroeconomic fluctuations seldom features in policy and academic debates, mostly because imputed rents are a

somewhat stable component of aggregate demand. If anything, they have risen as a fraction of either total consumption or GDP in almost all postwar recessions. The contribution of housing investment has been more often acknowledged, since housing investment is strongly procyclical, and strongly volatile

9. I will mention here some additional facts that did not make the cut in the list above: (a) The production of housing services can be thought of as the combination of housing structures and land (Davis and Heathcote, 2005). (b) The purchase of a house is typically financed with a down payment, with a mortgage making up for the difference between the purchase price and the down payment. (c) Housing services can be either purchased or rented, depending on preferences, life-cycle motives, and institutional arrangements. (d) Finally, contrary to what many seem to believe, the ratio of consumption expenditures to housing expenditures tends to fall over the life cycle: in other words, old people consume relatively more housing than young people (see Yang, 2009).
10. A search in Google scholar shows that as early as in 1996 some prominent researchers (Jordi Gali, Eric Leeper, Chris Sims, Tao Zha, Jinill Kim) were using the word DSGE to refer to real business cycle models that featured real or nominal rigidities. But it was probably the book of Mike Woodford on the one hand and the papers by Bernanke, Gertler and Gilchrist (1999); Smets and Wouters (2007), and Christiano, Eichenbaum and Evans (2005), as well as the toolkit by Harald Uhlig (written and circulated between the end of the 1990s and the early 2000s) that led to the popularity of DSGE models.
11. This effect occurs over and above the comovement coming from common shocks moving the two variables in the same direction.
12. To measure the cumulated output loss in the data, I detrend real GDP using one of the three methods described in the text. I then normalize the resulting series – regardless of what the detrending method says – so that GDP is right around trend in 2007Q4. I then compute the cumulated, annualized sum of all deviations from trend of the normalized series.

REFERENCES

Angeloni, Ignazio, and Ester Faia (2009). "A Tale of Two Policies: Prudential Regulation and Monetary Policy with Fragile Banks," Kiel Working Papers 1569, Kiel Institute for the World Economy.

Bernanke, Ben S., Mark Gertler, and Simon Gilchrist (1999). "The Financial Accelerator in a Quantitative Business Cycle Framework," in: J.B. Taylor & M. Woodford (ed.), Handbook of Macroeconomics, edition 1, volume 1, chapter 21, pages 1341–1393, Elsevier.

Brubak, Leif, Selim Elekdag, and Junior Maih (2007). "The Interactions Between Financial Frictions and Monetary Policy for Small Open Economies," working paper, IMF and Norges Bank.

Christensen, Ian, Paul Corrigan, Caterina Mendicino and Shin-Ichi Nishiyama (2009). "Consumption, Housing Collateral, and the Canadian Business Cycle," Working Papers 09–26, Bank of Canada.

Christiano, Lawrence, Martin Eichenbaum, and Charles Evans (2005). "Nominal Rigidities and the Dynamic Effects of a Shock to Monetary Policy," Journal of Political Economy, 113(1), February.

Davis, Morris A., and Jonathan Heathcote (2005). "Housing and the Business Cycle," International Economic Review, 46(3), 751–784.

Dib, Ali (2009). "Banks, Credit Markets Frictions, and Business Cycles," working paper, Bank of Canada.

Fernández-Villaverde, Jesus (2009). "The econometrics of DSGE Models." SERIEs vol 1.

Fisher, Jonas D.M. (2007). "Why Does Household Investment Lead Business Investment over the Business Cycle?" Journal of Political Economy, 115(1), 141–168.

Fuhrer, Jeff (2009). "Inflation Persistence," in preparation for the Handbook of Monetary Economics.

Gerali, Andrea, Stefano Neri, Luca Sessa, and Federico M. Signoretti (2009). "Credit and Banking in a DSGE Model," working paper, Banca d'Italia.

Gertler, Mark, and Peter Karadi (2009). "A Model of Unconventional Monetary Policy," working paper, NYU.

Gertler, Mark, and Nobuhiro Kiyotaki (2009). "Financial Intermediation and Credit Policy in Business Cycle Analysis," working paper, NYU and Princeton.

Head, Allen, and Huw Lloyd-Ellis (2008). "Housing Liquidity, Mobility, and the Labour Market," working paper, Queen's University.

Iacoviello, Matteo (2005). "House Prices, Borrowing Constraints, and Monetary Policy in the Business Cycle." American Economic Review, 95, 739–764.

Iacoviello, Matteo (2011). "Financial Business Cycles," working paper, Federal Reserve Board.

Iacoviello, Matteo (2012). "Housing Wealth and Consumption," International Encyclopedia of Housing and Home, Elsevier.

Iacoviello, Matteo, and Stefano Neri (2010). "Housing Market Spillovers: Evidence from an Estimated DSGE Model." AEJ Macro, April.

Kannan, Prakash, Pau Rabanal, and Alasdair Scott (2009). "Monetary and Macroprudential Policy Rules in a Model with House Price Booms," working paper, IMF.

Leamer, Edward E. (2007). "Housing is the Business Cycle," Proceedings, Federal Reserve Bank of Kansas City, 149–233.

Leeper, Eric M., Christopher A. Sims and Tao Zha, (1996). "What Does Monetary Policy Do?," Brookings Papers on Economic Activity, Economic Studies Program, The Brookings Institution, 27(2), 1–78.

Lombardo, Giovanni and Peter McAdam (2008). "Adding Financial Market Frictions to the NAWM," working paper, European Central Bank, June.

López Enciso, Enrique, and Andrés Salamanca Lugo (2009). "El efecto riqueza de la vivienda en Colombia," Borradores de economía, Banco de la República, Colombia.

Meh, Cesaire and Kevin Moran (2004). "Bank Capital, Agency Costs, and Monetary Policy." Bank of Canada Working Paper No. 2004–6.

Rappaport, Jordan (2007). "A Guide to Aggregate House Price Measures," Economic Review, Federal Reserve Bank of Kansas City, Second Quarter, 41–71.

Roeger, Werner, and Jan in't Veld (2009). "Fiscal Policy with Credit Constrained Households," working paper, European Commission, DG ECFIN.

Sellin, Peter, and Karl Walentin (2010). "Housing Collateral and the Monetary Transmission Mechanism," working paper, Riskbank.

Smets, Frank, and Rafael Wouters (2007). "Shocks and Frictions in US Business Cycles: A Bayesian DSGE Approach," American Economic Review, American Economic Association, 97(3), 586–606, June.

Sterk, Vincent (2010). "Home Equity, Mobility, and Macroeconomic Fluctuations," working paper, De Nederlandsche Bank and University of Amsterdam.

Uhlig, Harald (1995). "A Toolkit for Analyzing Nonlinear Dynamic Stochastic Models Easily," Discussion Paper 1995–97, Tilburg University, Center for Economic Research.
Woodford, Michael (2009). "Convergence in Macroeconomics: Elements of the New Synthesis." American Economic Journal: Macroeconomics, 1(1), 267–279.
Yang, Fang (2009). "Consumption Over the Life Cycle: How Different is Housing?," Review of Economic Dynamics, 12(3), 423–443.

3. Housing and business cycles in Korea: assessing the role of housing volume cycles*

Young Il Kim

1. INTRODUCTION

This chapter studies the role of housing volume cycles in macroeconomic fluctuations in the Korean economy. It is often argued that the housing boom and bust in major OECD countries (including the U.S.) served as a main cause of the recent global financial crisis. The abrupt rise of home prices and household debts up to the unsustainable levels and their subsequent fall resulted in failures of financial institutions and recessions. In addition, it is also argued that the significant contraction in residential buildings investment prior to the subprime mortgage crisis had contributed substantially to the recession (Leamer 2007, 2009).

Housing cycles may interact with macroeconomic fluctuations through changes in home prices, household debts and residential investments (Figure 3.1). Previous studies focused mainly on the role of house prices and household credits rather than the quantitative contributions of housing volumes in explaining the macroeconomic fluctuations. Studies on the relation between house prices and the real economy have often

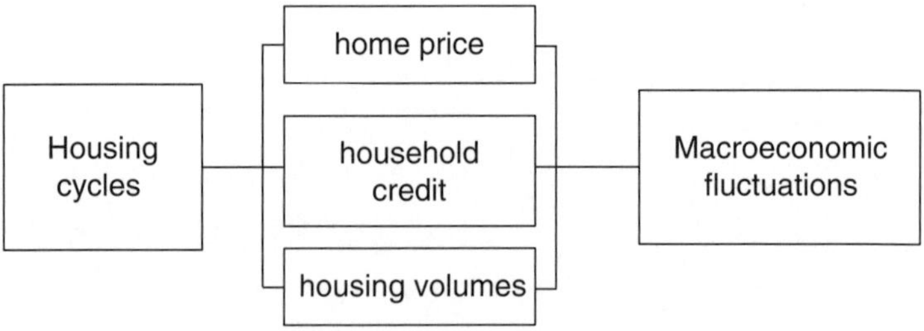

Figure 3.1 Interplay between housing cycles and macroeconomic fluctuations

focused on such channels as wealth effects and credit constraints through which changes in home prices may affect the real economy. In contrast, the role of housing volume cycles gained less attention until their quantitative contribution to GDP growth in the U.S. was emphasized in Leamer (2007). The present study focuses on the role of housing volume cycles in the overall economic fluctuations in the Korean economy, both a small open economy and an emerging market which may differ from other economies.

Wealth effects have been studied the most as important channels affecting real macroeconomic activity in previous studies, for example Case, Quigley and Shiller (2001), Catte et al. (2004), Iacoviello (2002), Lettau and Ludvigson (2000), Ludvigson and Steindel (1999), etc. In addition, credit constraints have gotten attention as channels for house prices to affect the real economy in such studies as Muellbauer (2007), Mian and Sufi (2009), Feldstein (2007), etc. More recently, the role of housing volume cycles in business cycles has been assessed for the U.S. economy by Leamer (2007, 2009) and for the European countries by Alvarez and Cabrero (2010), Alvarez et al. (2010), Ferrara and Koopman (2009), Ferrara and Vigna (2009), Knetsch (2009) etc. Regarding the Korean economy, an emerging market as well as a small open economy, such channels as house prices and credit constraints have been studied; however, less attention has been paid to the quantitative role of housing volume cycles in fluctuations of GDP. The present study investigates the missing part, the role of housing volume cycles in Korea's business cycles.

The remainder of this chapter is organized as follows. Section 2 characterizes and identifies business cycles and recessions in the Korean economy. Section 3 shows the cyclical property of home prices and household credits with related previous studies. Section 4 shows overall cyclical properties of housing volumes in comparison with other GDP components. Section 5 analyzes timing and magnitudes in contributions of housing volume cycles to GDP growth and to the depth of recessions in comparison with other components. Section 6 discusses further issues to be studied in this line of research. Section 7 provides a summary.

2. IDENTIFYING BUSINESS CYCLES AND RECESSIONS IN KOREA

It is necessary to characterize cyclical aspects of economic conditions and to date recessions in order to analyze cycles in housing in relation to the overall business cycles. However, there may not be a unique and easy way of identifying and dating business cycles and recessions. The present study uses the coincident composite index, the broadly cited indicator of cycles in macroeconomic conditions, which is released by Statistics Korea, the national statistical office in Korea. The coincident composite index is made and detrended by Statistics Korea to describe the Korean business cycles. Such components are included as industrial production index, operation ratio index (Mfg.), value of construction completed (real), index of services (excluding wholesale and retail sale), wholesale and retail sale index, producer's shipment index for domestic market, imports (real), and number of employed persons for the non-farm households. Figure 3.2 shows the cyclical components of the coincident composite index with the trend set at 100 and with periods between peaks and troughs shaded in grey. However, there are no officially available dates for recessions in Korea. Thus, the present study defines recessionary periods as periods below the trend as well as in declining phases from peaks to subsequent troughs of the detrended coincident composite index. Figure 3.2 shows the recessionary periods defined in this manner.

3. HOME PRICE, HOUSEHOLD CREDIT AND THE MACROECONOMY

Cycles in home prices and household credits tend to co-move with cycles in GDP. Figure 3.3 shows HP-detrended cyclical components of real GDP, real home prices and real household credits in logarithmic terms in Korea. Considerably strong co-movements are observed among those components.

Wealth effects and credit constraints are often argued as possible channels behind the co-movements and interplays. Changes in home prices may affect household wealth, which may be taken into account in households' consumption decisions so that GDP is affected. Changes in home prices may also affect the collateral values, which may influence borrowing limits, thus changing credit constraints and consumption. Price elasticities of consumption to housing wealth in Korea have been studied previously. The estimates for the long-run relationship are provided as 0.45 (Kim and Moon 2001), 0.13 (Choi and Kim 2007), or 0.05–0.17 (Kim 2010) depending on estimation periods and methods. The estimates for the short-run relationship are provided as 0.3 (Kim and Moon), 0.01–0.18 (Choi and Kim 2007), or 0.08–0.26 (Kim 2010) depending on estimation methods and sample periods. These estimates for the Korean economy may be compared with those of major OECD economies: 0.06–0.15 for the long-run elasticities and 0.04–0.14 for the short-run elasticities (Catte et al. 2004)

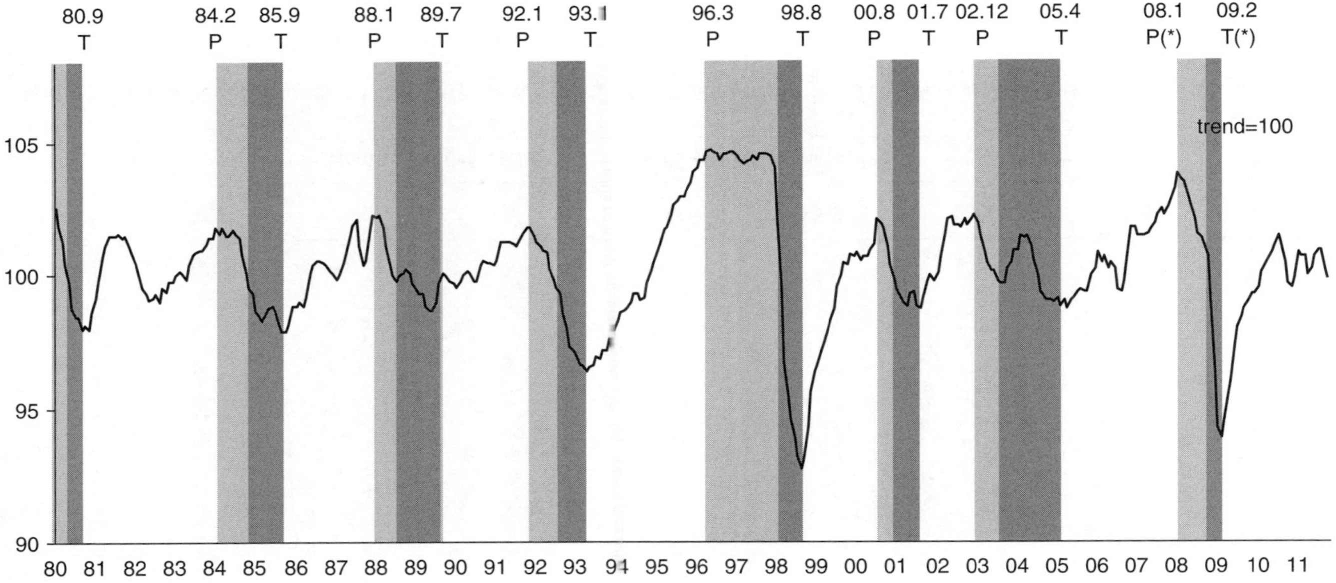

Notes:
Recessionary periods are shown by <shaded in dark grey>.
* The dates of the peak and trough for the 2008–09 cycle are preliminary.

Figure 3.2 Cyclical component of coincident composite index

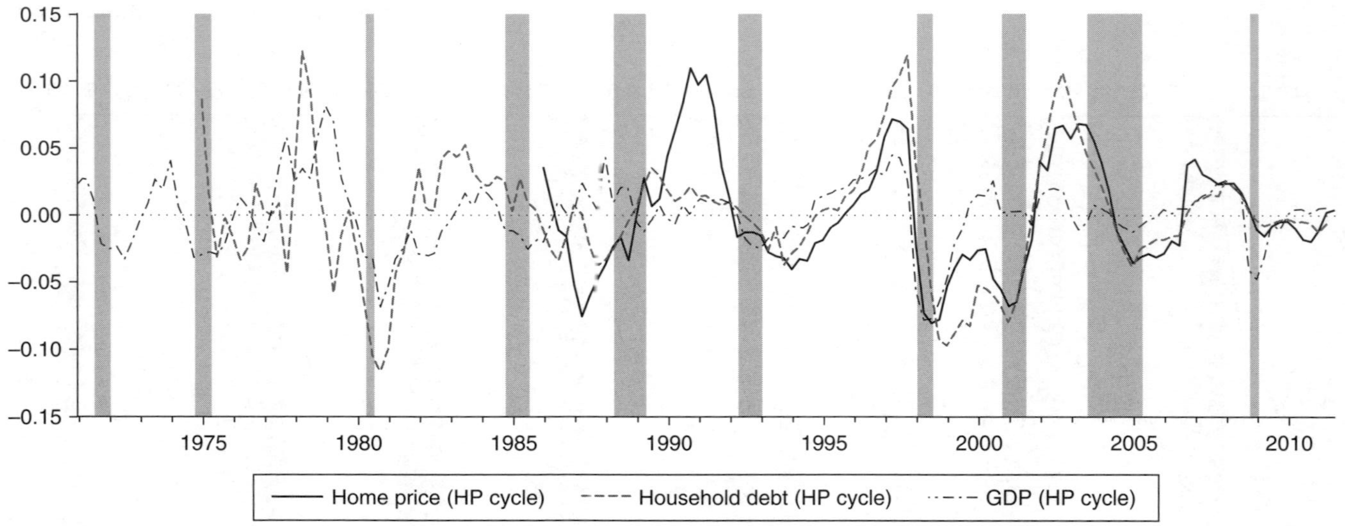

Figure 3.3 *Cyclical components of GDP, home price and household credit (HP-filtered cycles)*

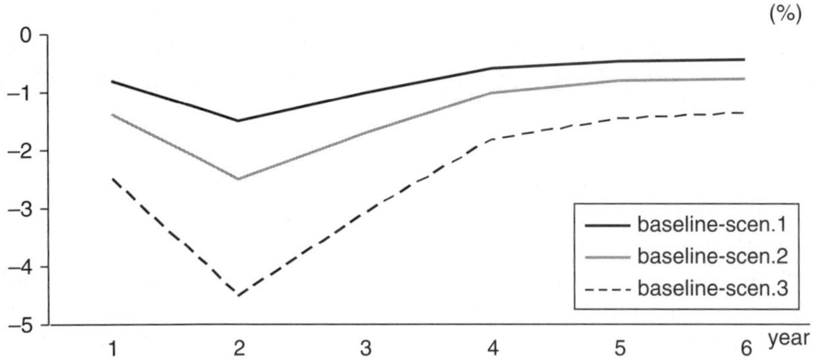

Figure 3.4 *Consumption responses under alternative scenarios against the baseline*

Table 3.1 *Scenarios for home price growth rates: baseline vs. alternative scenarios (%)*

House prices	Year 1	Year 2	Year 3
Baseline	5.79	5.79	5.79
Scenario1 (mild shocks)	0	0	5.79
Scenario2 (severe shocks)	−4	−4	5.79
Scenario3 (catastrophic shocks)	−10	10	5.79

which depend on sample countries, estimation periods and specifications of equations.

Kim (2011) has shown how private consumption may respond under alternative stress scenarios of home prices based on a simple error correction model with the long-run and short-run elasticities estimated as 0.039 and 0.282 respectively. Figure 3.4 shows the consumption path under alternative stress scenarios of house prices shown in Table 3.1.[1] It is demonstrated that more depressed housing markets may lead to more severe contraction in consumption. This effect may work through wealth effects or collateral constraint channels.

4. HOUSING VOLUME CYCLES AND THE MACROECONOMY: A BROAD VIEW OF CYCLES

Leamer (2007, 2009) argues that residential investments in the U.S. are a major leading indicator for recessions with relatively large quantitative contributions to the depth of recessions. However, the contributions of housing volume cycles to fluctuations of GDP may differ across countries. The present study investigates the quantitative role of housing volume cycles in relation to the overall economic fluctuations of the Korean economy, a small open economy with high trade volumes.

Figure 3.5 shows housing volume cycles and GDP cycles in Korea. The cyclical component of residential investment seems to co-move with that of GDP before the 1997–98 Asian financial crisis. However, their relationship has been much weaker since the Asian crisis. Table 3.2 shows volatility ratios of each component relative to GDP and their correlations before and after the Asian crisis. The correlation between cycles in GDP and residential investment has weakened greatly from 0.40 prior to the Asian crisis to −0.12 after the crisis while the volatility of residential investment relative to GDP has declined. As shown in Table 3.2, construction in general had been pro-cyclical before 2000, whereas it became somewhat counter-cyclical after 2000. It may be noteworthy that the volatility of exports and imports relative to GDP has increased, with their pro-cyclicality a bit more strengthened since 2000.

5. CONTRIBUTIONS OF HOUSING VOLUME CYCLES TO GDP GROWTH

5.1 Contributions to GDP Growth

Contributions to GDP growth by components, announced by the Bank of Korea, may be analyzed to understand what proportion of GDP growth could be explained by each component. Figure 3.6 shows GDP growth from previous quarters with recessionary periods shaded in grey. As indicated in the graph, annualized average quarterly GDP growth before 2000 was 6.5% while it is 3.7% after 2000. The GDP growth can be divided into parts based on how much of it may come from each demand component. Figure 3.7 shows contributions to GDP growth by such demand components as residential investment, private consumption, exports, and equipment investment with trends.

5.2 Trends and Cycles in Contributions to GDP Growth by Components

Contributions to GDP growth by components can be divided into trend and cyclical parts by such filters as the HP-filter. If trends in contributions to GDP growth by each domestic component are analyzed, domestic demands have been much weaker after 2000 while exports (external

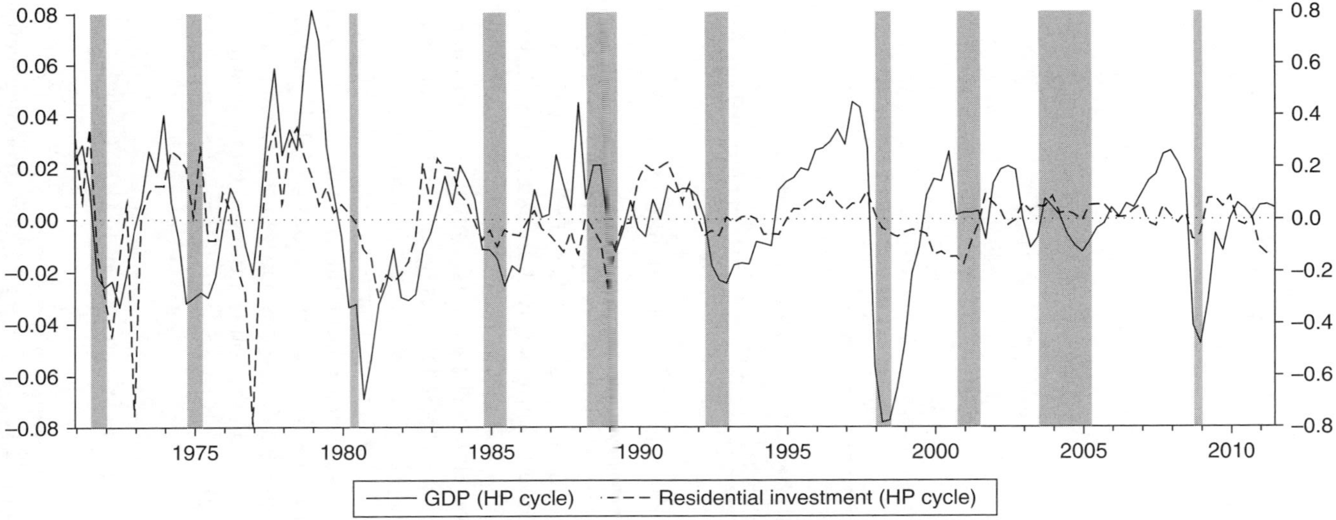

Figure 3.5 *Cycles in GDP and residential investment*

Table 3.2 *Volatility ratios and correlations between cycles in GDP and components*

	1971Q1–1999Q4		2000Q1–2011Q2	
	Volatility ratio	Correlation	Volatility ratio	Correlation
Durable Cons.	3.60	0.81	4.70	0.64
Quasi-durable Cons.	2.28	0.72	2.52	0.69
Nondurable Cons.	0.90	0.60	1.04	0.56
Service Cons.	0.83	0.68	1.04	0.37
Equipment Inv.	5.03	0.74	4.90	0.83
Residential Inv.	6.30	0.40	4.57	−0.12
Non-residential Inv.	4.93	0.51	4.13	0.15
Structure	3.62	0.23	2.57	−0.45
Imports	2.82	0.80	3.69	0.80
Exports	2.37	0.34	3.55	0.58

Notes:
Volatility ratios are standard deviations of each component relative to the standard deviation of the cyclical GDP.
Standard deviations of quarterly GDP growth before and after 2000 are 2.8% and 1.5% respectively.

demands) have maintained their contribution to GDP growth. The subcomponents of private consumption (durables, quasi-durables, nondurable goods, and services) have declined in their trends over time but with some unevenness. Equipment investment has declined in its trend over time while inventory investment has stayed around zero. Construction investment has also declined in trend in its contribution to GDP growth. Imports have declined over time while exports' contribution to GDP growth has been steady over time. These features reflect the rising share of trades out of GDP while the potential GDP growth has declined after 2000.

Since the purpose of this chapter is to analyze cyclical movements of housing and GDP and their relationships, we need to separate cycles out of each time series. Cycles in contributions to GDP growth by components may be defined as differences between the actual contributions and their trends. The cycles in the contributions to GDP growth may be called 'abnormal' contributions because the trends may be considered as 'normal' contributions.[2]

5.3 Cumulative Abnormal Contributions to GDP Growth

Because the abnormal contributions appear very choppy, it may be better to analyze the cumulative one. Summing abnormal contributions up from

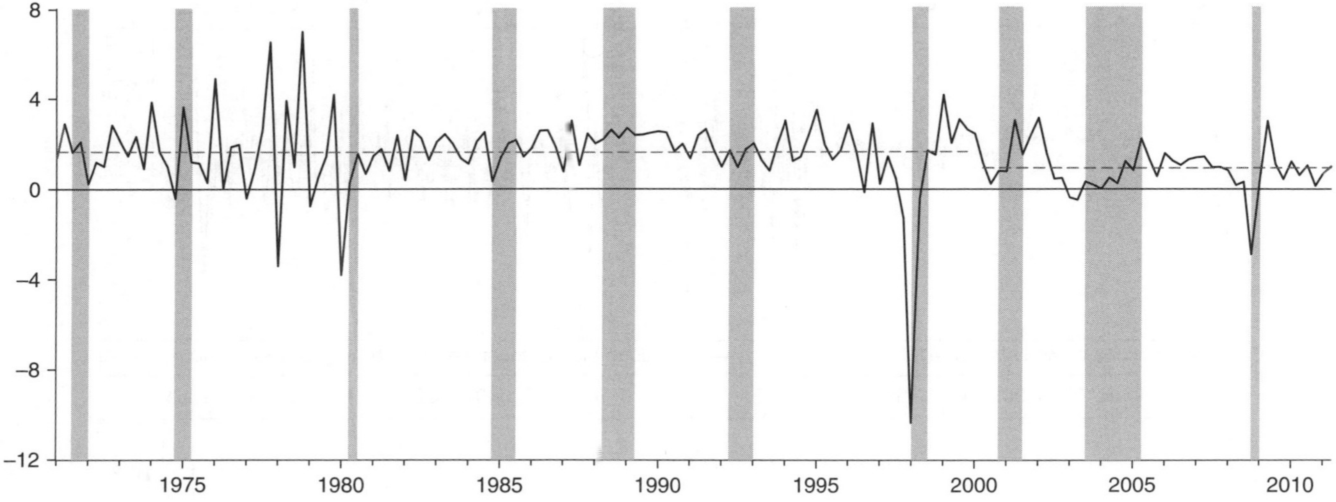

Note: Recessionary periods are shaded.

Figure 3.6 *GDP growth from previous quarters (in %)*

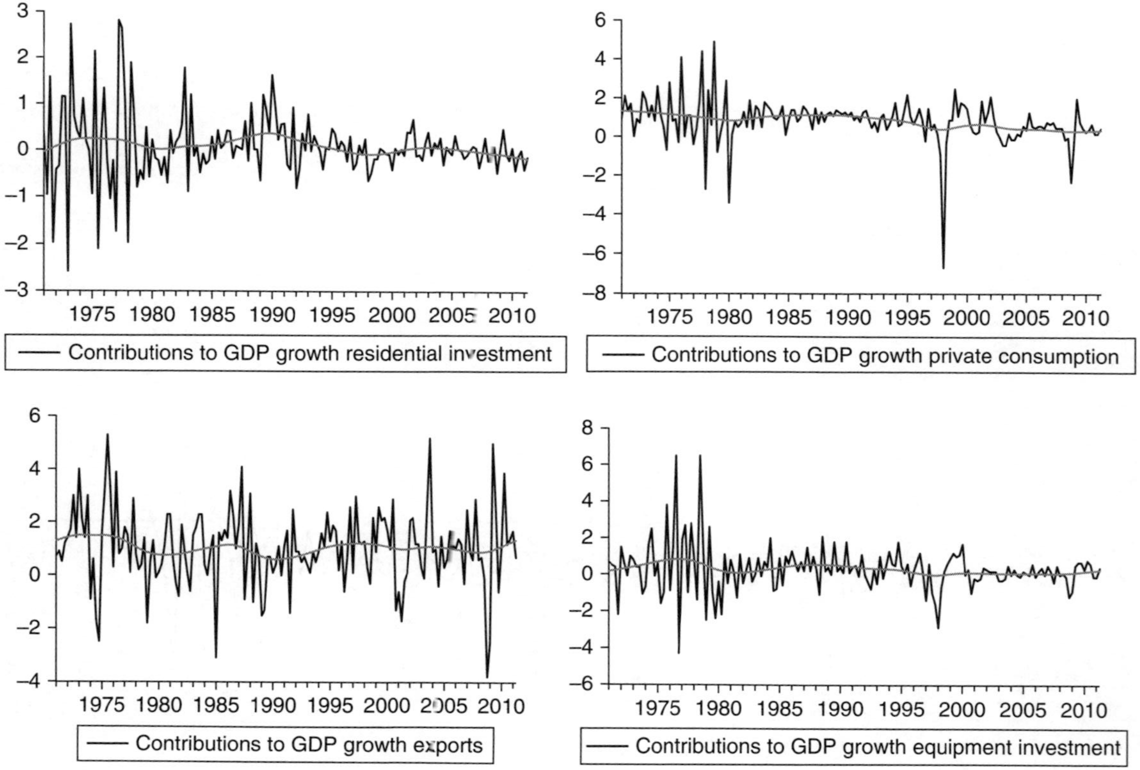

Figure 3.7 Contributions to GDP growth by components with trends

the starting point in time gives the cumulative abnormal contributions (Leamer 2007, 2009). Cumulative abnormal contributions may be flat, rising, or falling. If flat, actual contribution equals normal contributions, which is at the trend because abnormal contributions equal zero. If rising, actual contributions are above the normal, which is at the trend because abnormal contributions are positive. If falling, actual contributions are below the trend because abnormal contributions are negative.

Figure 3.8 shows the cumulative abnormal GDP growth. It falls during and around the recessionary periods, implying that the quarterly GDP growth around the recessions was below the normal (trend) GDP growth. The quarterly GDP growth had weakened by about 12% and 7% in total around the Asian financial crisis and the recent global financial crisis respectively compared with the normal growth pace. The cumulative abnormal GDP growth has been rising in the non-shaded periods, implying that the quarterly GDP growth was above the normal (trend) GDP growth outside the recessionary periods.

Figure 3.9 shows cumulative abnormal contributions to GDP growth by components. The contribution of housing volume (residential buildings) cycles to the amplitudes of GDP cycles has been declining over time especially after 2000 and their business cycle property has been much weaker. On the contrary, such components as exports, equipment, and services are still important in their contributions to the magnitudes of GDP cycles. Other components such as durables, quasi-durables, and imports are even stronger after 2000 than before in their contributions to the volatility of GDP cycles. Net exports seem to be counter-cyclical, implying that they tend to contribute to getting the economy out of recessions.

5.4 Average Cumulative Abnormal Contributions to GDP Growth by Components

We may analyze average cumulative abnormal contributions to GDP growth to assess each component's contribution to GDP growth on average. Figure 3.10 shows average cumulative abnormal contributions to GDP growth for the whole sample period and the period after 2000. Inventories are the strongest contributor to the weakness of GDP in recessions on average after 2000, while equipment investment is the next in its contributions. Net exports, construction, and government consumption boost the GDP during recessions after 2000. Net exports are earlier and stronger boosters while construction is a later and weaker booster after 2000, and they play important roles in getting the economy out of recessions. The countercyclical property of net exports reflects the fact that imports contract much more than exports during recessions on average.

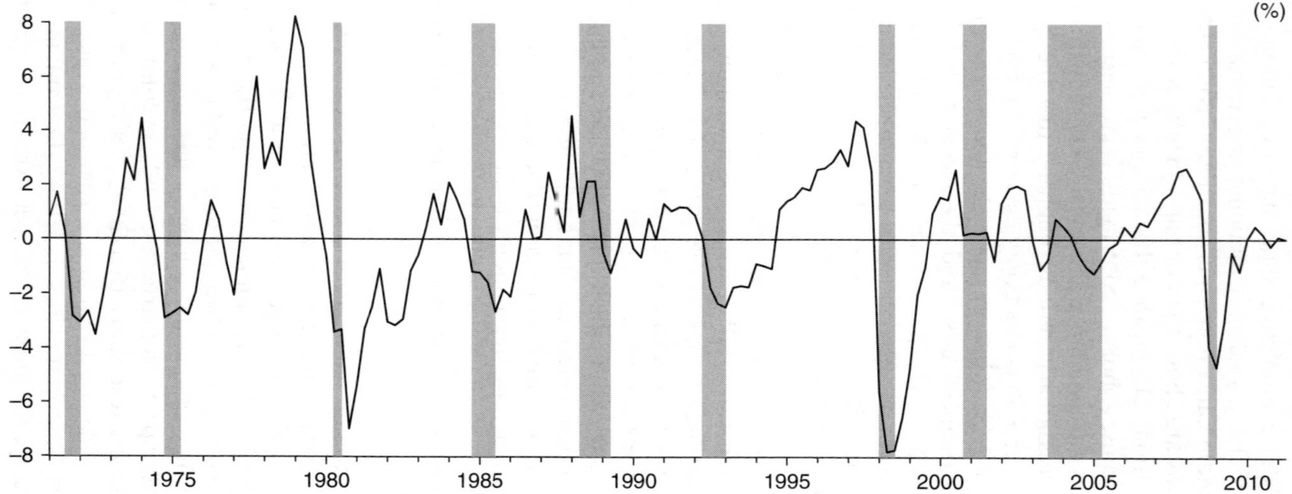

Figure 3.8 Cumulative abnormal GDP growth

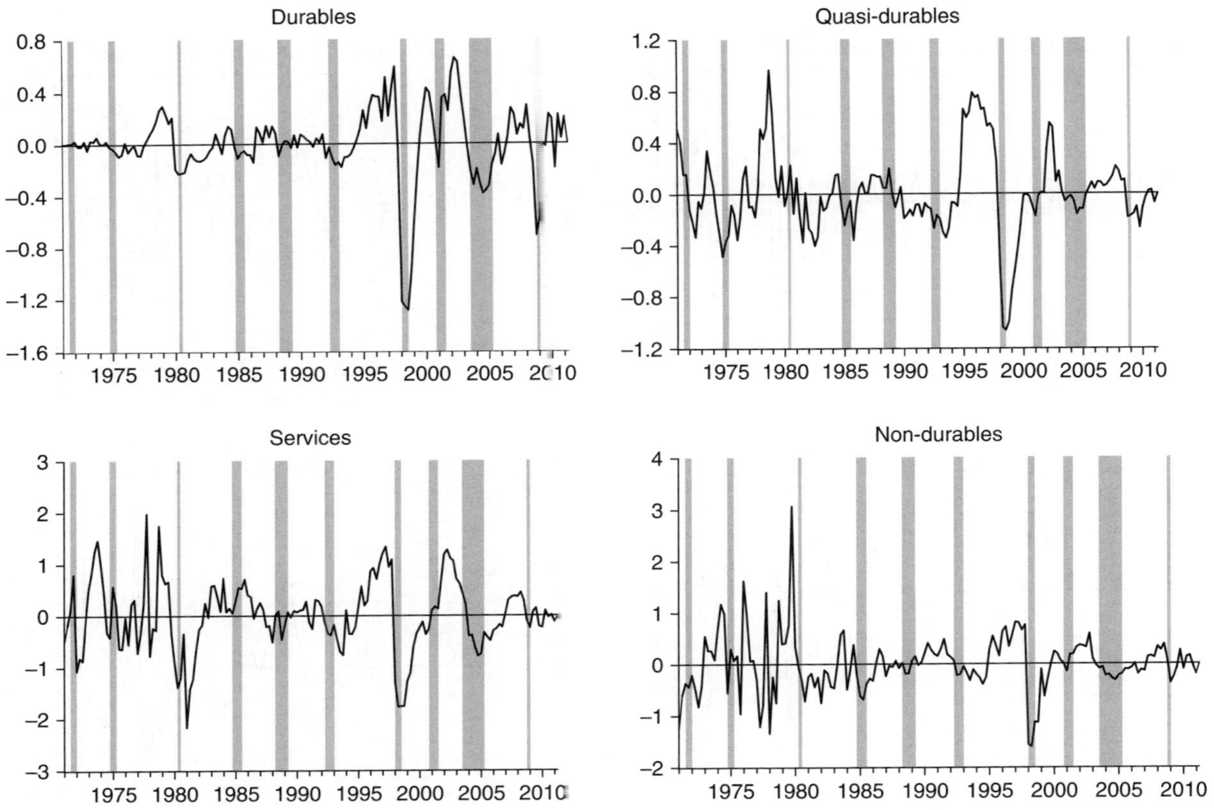

Figure 3.9 Cumulative abnormal contributions to GDP growth by components

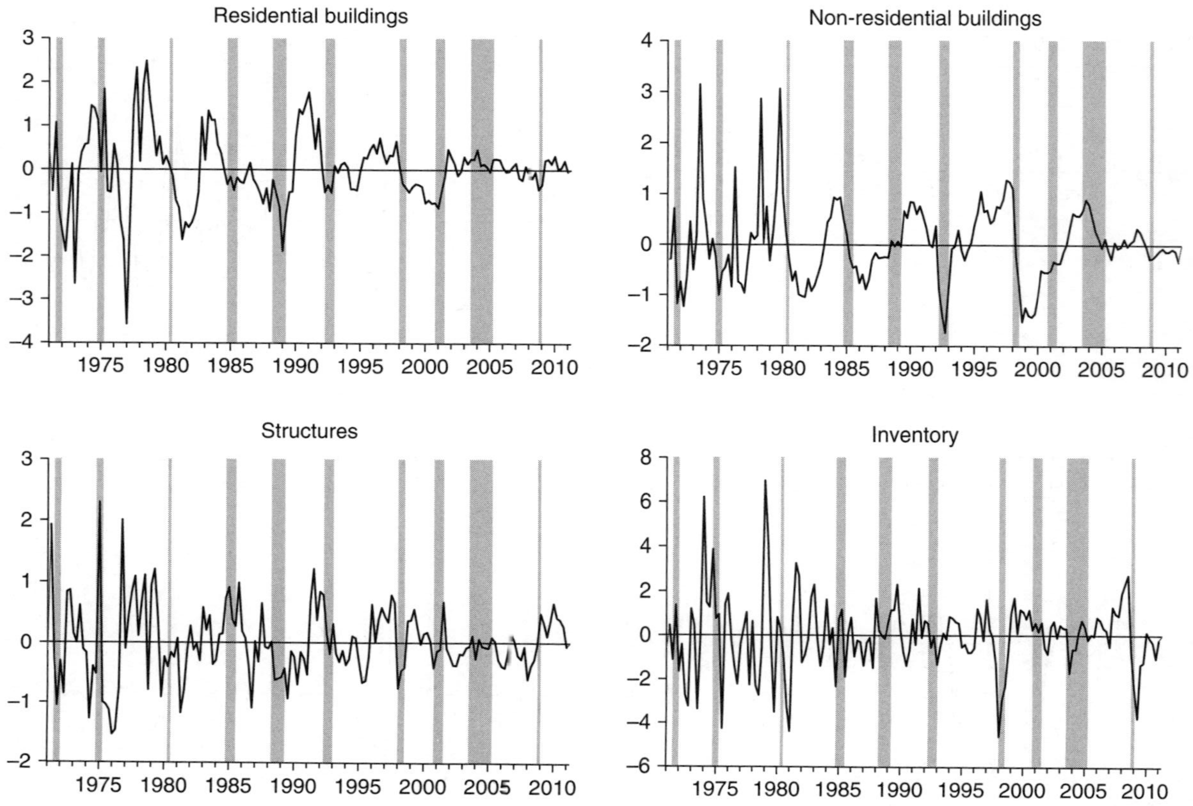
Residential buildings
Non-residential buildings
Structures
Inventory
1975 1980 1985 1990 1995 2000 2005 2010

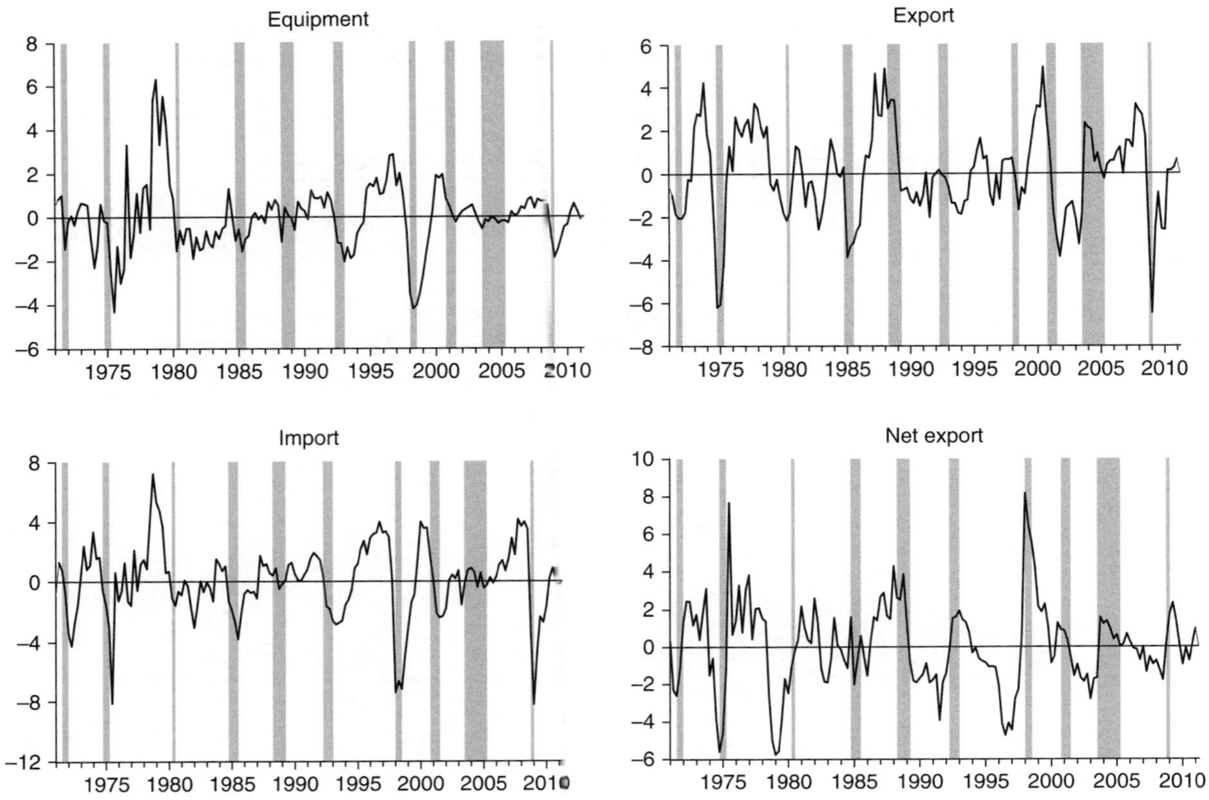

Figure 3.9 (continued)

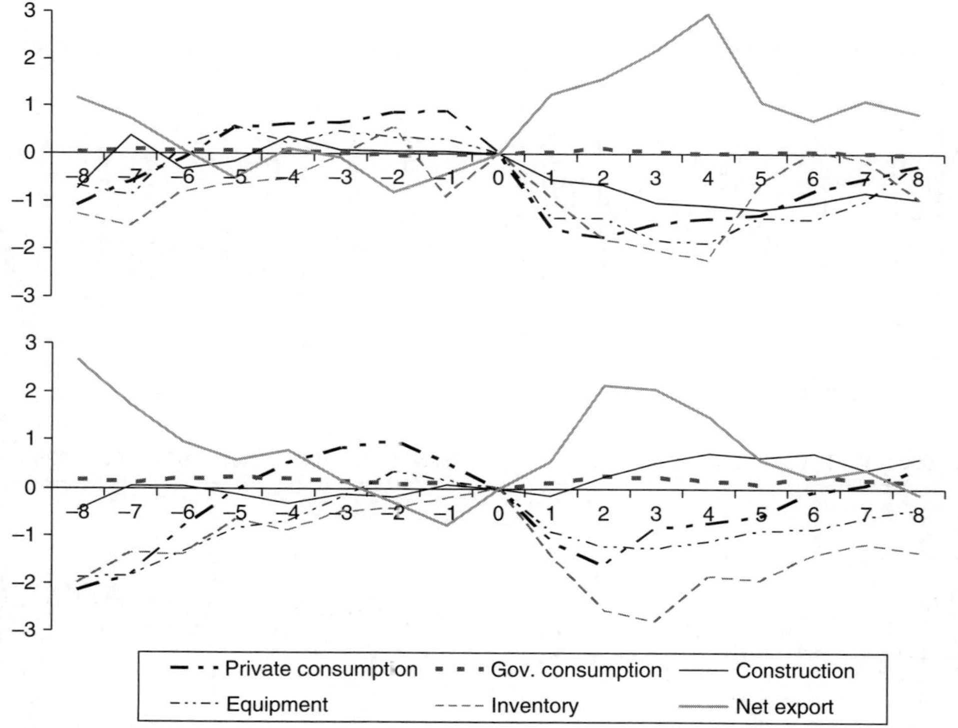

Figure 3.10 *Average cumulative abnormal contributions to GDP growth around recessions by components for the whole sample period (upper panel) and the period after 2000 (lower panel)*

Equipment and private consumption are leading indicators of recessions. They start to become weaker prior to the onset of recessions on average after 2000.

It may be shown that durables and equipment investment have been leading indicators for the incoming recessions as their contributions to GDP growth began weakening a few quarters before the onset of recessions on average after 2000. Figure 3.11 indicates that residential buildings do not show any predictive property for the incoming recessions on average after 2000. In addition, they contribute significantly to getting the economy out of recessions after 2000.

We may also arrange each component in order of the size of its contribution to GDP growth before and during recessions to assess the importance of each component in its contribution to the depth of recessions. Table 3.3 shows major components that contribute most to weakness in GDP before the onset of recessions and during recessions. Residential investment had shown some importance in adding weakness to GDP before the 1997 financial crisis; however, such important contributions are not found after the Asian financial crisis. Durable goods have shown significant weakness before the incoming recessions since the Asian crisis. Exports have been major contributors to weakness in GDP in more than half of the recessions, while equipment and inventory investments have been important contributors to weakness in GDP in most recessions.

6. DISCUSSION ON THE REMAINING ISSUES

It would be worth investigating why the co-movement between housing volume cycles and business cycles has weakened in Korea after 2000 while cycles in home prices and household credits show strong association with business cycles. Price elasticity of land supply for residential buildings may have changed so that the volume cycles have been more moderated than price cycles. The empirical analysis may show that volume cycles have been more moderated than price cycles after 2000. This feature may reflect that the land supply for residential buildings has become less elastic to changes in home prices, especially in Seoul, the most populated area in Korea.

In addition, public policy for residential buildings may have had effects in a manner different than the private market. The empirical analysis on the private share of new housing units constructed may show that the proportion of new housing units made by private sectors has changed over time while staying at around 60–70% recently.

The Korean economy may also have become more sensitive to external

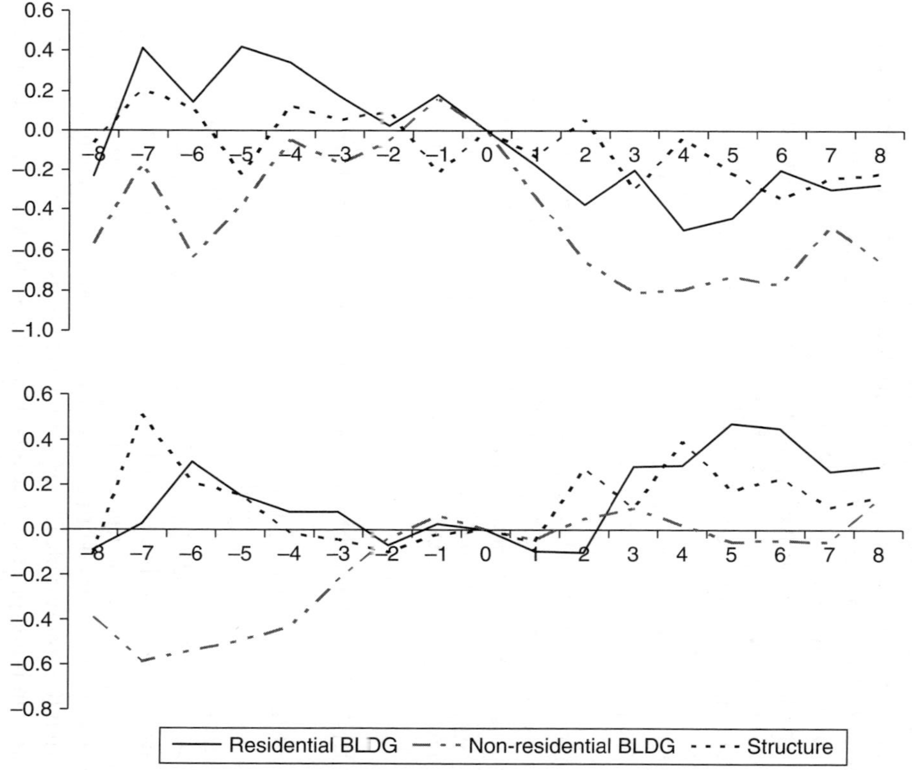

Figure 3.11 *Average cumulative abnormal contributions to GDP growth by construction components for the whole sample period (upper panel) and the period after 2000 (lower panel)*

Table 3.3 Major components contributing to weakness in GDP growth before the onset of recessions and during recessions

	1	2	3	4	5	6	7	8	9
	1974Q4	1980Q2	1984Q4	1988Q2	1992Q2	1998Q1	2000Q4	2003Q3	2008Q4
Before	XX/EQ	IV/ND/ NRI	XX/RI/ IV	ST/RI	RI/S	EQ/ IV/D	GC/S/D	XX/ IV/D/ ND	XX/D
During	EQ/XX	IV/EQ/ RI/ NRI	IV/ NRI/ EQ	XX/IV/ EQ	EQ/ NRI/ IV	EQ/IV/ NRI/S/ ND	XX/EQ	IV/S/ EQ/D	XX/IV/ EQ

Note: XX: exports, EQ: equipment investment, ND: nondurable goods, RI: residential investment, ST: structures, S: services, D: durables, GC: government consumption, ND: nondurables, NRI: nonresidential buildings, IV: inventories.

factors such as exports, exchange rates, etc. so that domestic factors such as housing show less contribution to GDP growth. The empirical analysis of the share of trades (export+import) out of GDP may imply that the Korean economy has become more exposed to external shocks in its overall economic fluctuations.

7. SUMMARY

This chapter investigated the role of housing volume cycles in macroeconomic fluctuations in comparison with other components of GDP for the Korean economy. Housing volume cycles showed significant co-movement with GDP cycles and had some predictability for the incoming recessions while contributing to the depth of recessions before 2000. However, housing volume cycles seem neither to co-move with GDP cycles nor to have predictability for the incoming recessions while contributing to boosting the economy out of recessions after 2000. Durable goods and equipment investment are significant leading indicators for the incoming recessions, while equipment and inventory investment contribute to the depth of recession by large amounts. Net exports are counter-cyclical and main contributors to the rebound of the economy from recessions.

The weakening co-movement between housing volumes and GDP may be due to the changing character of the Korean economy and government policies, suggesting that further studies on the phenomenon be needed. The weakness in the link between the housing volume cycle and the business cycle after 2000 is contrasted with the case of the U.S., where fluctuations in housing volumes may be an important source of macroeconomic instability. The Korean economy has shown a rapidly rising share of trades out of GDP since 2000 so that external factors such as exports, exchange rates, oil prices etc. have often destabilized the macroeconomy. In addition, the price elasticity of land supply for residential buildings may be different from that of the U.S. and may have changed as the number of houses has increased over time. Moreover, some proportion of residential investments is initiated by the public sector so that the government interventions in the housing market may have affected housing volume cycles in a manner different than before.

NOTES

* The author wishes to thank Dongchul Cho and seminar participants at the KDI conference in December 2011 for their useful comments. He also gives special thanks to Joohee Yoo for her helpful research assistance.

1. Alternative scenarios are cases corresponding to mild shocks, severe shocks and catastrophic shocks imposed on the housing market. All the stress scenarios assume two consecutive years of depressed house prices and a return to the normal growth phase of house prices.
2. The term 'abnormal' was previously used in Leamer (2007, 2009).

REFERENCES

Alvarez, L.J. and A. Cabrero, 2010. "Does housing really lead the business cycle?" Banco de Espana, Documentos de Trabajo No.1024.

Alvarez, L.J., G. Bulligan, A. Cabrero, L. Ferrara, and H. Stahl, 2010. "Housing cycles in the major euro area countries," Banque de France, Working Paper No. 269.

Bulligan, G., 2009. "Housing and macroeconomy: The Italian case," Banca d'Italia, mimeo.

Case, K., J. Quigley, and R. Shiller, 2001. "Comparing wealth effects: The stock market versus the housing market," NBER Working Paper No. 8606.

Catte, Pietro, N. Girouard, R. Price, and C. Andre, 2004. "Housing markets, wealth and the business cycle," Economic Department Working Papers No. 394.

Choi, Yo Chul and Eun Young Kim, 2007. "Analysis of the effect of changes in households' asset prices on consumption and implications," The Bank of Korea, Articles in Monthly Bulletin.

Feldstein, S. Martin, 2007. "Housing, credit markets and the business cycle," NBER Working Paper No. 13471, October.

Fernandez-Corugedo, Emilio, Simon Price, and Andrew Blake, 2003. "The dynamics of consumers' expenditure: The UK Consumption ECM Redux," Bank of England, Working Paper No. 204.

Ferrara, L. and S.J. Koopman, 2009. "Common business and housing markets cycles in the euro area: A multivariate component approach," Banque de France, mimeo.

Ferrara, L. and O. Vigna, 2009. "Evidence of relationships between macroeconomic and housing cycles in France," Banque de France, mimeo.
Iacoviello, Matteo, 2002. "House prices and business cycles in Europe: a VAR analysis," BC working paper 540.
Kim, Byung Hwa and So Sang Moon, 2001. "Stock market and consumption: The case of Korea," The Bank of Korea, Economic Papers Vol. 4.
Kim, Young Il, 2011. "Housing market depression and its impact on consumption," Chapter 3 in Stress Testing Long-Term Real Estate Market Decline Scenarios in Korea, Korea Development Institute.
Kim, Young Il, 2010. "Asset prices and consumption dynamics in Korea," Korea Development Institute, KDI Journal of Economic Policy, Vol. 32.
Knetsch, T., 2009. "Trend and cycle features in German residential investment before and after unification," Deutsche Bundesbank, mimeo.
Leamer, Edward, 2007. "Housing is the business cycle," Proceedings, Federal Reserve Bank of Kansas City, 149–233.
Leamer, Edward, 2009. "Homes and cars: Why are the cycles in homes and consumer durables so similar?" Advances in Economic Analysis & Policy, Berkeley Electronic Press, 9(3), article 5.
Lettau, M. and S. Ludvigson, 2000. "Consumption, aggregate wealth and expected stock returns," Journal of Finance, 56.
Ludvigson, Sydnet and Charles Steindel, 1999. "How important is the stock market wealth effect on consumption?" Economic Policy Review, Vol. 5, Federal Reserve Bank of New York.
Mian, Atif and Amir Sufi, 2009. "Household leverage and the recession of 2007 to 2009," Working Paper, October.
Muellbauer, John, 2007. "Housing, credit and consumer expenditure," Working Paper, Oxford University, September.

4. Global financial crisis and early warning system of Korean housing market

Seoung Hwan Suh and Kabsung Kim

1. INTRODUCTION

The perception that sustaining the stability of the housing market is necessary for sustaining the stability of the economy as a whole began to attract more attention especially after the recent Global Financial Crisis (GFC). For sustaining economic stability, carefully constructed and efficiently executed pre-emptive housing policies are necessary. However, examples of adequate pre-emptive housing policies are rare. There are many reasons why it is hard to implement housing policies in advance, but one of the main reasons is the lack of confidence in house price forecasts. This is especially true in the case of Korea, where the housing market is relatively thin and is highly dependent upon government real estate policies.

Both time series and structural models have some problems in forecasting real estate prices (Case & Shillar 1989, 1990; Clapp & Giaccotto 2002)). If the market is fairly stable, pure time series models can be safely used. But, since the Korean housing market is very unstable, the usage of the pure time series models cannot be safely suggested. In the case of structural models, serious problems are associated with adopting exogenous variables and adjusting constant terms. Even if theoretically and empirically appropriate exogenous variables are found, most of them are still very volatile. Therefore, forecasting the values of exogenous variables, which is imperative in forecasting house prices, is extremely difficult.

The Early Warning System (EWS) is a possible solution to prepare against housing market crises in unstable housing policy environments, especially with the limited availability of econometric tools (Beckmann et al. 2006). EWS permits timely monetary and fiscal policy interventions before housing market crises emerge (Lunde 2009). Numerous case studies have investigated the usefulness of EWS in providing signals to policymakers (Esteban & Sandra 2008; Mete 2004; Davis and Karim 2008).

Esteban & Sandra (2008) construct early warning indicators for Colombia using financial and real variables. They find that relevant information is embedded in these variables, and all indicators (except their new house price indicator) show significant deviations in the year(s) prior to the 1998–99 crises. Mete (2004) focuses on the Turkish financial crisis of 2001 and finds that the consumer price index, Turkish lira–US dollar exchange rate, and domestic credit are significant variables in explaining the financial crises. Davis and Karim (2008) seek to assess whether EWS in the U.K. and U.S. economies based on the logit and binomial tree approaches could have helped to foresee the 2007 GFC.

EWS performance is enhanced through the use of a logit model, shorter samples, and a regional approach (Beckmann et al. 2006; Davis and Karim 2008; Stock & Watson 1991). A signal approach model is a non-parametric method involving the selection of leading indicators (Suh et al. 2011). Considering the relatively large number of valid leading indicators, the easiness and flexibility of managing and modifying models, the use of a signal approach model is adequate in the case of Korea (Suh 2004). Suh (2004) finds 15 effective leading indicators in the case of a signal approach model, but only four leading indicators are found to be effective in the case of the probit model. For these reasons, we employ a signal approach in this study.

The purpose of this study is twofold. Firstly, characteristics of movements of Korean housing prices will be observed with a special focus on the situation after GFC. Secondly, EWS of the Korean housing market will be constructed in order to notice the housing market crisis before it happens by using the non-parametric signal approach model, which is the most convenient method in sustaining the system.

2. SOME ASPECTS OF KOREAN HOUSE PRICES

2.1 Movements of Korean House Prices

In this section, we will briefly introduce some empirical findings about the movement of Korean house prices, which will be helpful in understanding the characteristics of the Korean housing market. Monthly data for the Korean Housing Sales Price Index, HPI, is available from January 1987. The rate of changes in HPI with respect to the same month in the previous year, GHPI, is shown by Figure 4.1. Very high values of GHPI are observed in 1988–91, 2002–03, and 2007. The average of GHPI for each period is 14.4%, 12.8% and 9.1% with the maximum of 21.1%, 17.7% and 12.2%, respectively. Very low values of GHPI are observed in March 1998 – April 1999. The average of GPHI during that period is −9.9%

Figure 4.1 Movements of Korean housing sales price index

with the minimum of −13.1%. This housing market recession was mainly caused by the Asian Financial Crisis (AFC) of 1997.

Compared with the effects of the AFC from 1997 to –1999, the effect of the recent Global Financial Crisis (GFC) on the Korean housing market seems to be rather small. Values of GHPI showed the negative sign from April 2009, but the sign has been reversed to positive from November 2009. Also, values of GHPI are increasing and reached 7.1% in November 2011.

Recently, especially after GFC, the question of house price spillovers across countries has drawn more concerns. There are many empirical findings on both the intra-national and international synchronization and spillovers in housing prices (Vansteenkiste & Hiebert 2011; Klyuev 2008; Holly et al. 2011; Gros 2006; Setzer et al. 2011). Suggested reasons for synchronization and spillovers in house prices are endogenous interactions (Manski 2000), social interaction being dependent upon the mean housing demand (Ioannides & Zabel 2008), and belief diffusion of epidemiological models (Burnside et al. 2011).

In order to check this, we will compare the movements of GHPI and GHPI-US, which is the rate of changes in U.S. house prices obtained from the OFHEO's U.S. housing sales price index data. For both GHPI and GHPI-US, quarterly data between the first quarter of 1992 and third quarter of 2011 are used. As is shown by Figure 4.2, the co-movements of GHPI and GHPI-US seem not to be strong as a whole, but after around 2007, movements of GHPI and GHPI-US might be considered to be very similar.

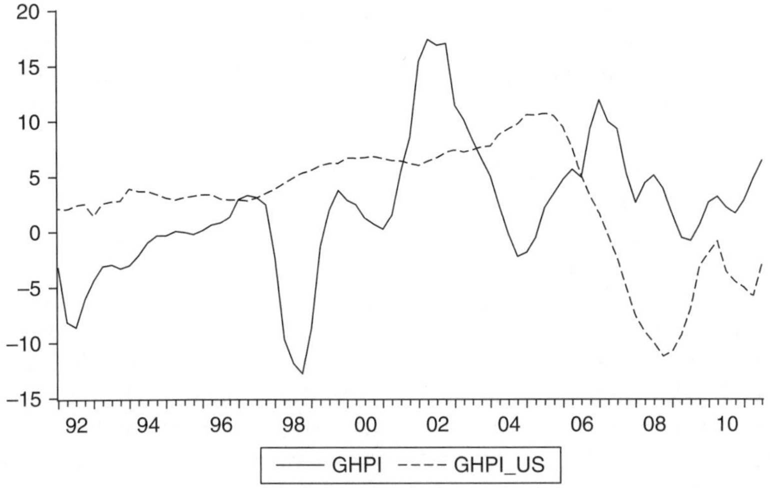

Figure 4.2 Movements of HPI and HPI-US

Table 4.1 Results of the variance decomposition

	GHPI	GNY	GHPI-US	GRR	GBLD
3Q 1992 – 3Q 2011	52.2	10.4	7.2	27.4	2.8
3Q 1992 – 3Q 2006	47.7	8.6	9.3	31.1	3.3
1Q 2007 – 3Q 2011	43.9	5.5	18.1	4.5	28.0

This casual observation can be confirmed by the results of variance decomposition analysis of unrestricted VAR. In estimating the unrestricted VAR model, GHPI, nominal GDP growth rate (GNY), GHPI-US, the rate of change in nominal interest rate (GRR) and the rate of change in residential housing building construction permits (GBLD) are used in this order. Here, GNY is used to represent market fundamental related factors and GRR is used to represent both the portfolio selection related factors and the cost of housing finance. GBLD may represent government real estate policies since tight real estate policies are always accompanied by the smaller GBLD. But, GBLD can also be interpreted to represent domestic environments surrounding the construction industry since pessimistic business expectations or depressed sales are usually accompanied by the smaller GBLD.

Results of variance decomposition for each period are summarized in Table 4.1. For the whole sample period, 52.2% of variance of GHPI is explained by itself and 27.4% is explained by GRR. Respectively 10.4% and 7.2% are explained by GNY and GHPI-US. Only 2.8% is explained by GBLD. Situations during 1992–2006 are similar to the whole sample period. Variances of GHPI are mainly explained by itself and GRR, 47.7% and 31.1%, respectively, and relatively small parts are explained by GNY and GHPI-US, 8.6% and 9.3%, respectively. GBLD only explains 3.3% of variances of GHPI.

After GFC, the situation becomes totally different. GBLD explains 28.0% of the variance of GHPI, which may imply that the Korean housing market after GFC is mainly affected by the real estate policies of the Korean government and Korean real estate market specific domestic factors. While the explanatory powers of GNY and GRR on the variance of GHPI decrease to 5.5% and 4.5%, respectively, that of GHPI-US drastically increases to 18.1%. But, it is not yet clear whether this implies that the international linkages of real estate prices have been increased after GFC.

Part of the circumstantial evidence for this doubt is that the movements of housing prices for different regions have been quite different in recent years. As is shown by Figure 4.3, movements of rate of changes in housing sales prices of Seoul and Busan, which is the second largest city of Korea, are quite similar up to around 2006. But then from the following year, the movements of the two cities are notably different. In Figure 4.4, it is shown that even though movements of rate of changes in the housing sales price of Seoul and Busan are quite different from that of the U.S. before 2007,

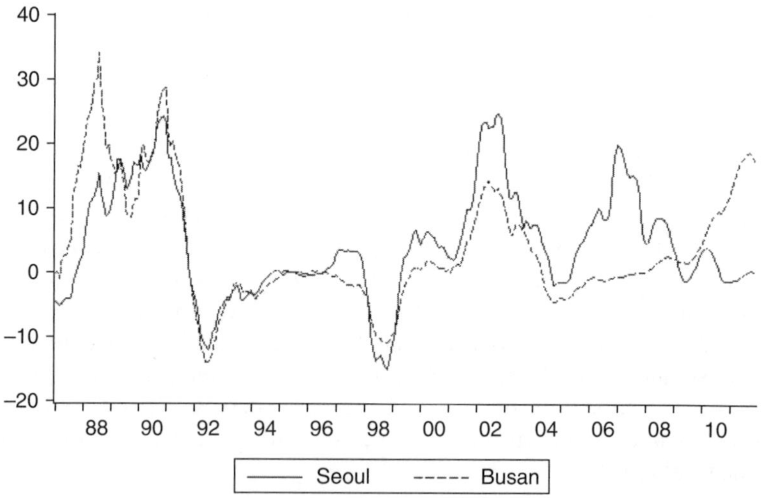

Figure 4.3 Movements of housing sales prices in Seoul and Busan

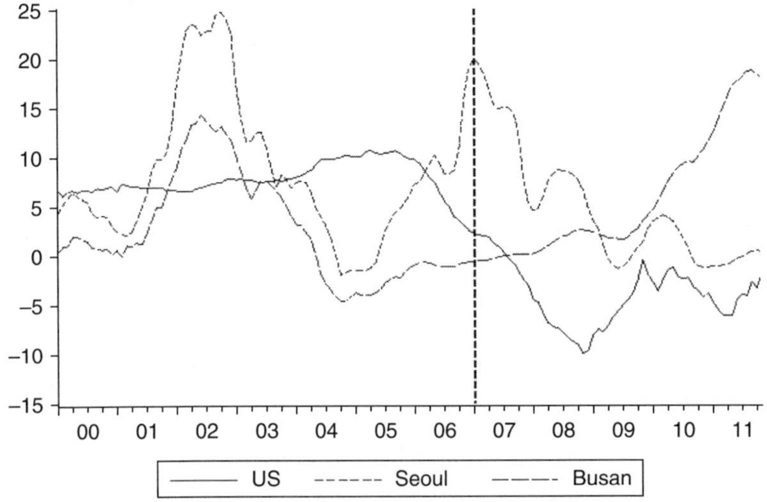

Figure 4.4 International comparison of movements of housing sales prices

we can find some similarities between movements of housing sales prices of the U.S. and Seoul after 2007. This may imply that the international linkages of real estate prices have been increased only for some regions, e.g., Seoul, not for the nation as a whole. This, however, might also imply that domestic regional factors are dominating in the case of Korea. Thus, whether the international linkages of real estate prices have increased after GFC is inconclusive in the case of Korea.

2.2 Korean Housing Market Business Cycle

As is shown by Figure 4.1, the Korean housing market clearly shows the business cycle. As for the choice of the object of housing market business cycles, two approaches are used. One is simply using the GHPI which was defined as above (Suh 2003). The other is to use the de-trended HPI obtained either by the residuals of the trend regression (Kim 1998) or by the HP-filter (Cho 1999).

In Figure 4.5, P1 is the GHPI and P2 is the HPI de-trended by the HP-filter. Movements of P1 and P2 are similar enough to conclude that using either P1 or P2 will make only limited differences in recognizing the housing market business cycle. If we run the Phillips-Peron unit root test about P1/P2, the test statistics will be obtained as −16.35, which implies that P1/P2 is $I(0)$ with 99% significance level.

By using P1 or P2, peak, trough and the length of the cycle can be

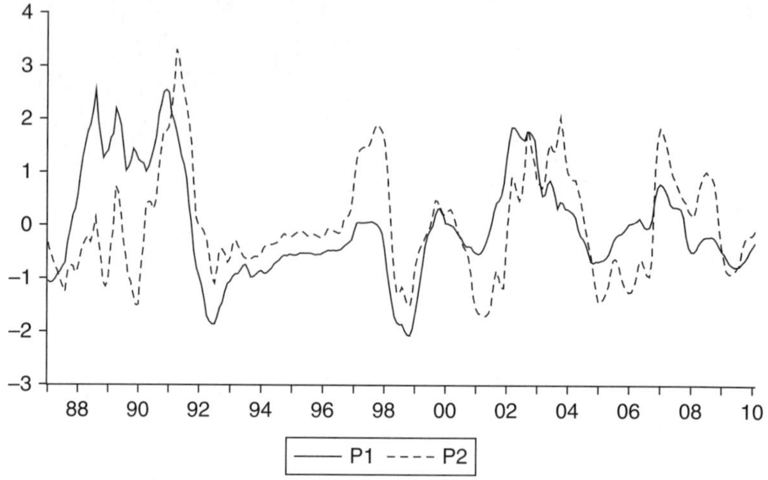

Figure 4.5 Comparison of P1 and P2

determined. Usually, peaks and troughs are determined by the casual look (Kim 1998; Cho 1999). In Suh (2003), CUSUM and squared CUSUM test results for residuals of recursive least squares regression are used in determining peaks or troughs of the land market business cycle. As for the Korean land market, it was found that the length of cycle is about 10–11 years. It was also identified that the length of the expansion phase is about 3–4 years and that of the contraction phase is about 7–8 years. Also, the length of the housing price business cycle is found to be 5–6 years.

2.3 Korean House Prices Forecasting Models

Three types of models are used in forecasting Korean house prices. These are the pure time series models, structural models and the models using the leading indicators. Pure time series models include ARIMA models and VAR models. Examples of ARIMA models are Kim (1998) and Yoon & Kim (2000). For these models, it was found that predictability of pure ARIMA models is poorer than the state space models or transformed functional models. This result may come from the fact that the Korean housing market is greatly affected by the government's real estate policies.

There are many examples of VAR models. Variables used in Suh (1994) are housing price, land price, consumer price index, stock price index, and manufacturing wages, and those used in Kang et al. (1997) are land price, money stock, per capita GDP, interest rate and exchange rate. Variables used in Suh & Kim (1999) are real GDP, stock price index, interest rate, inflation rate, manufacturing wage, money stock and building construction permits, and those used in Sohn and Kim (2002) are land price, house price, house 'Chonsei' price, real GDP, money stock, consumer price index, stock price index, interest rate, exchange rate, unemployment rate, building construction permits, construction investment and land exchange volume.

Results of impulse response analyses are generally fit to the theories. For example, the rise in interest rate causes the decrease in GHPI and the rise in stock price or GDP growth rate causes the increase in GHPI. According to the variance decomposition analyses, it was found that variance of a certain real estate price is mostly explained by related real estate price, and the explanatory powers of real GDP, stock price and interest rate are fairly low. As for the forecasting power of pure ARIMA and VAR models, VAR models have been found to have larger forecasting power.

Structural models include both simple regression models and macro-econometric models. Some models contain one or few regression equations (Kim & Choi 1992; Sohn & Kim 1993; Park et al. 2000), while some others have many equations (Suh 1994, 2000; Suh & Kim 2000; Kim Y.W. et al. 1993; Bank of Korea 2000). For example, the macro-econometric model used in Suh (1994) contained more than 100 regression equations and identities. Major variables used in structural models are housing price, land price, housing investment, housing loans, GDP, money stock, housing construction cost, volume of land supply, stock price, interest rate, building construction permits, unemployment rate, exchange rate, and so on.

In macro-econometric models, real estate market and the economy are linked by real estate prices. The rise in real estate prices increases consumption through the wealth or collateral effect. Also, the changes in real estate prices can affect the construction investment and the investment in machinery & equipment through the cost effect. Although the rise in real estate prices generally causes a decrease in the machinery & equipment investment, it has usually been found that the effect of a rise in real estate prices upon the construction investment is ambiguous because the cost and expectation effects are mingled. Since the change in real estate prices generally causes the change in general prices, it can affect the whole economy and the effects are simultaneous. The forecasting powers of structural models are generally found to be greater than the pure time series models.

Models using leading indicators include such indicators as the NBER index, Stock-Watson Index and the index obtained by using the principal component analysis. Kim & Chung (1993) construct coinciding and leading indicators for forecasting the construction cycles. Variables used to construct these indicators are building construction permits, sales volumes of cement and steel, domestic contract volumes of construction and machinery, volume of loans for construction and construction employment. Lim & Kim (1995) construct coinciding and leading indicators for forecasting the housing market business cycle. Variables used to construct these indicators are housing sales and 'Chonsei' price, land price, building construction permits, contract volumes of construction, shipment of construction materials, GDP, construction industry wage, stock price and consumer price index. Suh and Kim (2000) construct the leading indicator for land price by using macro-economic variables such as money stock, consumer price, producer price, GDP deflator, GDP growth rate, building construction permits, stock price and interest rate.

In Suh (2005), there is the forecasting power of pure time series model (PTM), pure structural model (PSM), time series model including the leading indicator (LTM) and structural model including the leading indicator (LSM). The Stock-Watson index is used as the leading indicator. Sample periods are first quarter of 1992 – fourth quarter of 2003. Each model is estimated by using the data of first quarter of 1992 – fourth quarter of 2001. By using estimated models, forecasting has proceeded for first quarter of 2002 – fourth quarter of 2003. Since there is the turning point from expansion to contraction phase around the first quarter of 2003, the forecasting period has been divided into two sub-periods. Case 1 is for 2002 and Case 2 is for 2003. Values of Root Mean Squared Error (RMSE) are used to compare the forecasting power of each model.

In Case 1, the averages of RMSE of PTM, PSM, LTM and LSM are 0.3613, 0.0326, 0.3636, and 0.0469, respectively. Also, in Case 2, the averages of RMSE of PTM, PSM, LTM and LSM are 0.6915, 0.3408, 0.1408, and 0.1904, respectively. When the business cycle phase is sustained, RMSE of PSM is the smallest and that of LSM is quite similar. But, when the business cycle is around the turning point, RMSE of LTM is the smallest and that of LSM is a little bit larger. At the point of making a forecast, it is not known whether there will be the turning point or not. Therefore, the safest method of forecasting Korean house prices might be LSM.

3. METHODOLOGIES OF CONSTRUCTING THE EWS

3.1 Definition of Crisis

In constructing the EWS, some terms should first be defined. In the case of the foreign exchange market, the market pressure index is the weighted average of the rate of changes in exchange rate, interest rate, and foreign reserves (Eichengreen et al. 1995; Goldstein et al. 2000; Kaminsky, Lizondo & Reinhart 1997). Crisis occurs when the pressure index surpasses the exogenously determined critical value. The critical value is the summation of the mean and *k* times the standard deviation of the pressure index. The value of *k* is dependent on the nature of the data (Suh et al. 2006, 2011).

Foreign exchange market crises are unidirectional. When drastic changes in foreign reserves (the decrease), interest rates (the rise), and foreign exchange rates (the depreciation) are observed, a foreign exchange market crisis is noticed (Edison 2003; Kaminsky 1998). In the case of the housing market, however, both the rapid rise and fall of house prices can be defined as housing market crises (Pace et al. 2000). EWS construction is basically the same for both expansion and contraction periods. In addition, Korean policymakers are more concerned about rapid increases than decreases in house prices because there are still many middle class non-home owners. Also, as is shown by Figure 4.1, the decrease in housing price after GFC is minimal and housing price increases picked up at a fast pace after 2010. Thus, despite current interest in depressions of housing markets, EWS construction for only the expansionary periods is considered in this chapter.

The housing market pressure index (HMPI) is determined using the house price change rate. In some cases, the weighted average of various house price indexes is used. In all cases, however, when the housing market pressure index exceeds the exogenously determined critical value, a housing market crisis is defined to occur (Suh et al. 2011).

3.2 Signal Approach Model

In the signal approach model, leading indicators, which are expected to have high explanatory powers on the occurrence of housing market crises, are chosen. When the value of a certain leading indicator exceeds the exogenously determined critical level, the signal is said to be generated by that leading indicator (Dua, Miller & Smyth 1999). Based on generations of signals of many leading indicators, the occurrence of a housing market crisis can be predicted.

3.2.1 Determination of leading indicators

Let X_t be any economic variable (t = 1, . . ., T). If the explanatory power of X_t (plural X_ts) is found to be high enough, it can be selected as one of the leading indicators. To determine this, we reshuffle X_ts in descending or ascending order. If the rise (or fall) in X_t and the occurrence of a crisis are positively correlated, X_ts are reshuffled in descending (or ascending) order. Reshuffled X_ts included between the top 10% and top 25% are equally divided into 14 parts. Thus, there will be 15 possible critical values, i.e., first critical value is the top 25% value of X_t, . . . etc. Among 15 possible critical values, the one with the lowest noise to signal ratio (NSR) is chosen.

Table 4.2 Relationships between crisis signal and crisis occurrence

	Crisis	No crisis
Crisis signal	A	B
No crisis signal	C	D

When the value of the leading indicator exceeds the critical value, the signal is defined to occur. If HMPI exceeds its own critical level within *k* months after the generation of the signal, a housing market crisis is defined to occur. Here, *k* is called the window.

After the signal occurrence, the housing market crisis may or may not occur. The same is true for the case of no signal occurrence. By using Table 4.2, good and bad signals can be distinguished. In Table 4.2, A, B, C, and D imply the number of occurrences for each case. The type 1 [type 2] error is defined as C/(A+C) [B/(B+D)].

When the increase in the leading indicator and the housing market crisis occurrence is positively correlated, the higher critical value of the leading indicator will cause the larger type 1 and the smaller type 2 errors. The lower critical value of the leading indicator will cause the opposite results. Because of these systematic changes in type 1 and type 2 errors, Kaminsky et al. (1997) define NSR as follows: NSR = type 2 error/(1 – type 1 error). In the signal approach model, the value of the leading indicator with the lowest NSR is set as the critical value. If the index randomly generates a signal, NSR becomes 1. Therefore, any economic variable with lowest NSR greater than 1 should not be chosen as the leading indicator in the empirical studies.

3.2.2 Composite crisis index and conditional probability of crisis occurrence

After all leading indicators are selected, the composite crisis index (CCI) is determined. Two methods are generally used. One is to use the number of signal occurring leading indicators. The other is to use the weighted number of signal occurring leading indicators, where NSR is used as the weight. If these two CCI values are very similar, the first can be selected for convenience.

I_t is the value of CCI at t, the value of which is found to be between the range (I_{min}, I_{max}). If we divide the range of I_t into N sub-divisions, each sub-division can be expressed as $D_1 \equiv (I_1, I_2), \ldots, D_i \equiv (I_i, I_{i+1}), \ldots, D_N \equiv (I_N, I_{N+1})$. Here, by definition, $I_{min} = I_1$ and $I_{N+1} = I_{max}$. When $I_t \in D_i$, the conditional probability of housing market crisis occurrence within k months after t, $Pr(C_{t,t+k})$ can be defined as (Kaminsky 1998):

$Pr(C_{t,t+k}: I_t \in D_i)$ = (# of months such that $I_t \in D_i$ and crisis occurrence within k months after t) / (# of months such that $I_t \in D_i$)

3.2.3 Explanatory power of composite crisis index

By using $Pr(C_{t,t+k}: I_t \in D_i)$ for each t, we can define the signal occurrence of CCI when the value of $Pr(C_{t,t+k}: I_t \in D_i)$ is over a certain value, i.e., the cutoff probability. Also, the explanatory power of CCI can be examined through the same process as explained in 3.2.2.

As the cutoff probability becomes larger, the ratio of signal occurrence during a crisis period (A/(A+C)) becomes lower, and the ratio of signal non-occurrence during a no-crisis period (D/(B+D)) becomes higher. Since these move systematically according to the cutoff probability; the ratio of correct signal and correct non-signal ((A+D)/(A+B+C+D)), the ratio of crisis occurrence after a signal occurrence (A/(A+B)), and NSR ([B/(B+D)]/[A/(A+C)]) become more meaningful.

4. EWS OF KOREAN HOUSING MARKET

4.1 Housing Market Pressure Index

In this section, HMPI will be determined by using various variables related to house price fluctuations. We adopt monthly house price data from January 1987 to December 2011, including the national housing sales price index (HPI), national "Chonsei" price index (HCI), Seoul Gangnam area housing sales price index (HPIS), Seoul Gangnam area "Chonsei" price index (HCIS), etc. "Chonsei" is a specific form of rental housings in Korea and the Gangnam area is where the volatility of housing price is the largest. The rate of changes in house prices with respect to the same month of the previous year is used in determining the HMPI. The optimal selection rule for combining these four price indexes must be determined. Through trial and error, we find that using the maximum value of the four price changes is the most appropriate.

$$\text{HMPI} = Max\ \{\text{GHPI, GHCI, GHPIS, GHCIS}\}$$

Here, "G" implies the rate of change as was defined above. The critical value is generally defined as the summation of the average and k times of the standard deviation of HMPI. If HMPI goes over a critical value, a housing market crisis is defined to have occurred. In the case of the foreign exchange market, k is generally set to 3 (Kaminsky et al. 1997). In the case of the Korean housing market, however, k is set to 1.1 (Park 2001).

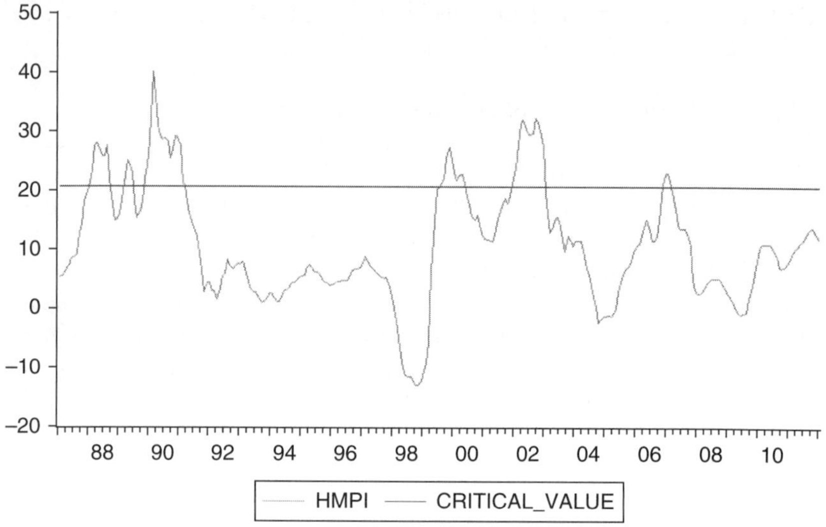

Figure 4.6 Crisis period in Korean housing market

As for determination of the critical value, no specific rule exists. Through repetitive trials, we choose 1 for the value of k.

$$\text{Housing Market Crisis Occurrence: HMPI} > \mu(\text{HMPI}) + \sigma(\text{HMPI})$$

Here, μ(HMPI) and σ(HMPI) are the average and standard deviation of HMPI respectively. By using this definition of housing market crisis occurrence, crisis periods over an expanding housing market can be determined, which is shown in Figure 4.6. There were housing market crises in around 1988, 1990, 1999–2000, 2002 and 2007.

4.2 Selection of Leading Indicators

The following macroeconomic variables are considered as the possible leading indicators: stock price index (PS), exchange rate of Korean won to U.S. dollars (ER), three-year government-issued bond rate (RR3), total currency circulation (M3), customer savings deposit (DEP), leading indicator (LIR), saving bank's saving/loan rate (DLR), consumer price index (CPI), industrial production index (IPI), manufacturing wages (W), etc. Moreover, the following housing market-related variables are considered: listed construction companies stock price index (PSCON), large scale construction contract amount (CONTL), and number of savings accounts for

Table 4.3 Selection of leading indicators

Variables	NSR	Explanatory Power
GPS	0.0270	0.9025
GER	0.0456	0.8457
XGRR3	0.0341	0.8719
GM31	0.1158	0.6834
GDEP	0.0291	0.8957
GLIR	0.0913	0.7324
GDLR	0.1085	0.6973
GCPI	0.2326	0.5180
GIPI	0.0738	0.7720
GW	0.1052	0.7038
GPSCON	0.1420	0.6378
GCONTL	0.0936	0.7276
GHSAV	0.6293	0.2843

new house purchases (HSAV). For any X, GX represents the change rate in X with respect to the same month of the previous year. Since the rise in RR3 causes the fall in HMPI, XGRR3 = −GRR3 is used.

After rearranging the leading indicators so that the value of a leading indicator and housing market crisis occurrence are positively correlated, the range between the top 10% and 25% levels of the leading indicator is equally divided into 14 parts. Thus, there are 15 possible critical values. Out of 15 possible critical values, the one with the lowest NSR is chosen as the critical value. As for the window, the length of 12 months is found to be the most appropriate.

In case of the random signal occurrence, the values of Type I and Type II errors become 1/2 for both cases, and the NSR is 1. Therefore, cases with an NSR greater than 1 are ignored. An explanatory power value below 0.25 is too low and is deleted. The chosen leading indicators are shown in Table 4.3.

4.3 CCI and the Conditional Probability of Crisis Occurrence

When all leading indicators are selected, the CCI can be calculated. Housing market CCI, HMCCI, can be determined in two ways. One is the simple summation of signal occurring leading indicators (HMCCI-1) and the other is weighted summation using the weight of NSR (HMCCI-2). As is shown in Figure 4.7, differences between HMCCI-1 and HMCCI-2 are minimal. Thus, it is suggested that HMCCI-1 is used, for the operational convenience. Hereafter, HMCCI-1 is referred to as HMCCI.

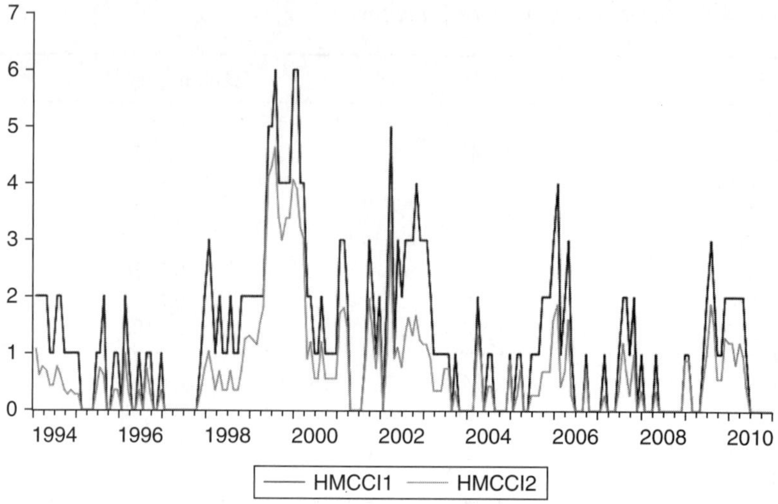

Figure 4.7 *Comparison of housing market crisis composite index*

Table 4.4 *Number of signal occurrences and conditional probability of crisis generation*

# of signal generation	# of total dates	# of total dates of crisis occurrence within 12 months	Conditional probability of crisis occurrence
0 or 1	132	9	0.0681
2	44	14	0.3182
3	14	10	0.7143
4	22	18	0.8182
5 or more	6	6	1.0000

Now, we consider the calculation of the conditional probability of crisis occurrence by using HMCCI. Values of HMCCI's range are from 0 to 6. Through trial and error, the most appropriate sub-division has been determined as Table 4.4. For each sub-division, conditional probability of housing market crisis occurrence can be calculated by the definition of $Pr(C_{t',t+k}: I_t \in D_i)$. Results of calculations are shown in Figure 4.8. Notice that the conditional probabilities are reported from 1994 because of the loss of sample points, which was caused by the differences in starting point of leading indicators and the needed lags up to 24 months in calculating the conditional probabilities.

As is shown by Figure 4.8, the conditional probability of housing crisis

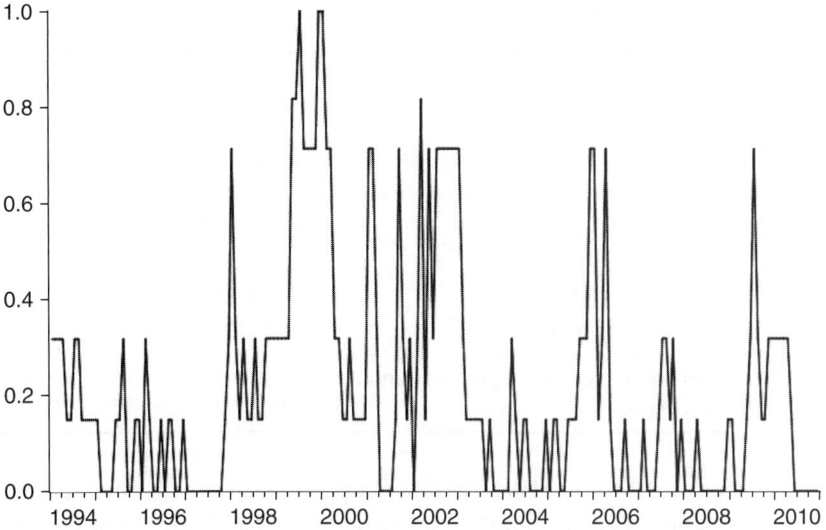

Figure 4.8 Conditional probability of crisis occurrence

occurrence in 1999, 2000–01, 2006 are very high as expected. Those high values of conditional probabilities may predict housing market crises in 1999, 2002 and 2007. The explanatory power of HMCCI can be examined by the conditional probability of housing market crisis occurrence. The evaluation of crisis prediction depends on the cutoff probability. The two cases of cutoff probability, i.e., 0.25 and 0.5 are considered.

If the cutoff probability is large, the ratio of signal indication (A/(A+C)) over a crisis period decreases due to the decreased number of signals, whereas the ratio of signal indication (D/(B+D)) increases over a no crisis period. Due to these systematic movements, the ratio of correct signal to correct no crisis signal ((A+D)/(A+B+C+D)), the ratio of crisis occurrence after signal indication (A/(A+B)), and NSR ([B/(B+D)]/[A/(A+C)]) are also considered. The results are summarized in Table 4.5. Even when the cutoff probability is as low as 0.50, the probability of crisis occurrence after signal indication reaches 0.82 (NSR is 0.04). Thus, we conclude that the signal approach model is appropriate for the Korean housing market EWS.

5. CONCLUDING REMARKS

In this chapter, movements of Korean housing market sales prices, HPI, before and after global financial crisis, GFC, have been observed. As for

Table 4.5 Prediction power of the signal approach model

Cutoff probability 0.25		
Correct signal + correct non-signal	(A+D)/(A+B+C+D)	0.74
Ratio of signal occurrence in crisis period	A/(A+C)	0.66
Ratio of signal non-occurrence in non-crisis period	D/(B+D)	0.76
Ratio of crisis occurrence after signal indication	A/(A+B)	0.51
Ratio of noise/signal	[B/(B+D)/(A/(A+C)]	0.36
Cutoff probability 0.50		
Correct signal + correct non-signal	(A+D)/(A+B+C+D)	0.82
Ratio of signal occurrence in crisis period	A/(A+C)	0.50
Ratio of signal non-occurrence in non-crisis period	D/(B+D)	0.97
Ratio of crisis occurrence after signal indication	A/(A+B)	0.86
Ratio of noise/signal	[B/(B+D)/(A/(A+C)]	0.06

the effects of GFC on HPI, the following two facts can be mentioned. Firstly, the effect of GFC upon HPI is found to be smaller than that of the Asian financial crisis, AFC, of 1997. As for the values of the rate of changes in HPIs, GHPI, very low values of GHPI are observed in March 1998 – April 1999. The average of GPHIs during that period is −9.9% with the minimum of −13.1%. But after GFC, negative values of GHPI are observed in April 2009 – October 2009 with an average of −0.6% and a minimum of −1.1%. Also, values of GHPI are increasing and reached 7.1% in November 2011.

Secondly, international synchronization or spillovers of house prices can be perceived after the GFC. In order to check this, GHPI and GHPI of U.S., GHPI-US, have been compared. After around 2007, movements of GHPI and GHPI-US are found to be very similar. This casual observation can be confirmed by the variance decomposition analysis of VAR. Variance decomposition analysis reveals that the effect of GHPI-US upon the variance of GHPI after 2007 has been significantly increased.

The tendency of synchronization or spillovers of international house prices after GFC does not necessarily imply that the foreign factors become the most important factor in determining the Korean house prices. In the case of Korea, it has been found that government real estate policies and regional specific factors might be more important. Relative importance of foreign and domestic factors in determining real estate prices of a nation needs further studies.

As is surveyed in section 2, like most other countries, it is extremely difficult to forecast the real estate prices. Thus, an early warning system (EWS), which is the non-parametric approach, is suggested to notice a housing market crisis before it occurs. By using the signal approach, a model EWS for the Korean housing market has been constructed. It has been found that the constructed EWS is considered to work appropriately. Three housing market crises, in 1999, 2002 and 2007, were able to be predicted as far as 12 months before they occurred. To sustain the favorable performance of the EWS, however, regular maintenance and reconstruction of EWS seem to be necessary.

REFERENCES

Bank of Korea, 2000, Macro-econometric model of Korean economy, Seoul (in Korean).

Beckmann, Daniela, L. Menkhoff, and K. Sawischlewski, 2006, Robust lessons about practical early warning systems, *Journal of Policy Modeling*, 28 (2), 163–193.

Burnside, C., M. Eichenbaum and S. Rebelo, 2011, Understanding booms and busts in housing markets, NBER Working Paper No. 16734.

Case, K.E. and R.J. Shillar, 1989, The efficiency of the market for single family homes, *American Economic Review*, 79 (1), 125–137.

Case, K.E. and R.J. Shillar, 1990, Forecasting prices and excess returns in housing market, *Journal of the American Real Estate and Urban Economics Association*, 18 (3), 253–273.

Cho, J.H., 1999, *Real Estate Business Cycle and the Factor Analysis*, KDI, Seoul (in Korean).

Clapp, J.M. and C. Giaccotto, 2002, Evaluating house price forecasts, *Journal of Real Estate Research*, 24 (1), 1–26.

Davis, E. Philip and Karim, Dilruba, 2008, Could early warning systems have helped to predict the subprime crisis? *National Institute Economic Review*, 206, 35–47.

Dua, P., S. Miller and D. Smyth, 1999, Using leading indicators to forecast U.S. home sales in a Bayesian vector autoregressive framework, *Journal of Real Estate Finance and Economics*, 18 (2), 191–205.

Edison, Hali J., 2003, Do indicators of financial crisis work? An evaluation of an early warning system, *International Journal of Finance and Economics*, 8 (1), 11–53.

Eichengreen, B., A. Rose and C. Wyplosz, 1995, Exchange market mayhem: the antecedent and aftermath of speculative attacks, *Economic Policy*, 21, 249–312.

Esteban, Gomez and Roza, Sandra, 2008, Beyond bubbles: the role of asset prices in early-warning indicators, *Ensayos Sobre Politica Econometrica*, 56, 114–48.

Goldstein, M., G. Kaminsky, and C. Reinhart, 2000, *Assessing Financial Vulnerability: An Early Warning System for Emerging Markets*, Institute for International Economics, Washington D.C.

Gros, D., 2006, Bubbles in real estate? A long term comparative analysis of housing price in Europe and the US, CEPS Working Document No. 239.

Gunterman, K.I. and R.I. Smith, 1987, Derivation of cost of capital and equity rates from market data, *Journal of the American Real Estate and Urban Economics Association*, 15 (2), 98–109.

Holly, S., M.H. Pesaran and T. Yamagata, 2011, Spatial and temporal diffusion of house prices in the UK, *Journal of Urban Economics*, 69, 2–23.

Ioannides, Y.M. and J.E. Zabel, 2008, Interactions neighborhood selection and housing demand, *Journal of Urban Economics*, 63, 229–252.
Kaminsky, G., 1998, Currency and banking crisis: the early warnings of distress, International Finance Discussion Paper no. 629, Washington: Board of Governors of the Federal Reserve System.
Kaminsky, G., D. Lizondo and C.M. Reinhart, 1997, Leading indicators of currency crisis, IMF Working Paper 97/79.
Kang, W.C., et al., 1997, *The Analysis of Land Price Fluctuation: Focused on IMF System and Land Price Movement*, KRERI (in Korean).
Kim, K.Y., 1998, A study on the housing market business cycle, *Journal of Korean Housing Association*, 6 (1), 5–32 (in Korean).
Kim, K.Y. and B.S. Choi, 1992, Changes of housing market business cycle and roles of housing finance, Proceedings of the 25th anniversary symposium, Korea House Bank (in Korean).
Kim, J.Y. and J.H. Chung, 1993, Study on effects of construction business cycle and housing and construction business cycle composite index, KRIHS.
Kim, Y.W., et al., 1993, *Korean Macro-Econometric Model: BOK-92*, Monthly Bulletin of BOK (in Korean).
Klyuev, V., 2008, What goes up must come down? House price dynamics in the United States, IMF Working Paper No. 187.
Lim, S.J. and Y.S. Kim (1995), Study on developing housing business cycle index, Korean Housing Corporation (in Korean).
Lunde, Jens, 2009, Financial soundness indicators for owner occupiers, *Housing Studies*, 24 (1), 47–66.
Manski, C.F., 2000, Economic analysis of social interactions, *Journal of Economic Perspectives*, 14 (3), 115–136.
Mete, Feridun, 2004, A probit model towards the prediction of financial crises, *International Economics*, 57 (4), 441–60
Pace, R.K., R. Barry, O. Gilley and C.F. Sirmans, 2000, A method for spatial-temporal forecasting with an application to real estate prices, *International Journal of Forecasting*, 16 (2), 229–246.
Park, W., 2001, Early warning system model in Korean foreign currency crisis, *International Economic Study*, 7 (1), 55–79.
Park, H.J., et al., 2000, *Structural Changes in Land Market and its Prospects*, KRIHS (in Korean).
Setzer, R., P. van den Noord and G. Wolff, 2011, Heterogeneity in money holdings across Euro area countries: Role of housing, *European Journal of Political Economy*, 27 (4).
Sohn, K.H. and H.S. Kim, 1993, *A Study on Housing Market: Housing and Housing Factor Market*, KRIHS.
Sohn, K.H. and H.S. Kim, 2002, *A Study on Structure Model of Real Estate Market*, KRIHS (in Korean).
Stock, J.H. and M.W. Watson, 1991, A probability model of the coincident economic indicators, in K. Lahiri et al. (eds), *Leading Economic Indicators: New Approaches and Forecasting Records*, Cambridge University Press, ch. 4, pp. 63–89.
Suh, S.H., 1994, Changes in capital gains of housing and its determinants, *Journal of Korean Regional Science Association* (in Korean).
Suh, S.H., 1994, *Macro-econometric Analysis of Korean Real Estate Markets*, Hongmun-sa, Seoul, Korea (in Korean).

Suh, S.H., 2000, An empirical study of behavioral changes in real estate prices, *Journal of Korean Housing Association* (in Korean).

Suh, S.H., 2003, Determinants of real estate business cycle and real estate policies, *Journal of Korean Regional Science Association*, 19 (3), 19–39 (in Korean).

Suh, S.H., 2004, A study on the construction of early warning system of Korean housing market, *Journal of Korean Regional Science Association*, 20 (3), 17–36 (in Korean).

Suh, S.H., 2005, Leading indicators of real estate prices and the construction of synthesized forecasting mechanism, *Journal of Korean Regional Science Association*, 21 (1) (in Korean).

Suh, S.H. and K.S. Kim, 1999, *An Empirical Study on the Structural Changes in the Real Estate Market*, SERI (in Korean).

Suh, S.H. and K.S. Kim, 2000, An empirical study of behavioral changes in real estate prices, Journal of Korean Housing Association, 8 (1), 5–26 (in Korean).

Suh, S.H. et al., 2006, *Early Warning System of Korean Real Estate Markets*, Ministry of Construction (in Korean).

Suh, S.H., K.S Kim and J.S. Jeon, 2011, Housing Market and Early Warning System: the Case of Korea, *European Journal of Scientific Research*, 56 (4), 539–547.

Vansteenkiste, I. and P. Hiebert, 2011, Do house price developments spillover across euro area countries? Evidence from a global VAR, *Journal of Housing Economics*, 20, 299–314.

Yoon, J.H. and H.S. Kim, 2000, *Housing Market Business Cycle and Short-Term Forecast*, KRIHS (in Korean).

5. Housing price and mortgage credit cycles: tales of two countries

Man Cho

1. INTRODUCTION

It is a historical fact that real estate boom-bust and cyclical bank lending are endogenously inter-connected. For example, the commercial real estate cycle in the U.S. in the 1980s was amplified by the lax underwriting in construction and development loans by lending institutions, in particular, by the Savings & Loan institutions, which is often termed an "unholy alliance" between lenders and developers (Litan 1992). More recently, Crowe et al. (2011) document that 35 out of 51 (almost 70 percent) housing price boom-bust episodes observed in 40 countries in recent decades were followed by a banking crisis; and two thirds of 46 "systemic" banking crises, i.e., those events that are disruptive not only to financial systems but to the economy as a whole, were preceded by the boom-bust patterns of housing prices. By contrast, only about 15 percent of stock market boom-busts preceded systemic banking crises, virtually all of which coincide with a real estate boom-bust.

With that as a backdrop, the last home price boom-bust in the U.S. (1997–current) is record-setting: the price cycle exhibits the highest total price growth rate (87% in real term), the deepest downturn (minus 35% so far), and the longest duration (14 years) in the country's recent history. And the boom-bust of the residential mortgage credit during the period was also unprecedented: having increased sharply from 2001, the total mortgage origination grew from about $100 billion (per quarter) to over $350 billion within a couple of years; in the secondary market, the share of Private-Label MBS, the vehicle for securitizing subprime and Alt-A mortgage loans, showed a lagged but even more dramatic boom-bust, rising from less than 10 percent in total MBS issuance in 2004 to over 30 percent in 2006 but dropping to almost zero after the Lehman Brothers' failure. As well documented in various academic and non-academic media, these housing and mortgage market cycles in the U.S. inflicted severe contagions to other sectors of economy, in particular, to private

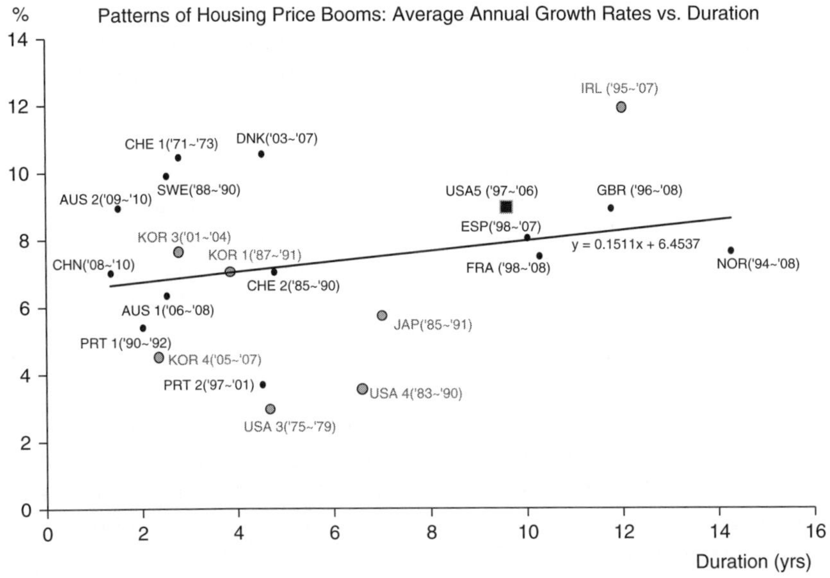

Note: Average growth rate is 53.2% and duration is 3.5 years in Taipei.

Figure 5.1 Cases of large housing price booms: an international comparison

consumption, residential and non-residential investment, and banking soundness.

There are similar episodes of large and contagious housing price cycles observed in other countries in different time periods. As shown in Figure 5.1, the recent price boom in the U.S. (1997–2006) surpasses the prior two cycles in the same country both in terms of the average annual growth rate during the boom and in terms of the duration of the boom. Nonetheless, it is not an outlier when comparing other international cases, although it certainly represents a fairly large one. For example, two price booms during roughly same time spans – Ireland (1995–2007) and Great Britain (1998–2008) – show the higher average growth rates and the longer durations. It is documented by a number of studies that some of these price booms interacted with a surge in residential mortgage lending in respective countries.[1] In general, the longer the price boom, the higher the average growth rate during the boom, as shown in the positive slope (0.15) of the trend line.

East Asian countries also experienced housing price boom-busts in different time periods, which tend to be smaller in size and shorter in duration than the recent cases observed in the U.S. and European countries.

In Korea, there were three price booms since the mid-1980s, which all entailed much shorter durations and lower average growth rates compared to the Western countries. Japan, on the other hand, had a reasonably long booming period (1985 to 1991), followed by two decades of price decline. It is also reported that, during the boom, there was a surge of mortgage credit in Japan with high-leverage (e.g., 120 percent loan-to-value ratio) loans being prevalent in the home mortgage lending sector. Last but not least, China recently experienced a sharp home price upturn from 2009, which to a large degree is explained by the rapid expansion of residential mortgage credit (Cho 2011). In particular, the ratio of mortgage debt outstanding to GDP in China has risen from 19 percent in early 2009 to 28 percent at the end of 2010, almost a 50 percent hike during only one and half years!

The main objective of this study is to measure and assess causal relationships between housing price and mortgage credit cycles of two countries – Korea and the U.S. To that end, we, first, attempt to conceptualize key causal relationships of the two cycles based on relevant literature and, second, present cases of two countries – Korea and the U.S. – in terms of evolution of, and recent milestone events in, the residential mortgage lending sector in each country, observed patterns housing price and mortgage credit cycles, and relevant empirical facts found from data analyses.

Our empirical results show that in the U.S., the housing price and mortgage credit cycles exhibit a statistically significant and, to some degree, explainable co-movement in the recent period (1997 2010), but not in prior cycles. That is, a regime shift is observed in terms of causal relationship between housing price movement and mortgage credit cycle, implying that the incidence of the subprime mortgage debacle in the U.S. is unique and would have limited policy implications for other countries.

In the Korean case, the relationship between two cycles is time-varying in that a very close co-movement is observed only in 2004–06, after which different types of mortgage lenders – banks and non-bank depositories – are shown to have divergent lending patterns. We interpret this as an outcome of differential regulatory controls on mortgage underwriting such as maximum loan-to-value (LTV) ratio and debt-to-income (DTI) ratio over those lending sectors. In particular, the leverage rate and other non-price terms in mortgage underwriting in Korea are very much conservative, making remote the possibility of a contagious housing price cycle and systemic banking crisis in the Korean context that is similar to the recent US experience. Nonetheless, our simulation results based on a dynamic stochastic general equilibrium macroeconomic model show that the LTV restriction in Korea does contribute to stabilizing private consumption and housing price movement.

From the public policy point of view, we argue that regulating the residential mortgage lending sector should consider both dimensions of ensuring macroeconomic and housing market stability via prudential regulations (i.e., managing housing sector driven systemic risk) and of enhancing housing affordability for first-time home buyers, self-employed borrowers, and other target consumer cohorts via affordable loan products (i.e., serving more underserved households). The recent U.S. experience demonstrates that the price boom-bust can be caused by various factors, e.g., exuberant home purchase by borrowers, weakened leverage and other underwriting conditions by mortgage lenders, and "the yield curve play" (or borrow-short-lend-long) by investors of mortgage securities. Therefore, we further argue that a regulatory design of the residential mortgage lending sector should impose control on a specific source of cycle amplification, whether it is an exuberant borrower, pro-cyclical lender, or yield-curve playing investor.

The rest of the chapter consists of the following five sections: a conceptual framework that links the housing price and credit cycles (Section 2); the U.S. case of the linkages that are observed and explained (Section 3); the Korean case of the linkages (Section 4); model-based policy simulations to quantify effects of LTV regulation in Korea (Section 5); and, policy implications and other concluding remarks (Section 6).

2. CONCEPTUALIZING KEY LINKAGES

There is a reasonably long history in the economic literature of examining collateralized lending and its linkages with asset price dynamics.[2] In the context of residential mortgage lending, the demand-side consists of borrowers, whose decision to purchase homes (or refinancing existing mortgages) is influenced by housing market conditions. Specifically, the user cost of capital for owning has been a key analytical tool in housing literature: that is, in a competitive housing market, the revenue generated from housing asset, i.e., per-period rental income, R, plus expected gain from future appreciation of asset price, $g^e \cdot P_h$, should be equal to the cost, $i \cdot P_h$:

$$R + g^e \cdot P_h = i \cdot P_h \tag{5.1}$$

In (5.1), i represents an after-tax cost of capital to be incurred by the home owner, which includes usual components such as financing cost, maintenance and depreciation, risk premium, along with relevant real estate tax rates. Under this equality condition, a marginal consumer should be indifferent between owning and renting.[3]

As one dis-equilibrating force, if $g^e > i$ (provided $R > 0$), then there will be an upward shift in demand for owner housing and, accordingly, its price will also increase. That is, a high expectation of future price appreciation on the part of the consumer can lead to a price boom, which, in turn, will increase demand for residential mortgage loans.

The consumer expectation on future capital gain, g^e, can be caused by various factors – shortage of housing supply (as observed in large cities in emerging market countries), inelastic housing supply with attractive locational attributes (i.e., "superstar cities" in the U.S.),[4] and rise of residential mortgage lending (which will be elaborated below). As g^e goes up, the user cost goes down (i.e., $R/P_h = i - g^e$), and, in consequence, both demand and price for owner housing will go up, a condition for a rise of irrationally-exuberant borrower-buyers. In downturn, however, consumer psychology can quickly change and g^e can be lowered rapidly, which is one of the main reasons for a regime shift in the price trend.[5]

The question is how to measure g^e. For that, Campbell, Davis, Gallin, and Martin (2009) offer an empirical model, with which one can infer g^e as a residual between realized R/P and three forward-predicted elements of i (risk-free interest rate, housing premium, i.e., housing return minus risk-free rate, and rental growth rate). We will follow their framework to estimate g^e as one of key explanatory variables in our empirical analyses.

On the supply side, the mortgage lender will determine two equilibrium lending conditions for each borrower – mortgage interest rate and leverage rate (amount of down payment relative to collateral value). In their theoretical exposition, Fostel and Geanakoplos (2008) and Geanakoplos (2010) describe how pro-cyclical lending by financial institutions and heterogeneous borrowers (with respect to g^e) can interact to create a leverage cycle. That is, in ebullient times, lenders tend to relax credit constraints by increasing equilibrium leverage rate, which, in turn, will increase the share of natural (or optimistic) buyers in the asset market. This rise of optimistic buyers, who are more risk-tolerant, will be bidding up the asset price because the larger the number of optimistic buyers in the market, the higher the willingness to pay for the asset by marginal buyers. In a downturn, the opposite can happen: that is, facing bad news from the marketplace, lenders lower the equilibrium leverage rate, which will reduce the share of optimistic buyers as well as collateral value.

In fact, the average loan-to-value (LTV) ratio among first-time home buyers in the U.S. sharply increased from about 87 percent in the early 2000s to almost 95 percent in 2005, dramatically reducing the down payment requirement. That, however, rapidly reverted back to its 1980s level after the housing price decline in 2006. Duca, Muellbauer and Murphy (2009) empirically show that the increase in LTV (hence increase in the leverage rate) reduces the user cost in the U.S. As another finding to this study, Duca et al. also show that the LTV trend in the U.S. closely tracks the rise and fall of the Private-Label MBS issuance.

Nonetheless, credit cycle is influenced by other micro details (other than the lending rate and LTV) of mortgage underwriting. For example, by using micro data, Haughwout, Lee, Tracy, and Klaauw (2011) document the surge of investor-borrowers in the U.S. mortgage market during the housing price boom, an evidence of the shift to more optimistic buyers (or "buy-and-flip investors"). During the boom, the flippers' investment behavior was enabled by weakened underwriting conditions, not only in terms of the leverage rate (as shown by the increasing LTV limit) but also in terms of other non-price terms (ONPTs) in mortgage underwriting (e.g., debt-to-income ratio, consumer credit rating, documentation requirements, and so on). Haughwout et al. also report that the multi-unit owning investors default more frequently than single-unit home owners during the downturn.

Another key player whose behavior should be examined is the investor of mortgage-driven securities. In the U.S. and other countries where the secondary mortgage market is well-developed, mortgage finance service is unbundled between lending and funding, and those who buy MBS or other mortgage related securities make their investment decisions based on their cost of capital, yield spread, and other financial market conditions.

The experience of the U.S. subprime mortgage lending sector demonstrates that, among others, the interest rate environment played a critical role in funneling a large quantity of liquidity to the residential mortgage lending sector between 2003 and 2006. That is, this particular time period was unprecedented in the recent history in two respects: between August 2002 and September 2004, the real Fed Fund Rate was negative, and the spread between long rate and short rate (10-year Treasury rate minus 1-year Treasury rate) continuously exceeded 200 basis points. This, which is unrivaled by any two-year period since 1950, offered a fertile ground for yield curve playing on the part of investors: those investors who had access to the money market could issue short-term securities such as ABCP and could have a windfall gain by investing the mobilized fund into the long-term bonds such as RMBS.[6] That favorable rate environment abruptly ended when the U.S. Fed rapidly increased the short rate from 2005, eventually creating an inverted yield curve between July 2006 and May 2007, ending the party of "yield-curve play" by RMBS investors.[7]

In this study, we attempt to systemically examine interactions between housing price and mortgage credit cycles in terms of the following factors in Korea and the U.S., as described in Figure 5.2: first, observed co-movement pattern (or lack thereof) between housing prices and mortgage

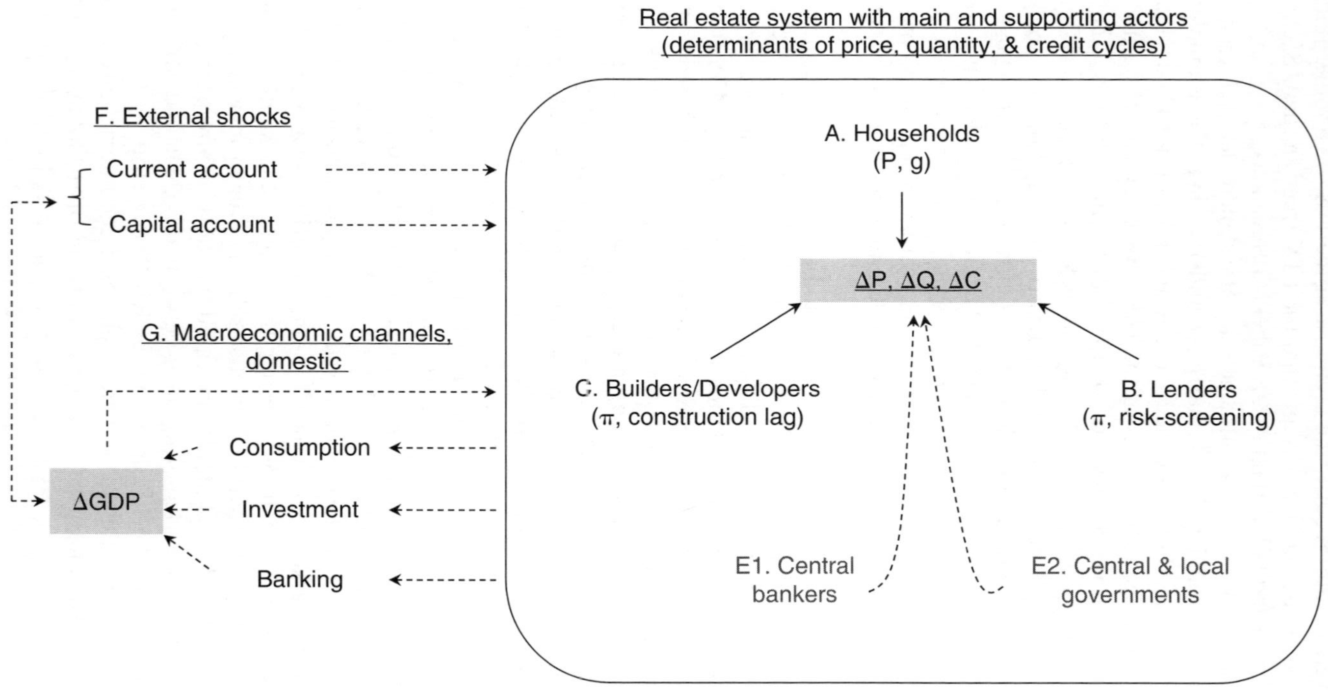

Figure 5.2 Three key cycle generators to be monitored

lending volume (ΔP and ΔC,[8] where C refers to mortgage debt outstanding (MDO) or new issuance in each country), second, trends of the key indicators of bubble-building and bubble-busting behavior by households and mortgage lenders (consumer psychology, g^e, leverage rate, other non-price terms in mortgage underwriting, and yield spread or others for interest rate environment), and, third, econometric analyses to identify causal relationships among those examined market outcomes and the indicators.

3. CASE 1: THE U.S. MORTGAGE MARKET

3.1 Evolution and Milestone Events

The first institutional mortgage lending in the U.S. began in 1835, with the "Terminating Building Society (TBS)" as the prevalent financial intermediary. TBS, whose origin goes back to 1775 in England, represents a "communal solution" to housing finance: that is, a small number of people from a town pooled savings and provided funds to one another for construction of houses; and the grouping ceased to exist once all members received the loans to build their respective homes. Later on, more formal lending institutions emerged out of TBS – to Permanent Building Societies (PBS), to Building and Loans (B&L), and eventually to Savings and Loans (S&L).[9]

Before 1980s, S&L was the predominant business model for residential mortgage intermediation. This model can be characterized as the localized lending and funding, and the bundled intermediation process (i.e., all three functions of funding, underwriting, and servicing being done internally within same financial institutions). Typical mortgage products, whose origin can be traced back to the Great Depression era, were long-term (either 15-year or 30-year maturity), fixed-rate (FRM), level-paying (constant payment each month), fully-amortizing (no balloon payment at maturity) mortgages with no prepayment penalty. Before the surge of the subprime mortgage market in 2000s, this product took more than 90 percent of market share. This plain vanilla FRM posed a low degree of uncertainty in projecting post-origination cash flows and, hence, was easy to administer (especially when being securitized), and involved with no payment shock during loan life. However, besides the problem of varying asset value as market interest rate changes, a FRM product of this sort also poses two additional cash flow issues, the well-known tilt problem (a higher payment burden early on for young borrowers) and the reinvestment (or prepayment) risk.

The first major shock in the U.S. mortgage market in recent years was the S&L crisis in the 1980s, which fundamentally changed the mode of

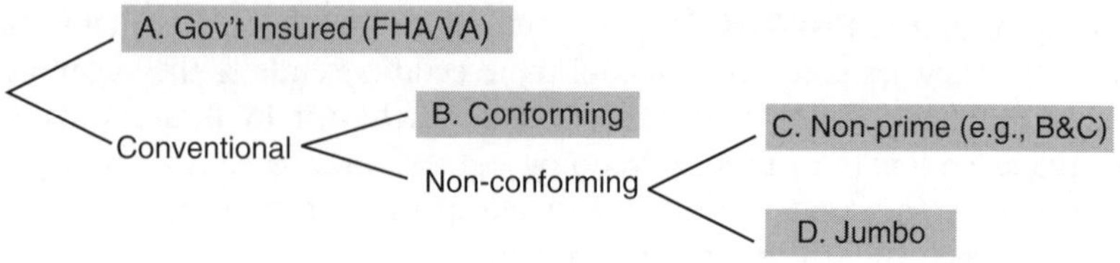

A. Gov't-insured (FHA/VA): Explicit gov't guarantee, & securitized by Ginnie Mae
B. Conforming conventional: Implicit gov't guarantee, & securitized by GSEs
C. Non-conforming non-prime: No gov't guarantee, & securitized by private-label (PL) MBS issuers
D. Non-conforming jumbo: No gov't guarantee, & securitized by PL MBS issuers

Figure 5.3 Segmentation of the U.S. mortgage market

mortgage funding in the U.S. The vacuum created in mortgage intermediation by a large number of failed S&L (more than 1,000) was gradually filled by GSEs (Government Sponsored Enterprises, referring to Fannie Mae and Freddie Mac) and Ginnie Mae, the government-run funding agency, through their issuance of MBS. The MBS market has grown steadily during the 1980s, and has steeply risen during the 1990s with its share in total origination reaching over 50 percent. The typical MBS products in the market of the plain vanilla FRMs were Pass-Through with no internal structure, and CMO (Collateralized Mortgage Obligation) with various tranches with different levels of call protection (or controls of prepayment risk) for investors. Borrower default risk was generally not a concern for MBS investors as it is guaranteed with external credit enhancements by GSEs and other service providers.

As the market for MBS grew, the GSEs' underwriting guidelines practically segmented the U.S. mortgage market. As shown in Figure 5.3, conventional loans (i.e., loans without a government guarantee) were divided into two segments: those that complied with the GSEs' underwriting guidelines, labeled as "conforming" or "A" loans; and, those that did not, referred to as "non-conforming" loans. The eligibility is essentially a bundle of loan characteristics such as the maximum allowable loan-to-value (LTV) and debt-to-income (DTI) ratios, acceptable borrower credit scores, documentation requirements, interest rate variability, and so on. The non-conforming segment is further divided into two groups, non-prime and jumbo loans. Non-prime loans, originally called "B&C" loans, are the origin of subprime and Alt-A mortgages. Jumbo loans are those that exceed the size of the GSEs' regulatory loan limit.

One major shock that occurred in the 1990s, which has not been discussed much in the context of the subprime mortgage crisis, was the IT-driven innovation in mortgage underwriting: namely, the introduction of internet-based Automatic Underwriting Systems (AUSs) that linked mortgage lenders in the primary market with securitizers in the secondary market. Both Fannie Mae and Freddie Mac implemented their AUSs in the mid-1990s (e.g., DesktopUnderwriter (DU) by Fannie Mae) and some large lenders followed suit (e.g., CAPES by Countrywide). Since then, the use of AUSs in mortgage origination and point-of-sale decisions rose sharply. For example, the share of Fannie Mae acquisitions processed through DU increased from less than 10 percent in 1997 to about 60 percent in 2002.[10]

The widespread use of AUS made mass production of residential mortgages possible, which is evidenced in the rapid rise of origination volume in the late 1990s and early 2000s.[11] Besides the dramatic reduction in transaction time and cost (e.g., the decline of processing time from a month to several minutes), it also had a profound impact in risk management, both positively and negatively. On the positive side, the assessment of credit risk became more scientific and data-driven. At the core of AUS there is a mortgage scoring model, a discriminant statistical method first used in car loan and credit card markets. It measures the level of creditworthiness of borrowers based on historical delinquencies by loan applicants and data specific to loan applications. The main improvement came from the fact that, in this model-based world, so-called "compensating risk factors" could be assessed and used more easily and accurately in loan underwriting and product development. That is, some of the risk drivers (e.g., borrower credit history, level of down payment, payment-to-income ratios, etc.) were examined in aggregate based on their risk weights from the model and, hence, overall risk for a given loan product could be assessed in a more holistic fashion both in underwriting and in pricing.

The challenge to this era of automation is potential increase in fraudulent loan applications, either via identity thefts or incorrect or invalid documentation (on employment, wealth, income, or collateral). It also increased "model risk" in that parameters of risk factors in the scoring model can be outdated, in which case projection of default risk can be fatally incorrect. The steep increases in delinquency rates, a lot higher than previously predicted, for the subprime and Alt-A mortgage loans during the global financial crisis in 2007–09 is a good illustration of this model risk.

As the last shock to mention, the widely-publicized accounting scandals of both Freddie Mac (in 2003) and Fannie Mae (in 2004) shifted the landscape in mortgage funding once again, away from GSEs toward the Private-Label (PL) MBS issuers. Those private funding institutions included investment banks (IB) and large commercial banks, including Lehman Brothers, Bear Sterns, JPMorgan, Goldman Sachs, Bank of America and Wells Fargo, as well as several major mortgage lenders such as Countrywide, Washington Mutual, and Indy Mac.[12]

Mortgage products in the subprime market are predominantly Adjustable Rate Mortgages (ARMs), in contrast to the prime market where Fixed Rate Mortgages (FRMs) are a majority. Those subprime ARMs also have various special features, often called "exotic" mortgages.[13] Such products as 2/28 Option ARMs have an additional option embedded, besides the default and prepayment options, in the form of possible refinancing decisions by lenders at the time of reset (hence, an asset to lenders but a cost to borrowers). That is, subprime lenders can waive the prepayment penalty to existing borrowers at, or right after, the reset, only if market conditions (home price appreciation, in particular) favor doing so. (Gorton, 2009) Due to this added possibility, the cash flow projection and risk assessment for subprime mortgage collateral were highly challenging to begin with.

3.2 Housing and Credit Cycles Observed

Figure 5.4 shows real annual home price growth rates in the U.S. from 1890 to 2011.[14] Over that period of a hundred or so years, a number of price cycles are observed. The first one was at the turn of the 20th century, showing a housing price boom-bust combined with the ramping up of the unemployment rate (from 4 percent in 1891 to 12 percent in 1897). Between then and the early 1970s, there were a number of cases of rise and fall, some of which appear to represent data-driven volatilities. Before, during, and after the Great Depression, there are cyclical price movements observed, which do appear to be coinciding with the macroeconomic shock.

After the 1970s, there are three more pronounced price cycles observed. During the first two – one in 1975–83 and another in 1983–93 – total price growth during the boom is followed by a fairly similar amount of decline in the downturn (in real terms). In the last one (1997–2011), however, the total cumulative real growth rate during the boom (87 percent) amounts to several times of those from the earlier booms, followed by a deep downturn of 34% price decline so far.

In the context of the credit cycle, the aspect that the price growth further accelerates from 2003 is worth noting. That propelled price boom from 2003 and the precipitous bust from 2006 is nicely coinciding with the PL-MBS issuance pattern as depicted in Figure 5.5. As shown in the figure, the mortgage origination itself started picking up rapidly from 2001, which is followed by a sharp reduction in 2004. The fall, I presume, is caused by the business shock that occurred to Fannie Mae and Freddie Mac as discussed earlier. However, the origination volume was rising again from 2004, which is co-moving with the rise and fall of PL-MBS issuance.

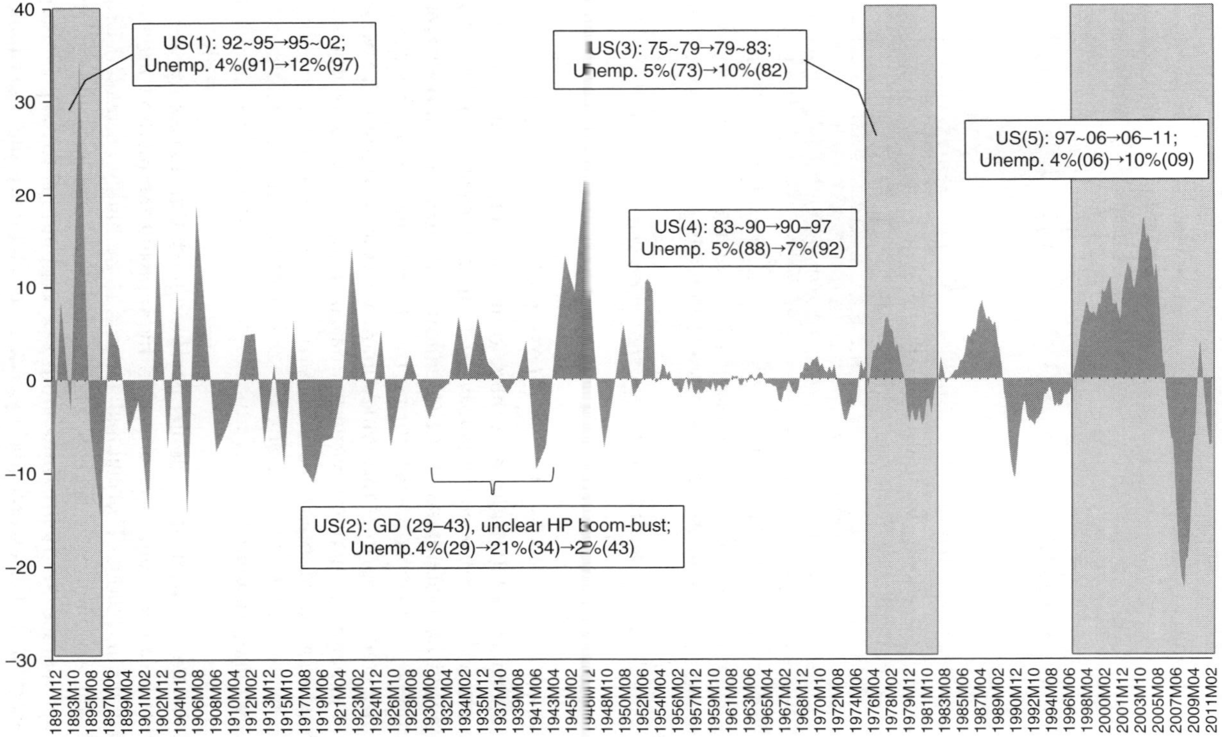

Figure 5.4 Real home price growth rates in the U.S. (1890–2011)

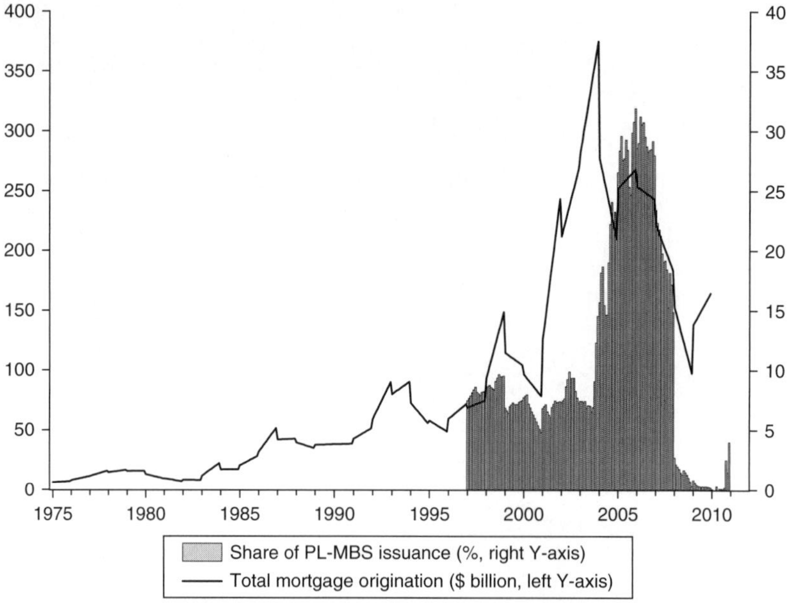

Figure 5.5 Total residential mortgage origination and Private-Label MBS Issuance in the U.S.

As reported by Mason and Rosner (2007), Gorton (2009) and Ashcraft and Schuermann (2009) among others, other non-price terms in mortgage underwriting have continuously weakened in early to mid 2000s, as evidenced by incrementally high delinquency rates from more recent origination-year loan cohorts. During the downturn, those geographical areas with high subprime and Alt-A loan origination during the boom tend to experience higher frequency defaults and distressed sales of foreclosed homes. (Mian and Sufi (2009))

3.3 Key Linkages Tested

To obtain the indicator of consumer psychology on future price appreciation, g^e, we fitted a rent-price equation by applying the method used by Campbell et al. (2009). The residual appears to be highly correlated with the housing price boom in the U.S. That is, the actual user cost trend starts declining from the late 1990s, from about 5 percent in 1997 to 3.6 percent in 2006, after which it rises very rapidly. The fitted trend, on the other hand, did come down from the early 2000s, but not as much as the actual ratio, creating the sizable residual in 2004–07.[15]

As a first step data analysis, we compiled the following housing and mortgage market indicators and performed pair-wise Granger causality tests among them (separately for 1980–97 and 1997–2010 to check a regime shift):[16]

Real annual home price growth rate in the U.S. (ΔHPI)
Residual of user cost, as a proxy for consumer psychology (RP_RES)
Annual growth rate of residential mortgage origination (ΔMORT)
Average loan-to-value ratios, as reported by Duca et al. (2009) (LTV)
Share of Private-Label MBS issuance (PL_MBS)
10-year vs. 1-year CMT yield spread (CMT_spread)
Real GDP growth rate (ΔGDP)

The results (Table 5.1) show that: three variables – expected price appreciation (RP_RES), average LTV, and share of Private-Label MBS (PL-MBS) – all Granger-cause (statistically significantly) housing price growth rates (ΔHPI) during the last cycle in 1997–2010, but not in the prior two cycles; and, the yield spread (CMT_spread) Granger-causes ΔHPI in 1980–1997 but not in the later period. For both time periods, CMT_spread Granger-causes expected price appreciation (RP_residual), but no other factor included does so. On the other hand, ΔHPI, RP_residual, LTV, CMT_spread all Granger-cause PL-MBS in 1997–2010 (no data on PL-MBS being available for the prior cycles). And ΔHPI, RP_residual, LTV, PL-MBS Granger-cause CMT_spread in the latter period.

Overall, a regime shift is detected in the latter period with more linkages between housing market indicators (ΔHPI and RP_residual) and mortgage sector indicators (PL_MBS, LTV, and CMT_Spread). The lending volume (proxied by MORT) shows no significant causality with housing or mortgage variable.

As a next step, we estimate a VAR model with all the variables listed as endogenous, also separately for the two time periods – (1) 1980–97, and (2) 1997–2010. The results (Table 5.2) generally confirm the regime shift observed: ceteris paribus, RP_residual, LTV, and CMT_spread are statistically significant determinants of ΔHPI in the latter period, but not during the prior two cycles. On the other hand, PL-MBS and CMT_spread are significant determinants of LTV in 1997–2010, while ΔHPI and LTV are key determinants of PL-MBS during the same price cycle. No significant relationship is observed between ΔHPI and the mortgage market variables in the earlier period.

Table 5.1 Granger causality tests

(1) 1980.1~1997.3

B\A	Δ(HPI)	RP_RES	ΔMORI	LTV	CMT spread	Δ(GDP)
Δ(HPI)	–	0.58	0.09	0.67	4.49***	0.11
RP_RES	0.77	–	0.10	0.55	2.98***	0.08
ΔMORI	1.50	2.14**	–	0.38	0.56	0.08
LTV	1.04	1.20	0.13	–	0.03	0.14
CMT spread	0.93	1.34	0.96	0.15	–	2.12**
Δ(GDP)	4.99***	1.59	2.10**	0.36	3.91***	–

(2) 1997.4~2009.3

B\A	Δ(HPI)	RP_RES	ΔMORI	LTV	PL/MBS	CMT spread	Δ(GDP)
Δ(HPI)	–	8.22***	0.18	3.79***	2.14**	1.59	0.68
RP_RES	1.25	–	0.10	0.19	0.44	2.08**	0.59
ΔMORI	1.13	0.74	–	0.98	0.66	0.29	0.87
LTV	0.21	0.66	0.04	–	0.59	1.66*	1.46
PL/MBS	3.93***	3.59***	0.21	2.09**	–	2.13**	0.49
CMT spread	2.33**	1.97**	1.01	2.38**	4.24***	–	3.46***
Δ(GDP)	3.82***	3.07***	1.08	1.88*	0.31	0.40	–

Notes:
1) A does not Granger Cause B.
2) ***, ** and *imply significant at 1%, 5% and 10% level, respectively.

Table 5.2 Results of VAR(1)

(1) 1980.1Q~1997.1Q

	ΔHPI	RP_RES	ΔMORI	LTV	CMT spread	ΔGDP
ΔHPI(t-1)	0.96***	0.00*	−0.57	−0.03	−0.02	0.15*
	(26.2)	(−1.7)	(−0.8)	(−1.0)	(−1.5)	(1.8)
RP_RES(t-1)	−0.01	0.84***	−9.55	0.99	0.04	4.33
	(−0.0)	(16.6)	(−0.4)	(1.0)	(0.1)	(1.5)
ΔMORI(t-1)	−0.001	0.0002	0.80***	−0.002	0.003	0.010
	(−0.2)	(1.3)	(9.1)	(−0.7)	(1.5)	(1.0)
LTV(-1)	−0.02	0.003	−1.49	0.74***	−0.02	−0.31
	(−0.1)	(0.6)	(−0.6)	(8.3)	(−0.3)	(−1.1)
CMT spread(t-1)	0.31	0.02**	2.07	−0.08	0.82***	0.05
	(1.5)	(2.6)	(0.5)	(−0.5)	(9.4)	(0.1)
ΔGDP(t-1)	0.01	−0.002	0.32	0.05	−0.001	0.18
	(0.2)	(−1.6)	(0.3)	(1.4)	(−0.1)	(1.5)
constant	0.01	0.00	1.27	0.22***	0.02	0.28
	(0.1)	(−0.6)	(0.6)	(2.9)	(0.4)	(1.2)
R-squared	0.93	0.94	0.69	0.64	0.79	0.28
Adj. R-squared	0.93	0.93	0.65	0.60	0.77	0.20

Table 5.2 (continued)

(2) 1997.2Q~2009.1Q.

	ΔHPI	RP_RES	ΔMORI	LTV	PL/MBS	CMT spread	ΔGDP
ΔHPI(t-1)	1.13***	−0.01***	1.18	−0.09***	0.37***	−0.02	0.07
	(24.3)	(−3.9)	(1.2)	(−4.1)	(3.9)	(−1.5)	(0.8)
RP_RES(t-1)	5.35***	0.88***	−4.83	−0.76	3.34	−1.03***	1.34
	(4.3)	(21.0)	(−0.2)	(−1.3)	(1.3)	(−3.8)	(0.6)
ΔMORI(t-1)	−0.01**	0.0001	0.72***	−0.002	−0.01	0.003***	0.01
	(−2.1)	(0.7)	(7.1)	(−0.8)	(−0.7)	(3.4)	(0.6)
LTV(-1)	0.44*	−0.002	−1.83	0.41***	1.48***	−0.08	−0.42
	(1.7)	(−0.3)	(−0.3)	(3.5)	(2.8)	(−1.4)	(−0.8)
PL/MBS(t-1)	−0.004	−0.004*	−0.92	0.11***	0.73***	−0.04**	0.14
	(−0.1)	(−1.7)	(−0.6)	(4.0)	(5.5)	(−2.6)	(1.1)
CMT spread(t-1)	0.53**	−0.01*	−8.98*	0.39***	0.15	0.85***	−0.15
	(2.2)	(−1.8)	(−1.7)	(3.6)	(0.3)	(16.1)	(−0.3)
ΔGDP(t-1)	−0.03	0.002	−4.46**	−0.09**	0.09	−0.02	0.24
	(−0.4)	(0.6)	(−2.5)	(−2.4)	(−0.5)	(−1.4)	(1.6)
constant	−0.38*	0.003	1.91	0.52***	−1.30***	0.08	0.38
	(−1.7)	(0.3)	(0.4)	(5.1)	(−2.8)	(1.5)	(0.9)
R-squared	0.99	0.99	0.69	0.95	0.93	0.95	0.48
Adj. R-squared	0.98	0.99	0.63	0.94	0.92	0.94	0.39

Notes:
1) t-statistics are reported in parenthesis.
2) ***, ** and * imply significant at 1%, 5% and 10% level, respectively.

4. CASE 2: THE KOREAN MORTGAGE MARKET

4.1 Evolution and Milestone Events

The Korean mortgage market represents one of the fastest-growing markets in the world, thanks mainly to the financial liberalization after the Asian Financial Crisis (AFC) in 1997–99. Before AFC, the access to mortgage credit was limited, mostly to selected groups of target households, and the lending rates were also a below-market subsidized level.

After AFC, two particular deregulations turned out to be catalysts in expanding the mortgage finance system in the country dramatically: first, the liberalization of both the lending rates and the deposit rates, which started from 1991 and accelerated after AFC; second, the removal of the restriction on real estate lending by private financial institutions.[17] These regulatory changes enabled the rapid growth in mortgage lending, as well as the creation of mortgage securitizer in 2003, the Korea Housing Finance Corporation (KHFC) as a wholly government-owned MBS issuer. As of the end of 2008, MDO-to-GDP in Korea amounts to 33%, a big jump from around 10% before the crisis.

In terms of mortgage product, Korea represents a typical ARM market, with over 90% of outstanding mortgage contracts as adjustable-rate, one of the highest ARM shares among OECD countries. As an additional risk factor, the majority of ARMs in Korea have short maturities (about 40% having three years or less) and are interest-only (or non-amortizing), although they are declining in new contracts in more recent years, posing a severe payment shock and rollover risk if and when housing and mortgage markets face a downturn. There are other product features that make mortgage lending in Korea less consumer-friendly, e.g., frequent rate reset (every three months), prepayment penalty for both FRM and ARM, and no cap structure.

The market for securitization is still being developed in Korea, with the total size of the ABS-MBS outstanding being about 11% of GDP (compared to 70% in the U.S.). Probably as a coincidence, in both countries, collaterals backing the securities are predominantly real estate loans, with 74% of securities in the U.S. being commercial or residential MBS and with about 72% in Korea being ABS or ABCP backed by construction loans (referred to as Real Estate Project Finance Loans) and residential MBS. The main difference between the two countries is the much shorter maturities of the securities in Korea (about 40% of them having less than one year maturity), implying that the securitization of residential mortgages has not yet helped in developing long-term bond markets in Korea.

4.2 Housing and Credit Cycles in Korea

Ever since economic growth took off in the 1960s, there have been several pronounced real estate price cycles in Korea. Although the housing price indexes in Korea do not go back before 1986, it appears that the cycle in the 1970s (based on the land price index) was the most volatile one. However, it would not be that meaningful to extend our analysis before AFC as the mortgage finance system went through an overhaul thereafter. In the 2000s, there were two major housing price cycles – one in the early 2000s and another in 2005–07, after which the price has been declining, or stagnating, since 2008 in response to the financial crisis.

Figure 5.6 shows that the co-movement pattern between two cycles in Korea is time-varying. That is, the MDO cycle was closely tracking the price cycle in 2003–07, confirming the linkage as hypothesized in Section 2 and as evidenced by the recent boom-bust in the U.S. However, the two tend to diverge after 2007. Specifically, both the price and MDO began decelerating from early 2007, which may reflect effects of the DTI regulation by the Korean government from January 2007, implemented in the prior year (which differentiates geographical areas depending on expected levels of speculative housing acquisition).

Another notable pattern observed is that, after GFC, the price cycle and the bank MDO growth rates are inversely correlated in the second half of 2008 until the end of 2009, while the non-bank MDO changes co-move with the price during the same period. Given that non-bank lenders in Korea are generally not penetrating the business lending sector, the deviation can be construed as a possible substitution in the lending portfolio of banks away from business lending and more toward consumer lending. Alternatively, the divergence may be caused by difference in supervision by banking authorities over primary vs. secondary banking sectors in Korea, which is to be confirmed by further research.

Although the mortgage lending sector in Korea faces product risk, i.e., the very high ARM share with its own special features (e.g., no cap structure) that can work as a risk factor during a downturn, the underwriting criteria are fairly, probably overly, conservative. As shown in Figure 5.7, the LTV and DTI trends in Korea are very low and stable: while the average (the top 90th percentile) LTV is hovering right below 40 (mid-50) percent, the average (the top 90th percentile) DTI is around 20 (30) percent. These conservative ratios imply that the mortgage lending sector in Korea can work as a stabilizer if and when a downturn in the economy occurs. At the same time, however, the sector would have room for further growth in serving more underserved households (or more borrowing-constrained consumers) without so much impairing the stability of the housing market and macroeconomy.

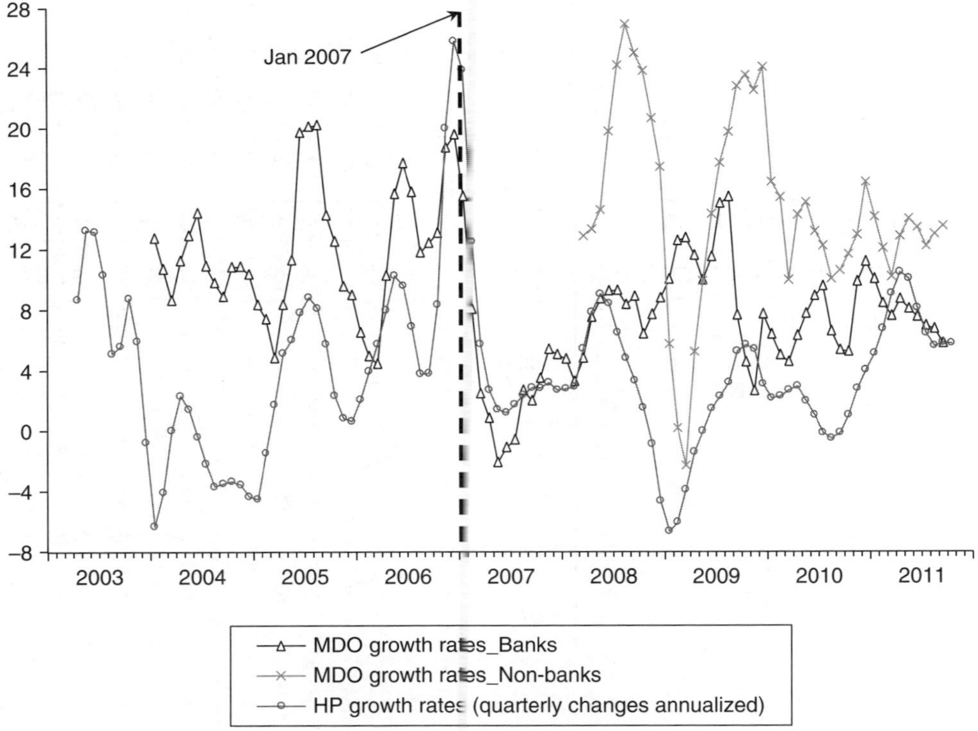

Figure 5.6 Home price and MDO growth rates in Korea (2003 to 2011; MDO by banks vs. non-banks)

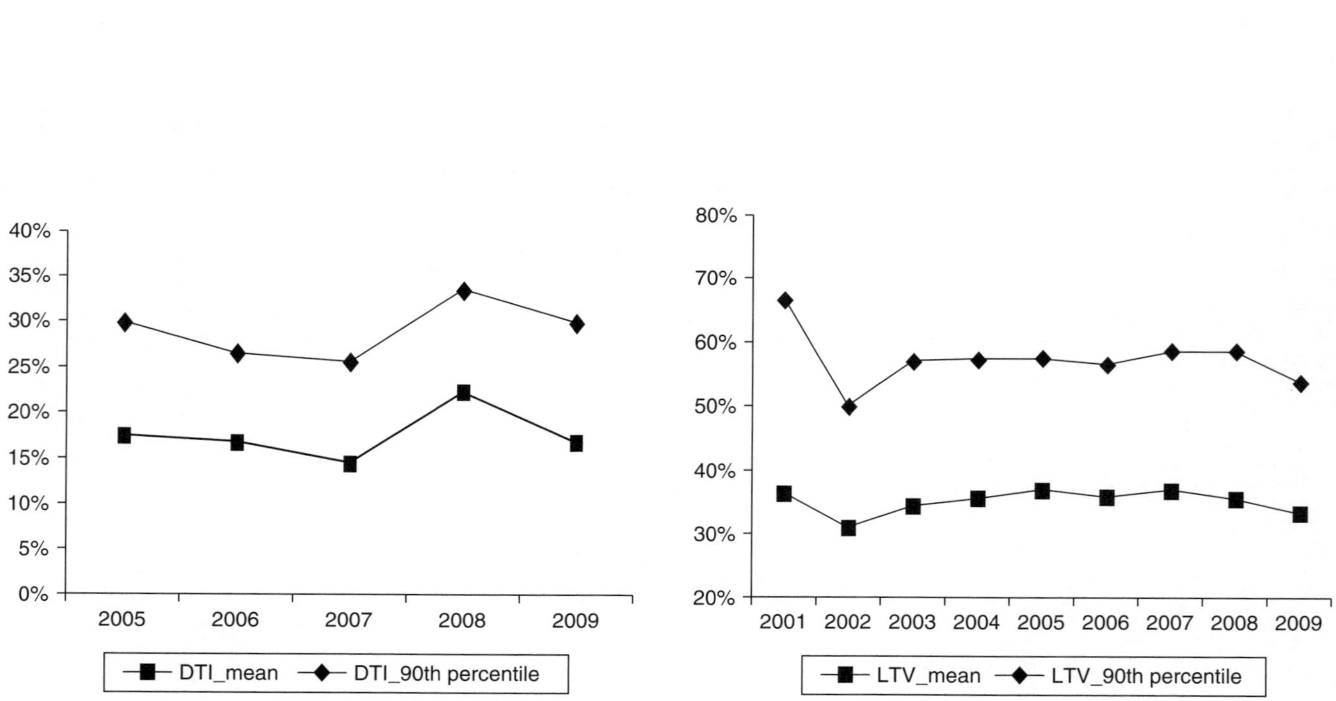

Source: Survey of Demand for Housing Loan (Kookmin Bank).

Figure 5.7 LTV and DTI trends in Korea

In the next section, we simulate effects of LTV restriction in Korea on housing price and private consumption, based on a similar testing framework employed by Crowe et al. (2011).

5. POLICY SIMULATIONS: THE KOREAN CASE

We test outcomes of differential regulatory controls on mortgage underwriting such as maximum loan-to-value (LTV) ratio by model simulations. Specifically, we use the DSGE model as developed by Song (2011) to perform the simulations. The economy, calibrations, and estimation follow the same structure as Song (2012). In simulations, we highlight the effects of the LTV restriction on both housing prices and consumption, so that we document that the control does contribute to stabilizing private consumption and housing price movement.

5.1 Tightening Monetary Policy, Loan-to-Values and Consumption

The high interest rate imposes restrictions in consumption on bigger debt holders, given all other conditions are constant. When we are in difficulty, such as an economy with bigger debt, a higher interest rate causes us to consume less. Figure 5.8 shows that when a rise in the interest rates takes place, bigger debt holders consume less. From the simulations, tightening monetary policy of a 1 percent rise in the interest rate with 50 percent loan-to-value ratios decreases aggregate consumption by 1.84 percent. As the loan-to-value ratio increases to 60 percent, a 1 percent rise in the interest rate decreases consumption by 2.04 percent. Moreover, as the loan-to-value ratio further increases to 70 percent, consumption falls by 2.6 percent. From this simulation, it is found that loan-to-value ratios play an important role in explaining significant changes in consumption through the shock of the rise in interest rates.

5.2 Tightening Monetary Policy, Loan-to-Values and Housing Prices

These simulations suggest that lower loan-to-value ratios reduce the risk of the housing market. Figure 5.9 shows that in the presence of tightening monetary policy, loan-to-value ratios amplify the volatility of housing price. Lower loan-to-value ratios show tradeoffs between the housing market stability and affordability of credit for credit-constrained households. Low loan-to-value ratios impose limitations of credit for wealth-constrained households. Hence the market stability through the loan-to-value ratio regulations sacrifice the affordable mortgage for the

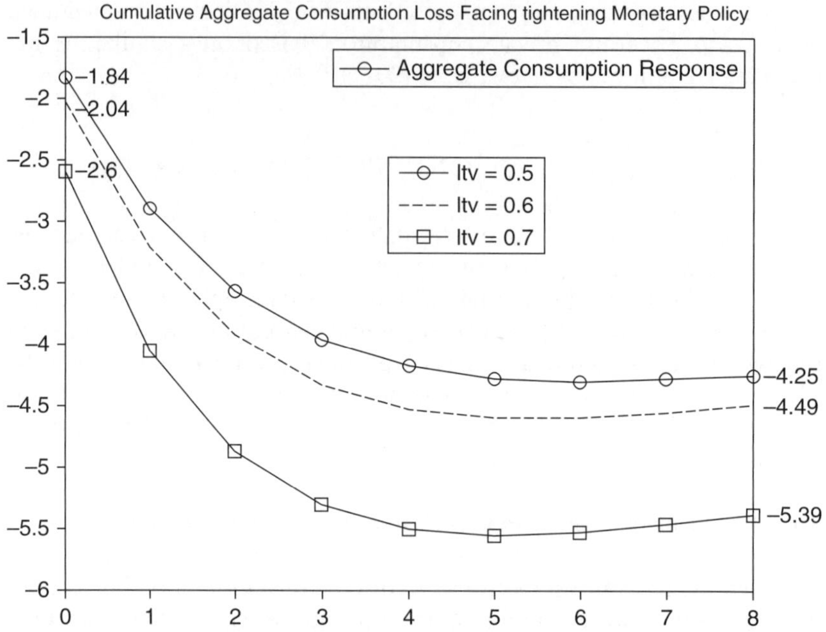

Figure 5.8 Tightening monetary policy, the loan-to-value ratios, and consumption

credit- and wealth-constrained households. In addition, we also see how much the loan-to-value ratios affect housing prices.

The rise in the interest rate with the presence of higher loan-to-value ratios serves to significantly decrease housing prices and investment. Tightening monetary policy of a 1 percent rise in the interest rate with 50 percent of loan-to-value ratios decreases housing prices and investment by 2.8 percent and 0.633 percent, respectively. Higher loan-to-value ratios increase the volatility of housing prices. Tightening monetary policy of a 1 percent rise in the interest rate with 70 percent of loan-to-value ratios decreases housing prices and investment by 3.1 percent and 1.21 percent, respectively. Loan-to-value regulations provide financial market stability.

On the one hand, this simulation shows that loan-to-value ratio regulations reduce the risk of market instability. Additionally, the investment volatility can be reduced through lower loan-to-value ratios. As a matter of fact, tightening monetary policy induces lower investment, while the speed of drop in investment can be faster in the presence of high loan-to-value ratios. Hence the loan-to-value ratio regulations play a macro-prudential instrument role in the economy.

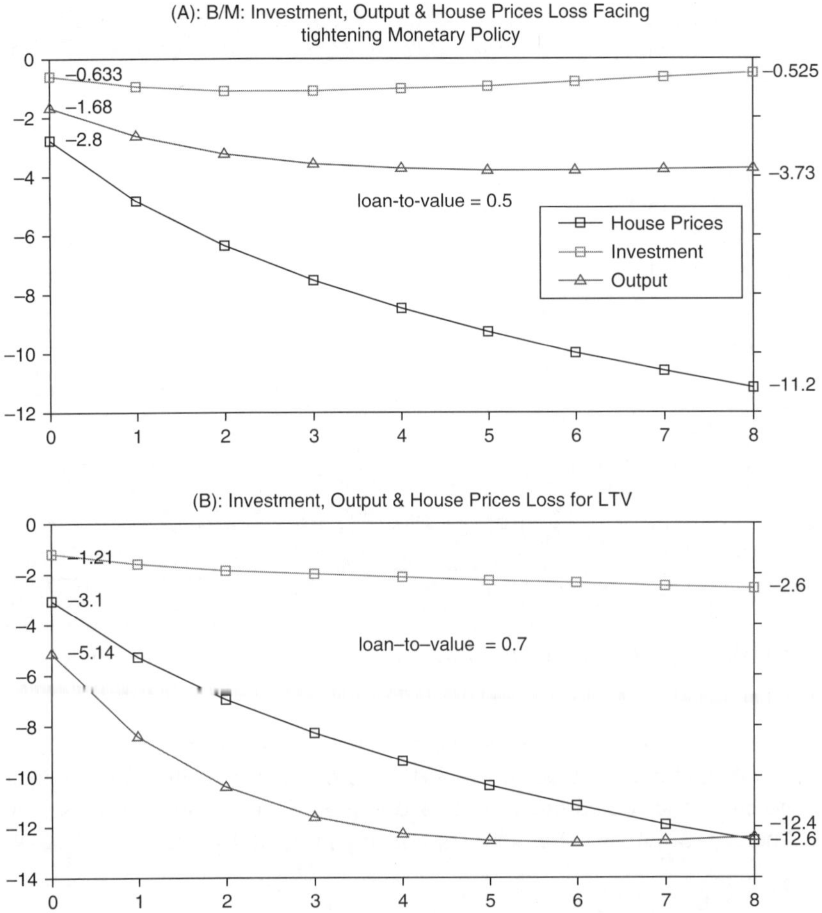

Figure 5.9 *Tightening monetary policy, loan-to-value ratios, and housing price*

5.3 Loan-to-Values, Housing Prices and Consumption

Figure 5.10 shows that housing prices rise with loan-to-value ratios. The existence of loan-to-value induces a collateral effect. The law of demand is subordinated to the extent to which housing is collateralized. Housing price boosts consumption through the collateral effect. A 1 percent rise in housing prices with 50 percent loan-to-value ratios increases consumption by 0.029 percent at impact, representing the triangle line. When loan-to-value ratios are set to 60 percent, consumption, which is denoted by the

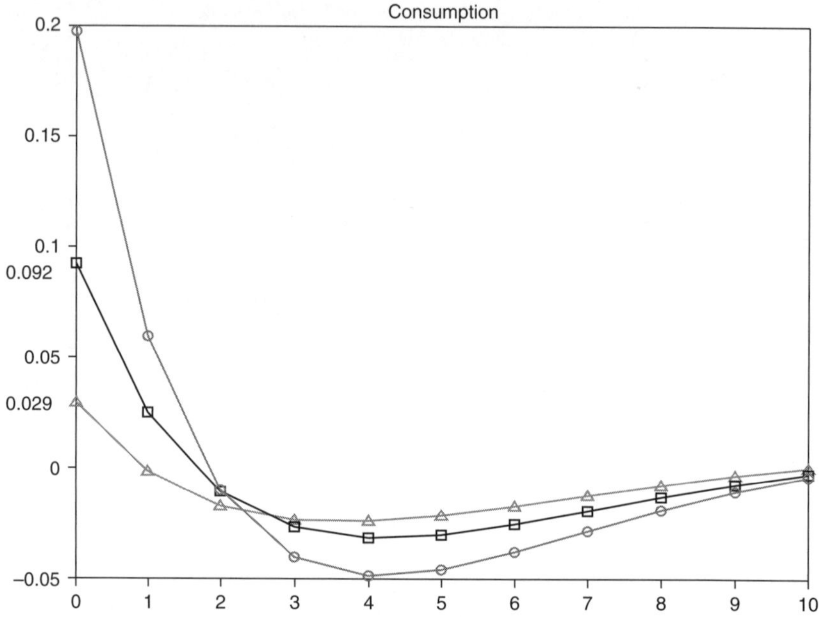

Figure 5.10 The loan-to-value ratios, housing price, and consumption

squared line, increases by 0.092 percent after a rise in housing price of 1 percent. As loan-to-value ratios further rise to 70 percent, consumption denoted by the circled line is more accelerated. Consumption increases by 0.2 percent at impact after a rise in housing price of 1 percent.

6. CONCLUDING REMARKS

This study attempts to explain linkages between housing price and mortgage credit cycles based on two country cases. From the U.S. case, we document that the last price cycle in 1997–current exhibits a statistically meaningful relationship between two cycles, implying that the impact of mortgage lending on a real estate cycle is far from uniform and tends to be time-varying. Based on our results, it is fair to say that future research, both theoretical and empirical, is warranted to explain more about endogenous linkages between the price and credit cycles as well as transmission mechanisms of mutual influence to each other. The U.S. experience in the recent cycle does show that it is imperative to properly monitor behavior of potential amplifiers of the real estate cycle, in particular, exuberant borrowers, pro-cyclical mortgage lenders, and yield curve playing investors of mortgage securities.

The Korean case also shows that the linkage between the two cycles tends to be time-varying, and that different types of lenders reveal different lending patterns. Given that the mortgage underwriting criteria in Korea are very much conservative and the boom-bust cycles do not entail a high volatility as observed in the U.S. and other countries, we can conclude that chances of a similar contagious real estate cycle and systemic banking crisis occurring in Korea are low. However, the subprime mortgage debacle also offers a lesson in that it is highly difficult to predict what would happen under a tail stress event. In that juncture, our simulation results provide a positive initial result as to stabilization effects of LTV restriction as a macro-prudence regulation. Obviously, there are many unresolved issues regarding such regulatory restrictions, e.g., what levels are proper thresholds (i.e., DTI and LTV limits), how one can interact those limits with product or borrower characteristics and market conditions (e.g., housing price volatility), when to activate (or not to activate) such restrictions (i.e., ex ante to a perceived price bubble or ex post), and so on. All these appear to be subjects for further analytical endeavor as well.

Finally, as we discussed in prior sections, the macro-prudential regulations to ensure housing market and macroeconomic stability should be balanced with the issue of housing affordability, in particular, for credit-constrained households. That is, government involvement in the mortgage lending sector should be two-track: on the one hand, properly containing a contagious lending cycle by getting to cycle amplifiers such as "flipper-borrowers" for investment, and, on the other hand, adequately expanding housing finance service to borrowing-constrained marginal consumers such as low-income and low-creditworthy first-time home buyers. In coming years, we plan to extend our research to various theoretical, empirical, and policy issues involved with this two-track policy initiative applicable to Korea and other countries.

NOTES

1. For empirical studies on linkages between housing price cycle and lending cycle, refer to Hofmann (2001) and (2003) for 20 or so countries in 1985–2001, Greef and Haas (2001) for the Netherlands, Davis and Zhu (2004) for 17 countries in 1989–2002, Oikarinen (2009) for Finland, Gimeno and Martinez-Carrascal (2010) for Spain, Gerlach and Peng (2005) for Hong Kong, Liang and Cao (2007) for China, and Park, Bahng, and Park (2010) for Korea.
2. Refer to Kiyotaki and Moore (1997), and Geanakoplos (1997) among others for the modern theory on the role of collateralized lending.

3. Refer to Himmelberg, Mayer, and Sinai (2005), Duca, Muellbauer, and Murphy (2009), and Muellbauer (2012) among others for details of this equilibrium condition.
4. See Glaeser, Gyourko and Saks (2005), Glaeser, Gyourko, and Saiz (2008) among others for the role of supply elasticity or regulatory restrictiveness in bubble-building in housing prices.
5. For example, a prolonged period of above-trend housing construction can result in overhang of excess supply, which depresses price decline (Ellis 2008). As to the effect of mortgage lending, a growing number of studies document evidences on the correlation between the recent price hike and the mortgage lending outcomes. That is, sub-national home price growth rates are shown to be positively (negatively) correlated with the amount of subprime mortgage lending in the localities during the upturn (the downturn) (Mian and Sufi 2009; Pavlov and Wachter 2011; Wheaton and Nechayev 2008; Coleman et al. 2008; Goetzmann et al. 2009).
6. ABCP and RMBS refer to Asset Backed Commercial Paper and Residential Mortgage Backed Securities, respectively.
7. There are certainly other factors that make subprime MBS investors' behavior cyclical, as reported in literature: the uncertainty caused by product complexity (in Subprime ABS CDO and Subprime ABS CDO-squared), which was the source of the liquidity spiral after the Lehman bankruptcy (Brunnermeier 2009; Fender and Mitchell 2009; Ashcraft and Schuermann 2008); and, the pro-cyclical bond ratings by rating agencies, which exacerbated the downturn from the second half of 2007 (Benmelech and Dlugosz 2009; Griffin and Tang 2009). It refers to the feedback loop driven: drop in asset value of subprime mortgage securities → fire sale by holders of such securities → increase in margin requirement by lenders (to security holders) → further fire sale and drop in security value, and so on.
8. In this study, we do include quantity (or construction) cycle, ΔQ, within our scope. As such, we do not explicitly examine the builder's behavior, another source of cycle amplification.
9. See Cho (2007) and (2009) for a detailed description of the evolution of the U.S. mortgage and MBS markets.
10. Cho (2007).
11. AUS has been contributing to further specialization in mortgage origination and in servicing, as key market participants achieve economies of scale in various intermediation steps. For example, the volume of loans originated by mortgage brokers has increased since the implementation of AUS because the cost of interfacing with the borrower and making the underwriting decision has been equalized for large and small lenders with the use of the AUS tools. Many large lenders are now focusing more on servicing with specialized AUS and IT solutions both in streamlining its administrative tasks (e.g., disbursing tax and insurance payments and reporting to investor and borrower) as well as in managing problem loans (deciding which loans present the greatest risk of default and then focusing their collection effort on them).
12. In fact, the competition between GSEs and the PL MBS issuers is rooted from the early 1990s and, more often than not, it went beyond the market place. That is, the public policy debate on the role of GSEs in the mortgage market frequently surfaced as a hot topic for both academic studies and media coverage. Some of the private MBS issuers even formed a trade organization, called "FM Watch," as a vehicle to lobby Congress for limiting the GSEs' function in the mortgage finance industry.
13. They include Interest Only (IO) ARMs, Option ARMs (for which borrowers have several options to choose in each payment mode including a negative amortization of principal), 2/28 or 3/27 Hybrids (that usually have below-market interest rates and non- or negatively-amortizing principal during first 2–3 years of loan life), and 40-year maturity ARMs. These exotic mortgage loans gradually increased their shares in total subprime origination between 2002 and 2006.
14. The price data before 1975 are from Shiller (2008), while periods thereafter use combined data from Federal Housing Finance Agency and Fiserv (the Case-Shiller indexes).

15. There is one policy shift in the U.S. that seems to be coinciding with the fall of the R/P ration: The Taxpayer Relief Act of 1997 practically made the capital gains tax rate close to zero for most home owners, by allowing home sellers to exclude $500,000 (or $250,000 for single filers) capital gains when they sell their homes and to potentially claim such an exclusion as often as every two years. Before this change, only those 55 years or older could claim a one-time exclusion of $125,000 against their capital gains, and a number of studies examine the effects of this particular policy change (Farnham 2006; Biehl and Hoyt 2007; Cunningham and Engelhardt 2008; Shan 2011).
16. Data sources of the included variables – to be included.
17. See Cho and Kim (2010) for details of the liberalization of mortgage lending in Korea.

REFERENCES

Adrian, T., and H. Shin, 2009, "Liquidity and Leverage," Journal of Financial Intermediation, forthcoming.

Ashcraft, A., and T. Schuermann, 2008, "Understanding the Securitization of Subprime Mortgage Credit," Federal Reserve Bank of New York Staff Report, #318.

Benmelech, E., and J. Dlugosz, 2009, "The Alchemy of CDO Credit Ratings," Journal of Monetary Economics, 56, 617–634.

Biehl, A., and W. Hoyt, 2007, "The Taxpayer Relief Act of 1997 and Homeownership: Is Smaller Now Better?" Paper presented at the annual meeting of the National Tax Association, Columbus, OH.

Brunnermeier, Markus K., 2009, "Deciphering the Liquidity and Credit Crunch 2007–2008", Journal of Economic Perspectives, 23(1), Winter, 77–100

Campbell, S., M. Davis, J. Gallin, and R. Martin, 2009, "What Moves Housing Markets: A Variance Decomposition of the Rent-Price Ratio," Journal of Urban Economics 66:2, 92–102.

Cho, M., 2007, "180 Years' Evolution of the US Mortgage Banking System: Lessons for Emerging Mortgage Markets", International Real Estate Review, 10(1), 171–212.

Cho, M., 2009, "Managing Mortgage Credit Risk: What went wrong with the subprime and Alt-A markets?" Working Paper.

Cho, M., and Kyung-Hwan Kim, 2010, "Structural Changes, Housing Price Dynamics and Housing Affordability in Korea," Housing Studies, Vol. 25, No. 6, November 2010, pp. 839–856.

Cifuentes, R., G. Ferruci, and H. Shin, 2005, "Liquidity risk and contagion," Journal of the European Economic Association, 3, 556–566.

Collyns, C., and Senhadji, A., 2001, "Lending booms, real estate bubbles and the Asian crisis," IMF Working Paper, No. 02/20.

Crowe, C., G. Dell'Ariccia, D. Igan, and P. Rabanal, 2011, "Policies for Macrofinancial Stability: Options to Deal with Real Estate Booms." IMF Staff Discussion Note SDN/11/02.

Cunningham, C., and G. Engelhardt, 2008, "Housing Capital-Gains Taxation and Homeowner Mobility: Evidence from the Taxpayer Relief Act of 1997," Journal of Urban Economics, 63(3): 803–815.

Davis, E., and Zhu, H., 2004, "Bank lending and commercial property prices: some cross country evidence," BIS Working Paper No. 150.

Duca, J., J. Muellbauer, and A. Murphy, 2009, "Housing Prices and Credit

Constraints: Making Sense of the U.S. Experience," Presented at the 2010 ASSA Meeting, Atlanta, U.S.A.
Ellis, L., "The Housing Meltdown: Why did it happen in the United States?," BIS Working Papers no.259, 2008.
Fender, I., and J. Mitchell, 2009, "The Future of Securitization: How to Align Incentives," BIS Quarterly Review, September, 27–43.
Fostel, A., and J. Geanakoplos, 2008, "Leverage Cycles and the Anxious Economy," American Economic Review, 98 (4) (September), 1211–44.
Geanakoplos, J., 1997, "Promises, Promises," in W.B. Arthur, S. Durlauf, and D. Lane, eds., The Economy as an Evolving Complex System, vol. 2, 285–320. Reading, Mass.: Addison-Wesley.
Geanakoplos, J., 2010, "Solving the Present Crisis and Managing the Leverage Cycle," FRBNY Economic Policy Review, August.
Gerlach, S. and Peng, W., 2005, "Bank lending and property price in Hong Kong," Journal of Banking and Finance, 29, 461–481.
Gimeno, Ricardo and Martinez-Carrascal, Carmen, 2010, "The Relationship Between Housing Prices and House Purchase Loans: The Spanish Case," Journal of Banking and Finance, 34, 1849–1855.
Goetzmann, W., L. Peng, and J. Yen, 2009, "The Subprime Crisis and Home Price Appreciation," Presented at the 2010 ASSA Meeting, Atlanta, U.S.A.
Gorton, G., 2009, "Securitized Banking and Run on Repo," NBER Working Paper 15223.
Gramlich, R., 2007, Subprime Mortgages: America's Latest Boom and Bust, The Urban Institute Press, Washington, D.C.
Greef, I.J.M. and Haas, R.T.A., 2001, "Housing prices, bank lending, and monetary policy," De Nederlandsche Bank Research Series Supervision Paper 31, 1–23.
Green, R., and S. Wachter, 2005, "The American Mortgage in Historical and International Context," Journal of Economic Perspectives, 19(4).
Glaeser, E., J. Gyourko, and A. Saiz, 2008, "Housing Supply and Housing Bubbles," Journal of Urban Economics, 64:2, 198–217.
Glaeser, E., J. Gyourko, and R. Saks. 2005, "Why Have House Prices Gone Up?," American Economic Review 95:2, 329–333.
Griffin, J., and D. Tang, 2009, "Did Subjectivity Play a Role in CDO Credit Ratings?" Presented at the 2010 ASSA Meeting, Atlanta, U.S.A.
Haughwout, A., D. Lee, J. Tracy, and W. van der Klaauw, 2011, "Real Estate Investors, the Leverage Cycle and the Housing Market Crisis," Working Paper, Federal Reserve Bank of New York.
Himmelberg, C., C. Mayer, and T. Sinai, 2005, "Assessing High House Prices: Bubbles, Fundamentals and Misperceptions," NBER Working Paper No. 11643.
Hofmann, B., 2001, "The Determinants of Private Sector Credit in Industrialized Countries: Do Property Prices Matter?" Working Papers BIS No. 108.
Hofmann, B., 2003, "Bank Lending and Property Prices: Some International Evidence," The Hong Kong Institute for Monetary Research Working Paper No. 22.
Iacoviello, M., 2005, "Housing Prices, Borrowing Constraints and Monetary Policy in the Business Cycle," American Economic Review, 95(3), 739–764.
Kiyotaki, N. and J. Moore, 1997, "Credit Cycles," Journal of Political Economy, 105, 211–248.

Liang, Q. and Cao, H., 2007, "Property Prices and Bank Lending in China," Journal of Asian Economics, 18, 63–75.
Mason, J., and J. Rosner, 2007, "How Resilient Are Mortgage Backed Securities to Collateralized Debt Obligation Market Disruptions?" Manuscript presented at the Hudson Institute, February.
Mian, A., and A. Sufi, 2009, "The Consequence of Mortgage Credit Expansion: Evidence from the U.S. Mortgage Default Crisis," The Quarterly Journal of Economics, November, 1449–1496.
Miranda, M., and Fackler, P., 2002, Applied Computational Economics and Finance MIT Press.
Muellbauer, J., 2012, " Housing markets and the macro-economy," International Encyclopedia of Housing and Home.
Oikarinen, E., 2009, "Interaction Between Housing Prices and Household Borrowing: The Finnish Case," Journal of Banking and Finance, 33, 747–756.
Park, S.W., D.W. Bahng and Y.W. Park, 2010, "Price Run-Up in Housing Markets, Access to Bank Lending and Housing Prices in Korea," Journal of Real Estate Finance and Economics, 40, 332–367.
Pavlov, A, and S. Wachter, 2011, "Subprime Lending and Real Estate Prices," Real Estate Economics, American Real Estate and Urban Economics Association, vol. 39(1), pp. 1–17, 03.
Rudebusch, G.D., and Svensson, L.E., 1998, "Policy Rules for Inflation Targeting," NBER Working Paper No. 6512.
Shan, H., 2011, "The Effect of Capital Gains Taxation on Home Sales: Evidence from the Taxpayer Relief Act of 1997," mimeo, Federal Reserve Board.
Shiller, R., 2008, The Subprime Solution: How Today's Global Financial Crisis Happened, and What to Do About It?, Princeton University Press, Princeton, New Jersey.
Song, I.H. (2011), Housing Prices and Consumption, Ph.D. Dissertation, The Ohio State University.
Song, I.H. (2012), A New Paradigm in Housing Policy After Global Financial Crisis (in Korean), KDI, forthcoming.
Uhlig, H. (1999), A Toolkit for Analysing Nonlinear Dynamic Stochastic Models Easily, Oxford University Press.
Wheaton, W., and G. Nechayev, 2008, "The 1998–2005 Housing 'Bubble' and the Current 'Correction': What's Different This Time?" Journal of Real Estate Research, 30(1), 1–26.
Yang, T., C. Lin, and M. Cho, (2009) "Collateral Risk in Residential Mortgages," Journal of Real Estate Finance and Economics, forthcoming.

6. Transatlantic mortgage credit boom and bust – the impact of market structure and regulation*

Hans-Joachim Dübel

1. INTRODUCTION

More than four years have elapsed since the U.S. subprime crisis broke out in 2007, taking with it hundreds of mortgage lenders. Since 2010 we find ourselves in a fully blown sovereign debt crisis in Europe, which to a substantial extent was caused by local mortgage credit booms with lending patterns and house price inflation very similar to those in the U.S. European countries in mortgage crisis include Ireland, Spain and Hungary. Waiting in the wings are others sitting on inflated house prices and hoping for a 'soft landing'.

Even though European mortgage default rates are below U.S. rates, the scale of problems, and as we will see the analogies of their causes, suggest that it is fair to speak of a transatlantic crisis. The weight of residential mortgage lending in balance sheets invariably means banking crisis, and where regulated banking has been replaced 'shadow banking' crisis.[1] As governments rescue lenders, the resulting pressure for fiscal and wage austerity, as well as higher unemployment, in a feedback effect enhances pressure on house prices and portfolio quality. With the two largest reserve currencies being affected, USD and EUR, systemic risk implications globally follow suit.

The financial sector development and macroeconomics professions overlapped only little in the past: the result has been that the former became notoriously weak at spotting (cross-border) liquidity and relative price shocks that destroyed even carefully designed financial institutions and regulations, and that the latter had little idea about the changing nature of the transmission channels between macro variables and their impact on the financial system. With the global financial crisis, greater interaction between the two professions is in demand, shown most clearly by the emergence of the concept of 'macroprudential' financial regulation.

Recent IMF empirical analysis (2011a, b) has therefore combined macro and financial sector micro analysis to explain credit booms and draw conclusions for regulation. It comes to quite different results regarding the relative weight of either factor for emerging and advanced economies that fundamentally differ in their financial systems' complexities. The dominant role of macro capital flows for credit in emerging markets with their typically shallow local capital markets, for example, is well documented.[2] However, for the advanced economies, the epicenter of the current crisis, the IMF suggests that financial market conditions have played a far larger role than capital flows.

This chapter moves further along this route by asking how the retail mortgage sector, which was small and virtually inexistent as a source of innovation and capital flows even by the 1980s, could turn into a central transmission mechanism for the global financial system. Specifically, it asks

> What has been the contribution of idiosyncratic supply and demand features of mortgage credit markets to boom and bust as well as cross-border flows? (Section 2)
> What can be done to reduce the mortgage finance systems transmission character for liquidity shocks and better protect financial systems? (Section 3)

The chapter concludes with a specific proposal regarding the principles of mortgage finance regulations.

2. STABILITY IMPACT OF MORTGAGE MARKET STRUCTURES AND REGULATIONS

2.1 Mortgage Finance System Design

European, and by extension the U.S., housing finance systems have been actively designed by policymakers historically to overcome the dearth of long-term funding sources that local markets, consisting of small savers, would not provide. The key principle adopted in the 19th century was to tap wealthier individuals and the beginning institutional investor sector via bonds, issued by specially chartered banks.

The European (covered) bank bond systems pioneered this principle: the Danish mortgage credit institution system founded in 1795, the first centralized mortgage bond issuer Credit Foncier de France in 1852, and the German system of specialized Pfandbrief issuers was created as early as 1769. Of these, only the Danish was targeted from the beginning to retail mortgages; the French and German systems funded first local large investors – aristocrats and communes – and later large developers that built the rental cities of Europe.

The classical European savings bank and later the U.S. Savings and Loans (S&L) for a long time were the prime suppliers of retail mortgages. They would, however, demand substantial savings prior to a loan takeout, both as a creditworthiness signal and as funding. Where savings were taxed away to fund governments, as in Britain before or in Germany after WWI, specialized building societies developed on the same mutual principles. Only after WWII did specialized mortgage banks gradually begin to fund retail mortgages on a larger scale.

A completely new design that separated credit risk from the lender level was born under the U.S. New Deal of the 1930s. The National Housing Act of 1934 created the first public mortgage loan insurer, the Federal Housing Administration (FHA). The FHA limited itself to insuring 20 year fixed-rate mortgages subject to interest rate ceilings and funded by Savings & Loans (S&L). S&L mortgage loans had been short-term only, which contributed to high default rates when roll-overs failed as lenders were afraid of the credit risk. Anglo-Saxon countries copied the U.S. insurance approach after WWII to establish either public or private mortgage insurance systems.

The U.S. in 1937 also created a national balance sheet for loan purchases from local 'mortgage banks' with limited access to deposits, via Fannie Mae. The fiscal pressures of the Vietnam War forced the government to abandon funding mortgages directly and privatize and convert Fannie Mae to a mortgage bond insurer. The S&L industry in 1970 received its own bond insurer, Freddie Mac. So the U.S. system became characterized by two layers of insurance, loan and bond.

The divergence between systems peaked in the 1980s. The high inflation of the 1970s had caused solvency and liquidity problems for special banks. In Europe this invited commercial banks into the market; in the U.S. the S&L crisis gave rise to a new public-private partnership, between Wall Street securities firms and the bond insurers Fannie Mae and Freddie Mac. The secondary mortgage market dis-intermediating origination, packaging, structuring, insurance and funding of mortgages via securitization was born.

The de facto public insurance-based setup of the U.S. housing finance system can be seen to bear great responsibility for the U.S. mortgage market crisis. The failure to abolish the New Deal's institutions after the economy had recovered by the 1950s created a giant policy lag. Semi-privatization of Fannie Mae and the similar status of Freddie Mac made matters worse, as profits could be privatized while losses would remain socialized. As such 'government-sponsored' enterprises (GSE) spread out in what regulations defined as 'conforming' mortgages, the true private sector was left with risky niches. Private mortgage insurance since the 1970s was insuring high loan-to-value (LTV) ratio loans ineligible for the GSE. In the 1990s and 2000s the sub-prime market developed for GSE-ineligible borrowers, funded mostly through Wall Street securitizations. And the 2000s added, again ineligible, high LTV home equity lending funded by both banks and securitizations. A substantial share of these 'private label' securitizations funding ineligible mortgages – 18% of the outstanding, by fall 2011 – found their way to the balance sheets of Fannie Mae and Freddie Mac. Their role in inflating U.S. housing debt went beyond the already massive expansion of the 'agency' securitizations, covering eligible mortgages only (Figure 6.1).

Both agency and private label mortgage securities during the 2000s became a key driver of capital imports into the U.S. As of 2011, some 14% of agency mortgage securities and 18% of private label mortgage securities are estimated to be directly held abroad, with likely substantial additional indirect holdings via money market and other U.S.-based foreign-owned funds.[3]

While much of the U.S. housing finance system design was copied by Canada and Australia, after the mortgage crisis of the 1990s the United Kingdom changed course and turned from third-party to lender self-insurance. This resulted in a considerable decline in the LTV-financed, and paid out in greater resilience in the current crisis (see Figure 6.2). Both in the U.K. and Ireland, the traditional housing finance system via building societies had seen a diminished role since the 1980s, vs. the rise of commercial banks.

There has only been a very limited role of public loan, let alone bond, insurance in Continental Europe.[4] Especially, high-LTV loan insurance is a missing element. An exception is the large, almost unconditional public insurance program run by the WSW in the Netherlands that also backs up large volumes of mortgage-backed securities issued in the country and which can be seen to have contributed to the high Dutch mortgage debt levels. The French FGAS program, in contrast, is targeted to non-prime borrowers only. In combination with a lesser role of mortgage interest deductibility in Europe, reduced and in many cases abolished during the interest rate compression phase of the 1990s, the absence of high-LTV insurance has moderated incentives favoring leverage.

The covered bonds used in Continental Europe have had a lesser funding relevance than securitization in the U.S. In the case of Denmark only, they still funded almost the entire mortgage portfolio. In Germany, Italy,

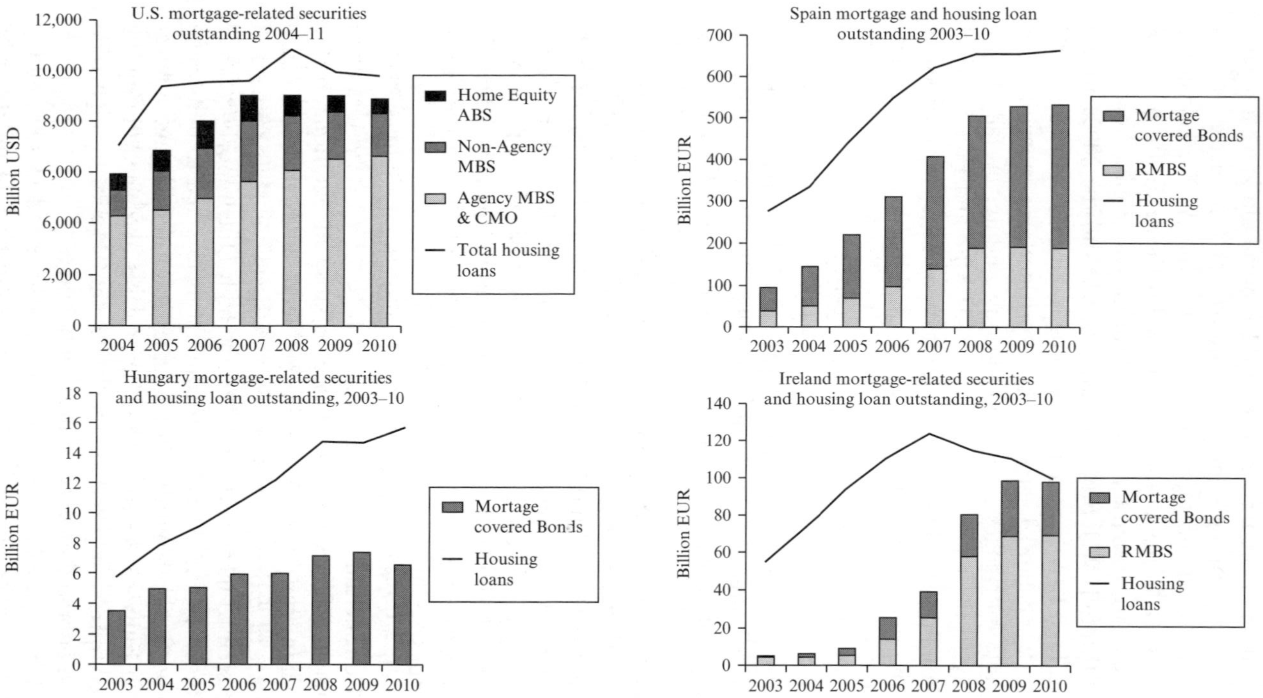

Note: the assessment is highly approximative as disaggregated funding analysis of the national housing loan portfolio is unavailable.

Sources: SIFMA, European Covered Bond Council, CEPS, author's computations.

Figure 6.1 Liquidity generation via capital markets in the U.S. insurance vs. European bank-based housing finance systems experiencing housing loan boom

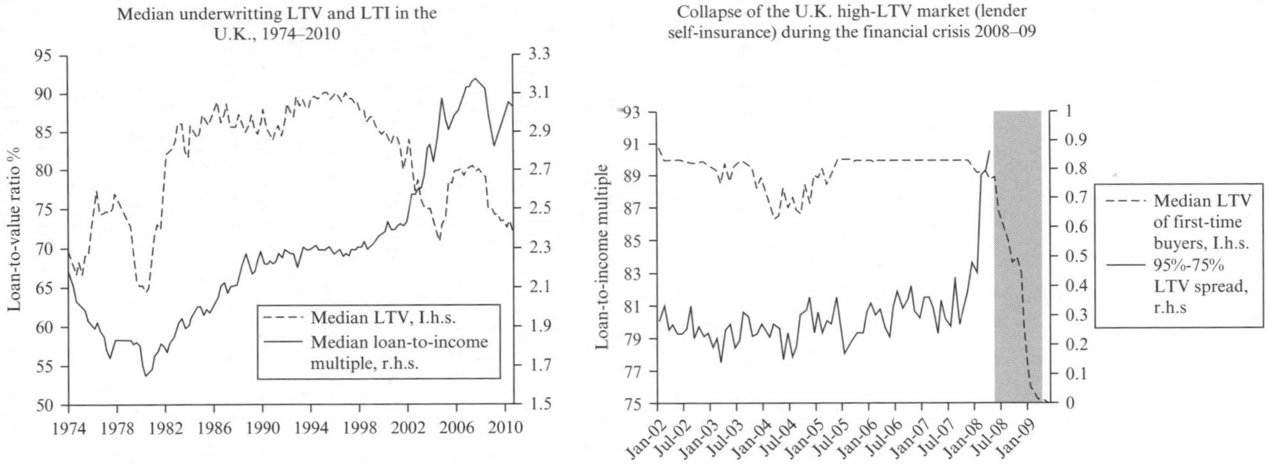

Notes: LHS: median LTV and LTI for all loans for house purchase. RHS: median LTV of first-time buyers and 95%–75% LTV interest rate spreads for 5-year initial fixed-rate periods 1995–2009. LTV – loan-to-value ratio, LTI – loan-to-income ratio. British mortgage insurers ceased new underwriting in 1990, initial LTV increase after 1990 was driven by falling house prices.

Sources: Bank of England, Council of Mortgage Lenders, Finpolconsult computations, Dübel (2011a).

Figure 6.2 Universal bank system and leverage – the British market

Spain and France, the historic strong reliance became diminished with the deregulation of the 1970s and 1980s, which allowed deposit-funded commercial banks to enter housing finance. Public ownership, dominating in France and Southern Europe until the 1980s, became reduced and over time the covered bond system in Europe became largely privately owned. The product started to appeal again in the 1990s, when Germany's issuers launched the 'Jumbo' Pfandbrief program with minimum issuance size of 1 billion Deutsche Mark. The success in attracting foreign investors into a corporate bond was unparalleled. Spain and Ireland modernized or adopted their covered bond laws in the 2000s, in order to address a shortage of domestic deposits amidst the lending boom and tap international markets. The U.K. started with 'structured' covered bonds.

Quite comparable to U.S. securitization, covered bond issuance activity in Europe financed some national housing booms, via the capital account. Figure 6.1 highlights the Spanish case: the deposit base had been depleted by high credit growth by 2002. With heavy issuance of both covered bonds and securitizations the boom was extended until 2007. Spain is estimated to have sold some 60% of covered bonds issued in the mid-2000s to foreign investors.[5]

Yet, Figure 6.1 also makes the opposite observation for Hungary, where covered bonds fell back over time. Here, liquidity for the housing finance boom was created via interbank and customer deposits in foreign currency, as well as the heavy use of swaps. The predominant Swiss Franc lending product required at least one swap to be contracted by a bond issuer, and foreign banks were willing to aggressively price cross-border funding.

Recent IMF analysis (2011a) has singled out the role of public guarantees in mortgage credit booms. This begs the question to what extent covered bonds are comparable with agency securities regarding implicit government guarantees. Technically, the implicit support framework for the U.S. GSE has been more analogous to the regime for bonds issued by public banks in Europe (e.g. Landesbanken). However, the covered bond product is at least as important in Europe politically, and during 2008 and 2009 the implicit guarantees turned explicit: almost all European covered bond markets were temporarily de-facto nationalized via guarantee commitments or ECB intervention. The two largest German issuers Eurohypo and Hypo Real Estate were even de-jure nationalized. In France and Switzerland, joint issuance vehicles of the banking industry took much of the activity temporarily. In Denmark, the fixed-rate covered bond market stayed open while the adjustable-rate covered bond market required the support of a public pension fund. Therefore, European covered bonds can be seen as implicitly publicly guaranteed instruments.

2.2 Banking and Insurance Regulation

It seems to be the consensus today that permitting extreme levels of borrower leverage has been the central micro regulation failure leading to the U.S. mortgage market crisis.[6] U.S. banks and thrifts had been gradually deregulated already during the 1970s. In 1971 U.S. S&Ls (savings and loans) were permitted to do 95% LTV lending, up from 80%, against protection provided by private mortgage insurance. Fannie Mae and Freddie Mac became allowed to increase their permissible loan purchase and bond insurance activities in the same way. That private high-LTV insurance provided questionable protection became clear with the collapse of the U.K. industry in the early 1990s.[7] The FHA limits were also pushed up and further into very high-LTV lending. Figure 6.3 on the right-hand side has an estimate by Pinto (2010) that indicates ballooning exposures already by the late 1990s.

A second deregulation measure encouraged subprime lending: the removal of interest rate usury limits in the early 1980s. Rather than simply adjusting the obsolete loan interest rate ceilings from low-inflation times to higher inflation levels, ceilings were removed altogether. This permitted very high interest rate lending. Supported by generally falling rates, later administrations only demanded enhanced disclosure on these loans.

In securitization, apart from transparency standards and legal liability enshrined in bond indentures, which has been extensively used only after the system collapsed, the private label market never became regulated. This was exploited to create derivative and multiplier structures.

Since public FHA-insured and 'agency' MBS mainly provided fixed-rate mortgage (FRM) lending and were impossible to compete against, the private label market focused on adjustable-rate mortgage (ARM) lending. With this strategy, available international capital supply was multiplied since short-term funding for ARM requires only a short-term investor commitment. Gaining access to low 'duration' mortgage assets was attractive in particular for U.S. money market funds, i.e. a large new investor class was added to the classical spectrum. Withdrawal of these funds played the central role in the liquidity crises of 2007 and 2008.

A second type of multiplier was credit-related: when 'BBB'-rated securitization tranches packaged into new mortgage products became more highly rated, the cost of credit protection of AAA-tranches was reduced. Questionable rating methodologies stipulated diversification effects where there were none. This meant that higher loan volumes could be funded.

The new types of bonds were finally sold by Wall Street to an increasingly diversified global investor base, i.e. global funding channels parallel to the GSE's distribution were created. A prominent investor was the system

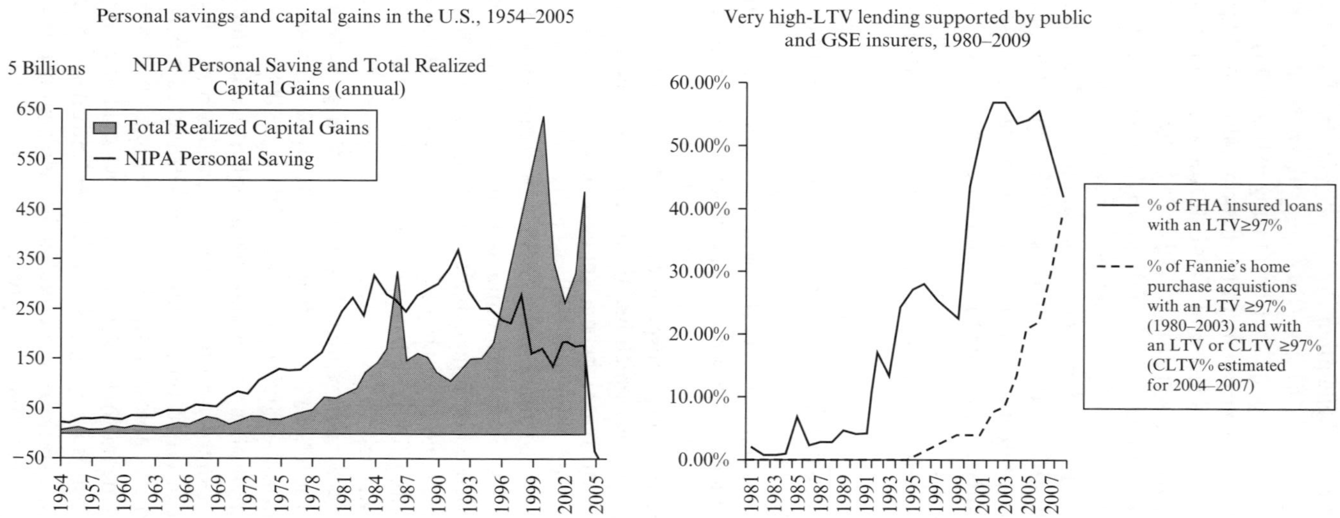

Note: NIPA = National Income and Product Accounts.

Source: LHS – Guidolin & de Jeunesse (2007); RHS – Pinto (2010).

Figure 6.3 Insurance-based housing finance system and leverage – United States of ABCP conduits run from offshore places such as Ireland that was sponsored primarily by European banks.[8] Banks acting as investors in the U.S. in this way enjoyed funding privileges (e.g. German Landesbanken) or had unprofitable core business or exacerbated return on equity goals (most European wholesale banks).

Some of the innovation seen goes back to a presence of unstable and costly unsecured bank funding conditions that weakened U.S. banks. In particular long-term bank bonds have hardly been used in the system, partly as a result of the powers given to the public deposit insurer Federal Deposit Insurance Corporation by the 1933 Glass-Steagall Act over bond investors. The introduction of covered bond legislation in the U.S. is trying to rebalance this.

Mortgage banking deregulation in Europe took place mostly in the 1980s. The U.K. had lifted LTV limits on building societies and admitted commercial banks to the mortgage market in 1984. This led directly to the Lawson boom of the late 1980s. The median LTV ratio on new loans increased within only five years during the early 1980s from 70% to 90% (see left-hand side in Figure 6.2). House price inflation combined with high-LTV lending resulted in a mortgage credit crisis unfolding after 1990.

Loan-to-value limits in seemingly conservative jurisdictions were liberalized at the time as well: in Germany, total LTV ratios were allowed to be higher than the Pfandbrief senior funding LTV limit of only 60%. Bausparen, a contract savings scheme inherited by Germany from the historic British building society model and designed to deliver safe high-LTV mortgages, came under pressure in the aftermath from cyclical high-LTV lending by both Pfandbrief issuers (mortgage banks) and commercial banks. In Denmark, commercial banks had been permitted to give personal loans to fill the gap left by the 80% LTV limit for covered bond funded loans, leading to an implicit rise in total LTV.

Outside the Netherlands, Ireland, the United Kingdom and Spain, securitization has played a minor role in Europe. MBS have in some markets not grown beyond the small high-risk niches, e.g. of non-performing (Italy) or high-LTV (Germany) lending. This has resulted in partial stigmatization of the product. European banks generally have preferred to keep high-quality loans on balance sheet, in particular those that use extensively covered bonds requiring high asset quality. In Ireland and Spain, the role of MBS has been considerable in attracting cross-border capital flows (see Figure 6.1). The impairment levels of European MBS have been low compared to the U.S., essentially for three reasons: very limited structuring, a selection bias in volume towards the more stable mortgage markets in the U.K. and Netherlands, and absence of high rate lending. There have been mispricing problems, however. In particular, Spanish and Irish MBS were endowed with too little subordination – lower than AAA-rated tranches – which mismatched with the increasing loss risk as house prices ballooned.

Mortgage funding stability of banks in Europe has been historically high as European states implicitly guarantee covered bonds and senior unsecured funding. The main mechanisms are high levels of overcollateralization accepted for covered bonds, and the absence of a seniority ranking for deposits (outside the U.K., which reformed only in 2011) expressed most clearly in the priority of general bank rescue funds over deposit insurance funds. The crisis has amply revealed the scale of this support, which in a negative feedback effect has weakened it via a decline in sovereign rating and prompted central bank interventions. Even before, long-term bank bond instruments were insufficiently used as a result of regulation failures allowing for mismatches. These are partly addressed with Basel III: McKinsey (2010) estimates that the top-12 European banks would need to issue €1.34 trillion in long-term bonds to fulfill the proposed 'net stable funding ratio' (NSFR)[9] requirements.

The British case is the most interesting when discussing the case for re-regulation after a crisis. At the peak of the house price cycle in 1989, median underwriting LTV stood at 85% with many lenders going beyond 100%, supported by mortgage insurance. With the subsequent collapse of house prices and rising defaults, in particular of high-LTV loans to 'right-to-buy' tenants, the mortgage insurance industry disappeared. Many building societies also went bankrupt, had to merge, or convert to universal banks. Lenders henceforth had to self-insure against high-LTV risks. Some learning effect on the part of the industry can be discerned from a closer inspection of Figure 6.2: after a short-term increase in LTVs in the immediate aftermath of the crisis resulting from falling house prices, LTV dropped back to almost pre-liberalization levels (of the 1980s) during the late 1990s. Even in the 2000s, characterized by strong house price inflation, LTV remained conservative compared to the 1980s.[10] This feature may have saved the U.K. from a full-blown mortgage credit crisis.

2.3 Competition Environment

Low regulation and competition levels do interact. A substantial contribution to the credit boom in the U.S. was made by 'charter competition'. Between 1980 and 2007 this supported the survival of the least regulated lender; the most prominent example being the rise of Fannie Mae and Freddie Mac which were completely unregulated until 1992 and later only lightly regulated. Many had blamed the S&L crisis on 50 years of rigid regulations leading to amnesia regarding interest rate risk in mortgages.[11]

Competition also intensified throughout the value-added chain and created the linkage between financial companies and investment banks, both e.g. exempt from capital requirements and operating under transparency regulations only. Insurers, usually tightly regulated, ventured from their core business areas into mortgages (esp. the large holding AIG, and the bond insurer MBIA). Both added pressure on banks.

Loan spreads over GSE funding cost for a long time were therefore near zero. Loan originators started living from points charged up-front instead; these were financed by being added to the debt consumers owed.[12] Servicing costs funded by the remaining spread were driven down by highly competitive specialists, such as Countrywide Financial. After the crisis banks promptly absorbed these. The servicers had played their own crisis genesis role by arbitraging the multiple funding exits available. For this purpose often borrowers were intentionally misclassified (e.g. from prime into subprime).

State Codes of Conduct governed the U.S. mortgage broker industry, but their existence could not prevent the active participating role of many brokers in misclassifying borrowers or selling high interest rate or risky products. Appraisal standards following the 'open market value' helped to maximize both intermediary and appraiser fees.

Europe during the boom years saw aggressive foreign market entry first in those markets traditionally open to competition, e.g. Britain, Ireland and Germany. In all three, brokers played a substantial role in altering the league tables. There was a surge of non-regulated financial companies in Britain, creating the 'non-conforming' market, and in the Netherlands. The British FSA holds them as co-responsible for declining lending standards. In Central and Eastern Europe, aggressive foreign entry brought product innovation with declining standards: examples are Swedish banks in the Baltics introducing Euribor lending, and a large Austrian and a large Portuguese bank introducing the new Swiss Franc product in Hungary and Poland, respectively. The desire to grow fast from low market shares has been a key motivation. The same banking groups showed both aggressive and passive entry strategies, depending on whether their investment in a given market was greenfield or whether they took over established lenders.

Brokers have a more limited, although increasing, distribution role in Europe. In the U.K., brokers were given incentives similar to those in the U.S. for selling the most profitable loan products and misclassifying customers. Brokers also are often tied by lenders in forms not directly visible to consumers. In some jurisdictions, such as Spain, Ireland or Poland, they have targeted the lower end of the credit curve not served by bank branches; in Germany, in contrast, primarily high income clients use brokers. Stability detriment was introduced under the 'bankassurance' concept: in Austria and the Netherlands, brokers charged commission for originating interest-only loans for banks and repayment vehicles for insurers or funds that were created to protect the loan principal repayment.[13] A holding company owning both bank and insurer could also book profit on two contracts.

2.4 Consumer Protection Regulation

2.4.1 Cyclical leverage changes

Loan officer survey data show that leverage in mortgage underwriting cyclically increases with house price levels.[14] Especially the equity of first time buyers, which rarely comes from selling existing property, does not keep pace with prices. At the price peak in 2006, an estimated 30% of U.S. new home purchase borrowers put no money down, and 40% had loan-to-value ratios in combination with other loans above 97%. Non first-time buyers withdrew their equity via second mortgage and home equity lending, which together reached some 40% of new originations in 2006. Figure 6.3 shows the cyclical nature of very high-LTV lending.

There is similarly considerable evidence for European cyclical LTV increases during the last credit boom. In Ireland, typical first-time buyer LTVs prior to the house price collapse were 95%, based on highly inflated house prices.[15] Spanish lenders had gradually abolished conservative LTV policies in the late 1990s when house price inflation picked up. Three years before the price peak, in 2004, regulations were pro-cyclically relaxed, leading to a quarter of loans originated in 2006 with original LTVs over 80%. In the U.K., the median LTV had been lower in the 2000s than in the 1980s, even though with 80% it was still higher than in Spain. Still we can see marked cyclical increases in LTV in the early 2000s that are a parallel to the increases during the Lawson boom of the late 1980s (see Figure 6.2).

2.4.2 Maturity extensions and negative amortization

Maturity extensions tend to come late in the mortgage credit cycle. The past cycle in the U.S. saw noticeable increases in initial interest-only (IO) lending in ARM products during 2005 (20% IO share) and in FRM products in 2006 (6% IO share). At the price peak in 2007, some 30% of total new originations were IO, with initial periods varying typically between 5 and 10 years. U.S. ARM lenders after 2005 tried to further reduce initial payments in areas with high house price inflation through 'option ARM'. In reality the borrower simply paid what he could afford in an inflated housing market and the residual payment due would be capitalized into the balance until a pre-specified amortization trigger was hit. Upon such a 'recast' event, the amortization would switch to regular and typically make the loan unaffordable (Figure 6.4).[16]

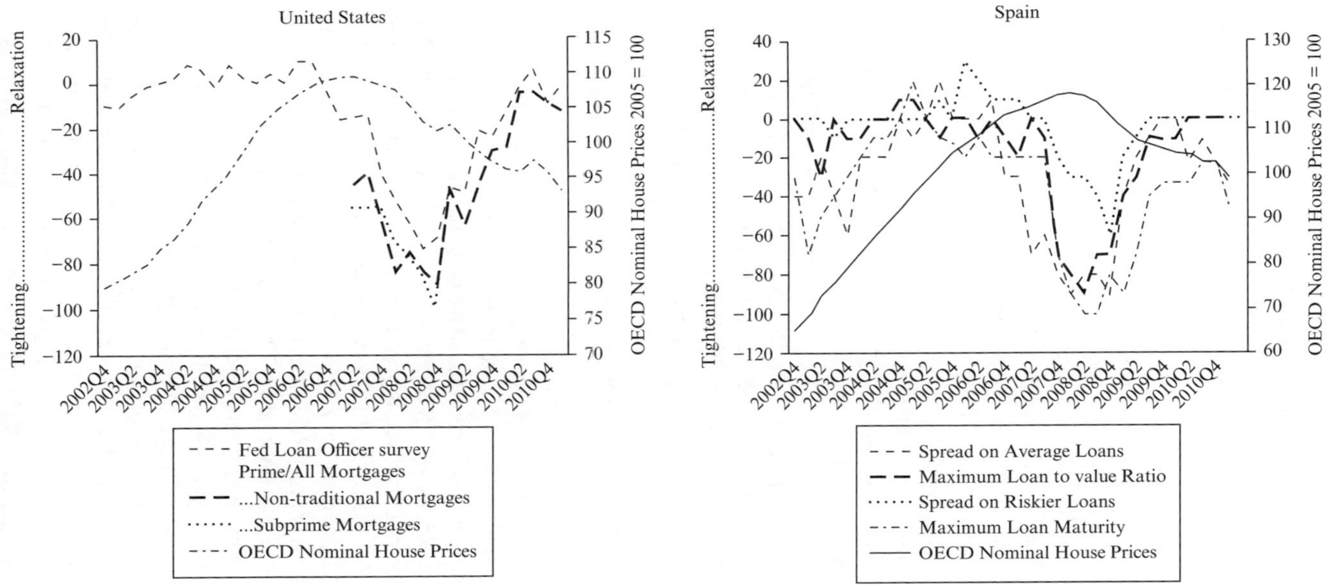

Notes: LHS & RHS – left-hand side: net percent of respondents reporting relaxation.

Sources: OECD (house prices), LHS – Federal Reserve Senior Loan Officer Opinion Survey on Bank Lending Practices, RHS – Bank of Spain Bank Lending Survey, author's computations.

Figure 6.4 Cyclical relaxation and tightening of mortgage underwriting – United States vs. Spain

Maturity extensions were both pervasive and played a crucial role in gradually increasing debt service risk in Europe, which is characterized by a higher ARM product share than the U.S. (see below). As amortization declines, the impact ('pass-through') of an interest rate shock on borrower debt service increases. The typical maturity of Irish amortizing mortgages according to the Central Bank of Ireland increased from around 20 years historically to 30 years by 2007. Interest-only mortgages rose from virtual insignificance in 2001 to 15% of new business in 2007. The typical maturity of loans in Spain, according to Fitch (2007) had increased from 17 years to 28 years within the decade before 2006, with maturities of 35 years becoming available in the end. In the Netherlands and Austria, a high share of interest-only loans was created through income tax preferences and combination with insurance products.

Negative amortization in local currency lending in Europe has been limited to Iceland, where accumulating mortgage balances in combination with a collapsing housing market significantly contributed to the banking crisis. However, foreign currency credit in Eastern Europe, and in particular Swiss Franc lending in Hungary and Poland, led to significant negative amortization in local currencies. The outstanding debt increased by 56% and 65% between 2007 and October 2011 in these two countries. It has been estimated that some 60% of Polish borrowers face negative equity as a consequence. Hungary in December 2011 was forced to restructure its entire Swiss Franc mortgage portfolio.

2.4.3 Adjustable- vs. fixed-rate mortgages

Adjustable-rate mortgages (ARM) have gained in market share in the United States since 1990, with both a trend and cyclical component. In the 1990s, the market share had still been sensitive primarily to the yield curve – a proxy for the relative price of FRM vs. ARM (Figure 6.5). In the 2000s, the house price boom put additional pressure on borrowers to lower initial payments by using ARM: the industry responded by adding initial teaser rates (e.g. 2/28 ARM), and so the ARM share rose even as the yield curve flattened. Structural factors contributed: the FHA de-facto withdrew from FRM low-income housing finance in 2003 and the opportunistic use of multiple funding exits by the private label securitization industry combined with generally higher margin achieved by intermediaries on ARM created mis-selling incentives. ARM were the basis product for risk layering with interest-only amortization or payment options. Most second mortgages and home equity loans at high LTVs were ARMs. ARMs were clearly mis-sold to low-income households with the least ability to withstand a rate shock, in addition with very low teaser rates for short periods. These loans were the first to default during 2007 and triggered the subprime crisis.

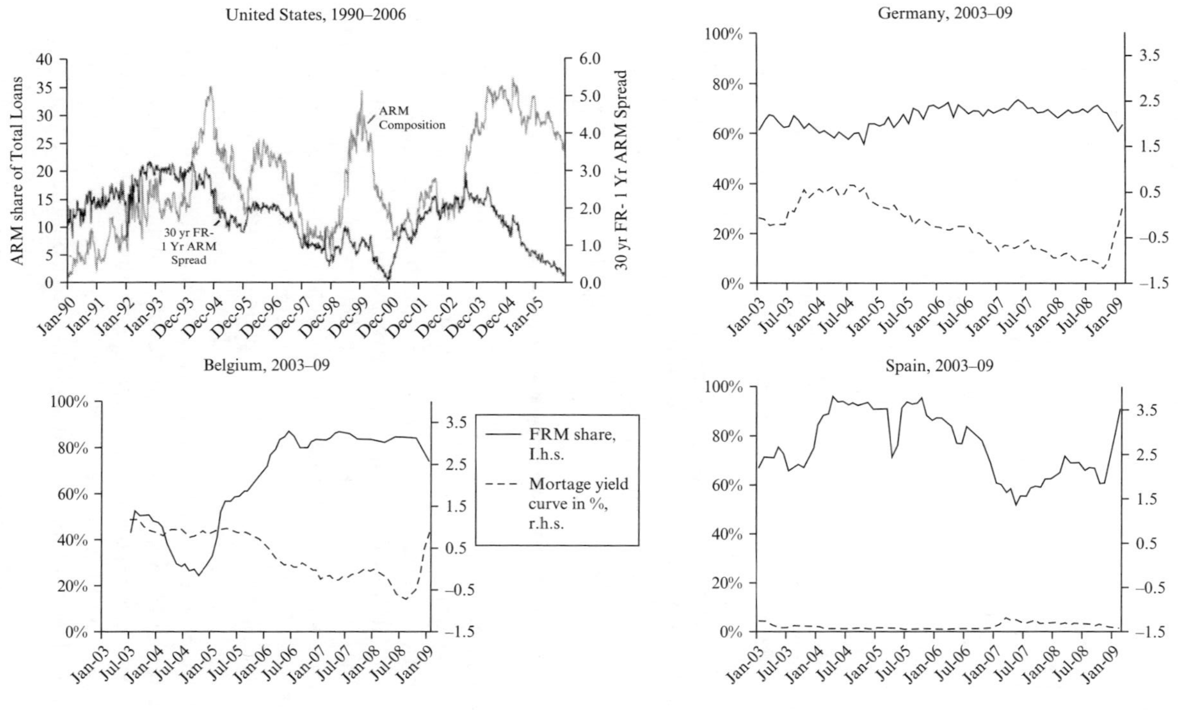

Notes: Except upper LHS – Market share of FRM with initial interest rate fixation period > 5 years (light line) vs. mortgage yield curve (interest rate differential of 5–10 yrs vs <1yr) (bold line).

Source: Upper LHS – MBA Weekly Application Survey, all others – ECB, author's computations.

Figure 6.5 Market shares of ARM vs. FRM and mortgage yield curve

Regulations bear their share of responsibility: FRM is expensive in the U.S., since the product, in contrast with most of Europe, carries a full prepayment option without indemnities via de-facto or de-jure prohibition of indemnities. The associated reinvestment risk for lenders raises borrowing cost for FRM – beyond the yield curve difference – on a 30-year loan by somewhere between 70 and 100 bp. In market stress situations as occurred after the refinancing wave of 2002/3 the option cost can be higher. A deeply divided market is the result that tends to allocate the 'more expensive', but protective product to upper income households and the 'less expensive' and less protective to lower-income households. A mezzanine product balancing risk and price of both extremes, such as e.g. a 5 or 10 year roll-over of fixing periods, typical for example in Canada and Germany, is not widely offered in the U.S.

ARM is already dominant in most European markets, outside the core of France, Germany, Belgium and the Netherlands where lending is mostly in FRM. While the U.S. ARM share in new lending averaged 25.9% over 2003–08,[17] the figure for the Eurozone was 59.8%. Adding the two largest European retail mortgage markets, both outside the Eurozone – the U.K. and Denmark, the ARM share in Europe should be closer to 70%. In transition countries, the predominant lending form of foreign currency (FX) lending can be interpreted as a form of ARM – in addition to the variable exchange rates, interest rates in the foreign currency are also generally variable. European borrowers thus are exposed to far greater market risk than their U.S. counterparts.

ARM or FX products not only permit maximal pass-through of falling interest rates 'benefiting' consumers (against inflating prices). Many European countries had pursued active policies discouraging FRM, which in the context of high inflation in local currency had required substantial subsidies. In Spain, as in many Southern European countries, in the 1980s the system was still dominated by a centralized mortgage bank, Argentaria, that was a quasi-monopolist and exclusively offered subsidized FRMs. Commercial banks entering the market around 1990 in the absence of long-term funding instruments – covered bond issuance then was a monopoly of Argentaria – lobbied strongly for the use of ARM. In 1994 Spain permitted ARM in a sweeping reform; since then, ARM using the interbank index Euribor have been dominating. Spain also capped prepayment indemnities for FRM at very low levels in order to facilitate borrower switching. This resulted in its disappearance from the market; even a flattening yield curve during the 2000s did not bring the product back. When the covered bond funding instrument became universally available it was issued as fixed-rate and swapped back to match the cash flows of the Euribor trackers.

Similar supply change, deregulation and subsidy issues supported FX lending in Hungary. Before Swiss Franc loans were introduced by foreign banks in 2003/4, Forint loans of domestic lenders had been deeply subsidized. Ballooning fiscal cost had forced the government to abandon these, leaving borrowers with no affordable alternative other than FX loans with low interest rates, but high negative amortization risk. That risk materialized with the financial crisis from 2008 onwards.

Cyclical factors stimulating the growth of ARM as in the U.S. were present also in Europe. Yield curve sensitivity can be shown for a number of countries. The stimulating impact of house price increases, as for the U.S., can be shown for Ireland, where the ARM share increased within six years from 60% (1999) to 80% (2005).

The 'savings' in initial payment that ARM provide come against future payment shock risk: in Spain, Euribor interest rates almost doubled between 2005 and 2007 and with them the interest burden of practically all existing mortgage borrowers. This happened although Spanish lenders were obliged to cap interest rates contractually; however, the typical cap was fixed at double-digit interest rate levels rendering it economically pointless. In Ireland, rates in the unilaterally reviewable section of the portfolio ballooned after 2008. In Hungary, both negative amortization risk and interest rate risk materialized, as Swiss Franc loan rates were unilaterally reviewable by the lender.

Figure 6.6 on the right-hand side suggests that caps protecting against such market risk are available in Europe only in markets that have larger FRM shares, i.e. are used to provide consumers with protection. This is most prominently the case in Belgium and France where permissible rate increases under an ARM are tightly limited. A Danish capped ARM market existed after 2000, but disappeared later in the house price boom, as increasing prices reduced the willingness to pay for the additional spread cost of the cap.

The behavioral change of both consumers and lenders that the described product changes induce should not be underestimated: in markets switching permanently from FRM to ARM, housing tends to be priced by buyers over the far more volatile and lower short end of the yield curve. This renders the discount factor in a discounted cash flow house price valuation formula more volatile. The result is higher house price volatility for countries dominated by ARM. While research remains to be done in this direction, early BIS analysis has already suggested such an effect.[18]

Volatility was exacerbated when index trackers replaced traditional unilaterally reviewable instruments, which allowed lenders to control the variations of rates according to cost changes and smoothen the interest rate cycle. The U.K. and Ireland started the 2000s with portfolios dominated by

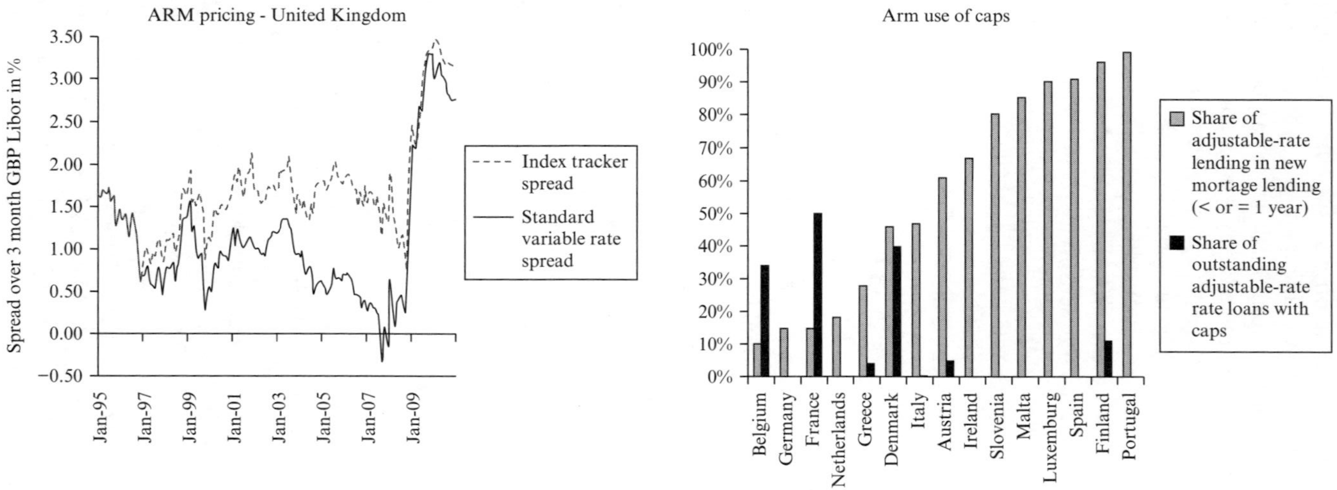

Source: LHS – Bank of England, author's computations. RHS – Table 2 of Drudi et al. (2009) / European Central Bank, author's rearrangement.

Figure 6.6 ARM regimes: pricing of index-tracker vs. reviewable and use of caps the latter product; in new lending those loans were almost entirely replaced by index trackers with declining spreads as house prices ballooned (see left-hand side of Figure 6.6). Often, governments or courts suspicious of banks' motives have demanded index-trackers for consumer protection reasons. Hungarian borrowers since 2008 were severely hit by reviewable CHF interest rates saddled with increasing bank funding cost while their Polish counterparts simultaneously enjoyed falling CHF index tracker rates. Default rates in Poland have been consequently significantly lower than in Hungary, even though the CHF appreciation shock was similar. Regulators therefore differ in their perspective of index trackers.

Finally, Europe like the U.S. has seen strong use of low introductory 'teaser' rates, a practice still widespread in the U.K., and to a lesser degree in Ireland.

2.5 Housing Affordability Policies

2.5.1 Non-prime lending

Borrower selection policies in the U.S. have been dominated by the politicized system set-up, and despite rhetoric in Codes of Conduct, the system lost track of responsible lending standards. When FHA was kept from increasing the house price limits for low-income households in 2003 by the Bush administration, the resulting gap was quickly occupied by private subprime lending. Subprime lenders overwhelmingly used ARM instead of FRM – the product to which FHA had been confined, creating risk layering.

As house prices further inflated, 'Alt-A' lending by the private sector replaced direct Fannie/Freddie lending to prime credit. Prime credit borrowers became classified as 'Alt-A' if they failed to meet one or several check boxes on Fannie/Freddie loan purchase checklists. Fannie/Freddie then purchased many 'Alt-A' bonds, i.e. de facto circumventing their own underwriting rules. Those bonds contained many 'liar' loans, with income quotes 'adjusted' to match runaway price levels.

Loan originators and servicers gamed the different capital market exits – prime, subprime, FHA, 'Alt-A', jumbo, bank balance sheets – to maximize profit. Investment loans to retail customers ('condo flippers') made up 1/3 of the subprime market. Finally, the scoring system failed in parts, e.g. by excluding credit-relevant factors such as LTV that could be indicative of the borrower leverage situation.[19]The labeling of the U.S. crisis as 'subprime' is oversimplifying and representative at most for the initial phase. Creditworthiness effects of rising house prices need to be separated from the structural effect of the additional credit curve penetration through subprime; the former could be called 'endogenous' subprime. This holds true both on the loan as well as mortgage securities market level.[20]

Borrower selection policies have been generally less aggressive in Europe compared to the U.S. Far fewer households are borrowers, and young and low-income households are typically renters. However, the claim that there have been no subprime practices in European markets would be incorrect. In the U.K., a market with analogous structures existed officially as 'non-conforming' and was funded dominantly by similar securitization deals. Lending especially to previously bankrupt borrowers, according to FSA (2010), has been a key contributing factor to elevated mortgage defaults. In Ireland, at least one large building society and a foreign entrant have been widely held to be engaged in lending activity to credit-impaired and vulnerable borrowers on a large scale. In Spain, a factor increasing defaults has been a wave of lending to immigrants to the big cities with scant or no credit histories that were served in particular by local Cajas. Spanish lenders have argued that such lending at low Euribor interest rates prevailing during 2005 and 2006 did not violate formal underwriting standards, which assumes the same low rate levels in perpetuity. Hungary and Poland in contrast have been portrayed as 'subprime' for some time, even though lending there primarily targeted higher-income groups.

Empirically more relevant for Europe than a narrow technical definition of subprime as lending to low-score borrowers has been risk layering for what under normal house price levels were creditworthy borrowers. These practices could be called the European version of 'Alt-A' lending. Versions of risk layering have been recorded essentially for all European countries with inflated house prices, and described above.

2.5.2 Fiscal incentives for leverage vs. savings

Since the U.S. had experienced permanent house price appreciation since the 1940s, taking out insurance in order to increase leverage was widely seen as preferable to greater savings, which would have meant deferring the house purchase and forfeiting capital gains. Firmly established in U.S. system design and financial regulation, leverage in addition was stimulated by fiscal measures such as mortgage interest deductibility. Saving for housing purposes ranked only sixth in a set of eight motives for savings quoted by U.S. households in 2010; in Germany, with a far lower homeownership rate than the U.S., it is routinely the third most important after cash for retirement and precautionary savings motives (see Table 6.1b). Both the FHA and the housing ministry HUD operated in the past 20 years without a single savings program for low-income borrowers.

The countries with the highest tax subsidies for mortgages in Europe, the Netherlands and Denmark, are similarly those with the highest mortgage to GDP ratios, both in excess of 100%. Where subsidies have been cut back, as in Britain after the housing market crisis of the 1990s, LTV has declined. However, without sufficient cash savings, either reliance on housing capital gains as the chief source of borrower equity, or pressure to borrow more, remains high. Table 6.1a compares available survey data on British and German sources of equity. In the British case, proceeds from the sale of a previous home dominate while in Germany it is cash and Bausparen, a form of contract savings for housing.

2.5.3 Broader housing policy design

The expansion of the mortgage credit curve since the 1980s has been the mirror effect of lower housing subsidies to lower-income households, on both sides of the Atlantic.

The U.S. government actively discriminated against urban tenement housing since the 1930s: FHA from its creation was prohibited from insuring private multi-family buildings. The urban riots resulting from decay and neglect at the end of the 1960s led to a temporary increase in public housing construction, which was terminated again in the 1990s in the context of welfare reforms. Today rental housing in the U.S. is supported via insufficient local programs and tax credit systems for landlords. Regulations permit short-term and symmetric termination options in rental law, providing only limited tenure security for solvent households which seek to buy as soon as possible.

Because rental housing is scarce, the first-time buyer age is low. This group needs a combination of high leverage, insurance support and direct subsidies. Examples for the latter in the U.S. are large property registration (stamp duty) and property tax exemptions. Once the first home has been bought, households rely on 'climbing the property ladder', i.e. producing early capital gains to fund down-payment for the next home. Such a system presupposes the presence of permanent house price inflation. Down-payment savings programs are ineffective in this context. Total recurring housing policy costs for the U.S. are safely in excess of 2% of GDP, most of which is spent on interest tax deduction and the cost of fixing the broken insurance system.

In Europe, housing policy budgets also steeply declined in the 1990s stimulated by the interest rate compression trend and Maastricht fiscal austerity requirements. Permitting ARM maximized the relief that the lending boom provided for state budgets because it meant immediate access to credit for many more households with risk being pushed into the future. Total housing policy program costs in European countries, including tax subsidies, today officially range between 0% (Italy) and 1.63% (France) of GDP, with a median below 1%.[21] Subsidy programs in the range of 3–4% of GDP were no rarity in the 1970s and still in existence in the 1980s (e.g. Germany, Netherlands, most of Scandinavia, France).

Table 6.1a Structural high-leverage policies: sources of equity finance in British (England) and German mortgage banking

Sources of equity	England	Germany
Data source	Communities & local gov	Infratest (private)
Period	2007/08	2004/07
Survey population	Owners	Buyers
Survey size	ca 20,000	1327
Proceeds from sale of previous home	52	>11
Savings	39	>71
Gift or loan from family or friend	6	23
Inherited money	4	
Loan to cover deposit/bridging loan/Bausparen	2	34
Money paid by local authority/ housing association	1	1
Windfall	1	n.a.
Money paid by private landlord	0	n.a.
Sweat money	n.a.	15
Other	3	n.a.
No other source	11	n.a.

Notes: Percentage of respondents using funding source. Comparable U.S. data not available.

Source: CML, Infratest, Finpolconsult rearrangements.

While some mortgage subsidies were cut, too, these trends have in particular gone to the expense of public rental housing.

The picture is not uniform: Spain has been struggling with the long-term effects of decades of rigid rent controls. This has reduced the share of non-owner-occupied tenure beyond what would be indicated by the structure of the building stock. Many young households and migrants were forced to buy apartments rather than renting. There has been no comprehensive public strategy to revive rental housing apart from some legal reform steps. The U.K., in contrast, after the crisis of the 1990s has successfully increased rental tenure, after the right-to-buy policy for tenants of the 1980s had reduced it to virtual inexistence. The subsequent governments were acutely aware of the causal relation between rental policy and sub-prime lending and supported the creation and funding of rental housing associations. These essentially replaced 'council' housing, and also private rental housing experiments. The improved rental sector conditions helped to expand first time buyer age and supported the reduction of LTVs.

Table 6.1b Structural high-leverage policies: motives for savings given by consumers in the United States and Germany

Motives for saving	United States		Germany	
Data source	Federal Reserve SCF		Infratest	
Period	2007		2010	
	Percent	Rank	Percent	Rank
Education	8.4	4	5	5
For the family	5.5	5	n.a.	n.a.
Buying own home	**4.2**	**6**	**46**	**3**
Purchases	10	3	58	2
Retirement	33.9	1	60	1
Liquidity	32	2	4	6
Investments	1.6	7	28	5
No particular reason	1.1	8	n.a.	n.a.
Does not save	3.3	n.a.	n.a.	n.a.
Homeownership rate-2009	**67.3%**		**55.6%**	

Source: Federal Reserve Board Survey of Consumer Finances, Infratest, Finpolconsult rearrangements.

There are clearly limits to rental policies. Countries with low urban densities such as Ireland or parts of the U.S. will build less apartment housing, have higher homeownership rates and remain more vulnerable to mortgage crises. Yet, the ongoing urbanization trend tends to support rental housing. Such corporate mortgage finance, via housing associations and private investors, in the current housing crisis has shown to be less vulnerable than retail mortgage finance.[22]

3. LESSONS FOR FINANCIAL STABILITY POLICY

We started by asking how macroeconomic imbalances interact with structural and regulation features to explain the dimensions of mortgage credit boom and bust seen in transatlantic economies. The evidence presented supports the view, expressed e.g. by the IMF (2011a, b), that both scale and length of boom/bust in these more developed economies must be seen as highly endogenous to structural and regulation features of the mortgage credit markets. Moreover, the fiscal policy setup stimulating or discouraging credit demand matters and both borrower and intermediary levels need to be taken into account. Table 6.2 provides a synoptic summary of the analysis by financial structure and regulation area.

Table 6.2 Summary: key structural and regulation features of mortgage finance systems and their crisis contribution – transatlantic perspective

Feature	United States	Crisis contribution	Europe	Crisis contribution
Macro prudential regulation	Global borrowing privilege, 30 years of large current account deficits. Asset price –consumer price inflation divergence (neglected by Fed).	High	Intra-Eurozone borrowing privilege, 15 years of large internal current account deficits. Consumer and asset price inflation differences between Eurozone members (neglected by ECB).	High
Capital market and intermediation structure	International sales of MBS (non-leveraged) & structured finance/CDO (leveraged). High explicit (agency) and quasi-explicit (GSE) public guarantee share. Public (agencies/GSE) and private (finance companies, conduits) shadow banking system in parallel to banking, leading to strong funding exit arbitrage. Strong disintermediation (originators, servicers, loan insurers, bond insurers, investors) leading to control problems.	High	International sales of MBS, covered bonds (non-leveraged), limited use of leveraged instruments with European assets. Explicit public guarantees only in isolated cases (NL, FR), however, strong implicit guarantees for too-big-to-fail banks (national champions). Some incidence of shadow banking in liberalized jurisdictions (e.g. Ireland, UK); however, mostly regulated banking with standard funding menu. Isolated cases of moderate disintermediation (NL, UK), mostly integrated bank intermediation.	Moderate

House price valuation	Open market method tracking inflation, fixed interest rate as implicit discount factor.	Moderate	Open market method tracking inflation, adjustable or foreign currency interest rate (lower, more volatile) as implicit discount factor in markets outside core.	High
Product structure regulation	Product dichotomy: callable FRM (fixed to maturity) for Prime, ARM with teaser rates for Subprime and with rising price level also for near-Prime / 'Alt- A' (payment shock risk) market segments. Reduced or no amortization in Subprime and near-Prime, some negative amortization ('option ARM').	High	Dominance of ARM & foreign currency loans (payment shock risk), in both Prime and non-Prime market segments. Only core (FR, BE, NL, DE) uses fixed-rate; near core countries have shifted from FRM to ARM (DK, AT). ARM interest rate caps only exist in FRM-dominated markets; foreign currency generally without caps (exception HU ex-post). Reduced or no amortization, negative amortization where foreign currency lending is used (HU, PL, AT).	High
Underwriting regulation	Structurally high LTVs (public/ private mortgage insurance, regulations), access to credit as political priority. Low-documentation %, rising with house price levels. Credit intermediaries and servicers with moral hazard problems.	High	LTVs changing cyclically with house price levels (IRE, UK). Isolated structural high-LTV lending (NL, DK; tax-driven) vs housing savings programs reducing LTV (DE, and Central Europe). Limited role of low-documentation lending. Limited role of credit intermediaries, some moral hazard issues (UK, AT).	Moderate

Table 6.2 (continued)

Feature	United States	Crisis contribution	Europe	Crisis contribution
Broader credit and housing policies	Large Subprime sector, replacing historic public loan guarantees and rental housing transfers. No significant corporate housing finance (rental).	High	No or small Subprime. High shares of lending to young/ immigrants and 'Alt-A' (affordable for Prime only in conjunction with ARM) correlated with low rental housing share (ES, IRE, UK). Core (DE, NL, FR, AT), Northern Europe (DK, SE, FIN) with strong private and public rental housing shares. UK rebuilding private rental.	Moderate
Foreclosure / consumer insolvency	Fast discharge in most states. Extra-judicial foreclosure dysfunctional in crisis.	High	Mixed discharge picture, but high barriers in crisis countries (ES, IRE, HU). Foreclosure politically pre-empted via moratoria (IRE, HU).	Low

Contrasting with IMF (2011a), in the transatlantic perspective the author finds little evidence for a strong causal role of *explicit public guarantees and ownership of intermediaries* for credit boom and bust, given that credit expansion was funded through all securities categories. There is little evidence of systematic bias also on the level of intermediaries: private and public owners alike failed to 'lean against the bubble' by tightening credit. Whether public intermediaries should have pulled out earlier should depend on their specific role, as investors or intermediaries, as well as their governance.[23] Primary *mortgage market regulation failures* can be seen as causal for the credit boom and bust in this vein only to the extent that they facilitated the pass-through of these capital market conditions into house prices.

Three flaws stand out:

1. *High 'borrower mismatch'* where cash outflows do not match with income (or saved rent) cash inflows. ARM instruments not only enhanced both the pass-through of monetary policy as well as short-term intermediary profit. They also eliminated market risk for intermediaries using short-term funds (money market or deposits) and – more subtly – helped to inflate lending volumes with limited additional investor commitment in terms of duration risk. Once high debt levels were created, ARM systems meant a straightjacket for central banks and governments: because of high pass-through, raising rates would mean immediate house price and default pressure.
2. Explicit *high borrower leverage policies* proliferating in particular under the insurance-credit split in particular in Anglo-Saxon countries. High leverage helped to avoid housing and social policy transfers as long as house price inflation was positive. A short-term fiscal gain was substituted by long-term fiscal cost. Remarkably, while Britain defacto abolished high leverage lending in the 1990s, the United States was still pursuing it almost two decades thereafter.
3. *Flawed house price valuation methods* simply tracking asset price inflation rather than attempting to assess long-term values (e.g. by simple metrics such as house price to rent or house price to income ratios). Inflated appraisal supports both short-term industry profits and government revenue.

These three flaws being in place, borrowers are set up financially as the miniature version of a highly leveraged hedge fund operating with questionable collateral. The liquidity or employment shock needed to create a crisis is far smaller than in the alternative of a highly capitalized and maturity-matched borrower. Unfortunately, the inadequacy of house price

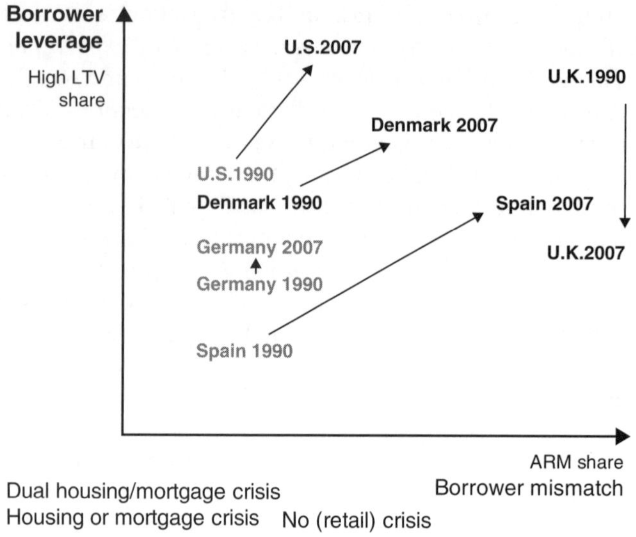

Notes: ARM – adjustable-rate mortgages; LTV – loan-to-value ratio (underwriting); borrower mismatch – degree of mismatch between rather fixed income or imputed rent cash inflows and loan cash outflows, rising strongly with the share of ARM.

Source: Author's assessment.

Figure 6.7 Stylized mortgage finance system trajectories in the key risk dimensions – 1990 vs. 2007

valuation standards is a universal risk in mortgages. It would then seem that the still lower share of ARM in the U.S. in comparison to Europe was 'compensated for' by substantially higher leverage. A stylized facts selection on both sides of the Atlantic (see Figure 6.7) suggests that avoiding only one of both factors does not greatly matter for stability: given even moderate macroeconomic shock, either high leverage *or* high borrower mismatch in isolation can establish sufficient conditions for a mortgage credit crisis.

Basic regulation failures going back generations are manifested in today's housing finance systems, and are frequently not even subject to serious debate among regulators.[24] Other mortgage market exuberances that have featured more prominently in the public debate, in contrast, are likely rather hard-to-avoid consequences of the credit boom and house price inflation (see Figure 6.4). These include in particular the hugely criticized mortgage product innovations and deeper credit curve penetration.

Mortgage product innovation can be shown to rise with credit booms with the aim to squeeze the last borrower cohorts into an inflated housing market. It is an open question to what extent such practices forced by inflation can be regulated away, since they have been a recurring feature over a long time and across very different market structures and shock situations. Surely, risk layering caused by innovation can be taxed by regulators.

Finally, excessive credit curve expansion can be both causal for and follow credit booms, as many prime borrowers over time 'fall down the credit curve' as a result of rising house prices (e.g. U.S. Alt-A market). A suitable test limiting expansion would measure affordability under underwriting standards prevailing in normal times, sufficient borrower equity and products protecting fully against interest rate risk. Rejecting lending despite a negative test can be difficult in economies lacking rental accommodation, especially for the young and migrants, insofar as much of the causality for credit booms comes from structural housing policy failures. If these cannot be addressed, this speaks in favor of focused low-income insurance or subsidy solutions rather than an aggressive regulatory approach.

4. CONCLUDING REMARKS

Mortgage credit boom and bust cannot be completely eliminated. Reducing systemic risk to more manageable levels has to be the goal. This implies measures that go beyond regulation, at least into monetary and fiscal (housing) policy, and possibly into redesigning the mortgage finance system, which was the historic approach.

The central focus of regulation reform should be to promote the shock absorption capacity of the system against a given liquidity shock, domestic or cross-border. Former U.S. Federal Reserve Chairman Paul Volcker has proposed a strict separation of proprietary trading by banks from their credit operations. The same reasoning can be applied to the mortgage sector with its specific long-term risk structure.

First Volcker Rule for Mortgages: 'Discourage leveraged interest rate risk speculation by borrowers with their most important financial asset, equity in housing'

Housing is a long-term asset promising fixed real returns whose financing should be matched and proportionally amortizing. This implies that the cash flow profiles of products should meet the utility stream in terms of saved rents derived from the property. Where markets are not in the position to produce mortgages with rates fixed to maturity, non-callable 'roll-over' FRM fixed e.g. for 5 or 10 years and ARMs with narrow caps should be second best. Demanding a minimum of protection will introduce risk pricing and reduce pass-through. Capital requirements should be raised for products carrying greater interest rate risk, and by implication borrower default risk.

Minimum borrower capital should be a sine qua non condition. High leverage amplifies all house price and interest rate shocks on the borrower balance sheet. Many regulation proposals shy away from demanding a hard minimum. Government programs can support at least first time buyer equity to make this feasible.

Stability-oriented house price valuation standards will be tied to regional rent and income levels as well as replacement cost. Reliance on open market valuation just tracking inflation should be discontinued for credit purposes. Reformed valuation standards would make a constant LTV rule anti-cyclical and a more useful measure for regulation.

Second Volcker Rule for Mortgages: 'Discourage (leveraged) interest risk speculation by mortgage lenders and force interest rate risk to be taken by institutions'

While we still have no systematic approach to borrower equity in most countries, governments are starting to demand higher minimum capital from mortgage lenders. Preferential treatments of residential mortgages should be discontinued in light of the crisis. Capital requirements should be differentiated by the risk profile of the product and risk layering features.

The key point of the rule is to discourage intermediaries from interest rate risk speculation to subsidize deficient credit risk margins and ultimately overbanking. Historic mortgage banking rules sought to achieve exactly this, by requiring full matching (S&Ls) and reserving the privilege for issuing specially designated covered bonds to special banks (special European mortgage banks). Analogous regulations can be constructed for today's universal banks; a first, albeit insufficiently calibrated, step 'back to basics' is the Net Stable Funding Ratio agreed on under Basel III.

Such moves could help to support the business of specialists, especially second tier lenders, and put the initial secondary mortgage market concept back on its feet. In this concept, credit risk would remain local and interest rate risk would be transferred to investors, via secondary market institutions or wholesale banks issuing covered bonds. Europe could develop cross-border specialist solutions going forward, given the small scale of national markets. These steps could reduce the role of commercial banks in mortgage finance again. They would also help to reduce interconnectedness between banks.

One attractive structural development option is a specialist system along the lines of Danish mortgage credit institutions that issues every loan directly on the capital market while retaining credit risk. Danish borrowers are protected by the market via prepayment options and the option to buy back their debt, potentially even below par if interest rates have risen (and house prices fallen). This structure avoids large wholesale banks and cleanly separates interest rate risk from credit risk at birth of the loan.

NOTES

* Hans-Joachim Dübel is founder of Finpolconsult.de, a consulting firm in the real estate finance sector based in Berlin. In the past 15 years he has co-authored a series of pan-European mortgage sector studies (download from www.finpolconsult.de). This chapter derives from the most recent "A New Mortgage Credit Regime For Europe – Setting the Right Priorities", CEPS special report, 6 July 2011, coauthored with Marc Rothemund, and from "Back to the Roots: Can Contractual Savings for Housing Help Terminating the High-Leverage Housing Finance System? A missing piece in the U.S. Housing Finance Reform Debate", a study commissioned by Bausparkasse Schwäbisch Hall.

1. Shadow banking can be defined as financial entities, infrastructure and practices beyond the reach of existing government monitoring and regulation.
2. For a recent analysis see Psalida and Sun (2011).
3. See Dorfman (2011).
4. For greater detail on structural differences, see Lea (2010).
5. See IMF analysis by Avesani et al. (2007).
6. See e.g. Levitin and Wachter (2010) and Villani and Hendershott (2012), from opposite sides of the political spectrum.
7. Calls on mortgage insurance contracts in particular by Fannie Mae and Freddie Mac were very limited during the current crisis, despite high default levels. Instead, loan originators and servicers were sued for mis-selling of loans. An immediate collapse of the mortgage insurance industry amidst declining house prices would have meant stopping high-LTV lending when it was needed most. Nevertheless by early 2012 all but one private insurer had exited the market.
8. See Arteta et al. (2009).
9. The NSFR compares credit and investment commitments of a lender with maturity greater than 1 year with his availability of funding with maturity greater than 1 year.
10. A drawback of self-insurance is lesser crisis resilience: in the current British mortgage market downturn the high-LTV market collapsed. The government in 2011 has been discussing public high-LTV insurance programs.
11. This argument overlooked the impact of the Garn-St.Germain Act of 1982 that permitted the S&Ls to engage in their terminally fatal activity: commercial real estate lending.
12. This is different in most European countries, where regulation or market standards pre-empt this practice.
13. The bank assurance concept postulated mergers between banks and insurance companies on the basis of synergy effects, including joint distribution of financial products to consumers.
14. See Dübel and Rothemund (2011) who find this for both European crisis and non-crisis countries.

15. See Doyle (2009).
16. Ironically, the recast thresholds used usually observed the historical U.S. federal negative amortization regulation limit of 120%, which had been lifted in the late 1990s.
17. See Dübel and Rothemund (2011).
18. E.g. Tsatsaronis (2005).
19. In the loan purchase and guaranty rules of Fannie Mae and Freddie Mac, scores were used together with LTV. However, both credit factors were treated as independently distributed, which ignored systematically the interaction effects ('risk layering').
20. BlackRock data looking into MBS rating transitions from AAA to junk in the private label universe reveal that the scale of subprime MBS downgrades was on par with the rest of the U.S. MBS portfolio for the house price peak vintages 2006 and 2007. For loans originated in those years, negative equity overrode all underwriting policy differences as risk determinant. The truly negative surprise of the crisis for MBS investors has been the performance of Alt-A, where AAA tranches were supported by little subordination.
21. See Ministry of Infrastructure of the Italian Republic and Federcasa (2006). Because of fears regarding the potential cost of housing policy programmes, there is no formal responsibility of the European Union in the sector.
22. In the U.K., insurance companies have progressively driven banks out of rental housing association funding because of lower perceived risk than direct or indirect (MBS) investment in retail mortgages.
23 A comparison between Landesbanken and FHA, both of whose debt was explicitly guaranteed by governments, highlights the point. The former institution group was autonomously investing German tax funds as an end investor in the global (mostly U.S.) capital markets, hence stopping this policy would have reduced credit boom and bust. The latter institution was operating as an intermediary in a competitive environment, with relatively safe products. Limiting its role has given rise to the (even) lower lending standards of the private label subprime market, and has unlikely contributed to lower credit creation.
24. The October 2011 Financial Stability Board Consultation Paper on Principles for Sound Residential Mortgage Underwriting Practices may serve as an example. While the paper issues warnings against high leverage, it proposes no specific limits and explicitly suggests the route of mortgage insurance for high-LTV lending. The paper, other than mentioning risk, is silent on specific measures curbing borrower mismatch via ARMs. It proposes open market valuation as one of several valuation methods.

REFERENCES

Aizenman, Joshua and Yothin Jinjarak (2008), "Current Account Patterns and National Real Estate Markets", NBER Working Paper 13921, October.

Arteta, Carlos, Mark Carey, Ricardo Correa, and Jason Kotter (2009), "Revenge of the Steamroller: ABCP as a Window on Risk Choices", Paper presented at the 2009 Financial Intermediation Research Society Meetings, Prague, 27–29 May.

Avesani, Renzo, Antonio Pascual, and Elina Ribakov (2007), "The Use of Mortgage Covered Bonds", IMF working paper, WP/07/20.

DeRitis, Chris and Mark Zandi (2010), "Restringing HARP: The Case for More Refinancing Now", *Moodys Economic and Consumer Credit Analytics*, 7 October.

Dorfman, Richard (2011). Statement Before the House Committee on Financial Services Subcommittee on International Monetary Policy and Trade "The

U.S. Housing Finance System in a Global Context: Structure, Capital Sources, and Housing Dynamics", October 13 http://www.sifma.org/uploadedfiles/correspondence/testimony/2011/sifmadorfmanhfsctestimony101311.pdf
Doyle, Nina (2009), "Housing Finance Developments in Ireland", *Central Bank of Ireland Quarterly Bulletin*, No. 04, October.
Drudi, Francesco et al. (2009), "Housing Finance in the Euro Area", Task Force of the Monetary Policy Committee of the European System of Central Banks, European Central Bank Occasional Paper No. 101, March.
Dübel, Achim (2011a), "Back to the Roots: Can Contractual Savings for Housing Help Terminating the High-Leverage Housing Finance System? A missing piece in the U.S. Housing Finance Reform Debate", Study commissioned by Bausparkasse Schwäbisch Hall. Download: http://finpolconsult.de/mediapool/16/169624/data/Duebel_US_Leverage_and_Savings_for_Housing_1_21_11.pdf
Dübel, Achim (2011b), "The Monetary Policy Transmission that Broke: the U.S. Interagency Conflict on Mortgages", mimeo. Download: http://finpolconsult.de/mediapool/16/169624/data/ US_Mortgage_Transmission_Agency_Conflict_Duebel_11.pdf
Dübel, Achim and Marc Rothemund (2011), "A New Mortgage Credit Regime For Europe – Setting the Right Priorities", *CEPS special report*, 6 July. Download: http://ceps.be/book/new-mortgage-credit-regime-europe-setting-right-priorities
Financial Stability Board (2012), "FSB Principles for Sound Residential Mortgage Underwriting Practices", April. Download: http://www.financialstabilityboard.org/publications/ r_120418.pdf
FitchRatings (2007), "Spanish Residential Mortgage Default Criteria", RMBS/Spain Criteria Report.
FSA (Financial Services Authority) (2010), *Mortgage Market Review: Responsible Lending*, Consultation paper 10/16, July.
Guidolin, Massimo and Elizabeth de Jeunesse (2007), "The Decline in the U.S. Personal Saving Rate: Is It Real and Is It a Puzzle?", *Federal Reserve Bank of St. Louis Review*, November/December.
International Monetary Fund (2011a), "Housing Finance and Financial Stability – Back to Basics?", Global Financial Stability Report, Chapter 3, April.
International Monetary Fund (2011b), World Economic Outlook, September.
Lea, Michael (2010), "International Comparison of Mortgage Product Offerings", Research Institute for Housing America monograph, Washington D.C., September.
Levitin, Adam and Susan Wachter (2010), "Explaining the Housing Bubble", Georgetown University Law Center. Business, Economics and Regulatory Policy Working Paper Series, Research Paper No. 1669401, August 31.
McKinsey (2010), "Regulatory changes and impact", presentation given to the Group of Experts in Banking Issues (GEBI) convened by Directorate General Markt of the European Commission, Brussels, 14 June.
Ministry of Infrastructure of the Italian Republic and Federcasa/Italian Housing Federation (2006), "Housing Statistics in the European Union 2005/2006" (available from Federcasa: federcasa@federacasa.it).
Pinto, Edward (2010), "Government Housing Policies in the Lead-up to the Financial Crisis: A Forensic Study", American Enterprise Institute, Washington, D.C.
Psalida, L. Effie and Tao Sun (2011), "Does G-4 Liquidity Spill Over?", International Monetary Fund, Working Paper No. 11/237, October 1.

Tsatsaronis, Kostas (2005), "What Drives House Price Dynamics – Cross-country Evidence", Presentation given at the EC Workshop on Housing and Mortgage Markets and the EU Economy, Brussels, November 21.
Villani, Kevin and Patrick Hendershott (2012), "The Politically Incorrect View of What Made the Financial Crisis Systemic: Government Housing Policy", Journal of Housing Research, 21 (1).

PART III

Market for construction financing

7. Financing real estate development: a case study of the US real estate market in the 2000s

Min Hwang

1. INTRODUCTION

Real estate development is a creative process that combines multiple disciplines. Like most creative work, real estate development is also risky. A real estate property under development is subject to market risk as a seasoned property is; a collapse of the real estate lease market or crash in the capital market imposes substantial risks for any real estate investors, regardless of their investments in seasoned properties or new development projects. In addition, a development project is also subject to idiosyncratic project risks that can lead to cost overrun or delay in construction completion resulting in higher carrying costs, shortfalls in funding or even incompletion. This chapter presents various arrangements made by developers, investors and lenders to manage those risks. Risk management efforts in real estate development range over development entity choice, cash flow allocations, construction loan underwriting process and various monitoring procedures used by lenders.

The current financial crisis appears to offer an ultimate testing ground for such risk management efforts in the real estate development industry and real estate capital markets. Since the current financial crisis started in 2008, there have been numerous reports and research papers on various problems in residential mortgage markets during the credit boom period in the 2000s. Many studies differ in terms of exact causes of the current crisis, but appear to agree that the start of the crisis is closely related to the housing bubble and its subsequent burst. In particular, many point out the lax underwriting as one of the main culprits for prevalent overvaluation in housing markets.

This chapter examines the development in construction lending markets during the credit boom period and the current crisis. We found that, even though most bank loans perform poorly during those years, the construction loans show particularly weak performance. The current magnitude of the deterioration in performance of construction loans brings to mind their similar performance during the previous financial crisis, the S&L crisis in the 1980s. What can explain the current performance of construction loans? To provide potential answers, we will first review the lending standards in real estate development loans during the period after 2000. Then we present an empirical analysis on the effects of changing lending standards and commercial real estate valuation on loan performance.

2. ECONOMIC IMPACTS OF REAL ESTATE DEVELOPMENT

The importance of real estate in the economy cannot be overemphasized. In the U.S., real estate generates over 28 percent of GDP, creates jobs for 9 million Americans, and is the source of nearly 70 percent of local government revenue (Ling and Archer, 2010).

Total size of commercial real estate in the U.S. is 84 billion square foot, excluding specialty properties (Table 7.1). The largest sectors in terms of size are the industrial sector and multi-family sector, which takes up 55% of the total space while the next two sectors (retail and office) take up about 35%. In terms of market capitalization, the two biggest sectors are retail and office sectors, taking up about half of total market capitalization.

Table 7.2 provides annual construction spending of various sectors from 2003–10. Impacts of the current crisis are clearly shown in both

Table 7.1 Market size by property type in rentable building area and market cap based on repeat sales indices, 2007–09 (excluding specialty properties)

Property type	Size (million sq ft)	Price/SF	Market cap
Office	12,058	$136	$1,639,940
Industrial	23,852	$45	$1,073,322
Flex	2,908	$91	$264,595
Retail	17,336	$172	$2,981,810
Health care	2,635	$490	$1,291,039
Hospitality	2,557	$97	$894,854
Mixed-use	108	$95	$10,227
Multi-family	22,644	$62	$1,403,897
Total	84,096		$9,559,684

Source: Florence et al. (2010).

Table 7.2 Construction spending (US$ million)

Type of construction:	2003	2004	2005	2006	2007	2008	2009	2010
Total private construction[a]	675,370	771,173	869,976	911,837	863,278	758,827	588,306	500,597
Residential	446,035	532,900	611,899	613,731	493,246	350,257	245,912	238,801
Nonresidential	229,335	238,273	258,077	298,105	370,032	408,569	342,394	261,796
Lodging	9,930	11,982	12,666	17,624	27,481	35,364	25,388	10,904
Office	30,579	32,879	37,276	45,680	53,815	55,502	37,282	24,231
Commercial	57,505	63,195	66,584	73,368	85,858	82,654	50,460	37,647
Health care	24,217	26,272	28,495	32,016	35,588	38,437	35,309	30,316
Educational	13,424	12,701	12,788	13,839	16,691	18,624	16,851	13,356
Religious	8,559	8,153	7,715	7,740	7,522	7,197	6,177	5,156
Public safety	185	289	408	419	595	623	471	207
Amusement/Recreation	7,781	8,432	7,507	9,326	10,193	10,508	8,402	6,541
Transportation	6,568	6,841	7,124	8,654	9,009	9,934	9,056	9,912
Communication	14,456	15,468	18,846	22,187	27,488	26,343	19,712	18,226
Power	33,619	27,603	29,210	33,654	54,115	69,242	76,064	66,601
Sewage /waste disposal	278	331	240	305	408	665	468	421
Water supply	393	405	326	477	516	466	319	664
Manufacturing	21,434	23,219	28,413	32,264	40,215	52,754	56,296	37,478

Note: a. Total private construction includes the following categories of construction not shown separately: public safety, highway and street, sewage and waste disposal, water supply, and conservation and development.

Source: U.S. Census.

residential and nonresidential properties. Residential construction sharply fell in 2007, and was still decreasing as of 2010. On the other hand, nonresidential construction spending dropped in 2009. The current total construction activities are still lower than the 2003 level. The major portion of construction spending decrease has come from the residential sector; its construction activities started to fall in 2007 after it peaked in 2006, and the current activities are less than half of the 2003 activities. The nonresidential construction activities were at their peak in 2008, and they are currently at the 2005 level.

Table 7.3 provides detailed estimates of economic impacts of construction spending by sector and by cost type. Hard costs include the direct cost of the physical components of the development project; soft costs include all the other costs such as design, legal and financing costs. In year 2009, the sector with the largest spending was the office sector which also has the largest effects on GDP, personal earnings and employment. Overall, $1 million spending in construction brings in about $3.15 million in GDP and 27 jobs.

3. SAVINGS AND LOAN CRISIS, 1980S

3.1 History of Savings and Loan Crisis

Probably the largest financial crisis in the U.S. prior to the current subprime crisis would be the Savings and Loan crisis in the late 1980s. Savings and Loan institutions (S&L) had existed since the 19th century, but it was the Great Depression in the 1930s that put them under regulation by the Federal Home Loan Bank Board (FHLBB) and at the same time under insurance by the Federal Savings and Loan Insurance Corporation (FSLIC). The main function of S&L institutions was to promote homeownership, supported by regional Federal Home Loan Banks which provide liquidity and low cost financing (Acharya et al., 2009). The main business model of S&L was simple: they borrowed with low interest rates on short term and lent for long term mortgages at slightly higher interest rates. The model worked fine as long as the yield curve was upward sloping. But as inflation accelerated in 1970 and short term interest rates started to rise,[1] not only were their funding costs rapidly increasing, but also many deposits left S&L for money market funds which promised higher interest rates.[2] In response to the S&L's funding squeeze, Congress and FHLBB relaxed regulations on S&L in various ways. First, they lifted caps on deposit rates. Next, S&L institutions were allowed to expand their business into consumer loans and commercial loans. The

Table 7.3 The impact of construction spending for hard costs, soft costs, site improvement and tenant improvement on the U.S. economy, 2009 (US$ billion)

Source	Direct outlays	Total output[b]	Personal earnings[c]	Jobs supported[d]
Office				
Hard costs	$19.56	$62.40	$18.75	516,444
Soft costs	$6.81	$19.96	$7.19	188,706
Site development	$5.91	$18.86	$5.67	156,120
Tenant improvement[a]	$7.14	$22.76	$6.84	188,385
Total	$39.42	$123.98	$38.45	1,049,655
Industrial				
Hard costs	$10.00	$31.89	$9.58	263,917
Soft costs	$2.44	$7.14	$2.57	67,464
Site development	$3.50	$11.16	$3.35	92,376
Tenant improvement	$2.53	$8.08	$2.43	66,881
Total	$18.47	$58.27	$17.93	490,638
Warehouses				
Hard costs	$4.11	$13.11	$3.94	108,474
Soft costs	$1.07	$3.14	$1.13	29,697
Site development	$1.34	$4.27	$1.28	35,319
Tenant improvement	$1.05	$3.36	$1.01	35,783
Total	$7.57	$23.88	$7.36	209,273
Retail				
Hard costs	$12.93	$41.26	$12.40	341,445
Soft costs	$4.36	$12.76	$4.60	120,669
Site development	$4.80	$15.31	$4.60	126,685
Tenant improvement	$3.94	$12.55	$3.77	103,876
Total	$26.03	$81.88	$25.37	692,675
Total				
Hard costs	$46.60	$148.66	$44.67	1,230,280
Soft costs	$14.68	$43.00	$15.49	406,536
Site development	$15.55	$49.60	$14.90	410,500
Tenant improvement	$14.66	$46.75	$14.05	394,925
Total	$91.49	$288.01	$89.11	2,442,241

Notes:

a. 'Tenant improvements' exclude furniture and equipment.

b. The total value of goods and services generated directly and indirectly as a result of the initial construction outlays within the United States.

c. The additional earnings generated within the United States from direct outlays during the construction phase.

d. The additional new jobs supported nationwide by the spending and re-spending of direct outlays associated with the outlays for new construction.

Source: Fuller (2010).

net worth requirement was also significantly weakened from 5% to 3% and even further weakened by allowing regulatory accounting principles (RAP), which are more lenient than generally accepted accounting principles (GAAP). On the legislative front, the Depository Institutions Deregulation and Monetary Control Act (DIDMCA) and the Garn-St Germain Depository Institutions Act were passed, which allowed federally chartered S&L to make acquisition, development and construction (ADC) loans and eliminated the previous statutory limit on loan-to-value ratios. DIDMCA also increased federal deposit insurance to $100,000 per account from the previous limit of $40,000. In response to Federal government's deregulation efforts, a number of states brought in even more liberal and lax regulation to keep state-chartered S&L from converting into federal chartered institutions.

In addition to substantial changes in banking regulations, Congress passed the Economic Recovery Tax Act (ERTA) of 1981 which greatly affected commercial real estate markets during the early 1980s. ERTA's most important provisions were to reduce ordinary income tax rates (70% to 50% for the highest earners) and capital gains tax rates from 28% to 20%. However, for commercial real estate investment, it was the change in depreciation rules that mattered the most. First, ERTA allowed the "Accelerated Cost Recovery System" (ACRS) which allowed the depreciation period (recovery period) of a commercial building to be 15 years, from 40 years of the previous regulation. Second, it permitted the use of 175 percent declining balance method in contrast to the previous straight-line method.

Therefore, in the early 1980s, there were two separate legislative efforts that led to a bubble in the commercial property market mainly fueled by loans poorly underwritten by S&L institutions. First, they brought in wide-range deregulation and substantially weakened supervision which allowed S&L institutions to pursue risky commercial and construction loans. Second, they made investment into commercial properties very attractive, not by investment strengths of the properties themselves, but by large, artificially-created depreciations. Investors flocked to the commercial real estate market, and financed their investments with loans on lax terms by S&L institutions. All of these led to a large-scale bubble in the commercial real estate market; property values were rapidly appreciating and construction activities were getting increasingly vigorous.

However, in 1986, another important legislation called the Tax Reform Act was passed. It lowered all marginal tax rates even further, but countered this with elimination of previous ACRS and prohibited the use of tax losses from passive investments in commercial real estate against income in other baskets. Also, by the late 1980s, the inflation rate was sharply reduced which led to a decrease in the demand for real estate as an inflation hedge. However, even at the signs of a weakening real estate market, construction and development still continued, and by the late 1980s, net supply of commercial properties far exceeded demand for these properties. This led to the burst of the commercial real estate bubble of the 1980s, and the real estate prices fell 30% to 50% in the short span of two years, the largest drop in property values in the United States since the Great Depression. More importantly, the burst of the commercial real estate market put substantial pressure on the S&L industry which was already suffering from bad commercial real estate loans, which ultimately led to many banking failures. By 1989, FSLIC closed about 300 institutions with 125 billion dollars.

3.2 Comparison with the Subprime Crisis

Even with many similarities, the two crises are quite different. The most important difference between the two is that it was the commercial real estate market that played the most significant role in the S&L crisis. Also, government regulation appeared to have played very important roles not only at the beginning of the cycle in terms of favorable tax treatments, but also in terms of lax regulation and weak supervision over the S&L institutions. On the other hand, during the recent commercial real estate cycle, the crisis was mainly driven by developments in the residential market, not by developments in the commercial market. Many of the factors suggested to account for the housing market bubble of the 2000s, such as securitization of bad quality real estate loans and various government subsidies for homeownership, do not appear relevant for the commercial real estate market. Instead, robust economic growth and the low interest rate environment drove the rapid appreciation of commercial properties.

The second difference is that the construction and development sector plays a much smaller role for the entire economy in the current subprime crisis. Figure 7.1 shows that private, non-residential spending has steadily increased over time, but at slower rates than the overall output. In the 1980s, the proportion of the construction spending in GDP was between 3.5% and 4% while it was only around 2.5% in the 2000s. Therefore, even if construction loans performed as badly during the current crisis as they did during the last S&L crisis, the overall effects on the whole economy would be much smaller.

One point to note in comparison of the two crises is the role played by securitization of commercial real estate loans. In contrast to residential mortgage loans which were securitized already in the 1970s, it was in the 1990s that RTC (Resolution Trust Corporation) securitized commercial

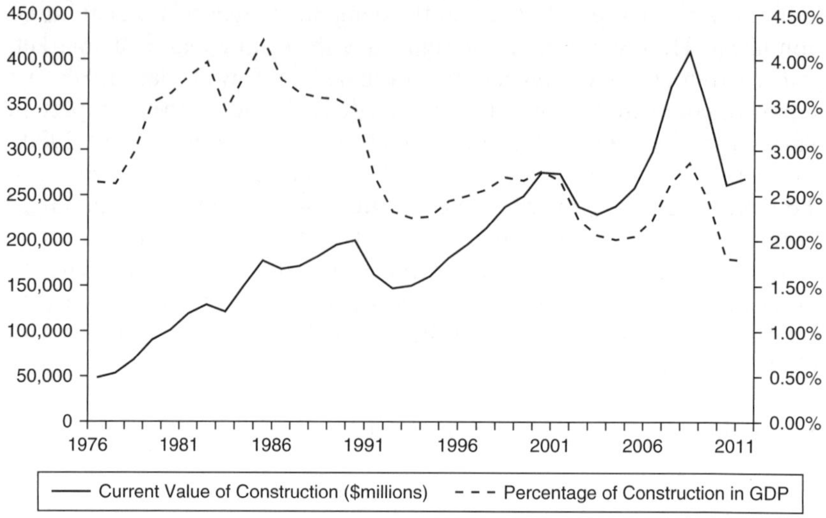

Figure 7.1 Value of construction put in place

mortgage loans on a large scale. The RTC was created to liquidate non-performing commercial real estate loans by failed S&L institutions and banks in the aftermath of the S&L crisis. Therefore, in the S&L crisis, securitization played no role in the boom and bust cycle in the commercial real estate market. Since the S&L crisis, CMBS gradually expanded in commercial real estate lending, but it followed quite a different path from residential mortgage backed securities. First, securitization of commercial real estate loans has been much slower. At its peak, the total face value of loans in CMBS pools was less than 30% of the outstanding commercial real estate loans. The majority of commercial real estate loans are still held by depository institutions as portfolio loans. In case of construction and development loans, effectively all the loans are portfolio loans. Second, most commercial real estate loans sold through CMBS were of high quality in sharp contrast to residential mortgage backed securities based on subprime and Alt-A loans. Moreover, commercial mortgages did not have government guarantees, unlike GSE residential mortgages, which have implicit guarantees, or FHA/VA loans, which have explicit government insurances. Therefore, securitization does not have direct effects on commercial mortgage performance in general, and more specifically on construction and development loans. However, there still appears to be an indirect link between securitization and performance of commercial mortgages (including construction loans) held by banks as portfolio loans. Since most high quality commercial mortgages were securitized and sold to investors in capital markets, banks have found that there were fewer good quality loans available, which might have forced them to rely on loans with lower quality or higher risks. There is some anecdotal evidence that failed, smaller, local banks tended to have higher concentration of risky commercial mortgages and construction loans.

4. REAL ESTATE DEVELOPMENT AND VOLATILITY

Cyclicality is one of the unique features of the real estate market. Other asset markets, especially markets for financial assets, do have cyclical fluctuations, but their magnitudes are much smaller compared to those of the real estate market. There are many studies looking into the nature of real estate cycles and the driving forces behind them.[3] In a widely accepted view, developers and their development activities play an important role. First, the real estate market initially reacts positively to favorable conditions in the macroeconomy, financial markets, or government regulations with rising valuations of the properties. Second, recognizing new opportunities, developers respond with development and construction activities. However, due to significant lags between the start of construction and its completion, excess demand for real estate properties persists at least for some time while property values are continually increasing. Third, supply of newly developed properties will soon catch up with the excess demand, starting to put pressures on property values. Depreciation of property values is more likely to accelerate now due to developers who "over-developed" properties based on their irrationally optimistic views. Under this view, real estate markets chronically experience excess demand and excess supply, creating a cyclical movement of property values. This view relies on two facts; it takes time to develop new properties and real estate developments are driven by irrational developers. Even though some assumptions underlying this view are questionable, it puts much emphasis on the role of developers to account for real estate market cycles and volatility.

The effects of real estate market volatility on development activities have long been recognized, especially in real options literature (Williams, 1991). When volatility or uncertainty is high in the real estate market, an option of delaying development becomes more valuable, and the hurdle value of properties that triggers development activity is high. It implies that, at the beginning of a real estate cycle triggered by positive effects of market fundamentals, development activities can be overly subdued due to high uncertainty in the market. However, as the market continues to improve, perceived uncertainty is gradually reduced, which will lead to increases in development activities. Depending on market conditions, this can potentially lead to development glut, called a "development cascade" by Grenadier (2002), creating potential for a downward cycle later on.

5. REAL ESTATE DEVELOPMENT PROCESS IN THE U.S.

Real estate development is a process of creating real estate properties. The process starts with a developer's search for suitable projects on land he or she already owns (site-looking-for-a-use type decision) or a developer's search for optimal location for a planned-out project (use-looking-for-a-site decision[4]). At the end of the process, the developer might seek to sell the finished property to investors, lease the property for a short period of time for subsequent sales, or manage the property as a long term investment. The closure process for development depends on developer characteristics, commercial property sector characteristics, capital market conditions and lease market development. If a developer decides to manage the property on a long term basis, the property might better be classified as a seasoned property. Even though the market for real estate development (or new properties) and the market for existing, seasoned properties are closely related, they are quite different in terms of investors, management practices and financing arrangement.

5.1 Real Estate Development Phases

A real estate development is a complex process, and each development project is, in a sense, unique. However, for most of the development projects, there are certain stages in which some tasks tend to be completed concurrently. Figure 7.2 describes a typical real estate development process in three steps.

5.1.1 Pre-construction phase

This is a preliminary stage where creativity and entrepreneurial efforts by the developer are required. The main task in this phase is an exploratory pre-construction planning which includes product design, site selection, due diligence on land, market analysis, project planning, financing analysis, and entitlement along with optioning land parcels if necessary. This process also includes the permitting process through which the developer files applications along with a thorough highest and best use analysis of the site for approval from public officials (Geltner et al., 2007).

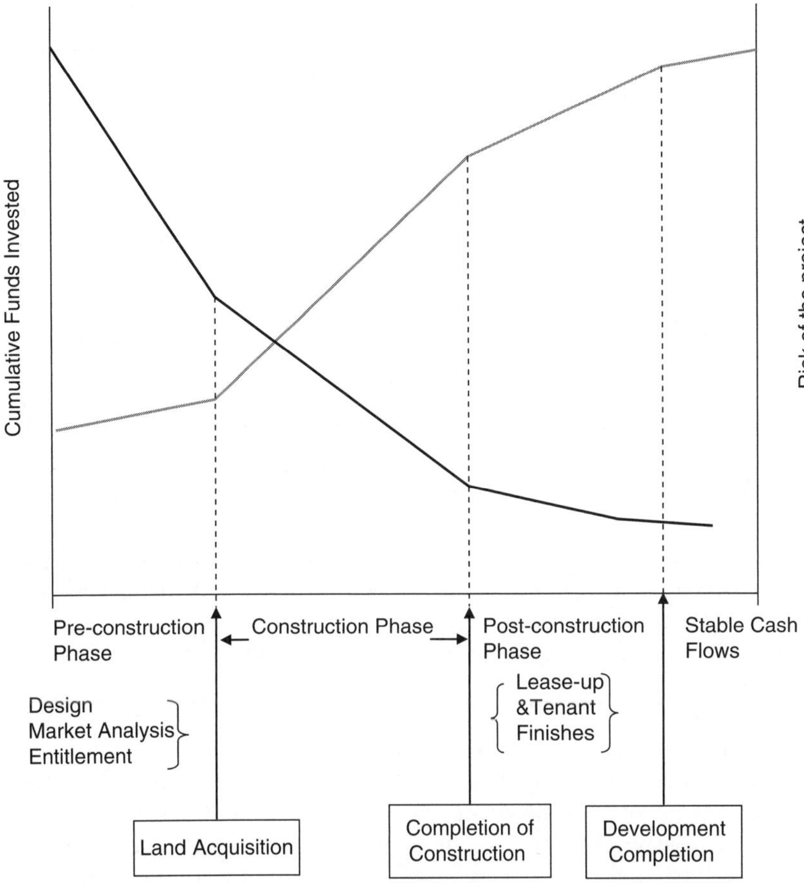

Figure 7.2 Real estate development process

This process can take somewhere between a few months and years, and entails the highest risks mainly due to much uncertainty involved in the project. It is often the case that a project may ultimately be determined not to be economically and administratively viable and either postponed or abandoned altogether. Due to the high degrees of uncertainty and risks involved, suitable risk premiums for financing in this stage can be as high as 40% (Geltner et al., 2007). Most of the costs involved in this process are soft costs, altogether in the range of 5–15% out of the total project budget. It is difficult to find financing arrangements for the costs involved in this stage and they are most often financed by the developer.

5.1.2 Construction phase

This phase consists of development and construction of the main project which starts with the closing of the land purchase. In some cases, developers purchase an option contract on the land rather than purchasing the land directly. The option contract the developer can enter into is a call option which provides the developer the right to purchase the land at the exercise price within the contract period, but not an obligation. This gives flexibility and additional room for further analysis to the developer for conducting any necessary engineering/soil testing, finishing the entitlement process, and securing financing from lenders and equity investors. If the developer decides to exercise the option, the purchase price of the land will be the original prices less the option cost.

Once the construction starts, it can potentially take from several months to a few years or longer depending on the project size. Cost-wise, 80–90% of total project budget is expected to be spent in this stage. Much of the uncertainty and risks have been already eliminated during market analysis and permitting processes, but there are still two remaining risks: market risk and project risk (Bruggeman and Fisher, 2011). Market risk faced by the development project is determined by market demand activities, leasing conditions and capital market development during the construction process. A drastic change in the market condition can potentially delay the project or even suspend it indefinitely. This risk will be greater for a developer who wants to retain the property on a long term basis after completion of the project since they will be exposed to longer-term risks of market cycles. Therefore, smaller developers prefer an exit strategy of selling the project to investors who specialize in managing those risks. However, large developers can potentially reduce some of the market risks by diversifying into different sectors and regions. In addition, they can benefit from property management since it can lead to future development opportunities by expanding existing tenant facilities and generating new opportunities in other areas and sectors by the same tenants when they expand into those areas or into different sectors (Bruggeman and Fisher, 2011).

In addition to the market risks, there are idiosyncratic project risks by which the construction process itself can be significantly delayed or construction costs can be substantially higher than the original plan due to unexpected site conditions, unexpected increase in material costs and design problems (Long, 2011).

Most of the costs in the phase are financed by equity investors or lenders. The usual expected return on equity investments is about 20% while interest costs for construction loans are about 200–300 basis points over LIBOR.

5.1.3 Post-construction phase

The main activities in this phase include marketing, lease-up, and sale of completed project. There can still be some finishing construction and tenant improvement, but the major costs involved are marketing and management costs, which range about 5–8% of the total project cost. The closure of this process depends on sectors and capital funding conditions. Some projects can be either preleased or presold depending on prior funding arrangements for permanent financing; others, especially those built "on spec" for speculation, have to be directly marketed to investors and tenants as the construction process is finalized. At this stage, however, most of the uncertainty has been removed, and required return for capital used for this phase should be around 10%.

6. FINANCING THE REAL ESTATE DEVELOPMENT PROCESS

In most development projects, developers seek equity financing and debt financing at the same time. However, as indicated by Figure 7.2, a development project goes through different phases, each of which represents different risks and uncertainty, and thus different capital structures are necessary.

During the preconstruction phase where most of the activities are concentrated on designing, planning and the permitting process, it is very difficult to obtain any form of financing due to high risks involved. It is often the case that the developer finances this process using his own funds.

Once the developer finishes planning, feasibility analysis and securing entitlement, the development project moves from pre-construction phase to construction phase. In this phase, the risks of the project have been substantially reduced, and it allows the developer to secure funding for land purchase and construction. Since lenders require a certain level of equity by the developer based on value of the project or the cost of the project, the developer without enough financial resources will need to seek equity investors concurrently. Most equity investment into the development project will take a form of joint venture, such as LLC (limited liability company) or LP (limited partnership). In such joint ventures, the developer will become a general partner and is expected to contribute development expertise and project management capability along with capital investment of around 10% of total equity, while outside equity investors will become limited partners of the project providing the rest of the equity investment in the venture. The total amount of equity investment is expected to be 30%–50% of the total project costs, including land costs.

6.1 Equity Financing in Real Estate Development

Since an equity investment arrangement for the development project brings in different types of capital (an intangible capital of the developer's expertise and a tangible capital of equity investors' funds) and there is asymmetry in information between the two parties, it is important to have a contract between the developer and equity investors to align their incentives while minimizing potential asymmetric information problems. In the U.S., different types of legal entities are available for an equity investment arrangement: partnerships, limited liability companies, S-corporations, or regular C-corporations. From a real estate investor's view, the following four factors highlight the major differences among the legal entities.

6.1.1 Taxation pass-through

Some legal entities such as C-corporations are subject to income taxation at the level of entity. However, in most real estate investment arrangements, investors usually use legal entities that allow avoiding double taxation such as limited partnerships, limited liability companies and S-corporations. Even REITs, which are C-corporations themselves, are allowed not to pay corporate income taxes once they satisfy certain requirements.

6.1.2 Limited liabilities

It is important to limit the liabilities for investors due to high risks involved in real estate development projects. Under legal entities such as C-corporations, S-corporations or limited liability companies, all the investors (including the developer) are not personally liable for any legal obligations or debt of the entity. On the other hand, under limited partnerships, limited partners (usually equity investors) are not personally liable, but general partners (which are developers) are.

6.1.3 Transferability of ownership interests

Naturally, equity investors prefer a legal entity that allows unlimited transfer of ownership interests. One extreme would be a listed public C-corporation whose shares are freely traded in very liquid stock exchanges such as NYSE. On the other hand, limited partnerships and limited liability companies have limited secondary markets for ownership shares. In addition, limited partnerships often impose the restriction that selling shares requires consent of other partners in the partnership.

6.1.4 Special allocation of ownership interests

One of the main advantages for partnerships and limited liability companies is that the ownership interests do not have to be divided proportionally

Table 7.4 Development entity comparison summary

	C-corporation	S-corporation	General partnerships	Limited partnerships	Limited liability companies
Avoid double taxation	No	Yes	Yes	Yes	Yes
Limited liability	Yes	Yes	No	Yes	Yes
Ease of transfer of interest	Yes	Yes	No	No	Yes
Allow special allocations	No	No	Yes	Yes	Yes

Source: Ling and Archer, 2010.

to capital investment. It allows the general partners in partnerships or some owners in limited liability companies to receive larger ownership shares for compensation of their efforts in organizing and managing the entities.

Table 7.4 taken from Ling and Archer (2010), summarizes how each entity fares on each of the factors. Even though all the entities have been used for equity investment arrangement in real estate development projects, limited liability companies and limited partnerships are the most flexible and preferred ownership form.[5]

6.2 Debt Financing in Real Estate Development

As discussed above, a real estate development process involves various uncertainty and risks. Usually debt financing is only available after the pre-construction phase. However, even at the construction phase which carries much less risk than the preconstruction phase, lenders still face substantial risks since (1) development projects can still experience unexpected delays and cost overruns, and (2) there is still considerable uncertainty in market conditions at completion of the project. In addition, development projects rarely generate cash flows which can be used for interest payments before completion of the project. Therefore, lending contracts for development projects come with peculiar loan features to address those concerns and risks. In practice, lending for a development project is typically done in two stages. Debt financing in the first stage is a short term bridge loan that covers financing needs only for the construction process itself. In the second stage, debt financing is based on long term contracts called permanent loans.

6.3 Permanent Financing

The permanent loans are usually granted for seasoned commercial properties with established performance and stabilized cash flows. For a newly constructed property, permanent loans might be accessible if it has a record of stable performance during the first few years or if it has a credible promise of future performance in terms of preleasing or preselling activities. Since permanent loans are less risky than construction loans, they are financed by a variety of lenders including commercial banks, insurance companies, conduit lenders of CMBS, private investors and government agencies such as GSEs and FHAs (in case of multifamily properties).

6.3.1 Financing terms

In contrast to what the name might imply, however, permanent loans have only five to ten year maturity terms, but are amortized over much longer periods such as 30 years. Therefore, most permanent loans are balloon mortgages, and need to be refinanced at the end of their terms. Permanent loans usually have fixed interest rates, but adjustable rate contracts are not uncommon. Most permanent loans also come with strong restrictions on prepayment. Unlike residential mortgages for which prepayment are often freely exercised, borrowers of permanent loans pay heavy penalties for prepayment.[6] Permanent loans have lower LTV ratios than residential mortgages, in the range of 50% to 80%, and are mostly non-recourse loans. Servicing of permanent loans is expected to be covered by property income rather than personal income.[7]

6.3.2 Lenders of permanent loans

In commercial mortgages (both of construction loans and permanent loans), commercial banks are the major provider of funds. Traditional non-depository institutional lenders include life insurance companies, property and casualty insurance companies and pension funds. Recently, securitization of commercial mortgages has become more active, and now it is the second largest source for funding of permanent commercial mortgages. Loans in CMBS pools tend to be of better qualities on average than permanent commercial mortgages held in banks' portfolios.

Figure 7.3 shows three major lender types, commercial banks, non-depository institutional lenders (insurance companies and pension funds) and MBS and ABS mortgage pools. Since the 1990s, commercial banks

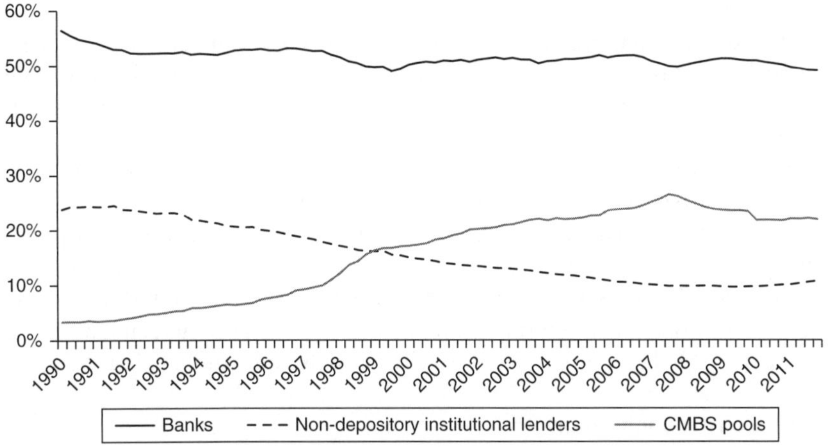

Figure 7.3 Lenders for permanent loans

have originated about a half of commercial mortgages, but there appears to be a slight downward trend. On the other hand, non-depository institutional lenders have been falling to 10% while CMBS pools appear to have picked up the lost share of loan volumes by them.

Given the dominant position of commercial banks in commercial mortgages, the share of non-depository institutional lenders such as pension funds, insurance companies and CMBS pools is much larger for permanent loans than for construction loans. The main reason for relatively stronger presence by non-depository institutional lenders in permanent loans is that those lenders are in a better position in maturity matching for loans with longer maturities than commercial banks are. Compared to banks, non-depository institutional lenders tend to have liabilities. One potential weakness of those lenders is that, since they most likely are not located in the vicinity of commercial properties for which permanent loans are made, they might not have enough knowledge of local real estate markets and are subject to more serious asymmetric information problems.

6.3.3 Underwriting of permanent loans

As in the case of residential mortgages, underwriting of a permanent loan is focused on the borrower and the property. However, since most permanent loans are non-recourse, and servicing of mortgage loans is based on cash flows generated from the property itself, the primary consideration is usually given to the property.[8] Two most important indicators for credit quality of the property are the debt service coverage ratio (DSCR) and the loan to value (LTV) ratio. Typical mortgage underwriting criteria rarely allow LTV ratio of a permanent loan to exceed 75%, and average LTV ratios of high quality CMBS pools are often lower than 65%. Since a typical permanent loan is expected to be refinanced at maturity, not only origination LTV, but expected LTV ratio at the end of the term is also an important factor to consider. On the other hand, a DSCR is the ratio of annual debt payment and net operating income, and it measures the debt servicing capacity of a given property. Sometimes DSCR is more important than LTV because the DSCR is more precisely measured compared to LTV (Lancaster, 2001). Since different property types exhibit different cash flow volatilities, it is difficult to pinpoint acceptable DSCR across the sectors, but the usual minimum DSCR for a typical commercial loan is 1.2 while high quality CMBS pools requires DSCR to be higher than 1.45.

6.4 Construction Loans

In many ways, construction loans are the opposite of permanent loans; they are usually short term interim loans, and are exclusively financed by commercial banks or an S&L association. Compared to permanent loans, construction loans are substantially more risky. Many financing terms of a construction loan are structured to protect the lender from those potential risks.

6.4.1 Maturity

Construction loans have short maturities which match with construction periods. A typical construction project ($1 million+) takes from nine months to twenty-four months from start to completion, and loans are granted with maturities between twelve to thirty months allowing for some unexpected delays in the construction process.

6.4.2 Interest rate and fees

Construction loans are usually based on adjustable interest rate, often using prime rates as index rate. It is partly because construction loans are rarely securitized in the secondary market, and more likely to stay on the banks' portfolio; it is more convenient for banks to carry adjustable rate loans on their books. The spread depends on various characteristics of borrowers, collateral and capital market condition, but has been between 1 and 3 percent. In addition to high interest rates, the bank also charges an upfront fee of 1 percent or more.

6.4.3 Maximum loan amount

The loan amount can be determined by expected appraised value at completion or costs of construction. When based on appraised values, LTV ratios are between 75% and 80%. When construction costs are used, developers can borrow 90% to 100% of total construction cost since lenders assume that the project will have a projected profit of 20% to 25% upon sales of the project. Usually, the land cost is not included in estimation of construction cost and often borrowers have to finance the land cost either by separate loans or by equity. In addition, lenders often put more emphasis on hard costs of construction such as materials and labor costs rather than soft costs of construction such as leasing costs, planning costs and management costs.[9]

6.4.4 Payment guarantee

Due to high risks involved, construction loans are usually recourse loans which require personal guarantees of developers, secured by a lien on the developers' assets as security (Long 2011).[10] More importantly, lenders usually ask for payment guarantee in the form of commitment by permanent lenders, called permanent commitment or take-out commitment.

In permanent commitment, another lender (other than the construction lender) makes a commitment in writing that a permanent loan will be provided to the developer at completion of the project to pay off the construction loan. The commitment comes with contingencies that the developer must satisfy for the commitment to become a legally binding contract. In the event where any of the contingencies are not met, the permanent lender does not have a legal obligation for the commitment. Common contingencies, listed by Bruggeman and Fisher (2011), include:

- The maximum period of time for the developer to secure a construction loan commitment.
- Completion date for project development
- Minimum lease-up requirements and approval of major lease contracts
- Provision for gap financing in case lease-up requirements are not met
- Approval of design changes and substitution of any building material

Because the performance of a construction loan ultimately depends on whether or not it is refinanced into a permanent loan, it is also important for the construction lender to make sure the loans satisfy the contingencies listed by the permanent lender. This requires the construction lender to actively monitor the developer and keep track of progress of the construction project.

This is why most construction loans are made by local commercial banks: they are familiar with real estate markets and economic conditions of the area where the development projects are located and thus have better capacity to monitor the development project. On the other hand, insurance companies and pension funds who do not have local presence are almost exclusively permanent lenders: they delegate monitoring to local lenders and take on lending for properties which have already established performance records.

6.4.5 Interest reserve

The disbursed portion of a construction loan accrues interest payments each month which are usually advanced through interest reserve account. An interest reserve can be lender-funded or borrower-funded. If it is lender-financed, then the lender advances the interest payments by adding them to the loan balance. Whether a loan can have a lender-funded interest reserve account depends on the feasibility of the project, the creditworthiness of the borrower and guarantors, and the protection provided by the real estate and other collateral.

6.4.6 Disbursement of funds

Unlike permanent loans on existing properties, construction loans are secured by a mortgage for future advances or by an open ended mortgage (Bruggeman and Fisher, 2011). Funds are disbursed periodically based on the progress of the development project, either by stage payment plan or by progress payment plan (Federal Reserve, 1997). In either case, a draw amount in a given month cannot exceed the construction cost of the previous month so that total disbursed amount of the loan is not greater than the economic value of the project. Under the stage payment plan, often used in residential construction projects or smaller construction projects, the fixed draw amounts are scheduled based on development stages. Under the progress payment plan which is more popular in larger commercial construction projects, draws are made after certain phases of projects are completed. The borrower requests a draw in the form of "construction draw" request or "certification of payment." In making a request for a draw, the borrower is required to demonstrate that all requested funds are to cover (or reimburse) the costs and the expenses occurred in the given stage of the project development and that all the suppliers and subcontractors were paid in full.

6.4.7 Monitoring the project progress

Closely related to period disbursement of the fund is the continual process of monitoring the borrower and the development project. The main purpose of the monitoring process is to ensure requested funds are justified by actual costs incurred during the previous period and verified by appropriate documentations. Also the monitoring process ensures that the development project is being progressed according to the project plan agreed by the lender and the borrower. It usually involves physical inspections (Federal Reserve, 1997) and is performed by the lender or by the independent construction consulting companies. It generates regular progress reports which detail quantity and quality of tasks performed and verifies the project's progress in terms of its original schedule and budget.

In addition, the monitoring process may involve verifying the borrower's current financial status and conditions and lien status of the project. OCC recommends banks to review the borrower's financial statements and accounts payable and receivable, updated credit reports and weekly legal reports and trade reports to detect potential financial problems (OCC, 1998).

7. EMPIRICAL ANALYSIS OF CONSTRUCTION LOAN PERFORMANCE

After the crisis, the development and construction loans turned out to be the worst performing loans for commercial banks. Figure 7.4 shows a sharp spike of noncurrent rate of construction loans as high as 17% during the current crisis. In contrast, noncurrent rates of permanent loans are around only 5%. Figure 7.4 implies, despite all the dramatic collapse of "toxic" residential mortgage backed security markets, it appears to be

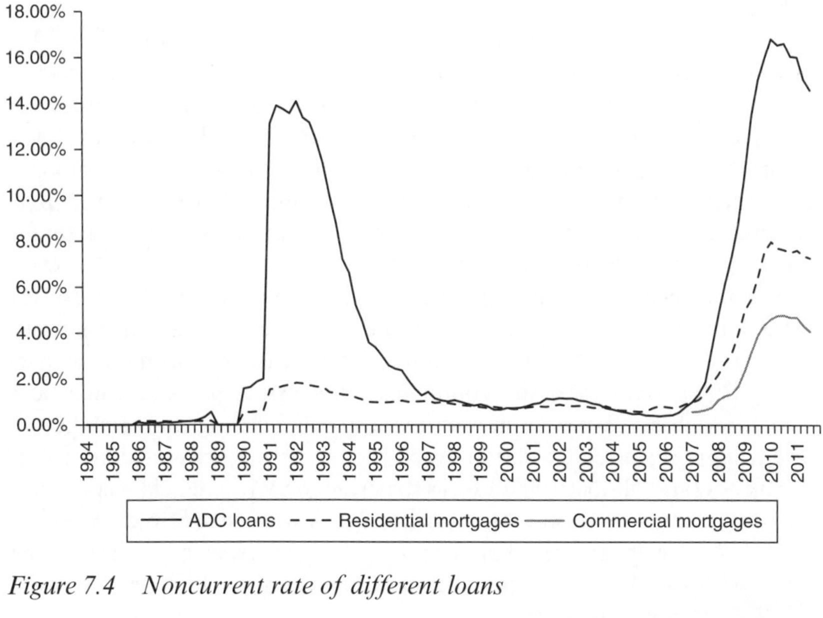

Figure 7.4 Noncurrent rate of different loans

commercial loans, especially development and construction loans, that greatly contributed to bank failure for smaller depository institutions nationwide (Cole and White, 2010). Unfortunately, this is not a new phenomenon. As discussed, during the earlier S&L crisis, commercial real estate loans, especially construction loans, played the most important role for bank failures (Cole and Fenn, 2008).

Why do construction loans perform so badly during the crisis? Note that development and construction loans have a high level of risk compared to other loans by nature. Compared to permanent loans to existing properties, construction loans have an additional layer of idiosyncratic project risks, and should be more prone to bad performance. Therefore, bad performance of those loans compared to other loans "on average" should not be surprising as long as interest rates and reserves are adequate for perceived risks.

Bad performance of development and construction loans can be due to unexpected worsening of commercial property markets. In this case, even if a construction loan is well underwritten in the sense that it is lent to a creditworthy borrower with a strong development project, it can perform badly simply because the underlying real estate market performs badly. On the other hand, a construction loan might perform poorly due to weak underwriting, either in terms of financially vulnerable borrowers or in terms of a badly conceived project. If construction loans perform badly on average due to the latter case, it is the bank's lending standard that is to blame.

Note that lending standards are not fixed. Market conditions that surround lenders are constantly changing, and lenders often respond to changing conditions by actively adjusting their lending standards. For example, the 2004 Survey of Credit Underwriting Practices by OCC reports that banks were easing on lending standards of commercial loans due to stronger competition, improving economic outlook and risk appetite, and that banks were easing standards by lowering pricing, lengthening maturity, increasing the credit line and adjusting covenants (OCC, 2004). The importance of lending standards is directly related to the nature of the current crisis. It is often believed that the current crisis is at least partially due to massive securitization of badly underwritten subprime mortgages during 2000s. However, the commercial real estate market, which also went through a similar boom and bust cycle as housing markets, did not have a large scale securitization of bad loans. A majority of commercial mortgages (and almost 100% of construction loans) were held as portfolio loans by lenders, and only high quality loans were securitized. After the crisis, however, it appears that commercial loans, especially construction loans, perform even worse than residential mortgages. Is it because weak construction loans were originated or is it due to the collapse of the commercial property market even though loans themselves were appropriately underwritten? One important implication of this question is what would be the role of government supervision of banks. Unlike private label securitization of subprime loans, many lenders, especially commercial banks, were regularly examined by supervisory institutions such as Federal Reserve or OCC. If loans were originated under weak underwriting standards, why didn't supervisory institutions intervene? To answer such questions, it is important to understand potential factors of construction loans performance.

In understanding performance of real estate development loans and how they are related to changing lending standards, we will use the Federal Reserve's Senior Loan Officer Opinion Survey. The survey is conducted on a quarterly basis, and 60 major banks participate. Lown and Morgan (2006) reported that participating banks accounted for about 60% of all loans by U.S. banks and about 70% of all U.S. bank business loans. Even though the survey has existed since 1967, the current format of survey questions was introduced in 1990. The survey asks senior loan officers of participating banks if they have changed the lending standard for loans since the last quarter in six categories: C&I, commercial real estate, residential real estate, home equity line of credit, credit cards and consumer loans other than credit cards. Participating banks' responses are recorded in one of the following five discrete answers: "eased considerably", "eased somewhat", "remained about unchanged", "tightened somewhat", and "tightened considerably." Federal Reserve reports the survey results in terms of "net percentage of banks tightening standards," the number of loan officers reporting tightening standards less the number of banks reporting easing divided by the total number of reporting loan officers.

Figure 7.5 presents the lending standards for commercial real estate loans since 1990. First, there are wide swings in lending standards for CRE loans: gradual easing during the early '90s, faster tightening during 1997 to 2001, sharp fall in standards in 2001 through 2005 followed by rapid tightening in 2005 to 2009. Second, even with wide cyclical trends in standards, lending standards appear to be tightened almost always except for a few brief periods of net easing. Among those rare easing periods, the two year period from 2004 through 2005 seems to be the longest and the largest. Third, standards for CRE loans and those for residential mortgages tend to move in the same directions. However, the volatility of changes in standards for CRE loans is generally much larger than volatility for residential mortgages. Especially during the early to mid 2000s, while lending standards for residential mortgages appeared rather stable, those for CRE loans exhibit more extreme shifts. Often, the period of 2004 through

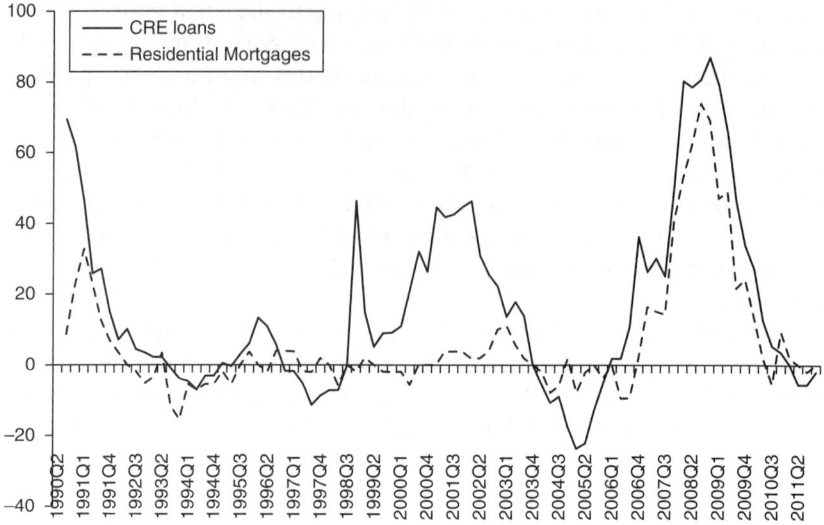

Figure 7.5 Lending standards for CRE loans and residential mortages

2006 is characterized as one of extremely lax underwriting for residential mortgages in the media and academia. During the same period, CRE loans appear to have had even more lax lending standards. Implications of apparent lax lending standards are the focus of this empirical section. What are the consequences of lax standards? Did loose lending standards play a role in subsequent loan performance, and what can explain such loose standards during the period of 2004 and 2005?

Our main interest is to explain bad performance of construction loans; especially, we are interested in whether the bad performance is driven by collapse of commercial real estate values or by weak underwriting. For this, we will use regression analysis on ADC loan performance by regressing lending standards with other control variables on loan performance. We first measure the loan performance by net charge-off rates by commercial banks and savings institutions. The loan performance can be measured in different ways: loss given default after foreclosure sale, probability of continuous accumulation of delinquencies over 90 days or 120 days. Especially, in residential mortgages, 90 day delinquency has been a popular measure for loan performance, partly because lenders can proceed with the foreclosure process once the loan passes either a 60 or 90 day delinquency. However, construction loans are mostly on much shorter maturities, and there does not appear to exist any established guideline for foreclosure initiation for ADC loans. Another reason is that, even in the residential mortgage market, it is not difficult to find loans that cured themselves from a 90 days or longer delinquency status, which implies that using 90 day delinquency can potentially over-estimate the probability of loan defaults.

The control variables used in the regression analysis include interest rates (Federal Funds rate and 10 year constant maturity date treasury rate) and appreciation return on CRE. The interest rates are included to capture effects from general lending conditions around the time of delinquency. The general lending conditions are reflected in the current lending standard, but since lending standards are persistent, it can potentially mask the effects of lending standards at origination. Instead we use short term interest rates and long term interest rates as instruments to control for effects from the current lending standards, both of which are used in Maddaloni and Peydró (2011) to explain lending standards. The appreciation return on the CRE, captured by MIT's transaction based index (TBI), is included to reflect effects of changes in existing CRE property values between loan origination and delinquencies. The dependent variable is the net charge-off normalized by ADC loan balance at the same quarter.

Table 7.5 presents estimation results for the effects of CRE lending standards on ADC loan performance, measured by net charge-off rate. We estimate three specifications, one for only 12 quarter lag, another for 11 and 12 quarter lags and the last for 10, 11 and 12 quarter lags. The estimation model performs consistently over a different lag length. First, the CRE lending standard three years previously is related to the performance of a construction loan. That is, construction loans that were originated during the time of easing standards tend to perform worse later. The effect is not only statistically significant, but also economically significant. When the CRE lending standards change by one standard deviation, net charge-off changes by half standard deviation. Appreciation of commercial real estate values has an expected effect. When CRE values go up, net charge-off will decrease either because development projects tend to default less often or project values at default increases so that loss given default decreases. When the model includes more lags for variables, some estimated coefficients are no longer significant, but it might be due to potentially high correlation among lagged variables. For example, when lagged variables are added for lending standards, either one lagged variable becomes insignificant (lag of 11 and 12 quarters) or all three lagged variables become insignificant (lag of 10, 11 and 12 quarters). However, the lending standard variable is highly persistent, and correlation among the lagged variables might have made standard errors large. However, when we test significance of lagged lending standards jointly, the null is always rejected. In case of two lagged variables, lending standard lagged at 11th quarter is statistically insignificant. But the log likelihood test shows that

Table 7.5 Development (ADC) loan performance

Loan growth t-12	0.007117	−0.0476311	−0.0340328
	(6.08)	(3.71)	(1.68)
Loan growth t-11		0.0595341	0.0165084
		(4.26)	(0.41)
Loan growth t-10			0.0305349
			(1.33)
Lending standard t-12	−.0001041	−0.0000658	−0.0000494
	(4.38)	(2.13)	(1.61)
Lending standard t-11		−0.0000155	0.0000142
		(0.49)	(0.39)
Lending standard t-10			−0.0000535
			(1.53)
Federal funds rate t-4	0.0007126	0.0002835	0.0001343
	(1.95)	(3.84)	(0.39)
10 year Treasury t-4	−0.003565	−0.0019506	−0.0015794
	(7.89)	(3.34)	(2.69)
CRE value changes between t-4 and t-12	−0.00979 (3.60)	0.0058795 (0.78)	0.0039867 (0.52)
CRE value changes between t-4 and t-11		−0.0097016 (1.18)	0.0034877 (0.35)
CRE value changes between t-4 and t-10			−0.0135232 (1.56)
Constant	−0.003833	0.005995	0.0058855
	(7.18)	(1.02)	(0.91)
Number of observations	71	71	71
F-statistics	32.07	29.41	23.72
Adj R square	0.6893	0.7645	0.7812
Root MSE	0.0027	0.00235	0.00227
Sum of coefficients on lending standard	−.0001041	−0.0000813	−0.000089
Likelihood ratio test	38.905583	40.186119	51.701455
Difference in Adj R square	0.2701	0.2063	0.1349

two lagged lending standards are jointly significant with chi square value of 40.2 and p-value of 0. Adjusted R-square also increase sharply by 0.20. In addition, the sums of coefficients (over two quarters and three quarters) are always negative, strongly indicating that lax lending standards lead to worse performance of construction loans.

The results indicate that performance of construction loans is affected both by valuation of commercial real estate, and by lending standards at the same time. The results imply that deteriorating lending standards, either in terms of loan quality or in terms of inappropriate loan terms, were at least partially to blame for bad performance of construction loans. This also implies that weakening lending standards in general might be less related to securitization but rather more to a low interest rate environment (Maddaloni and Peydró, 2011) because construction loans were rarely securitized and almost always kept as portfolio loans. Under the current model, it is difficult to separately estimate the effects of lending standards from the effects of market valuation. However, if we assume permanent loans and construction loans are equally subject to the market valuation effects, the difference between loan performance will be a lower bound for the effect of weak lending standards. As of 2010, the difference between net charge-off rate is larger than 10%, which indicates a potentially large effect of lending standards.

8. POLICY IMPLICATIONS

Development and construction loans are risky loans. They are subject to the same market risk as permanent loans for existing commercial properties. However, there is another layer of risk unique to construction loans: idiosyncratic project risk. The idiosyncratic project risk which encompasses most of the uncertainty during the pre-construction phase and the construction phase can be substantial, and even greater than the market risk itself. Lenders have recognized this additional risk; they not only charge higher interest rates but also structure terms and covenants of construction loans to minimize this risk. The unique risk structure of a construction loan requires careful underwriting prior to loan origination as well as active monitoring after origination.

8.1 Monitoring Underwriting Standards

Commercial mortgages, including construction loans, are complex contracts which come with many covenants and terms. The lending standard is an aggregate measure of all the numerous covenants and terms, indicating the quality of loans. Literature shows that lending standards such as borrower's financial conditions, LTVs, terms and various covenants have substantially fluctuated over time even though there is still much debate over what led to such variation in standards. Certainly loan size and loan to value ratios are important parts of lending standards, but lenders have substantial discretion in adjusting loan qualities by controlling various loan terms and covenants. For loans that are standardized in loan terms, such as securitized residential mortgages, macroprudential regulations based on a few representative loan characteristics can be effective. However, for loans that are not standardized and are held by lenders directly, substantially more active supervision might be necessary. Commercial real estate loans are a typical example of such loans. Even though many high quality commercial loans have been actively securitized into CMBS pools, a majority of commercial mortgages are still kept as lenders' portfolio loans. Many of such mortgages are made based on an established relationship between lenders and borrowers; their loan terms and covenants are flexible, and can be adjusted toward a borrower's unique conditions. Development and construction loans are, in a sense, an extreme example of such portfolio loans. Since those loans require lenders to be well-informed not only about local real estate markets and regulations but also developers themselves, lenders often maintain close, long term relationships with developers. Therefore, active supervision of lending standards on such loans is very important. Currently, Federal Reserve surveys senior loan officers for lending standards. OCC, on the other hand, surveys bank examiners on lending standards and risks of loan portfolios of large national banks. Those surveys do provide important information on lending standards, but there are some limitations. First, the surveys are limited to 50–60 largest banks, which leaves out mid-sized banks that can have substantial effects on local economies. Second, information from the surveys on lending standards may be limited due to the nature of such surveys. Since the surveys ask the subjective opinions of senior loan officers (Federal Reserve) or of bank examiners on overall loan quality, they are subject to individual discrepancies and biases. The empirical section of this chapter shows even those surveys have considerable prediction on loan performance, which implies better measurements of lending standards can be substantially more effective.

Since loan terms and covenants are very diverse, it is too costly and probably impractical to monitor all those terms. One possibility is to create an index based on actual loan terms, and include it as a part of macroprudential regulations. If the index is carefully created in a way to encompass diverse loan terms, the index can be aggregated by region and by industry to the national level to provide aggregate risks posed by such loans. The index can be further used for dynamic provisioning as well, requiring a lender's capital to be tied to average lending standards by the lender. The index can also include post-origination changes in loan terms and covenants as well, as a part of the single index or as a separate index.

8.2 Monitoring the (Post-origination) Monitoring Process

In construction loans, the role of lenders goes beyond negotiations over loan terms with the borrower before origination; lenders are required to actively monitor progress in the development project and borrowers' financial conditions after loan origination. There is much room for discretion with loan covenants in terms of flexible monitoring and delinquency management after loan origination. Since funds are disbursed in stages in construction lending, it is still possible for lenders to limit their potential losses by stopping disbursement at the early sign of troubles for developers. But there are some potential reasons for lax monitoring by lenders. First, construction loans are often based on relationship lending, which might lead to overconfidence of the lender in an underperforming borrower. Second, the lender might have an incentive to hide the true delinquency of construction loans since it might affect evaluation of their performance. One example is the abuse of interest reserves by lenders (FDIC, 2008). Loan-funded (or lender-funded) interest reserves are used for construction loans since it is difficult for a development project to generate cash flows to service interest payments even if the project is well-planned and promising. They are designed to effectively postpone interest payments until successful capital event of the project. However, in some cases, lenders continued to advance interest payments to delinquent construction loans. Sometimes, lenders even extended, renewed or restructured the terms of delinquent loans. This leads to much larger losses eventually for the lenders. This illustrates how the post-origination monitoring process which can potentially help reduce losses by detecting early signs of troubles for construction loans can be equally likely abused to magnify loan losses instead. Therefore, it is necessary and important to establish risk management procedures even after a construction loan is originated. This includes close monitoring of compliance with loan covenants, periodic review of financial conditions, progress reports on the development project, and regular and vigorous evaluation of market conditions.

9. CONCLUSION

Real estate development is a unique opportunity in real estate investment, the importance of which cannot be overemphasized. From an investor's point of view, a development project offers an investment opportunity that comes with substantial risks, but also with considerable returns at the same time. A typical real estate development project faces two types of risks: the market risk and idiosyncratic project risks. Therefore, any financing arrangement for real estate development projects, equity or debt, should be designed to manage those risks.

The ownership interests of a development entity are shared between the developer responsible for operation and management of the project and investors who finance the equity of the project. Investors choose a legal entity for the project in a way that minimizes tax obligations, brings only limited liabilities and allows flexible transfer of ownership interests. In sharing project returns, equity investors are given preferred returns (smaller but less risky returns), while developers are given more risky, but incentive driven promotional returns. On the other hand, construction loans are structured as adjustable rate based recourse loans. Loans are originated usually with permanent commitment or take-out commitment by permanent lenders, and disbursement of funds follows the progress of the project.

Currently, construction loans are the worst performing loans for commercial banks with delinquency rate of 16% or higher. We found that recent poor performances of construction loans are mainly due to the collapse in commercial real estate markets but also weakened underwriting standards during the boom period, and. The recent experience shows how important it is to have appropriate underwriting standards prior to loan origination as well as proper monitoring procedures post origination.

NOTES

1. Most of S&L institutions' loans were 30 year fixed rate mortgages. Interest payments from those mortgages received by S&L were fixed, but interest payments they had to make for funding those mortgages were rising.
2. Interest rate ceilings were imposed on deposits at S&L, but there were no ceilings on deposits at money market funds.
3. For review of the literature on real estate cycles, see Dokko et al. (1999).
4. This classification comes from James Graaskamp, a famous former real estate professor at University of Wisconsin (Geltner et al., 2007).
5. In recent years, LLC became more popular since it is more flexible in structuring management and less costly to set and run (Ling and Archer, 2010).
6. Yield maintenance clause and defeasance are popular penalties for prepayment in commercial mortgages. However, most permanent loan contracts do allow prepayments during the last few months of their terms, partly helping borrowers to search for term-refinancing opportunities.
7. Due to this, permanent loans rarely have problems in income documentation problems in "stated income" loans for residential mortgages.
8. A potential offsetting factor of importance for borrowers is that permanent loans tend to be more relationship-based. Due to relatively short maturities of permanent loans, compared to residential mortgages, borrowers are often repeat customers. Many investors of commercial properties are locally based and it is important for them to establish a good relationship with lenders for future business and investments (Geltner et al., 2007).
9. Lenders are reluctant to finance soft costs and off-site improvement costs since they may not be recoverable when the development projects default and are subject to foreclosure (Bruggeman and Fisher, 2011).
10. Even though non-recourse construction loans are rare, they were available for development projects with much lower loan-to-cost ratios in the early 2000s (Long, 2011).

REFERENCES

Acharya, Viral, Thomas Cooley, Matthew Richardson and Ingo Walter, 2009, Market Failures and Regulatory Failures: Lessons from Past and Present Financial Crises, Working Paper.

Bruggeman, William and Jeffrey Fisher, 2011, *Real Estate Finance and Investment*, 14th ed. (McGraw-Hill/Erwin).

Cole, Rebel, and George Fenn, 2008, The Role of Commercial Real Estate Investments in the Banking Crisis of 1985–92, Working Paper.

Cole, Rebel, and Lawrence White, 2010, Deja Vu All Over Again: The Causes of U.S. Commercial Bank Failures This Time Around, *Journal of Financial Service Research*.

Dokko, Yoon, Robert Edelstein, Allan Lacayo and Daniel Lee, 1999, Real Estate Income and Value Cycles: A Model of Market Dynamics, *Journal of Real Estate Research*.

FDIC (Federal Deposit Insurance Corporation), 2008, Supervisory Insights, Washington D.C.

Federal Reserve Board of Governors, 1997, *Branch and Agency Examination Manual*, September.

Florence, Andrew, Norm G. Miller, Jay Spivey and Ruijue Peng, 2010, Slicing, Dicing and Scoping the Size of the U.S. Commercial Real Estate Market, Working Paper.

Fuller, Stephen, 2010, *The Contribution of Office, Industrial and Retail Development and Construction to the U.S. Economy*, NAIOP Research Foundation.

Geltner, David, Norman Miller, Jim Clayton and Piet Eichholtz, 2007, *Commercial Real Estate Analysis and Investment*, 2nd ed. (Cengage Learning).

Grenadier, Steve, 2002, Option Exercise Games: An Application to the Equilibrium Investment Strategies of Firms, *Review of Financial Studies*, 691–721.

Lancaster, Brian, 2001, Introduction to Commercial Mortgage-Backed Securities, *Investing in Commercial Mortgage Backed Securities*, ed. Frank Fabozzi (Frank J. Fabozzi Associates).

Ling, David and Wayne Archer, 2010, *Real Estate Principles*, 3rd ed. (McGraw-Hill/Erwin).

Long, Charles, 2011, *Finance for Real Estate Development* (Urban Land Institute).

Lown, Cara and Morgan, Donald, 2006, The Credit Cycle and the Business Cycle: New Findings Using the Loan Officer Opinion Survey, *Journal of Money, Credit and Banking*, 38, 1575–1597.

Maddaloni, Angela and José-Luis Peydró, 2011, Bank Risk-Taking, Securitization, Supervision, and Low Interest Rates: Evidence from the Euro Area and U.S. Lending Standards, *Review of Financial Studies*, 2121–65.

OCC (Office of the Comptroller of the Currency), 1998, Commercial Real Estate and Construction Lending: Comptroller's Handbook, March.

OCC, 2004, Survey of Credit Underwriting Practice, National Credit Committee.

Williams, Joseph, 1991, Real Estate Development as an Option, *Journal of Real Estate Finance and Economics*, 191–208.

8. Construction financing in Taiwan: current state and policy regime

Chin-Oh Chang and Ming-Chi Chen

1. INTRODUCTION

Many literatures (for example, Jin and Zeng, 2004; Goodhart and Hofmann, 2008) have suggested that the financial environment and policy both have enormous influence on the real estate market. From the perspective of market demand, interest rates affect the purchasing power of home buyers. From the viewpoint of market supply, interest rates affect the investment and operation of construction businesses (Blackley, 1999; Berger-Thomson and Ellis, 2004). Governments typically use interest rates or credit control to regulate the boom or bust of the real estate market. However, many countries around the world are currently in environments of low interest rates under policies of quantitative easing, whereby borrowers have easy access to funds. This could lead to over investment and cause prices to rise sharply in the real estate market. One of the major causes of the U.S. subprime mortgage was the over investment in real estate, which caused housing prices to surge upward. When economic growth abated and the flow of funds began to reverse, housing prices declined and borrowers were unable to repay their mortgages, resulting in a crisis in the financial industry.

Literatures have argued that the inadequately applied monetary policy of the U.S. is responsible for this crisis. To stabilize the financial environment, governments must consider changes in the real estate market when formulating monetary policy. Taiwan has long been in an environment of an easing monetary policy. People tend to ignore market risk, credit risk, or macroeconomic risk. However, the Taiwanese real estate market has been expanding from 2004 (Chang, 2010), and the chance that the market may begin to shrink is increasing. The government needs to consider the possible consequences of a shift in economic cycle.

The usual channel for construction businesses to obtain financing in Taiwan is to directly apply to banks for construction finance. However, because the financial institutions are relatively conservative in the early years, Taiwanese construction businesses usually end up having to raise funds on their own. Project financing operation and a special financing method called the pre-sale system, which still prevails in the Taipei area, successfully helped the development of the housing market in Taiwan. However, banks were still most critical to the access to construction funds. Because of great fluctuations observed in the real estate market, the construction businesses are in an environment of instability. During this period of economic downturn, many construction businesses may close down and have a negative influence on bank operations. Therefore, the government must examine development in the construction industry with greater scrutiny.

Since 2004, the real estate market in Taiwan has regained its energy and housing prices have again increased dramatically, especially in the Taipei area. This upward trend has continued through 2011. This upward trend was the longest in many years and has caused heavy burdens on ordinary home buyers.[1] Furthermore, this trend may continue into the near future. According to the national population census of 2010, the percentage of vacant houses (vacancy rate) had a high of 20 percent, a total of about 1,560,000 vacant homes. This indicated that a huge amount of capital is currently invested in vacant real estate. This idle capital might come from mortgage investment, the savings of rich households, or an inflow of international capital. When interest rates increase or other higher-return investment instruments exist, this capital would eventually flow outward. As a result, many vacant homes were released, causing housing prices to decline. After continuously increasing for 7 years, housing prices now had an increasing probability of falling. For the construction industry, operations risk had reached its threshold.

The construction industry is considered to be the engine of Taiwanese industry and has significantly contributed to housing development in Taiwan. However, the Taiwanese construction industry arose in a different environment than is found in other countries. The first unique characteristic of this environment is that the Taiwanese construction industry was developed under the auspices of a conservative financial system. Given these conditions, construction firms experienced great difficulty in obtaining funding from financial institutions by relying strictly on their own creditworthiness; thus, project financing operations involving preferred collateral and informal measures of acquiring capital, such as the pre-sale system, were essential for the development of the Taiwanese construction industry. Despite the restrictive financial circumstances, construction businesses in Taiwan have provided 95 percent of the housing supply in the market. Public housing provided by the government has had no major influence on the market supply. Thus, despite difficult circumstances, the evolution and maturation of the Taiwanese construction industry are an intriguing topic with ramifications that have impacted virtually all Taiwanese residents.

In addition, the Taiwanese government lacked a specific housing policy until the Housing Act was finally enacted in 2011. Compared to other governments, the Taiwanese government has intervened relatively little in the housing market. The government put the greatest emphasis on economic development. As a result the public housing department was ignored and the housing development was led by the private sector. On several occasions, the government failed to take any measure to stabilize housing prices, until the prices were heightened to a level that caused public indignation. By then, the construction industry was also already over-invested. When observing the changes in each housing business cycle, we found it obvious that housing prices increased in the short term and then contracted slightly over the long term, indicating a short period of expansion and a long period of contraction. Whether the construction industry would face many years of difficult operations because of an oversupply becomes an issue to be addressed. With this in mind, this study analyzed the development of the Taiwanese construction industry and the influence of the financial environment and government policy on this industry.

This chapter seeks to analyze the current conditions and policy regime of construction financing in Taiwan. Following a review of the literature, we first describe the development of the construction industry. Next, we address the focus of this study, namely, the analysis and discussion of the influence of financing and government policy on the development of the Taiwanese construction industry. Finally, we draw our conclusions and implications.

2. LITERATURE REVIEW

Building permits and housing prices show a cyclical behavior in Taiwan, which implies that underbuilding and overbuilding occur continually in the housing market. McNulty (1995) used economic base theory to evaluate the causes of overbuilding and found that construction decisions depended on the strength of the local economy. Because basic activity is cyclical, a significant lag in the multiplier process can result in overbuilding, which is also caused by false signals of imminent growth in the local economy perceived by builders, developers, and lenders at the time a project was conceived. Tan (1987) considered the decision of builders as crucial to a supply-side explanation. In essence, individual rationality creates group irrationality. Hence, overbuilding is the result of group irrationality. DeCoster and Strange (2011), however, focused on rational overbuilding, wherein developers make decisions under uncertainty. They showed that two types of herding, statistical and reputation-based, can lead developers to overbuild. Statistical herding arises because developers learn from each other's decisions. If initial developers obtain inaccurate signals that the market is strong, it can set off an information cascade wherein later developers choose to ignore the signals, which leads to overbuilding. Reputational herding arises when developers want to frustrate bank attempts to discern their true quality or because they are afraid the bank will draw incorrect inferences on their quality, leading them to ignore their signals and overbuild in particular markets. For Taiwan, Hsieh (2005) studied an unprecedented boom in Taiwanese residential unit production, and described it as a supply side phenomenon. Hsieh indicated that builders' construction investments vary with business profits and future expectations.

Many studies have addressed the housing supply and the boom and bust cycle in the construction industry. Construction costs are fundamental costs of suppliers building the new housing. Somerville (1999) stated that higher construction costs reduced residential construction. Mayer and Somerville (1996) observed a lagged effect of construction costs in housing starts. They also described a supply function for new housing that is consistent with land development (Mayer and Somerville, 2000). Saiz (2010) indicated that land constrained by geography was a key factor in contemporaneous urban development. Interest rates are also a significant variable that affects construction investment. In earlier studies, Muth (1960), Follain (1979), Schwab (1983), and Topel and Rosen (1988) showed that nominal and real interest rates had a strong influence on construction investment. Recent literature by Agnello and Schuknecht (2011) further suggested that interest rates had different effects during different times, and they have significantly influenced the probability of booms and busts. The government usually uses interest rates or other financial instruments to regulate the housing market. Tse and Raftery (2001) examined the extent to which fluctuations in the money supply led to fluctuations in real construction in Hong Kong. They indicated a specific and strong causal relationship between construction activity and the broadly defined money supply. Their empirical results also suggested that construction activity flows and construction loans were cointegrated, but their lead-lag relationship could not be established.

3. DEVELOPMENT AND OPERATION OF THE CONSTRUCTION INDUSTRY

According to the definition provided by the Ministry of the Interior, the construction industry includes construction companies, building development companies, and building investment businesses which provide capital for the development of land that is designed, planned, developed, and sold for profit upon completion. The construction industry is considered the leading industry in Taiwan because it involves various related industries and receives extensive attention from the government, businesses, and general investors. Under this definition, the construction industry in Taiwan, as discussed in this study, refers to industries known as construction companies or construction businesses. Below is a brief description of the development and operation of the construction industry in Taiwan.

3.1 The Historical Development of the Construction Industry

According to Chang (1996) and Huang (2003), we can divide the development of the construction industry in Taiwan into several stages:

3.1.1 The period of military dependent villages (from the recovery of Taiwan until 1961)

After the recovery of Taiwan from Japan, housing demand increased dramatically due to economic development, the immigration of a large population which came to Taiwan with the nationalist government, and reconstruction works after the war. To help these immigrant soldiers and their dependents settle down, the government constructed numerous military dependent villages and began paying attention to housing construction, and hence attracted participation from the private sector. There were increasing numbers of businesses which joined in the construction activities and contributed to the development of the construction industry. This was called the period of military dependent villages.

3.1.2 The apartment period (1962–71)

As national income increased following economic development, demand for residential quality increased accordingly. To cater to greater demand for comfort, standards for apartment construction and residential facilities were also increasing. Various professional investors appeared who operated as corporations to plan land and construct all types of housing. This was also called the growth period of the construction industry in Taiwan.

3.1.3 The start of the high-rise housing period (1972–81)

In this period, the prevailing pre-sale system changed the trading pattern of the entire newly constructed housing market. The global economic recession and the oil crisis resulted in global inflation. Expecting the prices to rise, people rushed into the housing market with the belief that this market was most able to retain investment value. As a result, the real estate prices surged dramatically upward. To stabilize the domestic situation, the government introduced the program for the stabilization of the present economy. Influenced by the government suppression and by economic factors, real estate in Taiwan entered into the first wave of a recession cycle. In 1974, the government lifted the ban on construction and opened up high-rise housing in downtown areas. Residential buildings of seven to ten stories and higher began to appear, and buildings gradually extended into suburban areas.

3.1.4 The height of the high-rise housing period (1982–91)

After two upward trends in both housing and land prices, low-rise buildings were no longer economically feasible given the increased cost of land. Under such circumstances, high-rise residential buildings sprang up and became common in the market.

3.1.5 The period of diversified housing products (1992–2003)

From the end of 1991, 15 new private banks opened in succession, with their lending operations focused on mortgage and construction financing. Moreover, construction related policies such as plot ratios were implemented beginning in 1992. As a result, construction businesses rushed to apply for licenses and promoted numerous housing projects, which led to later problems of oversupply. The sales rate of pre-sale housing gradually declined, bringing the construction industry into a period of stagnation. To overcome this difficult situation, businesses diversified the design of housing products and constructed not only residential buildings, but also recreational housing, housing for seniors, shopping malls, office buildings, hi-tech housing, luxury housing, cross maisonette housing, composite sandwich housing, and more.

3.1.6 The period of polarized housing products (2004–11)

After more than a decade of recession in the real estate market, the outbreak of Severe Acute Respiratory Syndrome (SARS) in 2003 bottomed out housing prices. With a background of low interest rates and an inflow of foreign and Chinese capital, the housing market regained its upward momentum in 2004. Because Taiwan was becoming an M-shaped society, construction companies preferred constructing studios and luxurious mansions with large interior spaces for higher profits and sales rates. During this period, a large quantity of expensive and luxurious mansions emerged in Taiwan. Compared with housing prices in other cities, those in Taipei all increased to a level of luxury, and were more than five times the housing prices in the second largest city of Kaohsiung. Most peculiarly, the prices of residential real estate were higher than those of commercial real estate in Taipei areas.

3.2 Housing Investment and the Construction Industry

Figure 8.1 presents Taiwan's housing investment and fixed capital formation from 1968 to 2010. The ratio of housing investment to GDP in Taiwan was not stable during these years, varying from 1.15 to 4.4 percent. However, this ratio underwent an obvious decrease after 1997, dropping below 2 percent. This ratio is generally lower in Taiwan than it is in other developed countries; although housing investment in Taiwan appears to be relatively low in magnitude, the construction sector is commonly regarded as a leading sector in the Taiwanese economy. Su, Lin and Wang (2003)

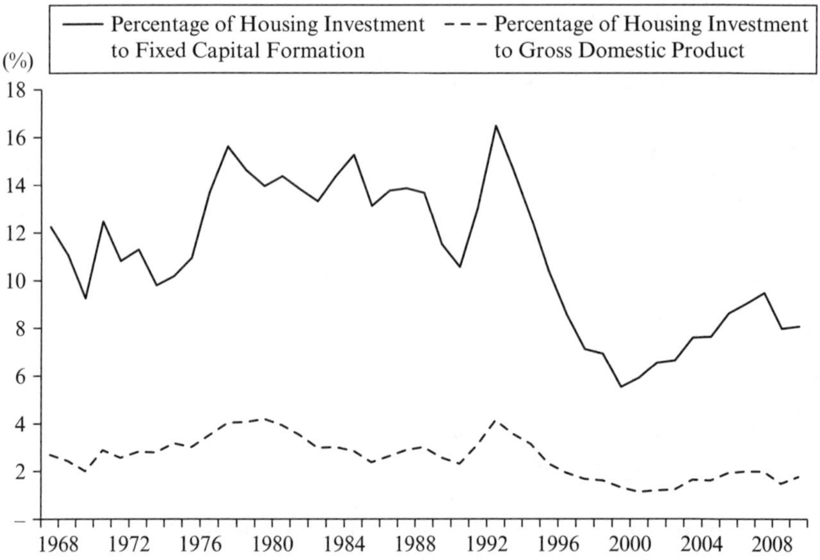

Source: Urban and Regional Development Statistics, Council for Economic Planning and Development Executive Yuan, R.O.C. (Taiwan).

Figure 8.1 Percentage of housing investment to fixed capital formation and gross domestic product suggest that the construction industry in Taiwan has both "pull" and "push" effects on the national economy, which is why the Taiwanese government considers the construction industry to be extremely important. Those researchers utilize input-output analysis for the Taiwanese construction industry from 1964 to 1999 and indicate that, as the Taiwanese economy matures, Taiwan's share of construction in GNP versus GNP per capita demonstrates a two-stage inverted U-shaped relationship.

In the Taiwanese housing market, most of the housing has been built by the construction industry, and public housing supplied by the government comprises less than 5 percent of total housing. Figure 8.2 illustrates the cumulative area of construction licenses issued annually over the course of the past thirty years, which demonstrates changes in the housing supply cycle in Taiwan. The production period between the start and completion of a new building is generally approximately two to three years. Overbuilding typically occurs in the Taiwanese housing market in response to strong short-term housing demand, which causes cyclical construction development and housing price fluctuations. Barras and Ferguson (1985) identified a short building cycle of three to four years in the UK for the

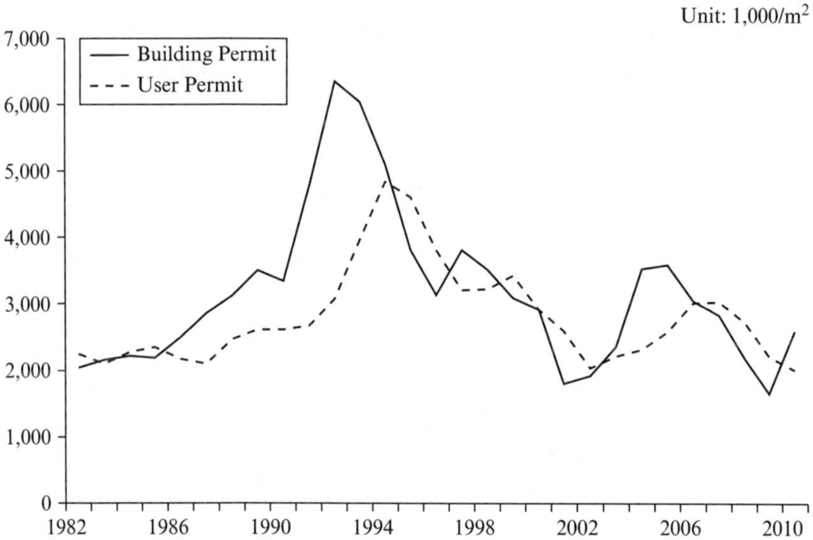

Sources: The Statistical Yearbook of Construction and Planning Agency, Ministry of Interior, Executive Yuan, R.O.C. (Taiwan).

Figure 8.2 Total floor areas of building permits and user permits in Taiwan

period following World War II. Chen, Kawaguchi and Patel (2004) examined four Asian countries and suggested three- to four-year housing price cycles caused by construction lag times. The differences between high and low levels of supply in Figure 8.2 appear to be quite large, which indicates the instability of the Taiwanese construction industry. However, the number of building permits issued generally remains between 1.5 million and 3.5 million each year, except for a distinct peak around 1992. This peak occurred because the Taiwanese government implemented floor area ratio control for the entirety of Taiwan in 1992; thus, construction companies rushed to apply for permits before this regulation went into effect. Hsieh (2005) suggests that the resulting construction boom caused subsequent housing price slumps and high vacancy rates.

Table 8.1 presents descriptive statistics for permits, housing prices and several related macroeconomic variables, such as the number of construction loans, interest rate (basic lending rate), inflation rate, stock price index and the building material and construction price index from 1973 to 2010.[2] We observe that the numbers of building and use permits issued grow at approximately 6 and 4 percent annually, respectively. The growth rate and standard deviations of building permits are higher than those of use permits. Construction loans demonstrate 20 percent annual increases, suggesting either that the construction industry has strong financing demand or that construction loans are favorable for banks. Real housing prices increase at approximately 6 percent annually, and the inflation rate is approximately 4 percent.

Table 8.2 presents the correlations of these variables in level and growth rate. The signs of correlation between these variables are mostly as expected. We observe a negative relationship between permits and housing prices but a positive correlation between construction loans and permits. Regarding temporal relationships, we observe from Figure 8.2 that the issuance of use permits appears to lag the issuance of construction permits by approximately one to two years. Peng, Chang and Lin (1998) indicate that the duration of the lag between these two metrics depends on market conditions and, specifically, that the lag between the issuance of building permits and the issuance of use permits is longer during market downturns. However, housing prices and permit issuance do not show any clear temporal relationship.

As mentioned previously, the financial environment during the development of the construction industry in Taiwan was highly conservative. However, shortages in the housing supply were rarely observed, indicating that the construction industry met housing demand. Table 8.3 presents the results of seven population censuses. The census data indicate that, since 1966, no shortage in housing supply has been reported in Taiwan, except

Table 8.1 Descriptive statistics for the selected variables

	Building Permit	User Permit	Housing Prices	Construction Loan	Consumer Price Index	Building Material and Construction Price Index	Stock Price Index
Level							
Mean	4,399,066	4,092,388	204,500	570,486	76	232	4,140
Std.	1,808,103	1,501,388	107,751	329,222	23	160	3,137
Max.	8,515,392	6,933,154	434,011	1,273,635	105	723	9,624
Min.	1,133,705	1,590,541	62,128	54,876	23	55	193
Growth Rate							
Mean %	6.06	4.46	6.17	20.53	4.42	17.59	16.33
Std. %	43.48	32.23	15.16	41.52	8.39	52.25	44.09
Max. %	153.90	156.10	57.12	131.55	47.47	137.25	125.18
Min. %	−55.60	−27.57	−9.80	−17.85	−0.87	−62.69	−61.03

Sources: Housing prices were obtained from Cathay Real Estate Company. Household number, household income, building material and construction price index and consumer price index were obtained from the Directorate General of Budget, Accounting and Statistics. Building and user permits were obtained from the Construction and Planning Agency. House-purchase loan, and construction loans and stock price index were obtained from the Financial Statistics Monthly.

Table 8.2 Correlation matrices for the selected variables

	Building Permit	User Permit	Housing Prices	Construction Loan	Consumer Price Index	Building Material and Construction Price Index	Stock Price Index	Interest Rate
Building Permit	1	0.571	−0.282	0.003	−0.393	0.081	−0.315	0.342
User Permit	0.454	1	−0.301	0.490	−0.275	−0.148	−0.354	0.227
Housing Prices	0.085	0.098	1	0.675	0.872	0.510	0.898	−0.713
Construction Loan	0.268	0.010	−0.058	1	0.858	−0.236	0.422	−0.718
Consumer Price Index	−0.123	0.084	−0.053	0.412	1	0.139	0.820	−0.847
Building Material and Construction Price Index	0.279	0.176	0.405	0.044	−0.146	1	0.667	−0.056
Stock Price Index	0.207	0.029	0.499	0.148	−0.336	0.776	1	−0.688
Interest Rate	−0.179	0.165	0.224	0.056	0.792	−0.093	−0.222	1

Note: Correlations for level are at upper right and correlations for growth rate are at lower left.

Table 8.3 Census statistics related to housing

	1966	1970	1975	1980	1990	2000	2010
Population	13,348,096	14,693,013	16,206,183	17,968,797	20,286,174	22,226,879	23,056,788
Household Number	2,272,161	2,625,682	3,071,101	3,733,522	4,943,029	6,481,584	7,959,088
Average Persons per Household	5.7	5.5	5.3	4.8	4.0	3.4	3.0
Home Ownership (%)	66.2	66.1	70.1	79.1	78.5	82.5	83.8
Housing Unit	2,292,191	2,623,265	3,06,8420	3,665,122	5,073,909	6,977,770	8,054,184
Household Number/ Housing Unit	1.01	1.00	1.00	0.98	1.03	1.08	1.01
Vacant House	21,928			479,839	674,317	1,228,798	1,561,275
Vacancy Rate (%)	1.0			13.1	13.3	17.65	19.4

Sources: Population and Household Census, Directorate-General of Budget, Accounting and Statistics, Executive Yuan, R.O.C. (Taiwan).

in 1980 (when there was a 2 percent shortage). In all other census years, the number of residential units was higher than the number of residents, indicating that the housing supply was sufficient. However, this sufficiency of supply does not imply that each household could own a home, although home ownership rates increased from 66.2 percent to 83.8 percent between 1966 and 2010. Housing vacancies were relatively frequent, particularly during the latter part of the time period examined. In particular, Table 8.3 indicates that the vacancy rate reached 13.1 percent in the 1980s and increased to 19.4 percent by 2010. This high vacancy rate reflects not only overbuilding by the construction industry but also that certain affluent households owned multiple residences at the same time. The high vacancy rate data revealed that many real estate resources in Taiwan were left unused and wasted. The oversupply of residential buildings and the underinvestment in infrastructure explain Taiwan's relatively low ratio of housing investment to GDP compared with other countries, along with significant numbers of vacant houses; in fact, the World Competitiveness Yearbook (IMD, Switzerland) indicates that Taiwan's infrastructure is consistently rated as falling far behind that of other advanced industrial countries.

3.3 Methods of Project Construction

Several methods of project construction exist in Taiwan's construction industry. The first type is to purchase and develop the land on one's own, meaning that the constructor purchases land, completes construction and sells it independently. The second type is joint construction, meaning that the constructor provides funding, and the landlord provides the land to construct the residence jointly. After the construction is completed, the residence and the land or profits are distributed according to the ratio agreed upon. The third type is joint investment construction, meaning that more than two constructors exist. These constructors jointly construct the residence and pay the building costs and fees. As with joint construction, the residence and the land are distributed according to the agreed upon ratio after construction is complete. The last type is commissioned construction, in which a constructor is commissioned to construct the residence by a client who owns the land. The house is delivered to the client after the construction is completed.

3.4 Types of Construction Companies and Processes of Construction

Construction companies in Taiwan can be divided into two broad categories based on firm size. In the first category, larger construction companies are typically established corporations listed in the stock market or supported by syndicates. The first construction company was listed in 1964. Not many construction companies were listed[3] in the Taiwanese stock market until 1995, however, when the Taiwanese government imposed increased restrictions on public offerings for construction companies. As of 2011, there were 43 companies listed in the "Building Material and Construction" industry of a total of 790 companies listed in the Taiwanese Stock Market Exchange. Among these 43 companies, 34 are construction companies. Table 8.4 shows the financial data for these construction companies over the past 26 years. These companies have generally recovered from the recent recession.

These large construction companies have integrated operations for tasks ranging from land acquisition and development planning to supervision of construction and sales. They also have their own technical departments, addressing civil engineering, plumbing, electrical engineering, decoration, and related operations. Moreover, these large construction companies typically have affiliated companies that can perform related work and share profits, and these affiliates can cooperate with each other regarding financial and operational tasks to minimize their tax burdens and increase profits.

In the second category, small and medium-sized construction companies account for the majority of the Taiwanese construction industry. There are no accurate data regarding the number of construction companies in Taiwan. However, according to the Census of Industry, Commerce and Service, there were 4,291 real estate developers in 2001, and this number increased to 7,622 in 2006. The total number of employees working for real estate developers was 31,818 in 2001 and 32,072 in 2006. However, this number equates to only 7.4 and 4.2 employees per real estate development company in 2001 and 2006, respectively, suggesting that Taiwan's construction companies are generally very small. Because of the cyclical behavior in the Taiwanese real estate market, the numbers of small and medium-sized construction companies fluctuate in accordance with market conditions. In addition, a distinctive characteristic of Taiwan's construction industry is that it includes many one-project companies. It has been estimated that more than 60 percent of construction companies in Taiwan close after developing only one project.

The typical process of construction investment in Taiwan includes market analysis, raising funds, land acquisition, project planning, construction and sales. The market analysis is usually conducted by a sales agent or consultancy company, and investment feasibility is analyzed by the construction company based on its own financial conditions and access to the land. The funds to be invested in the construction come partly from the equity fund of the construction company, and partly from loans made by financial

Table 8.4 Financial data of listed construction companies

Year	Number of Companies	Sale Revenue	Net Profit Before Tax	Total Asset (A)	Total Net Worth (B)	B/A(%)	Capital
1986	13	13,425,208	1,319,900	21,180,906	78,260	39.15	5,527,956
1987	18	16,914,205	2,528,952	28,354,543	102,543	30.23	6,489,988
1988	24	17,548,450	3,118,160	44,911,358	141,410	33.03	8,921,848
1989	25	23,328,110	3,544,970	70,199,157	283,579	37.25	15,340,658
1990	27	31,841,910	6,305,370	99,403,096	392,409	43.67	20,293,538
1991	29	42,549,298	6,774,184	123,440,471	507,482	48.42	28,316,688
1992	33	48,852,130	7,184,746	143,495,802	594,606	39.51	36,275,605
1993	33	54,504,298	7,364,592	166,522,063	689,887	35.80	44,285,044
1994	33	63,095,170	11,176,581	194,258,446	828,742	39.01	53,082,346
1995	33	65,773,809	4,396,387	206,385,120	967,655	44.02	68,582,999
1996	33	67,604,364	6,932,305	230,515,576	1,079,388	46.85	78,121,010
1997	34	82,814,197	13,426,907	301,648,842	1,533,498	52.71	97,093,418
1998	34	86,757,087	−1,887,484	376,227,544	1,618,176	46.24	118,197,134
1999	34	86,701,603	−2,000,457	360,945,467	1,572,590	45.39	121,456,477
2000	34	85,124,350	−2,446,691	356,886,438	1,508,188	43.81	126,765,524

2001	34	71,063,424	−7,681,877	323,033,616	1,379,624	45.28	122,520,888
2002	34	63,903,119	−18,774,823	275,457,825	1,167,769	46.39	117,544,058
2003	34	58,495,366	−1,511,715	256,118,929	1,166,912	44.75	113,639,851
2004	34	70,548,977	3,404,281	285,719,656	1,220,779	41.87	107,955,111
2005	34	76,387,554	6,209,820	297,343,433	1,257,237	41.63	108,843,389
2006	34	114,055,744	22,843,121	340,004,432	1,536,068	44.56	110,180,739
2007	34	117,244,297	25,716,767	376,679,298	1,697,820	45.99	117,453,229
2008	34	103,427,001	15,723,171	406,167,854	1,693,557	44.01	124,313,957
2009	34	123,680,750	30,267,633	440,144,990	2,005,758	50.67	130,964,172
2010	34	139,469,491	40,870,425	486,141,539	2,274,162	52.14	130,574,806
2011	34	136,359,226	43,296,762	591,132,623	2,614,138	46.59	133,807,332

Source: Taiwan Stock Exchange.

institutions. Land can be acquired through numerous methods, including purchasing it from or reaching a mutual agreement with the landlord, or by acquiring it through the government or through judicial foreclosure. In a real estate project, the party investing in construction typically is responsible for project initiation, decision-making, and project implementation. The planning is mostly outsourced to other related businesses. For example, the sales plan is drafted by the sales agent, and the construction plan is drawn up by the architect or the engineering consultancy company. The construction process includes design, contracting, construction, and construction management. Design is mainly implemented by the architect, whereas contracting is done by the construction investors themselves. The construction is done by various levels of construction companies, professional engineering companies, and contractors. The later sales process includes marketing, sales, contract signing, and transfer of ownership. The marketing and sale of real estate is mostly delegated to professional sales agencies.

4. FINANCING OF THE CONSTRUCTION INDUSTRY

4.1 Historical Development

Construction financing was quite conservative prior to 1974 (the initial stage), and followed the procedure for ordinary corporate loans. From 1974 to 1976, the global energy crisis drove up real estate prices and hence commodity prices. The government implemented the program for the stabilization of the present economy and suspended pledge and secured loans to housing construction projects. This measure limited the sources of financing, so the construction industry was not able to obtain enough financing from lending institutions. As a result, the construction industry tended to raise its development capital by means of pre-sales. Therefore, the pre-sale system prevailed and became a characteristic of the real estate market in Taiwan. Housing prices later stabilized. To stimulate the real estate market and to rectify trading orders in the market, the government issued the "Essential Points for Improving the Investment Environment" in 1977 and restored construction finance.

When international oil prices rose again and the second oil crisis occurred, market prosperity reached another peak between 1979 and 1980. Thus, the government announced a restriction on the construction of vacant lands and traced the sources of capital that were invested in purchasing more than three residences, resulting in the bankruptcy of many construction companies. In 1981, the "Measures to Mitigate Current

Difficulties in Industry and Commerce" were issued, giving the Land Bank of Taiwan the authority to make special construction loans. In 1985, the restraints on construction financing in lending institutions were gradually eased. During the housing bull market between 1986 and 1989, financial institutions increased credit to the construction industry under the pressures of a prosperous real estate market and large amounts of savings. Construction finances expanded dramatically, resulting in soaring housing prices. Therefore, the government implemented selective credit control measures in 1990 to limit the maximum quota and terms of construction financing, and also to suspend unsecured loans for the purchase of land and loans for vacant land without an objective for use. After the 1990 real estate boom subsided, the central bank announced its termination of selective credit control and widely eased up construction lending. The volume of construction loans increased greatly in response. Under the pressure of floor area ratio control since 1992 and reforms on land taxes, construction companies launched numerous projects. In addition, the establishment of many private banks also helped to increase construction financing (Wong and Chang, 1993). Nevertheless, the real estate market had plunged into a long term bear market since 1990. Therefore, the government proposed a succession of nine times of mortgage interest rate subsidy policies after 1999. Though these policies subsidized mortgages for home buyers in the purchase of primary residences, subsidizing mortgage interest seems to be less important, because Taiwan had been in an environment of low interest rates for a long time. The purpose of the government was to avoid the closing down of construction companies in the long term, which could cause a depression and affect the financial order. Figure 8.3 shows the statistics of construction loans and house-purchase loans over the years. We discovered an upward trend and cyclical behavior in the balance of construction loans, but house-purchase loans increase steadily.

4.2 Financing Methods of the Construction Industry

Essentially, the financing measures of the construction industry can be divided into three categories: corporate financing, project financing and real estate securitization, as shown in Figure 8.4. As stated in the previous section, prior to 1970, corporate loans were the main sources of capital for construction companies. In addition, construction companies can enter the securities markets if they possess more than 300 million Taiwan dollar (TWD) in capital, or they can enter the over-the-counter market with at least 50 million TWD in capital. Real estate securitization is another financing method that opens up new sources of capital through public market listings; however, the current Real Estate Securitization Act still

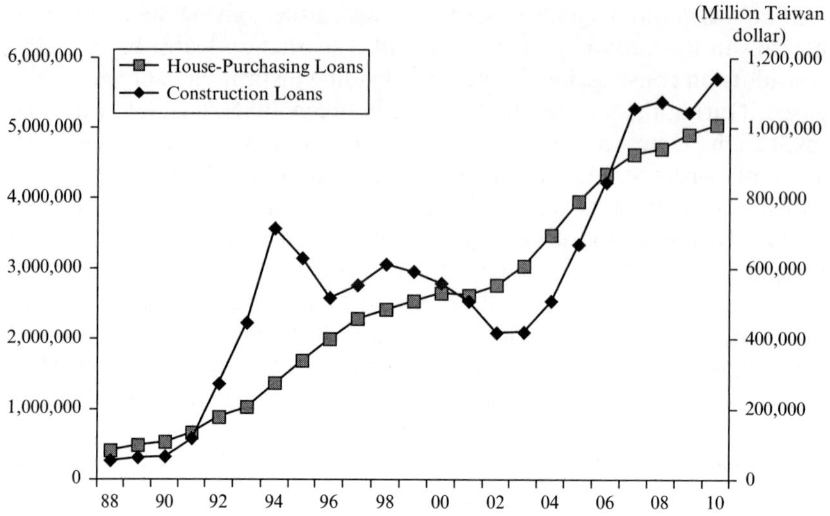

Note: RHS: construction loans; LHS: house purchasing loans.

Source: Financial Statistics Monthly, Central Bank of the Republic of China (Taiwan).

Figure 8.3 Construction loans and house-purchasing loans in Taiwan

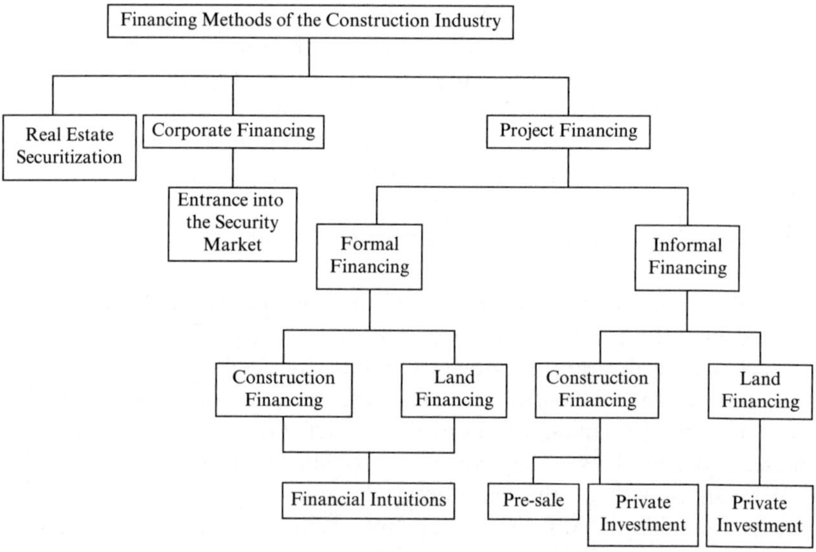

Figure 8.4 Financing methods of the construction industry

incorporates limitations for developers' fundraising activities. Because of the strong demand for capital to satisfy high housing demands and the preferences of financial institutions, project financing became a more dominant funding source after 1970. Project financing, which includes construction and land financing, remains the main method of financing for construction companies. One project financing option is "formal financing," which refers to loans from financial institutions. The other project financing option is "informal financing," which refers to funds raised by the construction industry via private investment and income from pre-sales.

Financial institutions make formal loans to the construction industry that comprises a portion of those institutions' credit business. These are mainly circulating loans to the development projects of the construction industry and represent a type of project financing. These formal loans can be categorized as either land or construction financing.

Land financing refers to loans for the purchase of land. Because this is a type of secured loan, the loan-to-value ratio is higher than that of a construction loan. Depending on market condition, up to 90 percent of value of the collateral can be borrowed in land financing. Banks are more willing to approve land financing because of its secure nature. As a result, some construction businesses reserve land for future development while the interest rates are still affordable. When housing prices are too high, the central bank usually asks banks to set restrictions on loans to the construction industry (construction must begin within a certain period after the loan is granted, or the bank would increase the interest rates or even recall the loan) to avoid speculative behavior in the construction industry.

Construction financing refers to loans for the construction of residences, which are short term loans which last from one to three years, or no longer than five years. The loan-to-value ratio and the amount of the loan depend on the marketing of projects, the credit of the investor, collateral, etc. Generally, the total limit for construction financing (including secured and non-secured loans) is 60 percent of the estimated construction value. In addition, unlike other loans which are paid in a single payment upon approval, construction financing is paid in installments according to the progress of the construction. This is because financial institutions hope to reduce the financing risk and ensure that the borrower utilizes the loan for construction.

Informal financing refers to funds privately raised by the constructor or capital income from a pre-sale system used as the financing capital of the project. The reason for the prevalence of the pre-sale market in Taiwan is because of an insufficient supply of construction funding from financial institutions. To continue construction to complete the project, the construction industry had to rely on the pre-sale system to acquire capital.

In the pre-sale system, the constructor could collect funds by pre-selling houses to serve as operating capital. This was a type of portfolio selling strategy of constructors (Chang and Ward, 1993) because they could distribute one third of the houses in each of the three stages, including pre-sale, construction, and completion. Home buyers could buy their houses by means of installments and mortgages. This could increase their purchasing ability. The pre-sale system allows constructors to be aware of selling conditions, and for home buyers to accrue a sense of participation during the construction process.

The process of the pre-sale system is shown in Figure 8.5.

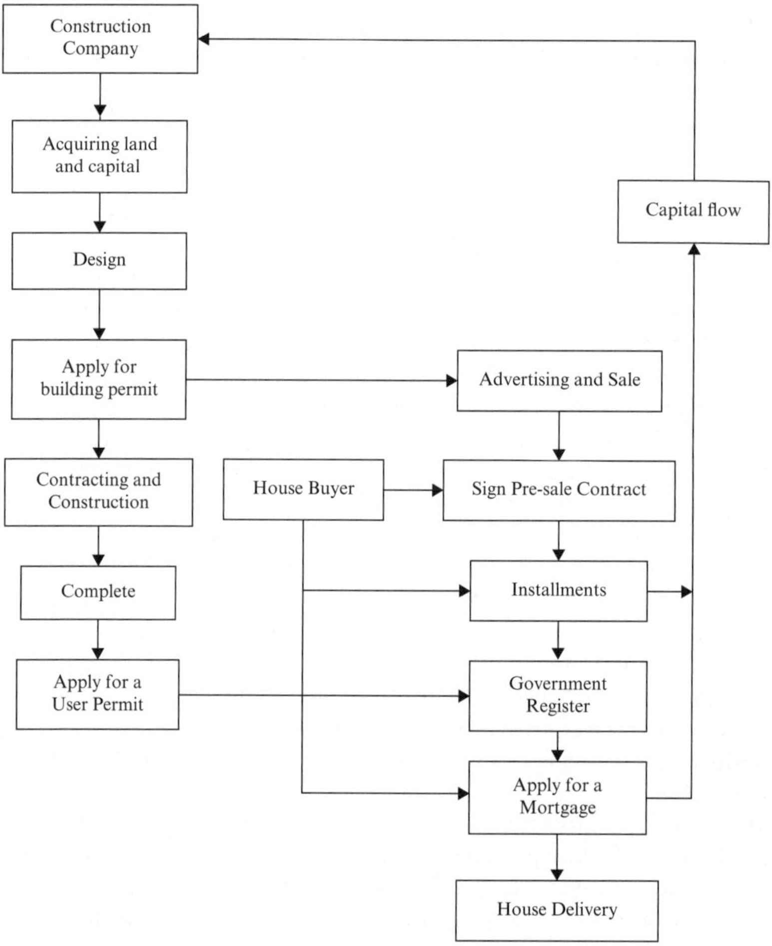

Figure 8.5 The process of the pre-sale system

4.3 Major Default Risks in the Construction Industry

According to Taiwanese banking law, the upper limit of the ratio of construction and land loans to total loans is 30 percent for financial institutions, a requirement that limits the credit risk of financial institutions. Over the four-year period beginning in 2007, this ratio has been approximately 21 percent, which is below the upper bound established by banking regulations. The ratio of home purchase, construction and land loans to total loans of financial institutions was 34 percent in 2010. This ratio has increased significantly from its 20 percent value in 2004, presumably because of the rapid increase in housing prices that has occurred during the intervening time. However, low delinquency ratios of only 0.47 percent for home purchase loans and 0.33 percent for construction and land loans were observed in 2010.

The construction industry in Taiwan is highly dependent on financing from financial institutions. The land and construction financings are also the major credit operations of banks. Banks should consider the problems and risks related to providing construction financing. Difficulties encountered by the construction industry have direct influences on the safety of credited assets of the bank, and whether the capital can be recovered successfully. The major risks related to construction financing made by banks in Taiwan include:

- The financial ability of the constructor is unsustainable due to unfavorable sales rates.
- Falling real estate prices which result in problems of insufficient collateral.
- The operations of the constructor expanded too rapidly and triggered a credit crisis.
- The capital flows to affiliated businesses or other purposes, affecting the implementation of construction projects.
- Risks related to disputes occur upon delivery of the houses.

5. REGULATIONS AND POLICIES REGARDING THE CONSTRUCTION INDUSTRY

The legislative environment of the construction industry is based on the regulations of the Building Act and the relevant regulations in the Civil Code and Land Act. These regulations are modified periodically to adjust to changes in the economic environment and policy implementation. Because of various changes in the market and demands from industrial developers, numerous related regulations have been recently added or modified to promote the healthier development of the construction industry. For example, the Consumer Protection Law, enacted in 1994, brought positive influences and improvement to housing transactions; the 1995 Condominium Management Ordinance became the basic source of laws regarding community management; and the 1999 Real Estate Broking Management Act and the 2000 Real Estate Appraiser Act both improved the management and safety of real estate transactions. In addition, the Urban Renewal Act, enacted in 1998, became the source of regulations related to urban renewal, including those for the establishment of urban renewal trust companies and the securitization of real estate. The Real Estate Brokering Management Act was enacted in 1999 as the basis for the management of real estate brokerages and sales agents. Furthermore, the 2003 Construction Industry Act established a complete system for the manufacturing aspect of the construction industry.

The regulations related to land use and construction were gradually established as the real estate market developed. Volatility in the macroeconomic environment and the real estate market has led the government to implement various policies to stabilize the market and to adjust the development of the construction industry. Specific policy measures regarding the industry can be summarized as follows.

5.1 Policy Measures Restricting Over-investment by the Construction Industry

The government has taken direct measures to restrict overinvestment by the industry during times of high inflation or booms in the real estate market. These measures include the following:

- Imposing a time limit for construction on vacant lands
- Executing selective credit control, such as suspending unsecured loans for the purchase of lands, limiting the amount of construction financing to certain multiples of the publicly appraised value of the land, limiting loan term periods, and restricting loans for construction working capital to below a certain percentage of the building cost;
- Controlling the prices of construction materials;
- Restricting the construction of tall buildings;
- Increasing interest rates on loans;
- Reducing the loan-to-value ratio; and
- Constructing public housing.

Indirect measures were also adopted to restrict demand for real estate investment, such as tracing the source of funds for the purchase of homes, limiting the loan-to-value ratio, and levying a luxury tax (Selected Goods and Services Tax Act). However, the Taiwanese government has typically failed to take any policy measures until major changes in market prosperity or serious public indignation have occurred. Essentially, the Taiwanese government has intervened less in the market than have governments in neighboring countries, such as Hong Kong, Singapore, Korea, and China.

5.2 Policy Measures to Prevent Construction Businesses from Closing

To restrict the increase in housing prices, the government has usually taken certain measures that have caused difficulties for the construction industry. After governmental intervention in both the second and third waves of soaring housing prices mentioned in section 3, thousands of construction businesses closed. Therefore, after implementing these measures, the government typically removed controls on credit and took other measures, such as the passage of the "Tax and Financial Measures Related to the Healthy Development of the Construction Industry". The government may also take certain indirect actions to stimulate the demand for housing to help the construction industry. These measures include releasing control over farmland, suspending the construction of public housing, subsidizing mortgage loans, allowing foreign and even Chinese investment in Taiwanese real estate, cutting the land value increment tax, and extending the applicable range of preferential rates for this tax.

6. CONCLUDING REMARKS AND IMPLICATIONS

Over the past four decades, the housing market in Taiwan has demonstrated a long-term upward trend and cyclical fluctuation. Large quantities of resources and capital were attracted into the construction industry, and this industry became the engine of economic development in Taiwan. However, the construction industry was developed under a conservative financial system. Project financing and informal measures, such as the pre-sale system, were utilized to acquire sufficient funds to complete development. When housing prices soared, the government rarely took action to control housing prices because most political parties and elected representatives had support from construction companies. After housing prices soared excessively, the government then was forced to employ certain measures to suppress prices. These measures typically affected construction companies that were overinvested and caused them to go bankrupt. However, the government duly provided assistance to avoid impacting the job market or increasing the number of non-performing loans issued by financial institutions. Currently, housing prices have been on the rise for seven consecutive years. The chance that housing prices will enter into a period of contraction is increasing. If this contraction occurs, it will be another challenge to the operation of construction businesses and to the government.

Taiwan's construction development process is generally similar to that of other countries, but there are certain different and unique characteristics. Taiwan's experience can suggest implications for other countries, and Taiwan can also learn from other countries' experiences.

6.1 Taiwan's Pre-sale Experience Can Provide Reference for Other Countries

The most special characteristic for Taiwanese construction financing is the pre-sale system. Other Asian countries such as Korea, and the U.S., also use forms of pre-sales. Taiwan's system, which started almost half a century ago, helps to solve the problem of lack of capital for the construction industry and accelerate Taiwanese housing development without a housing shortage problem. Although the pre-sale system caused some problems in the early years, Taiwan has developed an escort scheme and other regulations for pre-selling to avoid these problems.

6.2 Experiences of Other Countries: Practices to Adopt or Avoid

Taiwan can learn from the experiences of other countries and thereby improve the development of its construction industry. For example, in Taiwan, collateral is important when construction companies borrow money from banks. However, a U.S. developer can seek a mini-perm loan or refinance the construction loan with a long maturity of 10 years and a lower interest rate, whereas Taiwanese construction companies are not likely to refinance their loans through banks. In addition, the LTV ratios for Taiwanese construction companies are typically lower than the LTV ratios for U.S. construction firms. Taiwan can learn from the U.S. practice of developing "commitment schemes to the lender" to increase the LTV ratio. Moreover, some U.S. banks establish high lending standards that Taiwanese banks would do well to adopt. In particular, Taiwanese financial institutions should improve their review process for construction financing, establish a credit evaluation system that addresses the construction industry, and refuse to approve loans based on the relationship between the bank and the construction company. Korea's credit rating methods for construction companies or third-party guarantors are also good principles for Taiwan to emulate. However, given the experience of the U.S. financial crisis, Taiwan should avoid subprime mortgages or the development of overabundant derivatives. An overly liberalized financial system could produce a crisis; even in the U.S., the excesses of the finance system eventually upset the real estate market and the overall economy.

6.3 Tradeoffs Between Project Financing and Corporate Financing

Project financing generally involves higher credit risk than corporate financing because project financing involves higher leverage ratios. In Taiwan, although project financing involves higher risk, it is the main financing method for Taiwanese housing development and has contributed significantly to that development without producing a housing shortage problem for the past forty years. By contrast, Korea suffers from housing shortage issues. Korea had relied on corporate financing but began to practice project financing after the year 2000. Project financing has therefore contributed to the rapid expansion of housing in Korea over the past ten years. However, project financing overheats the Korean real estate market and also exposes financial institutions to higher risk, as observed during the financial crisis in 2008. Project financing appears to be more effective for construction development, despite its inherently higher credit risk. Corporate financing may be a safer method when the real estate market is sluggish, but when the market is prosperous and risk is lower, project financing can be used to speed development. Thus, the choice between corporate and project financing entails a tradeoff between greater risk and faster development, and careful consideration should be used to determine the better option for a given economic situation.

NOTES

1. According to the Housing Demand Survey (Institute for Physical Planning and Information, 2011), the Taipei housing price to household income ratio is 16.2 in the second quarter, 2011.
2. Certain variables are displayed over shorter time spans due to data limitations. In particular, the construction loan data begin in 1988, and the building materials and construction price index data begin in 1980.
3. Only six building material and construction companies were listed in the Taiwan stock market before 1995.

REFERENCES

Agnello, L. and L. Schuknecht (2011), Booms and Busts in Housing Markets: Determinants and Implications, Journal of Housing Economics, 20, 171–190.
Barras, R., and D. Ferguson (1985), Spectral Analysis of Building Cycles in Britain, Environment and Planning, 17, 1369–1391.
Berger-Thomson, Laura and Luci Ellis (2004), Housing Construction Cycles and Interest Rates, Research Discussion Paper 2004–08, Economic Group, Reserve Bank of Australia.
Blackley, Dixie M. (1999), The Long-Run Elasticity of New Housing Supply in the United States: Empirical Evidence for 1950 to 1994, The Journal of Real Estate Finance and Economics, 18(1), 25–42.
Chang, Chin-Oh (1996), Real Estate Investment and Decision Making – Theory and Practice, Hwa Tai Publishing (in Chinese).
Chang, Chin-Oh (2010), Real Estate Cycle Indicators of the Third Quarter 2010, Architecture and Building Research Institute, Ministry of Interior.
Chang, Chin-Oh and Charles W.R. Ward (1993), Forward Pricing and the Housing Market: The Pre-sale Housing System in Taiwan, Journal of Property Research, 10, 217–227.
Chen, Ming-Chi, Yuichiro Kawaguchi, and Kanak Patel (2004), An Analysis of the Trend and Cyclical Behaviours of House Prices in the Asian Markets, Journal of Property Investment and Finance, 22(1), 55–75.
DeCoster, G.P. and W.C. Strange (2011), Developers, Herding, and Overbuilding, Journal of Real Estate Finance and Economics, online.
Follain, J.R. (1979), The Price Elasticity of the Long-Run Supply of New Housing Construction, Land Economics, 55(2), 190–199.
Goodhart, C. and B. Hofmann (2008), House Prices, Money, Credit, and the Macroeconomy, Oxford Review of Economic Policy, 24(1), 180–205.
Hsieh, H.H.Y. (2005), The 1990s Taiwan Residential Construction Boom: A Supply Side Interpretation, Construction Management and Economics, 23, 265–284.
Huang, K.R. (2003), General Situation and Trend of Taiwan Construction Industry, Industrial Economy, 258, 1–34 (in Chinese).
Institute for Physical Planning and Information (2011), Housing Demand Survey of the Second Quarter 2011, Construction and Planning Agency, Ministry of Interior, Executive Yuan, R.O.C. (Taiwan).
Jin, Y. and Z. Zeng (2004), Residential Investment and House Prices in a Multi-sector Monetary Business Cycle Model, Journal of Housing Economics, 13, 268–286.
Mayer, Chris and C.T. Somerville (1996), Land Development and the Supply of New Housing: Unifying Empirical and Theoretical Models of Housing Supply, Working Paper, UBC Centre for Real Estate and Urban Economics.
Mayer, C. and C.T. Somerville, C.T. (2000), Residential Construction: Using the Urban Growth Model to Estimate Housing Supply, Journal of Urban Economics, 48, 85–109.
McNulty, J.E. (1995), Overbuilding, Real Estate Lending Decisions, and the Regional Economic Base, Journal of Real Estate Finance and Economics, 11(1), 37–53.
Muth, R. (1960), The Demand for Non-Farm Housing. In A.C. Harberger (ed.), The Demand for Durable Goods, Chicago: University of Chicago Press.

Peng, Chien-Wen, Chin-Oh Chang, and Antsong Lin (1998), The Impact of Real Estate Cycles on Construction Lags, Taiwan Economic Reviews, 26(4), 409–429.
Saiz, A. (2010), The Geographic Determinants of Housing Supply. The Quarterly Journal of Economics, 125(3):1253–1296.
Schwab, R.M. (1983), Real and Nominal Interest Rates and the Demand for Housing, Journal of Urban Economics, 13, 181–195.
Somerville, C.T. (1999), Residential Construction Costs and the Supply Of New Housing: Endogeneity and Bias in Construction Cost Indexes. Journal of Real Estate Finance and Economics, 18(1), 43–62.
Su, C.K., C.Y. Lin and M.T. Wang (2003), Taiwanese Construction Sector In A Growing "Maturity" Economy, 1964–1999, Construction Management and Economics, 21, 719–728.
Tan, W. (1987), GNP, Interest Rate and Construction Investment: Empirical Evidence from US Data, Construction Management and Economics, 5, 185–193.
Topel, R. and S. Rosen (1988), Housing Investment in the United States, Journal of Political Economy, 96(4), 718–740.
Tse, R.Y.C. and J. Raftery (2001), The Effects of Money Supply on Construction Flows. Construction Management and Economics, 19, 9–17.
Wong, Y.C. and Chin-Oh Chang (1993), An Investigation of Construction Finance System From the Change of Construction Capital, Taiwan Land Finance Quarterly Journal, 30(1),181–198 (in Chinese).

9. Korea's development finance at the crossroads

Jae-young Son*

1. INTRODUCTION

Before the Asian economic crisis the Korean government had effectively blocked financial resources channeled into the real estate sector, since it tried to mobilize as much resources as possible to promote the export-oriented manufacturing sector. Banks were banned from making loans for purchase of land (except as sites to build small houses and factories), for construction or purchase of large houses, and for other real estate businesses.

Since official housing finance could only partially support real estate developers and home buyers, peculiar financial instruments which do not involve financial intermediaries have been developed and widely used. For home owners, the Chonsei rental system with which an owner of a house effectively borrows from the tenant has been popular. For home builders, the pre-sale of new houses has been the norm. The rules on housing development and supply allow the home builders to be paid the contract deposit and interim payments by the home buyers before the houses are completed. In effect, home buyers directly supply funds to the builders without the involvement of financial intermediaries. In 1994, such contract deposits and interim payments amounted to 26 trillion won, 3.5 times as much as the housing construction loans supplied by financial institutions in that year (Lee and Cho, 1995).

In the wake of the Asian economic crisis, as part of the sweeping economic reform to cope with the crisis, major deregulation of the real estate sector was taken in 1998 and the following years. In February 1998, the government abolished the restriction on real estate loans as part of financial sector deregulation measures. It was expected and subsequently proved to benefit home building, non-housing real estate development, and acquisition of existing houses. In addition, the government established a legal framework for issuing asset backed securities in September 1998 and mortgage-backed securities in January 1999, and introduced real estate investment trust (REIT) in April 2001.

New players entered into the real estate sector and new financial instruments proliferated which served home buyers' and developers' needs. Mortgage loans and related products are discussed elsewhere in this volume. This chapter deals with the development finance. Since the deregulation, the Korean version of project finance (hereafter, K-PF) has dominated development finance. Now, after about a decade, flaws of K-PF are increasingly pronounced, and the search for new financial instruments is a major task both for the government and for the industry.

We conducted a survey on real estate developers, contractors, and financiers asking about the problems of the current K-PF structure and possible alternatives to it. From the survey results as well as from discussions in the literature, we propose ways of improving development finance.

Section 2 explains the structure of K-PF and the role of each player. Section 3 discusses the market wide trend of K-PF and related problems. Section 4 examines possible alternatives to K-PF for future development finance, and section 5 concludes the chapter.

2. KOREAN PROJECT FINANCE

2.1 Structure

Every development project has its own peculiarity, and the financial structure of development projects has infinite varieties, but the textbook definition of project finance is "the long term financing of development projects based upon the projected cash flows of the project rather than the balance sheets of the project sponsors, i.e. equity investors". The loans are commonly non-recourse loans, which are secured by the project assets and paid entirely from project cash flow, rather than from the project sponsors (Figure 9.1).

K-PF has the appearance of the textbook project finance, but differs from it in several critical aspects (Table 9.1). Firstly, K-PF is used in conjunction with the pre-sale of houses with which the developer borrows from prospective home buyers to finance construction costs. K-PF's role is to finance purchase of land and other initial costs, before the pre-sale is offered and cash-inflow begins. Depending on the risks involved, savings banks and commercial banks play separate roles. Savings banks usually provide the land loan, which is called the bridge loan, and after completion of land purchase and securing of development permits, the developer takes out loans from commercial banks, which is called the main-PF, to retire the bridge loan and to cover costs not paid by pre-sale payments.

Secondly, since most of the construction costs are paid by home buyers, the developer can initiate a project with an equity as little as the contract

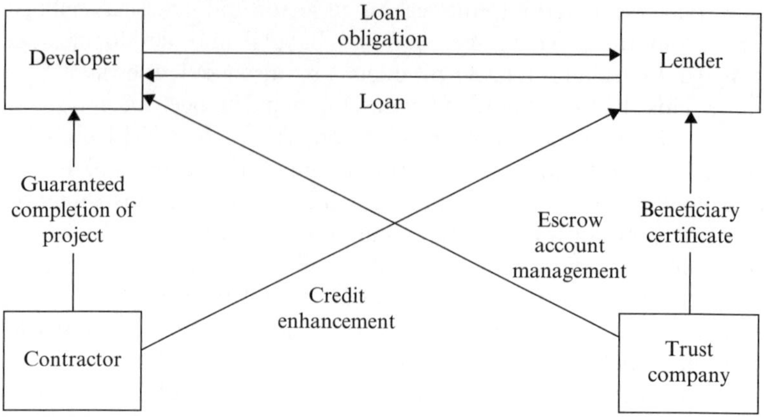

Figure 9.1 Structure of project finance

Table 9.1 Summary of differences between textbook PF and K-PF

	Textbook PF	K-PF
Borrower	Developer (mostly, SPC)	Developer (corporation, sometimes SPC)
Funds for repayment/ security	Cash-flow from project	Cash-flow from project. Guarantees by contractor and developer
Recourse	Non- or limited-recourse	Full-recourse
Cash management	Escrow account	Escrow account with real estate trust company
Borrowing cost	Higher than corporate loan/ profit sharing common	Depends on credit rating of contractor which provides credit enhancement
Project evaluation	Thorough feasibility study essential	Valuation of collateral and contractor's credit worthiness more important
Risk allocation	Dispersed among participants	Concentrated on contractor

deposit for land purchase, usually 10% of the land price. Entry into the development industry thus has little financial barriers for aspiring developers, and most indeed have equity as small as the contract deposit for land, and in some cases not even that much.

Thirdly, Korean financial institutions prefer making straight loans to providing equity, unlike investment banks which act as sponsors in the textbook project finance. However, they certainly do not believe that those small developers can pay back loans in case the project fails. Contractors fill the gap. Contractors have much larger equity and higher credit ratings than developers. They usually provide the triple-guarantees to pay back loans, to carry out and finish construction works, and to complete sales of houses being built. Lenders' attention is mostly focused on these guarantees in assessing loan applications. With the triple-guarantees the loan is certainly not non-recourse, and K-PF is more of a corporate loan to the contractor, whoever the nominal borrower may be, rather than the text book project finance.

2.2 Participants

Developer

The developer is a rather new profession, a creation of the Asian economic crisis and ensuing deregulation. Before the crisis, only well-capitalized large construction companies could afford to buy up land and hold it for future development, since banks did not lend directly for land purchase. Construction companies assumed the role of the land speculator, the developer, and the contractor all at the same time.

The economic crisis changed the structure of real estate development. Firstly, all large Korean companies, including those in the construction sector, emerged from the crisis as much more transparent entities with much lower debt to equity ratios than before. Construction companies, usually well-known large firms, could no longer hold onto future development sites for a long period, since such land inventory and related expenses negatively affected their balance sheets. Secondly, construction companies found that owners of development sites charged higher prices as they believed large firms can afford to pay more. Small unknown developers could buy up land at lower costs. These small entities also have advantages in dealing with local government officials to acquire development permits. Thirdly, developers could now finance the purchase of land, since financial institutions began to lend for such purposes. K-PF was precisely the financial instrument for these new entrepreneurs.

Figure 9.2 represents the procedure a developer follows in most projects, although one must bear in mind that no two developments are identical. The developer searches for a potential development site; secures the site by signing a contract after paying contract deposit, usually 10% of the purchase price; finds a savings bank willing to make a bridge loan amounting to 90% of the land price; gets development permits from the local government; finds a contractor willing to provide the triple-guarantees; arranges a commercial bank loan to retire the savings bank loan; gets approval for pre-sale and offers to-be-built houses to the general public;

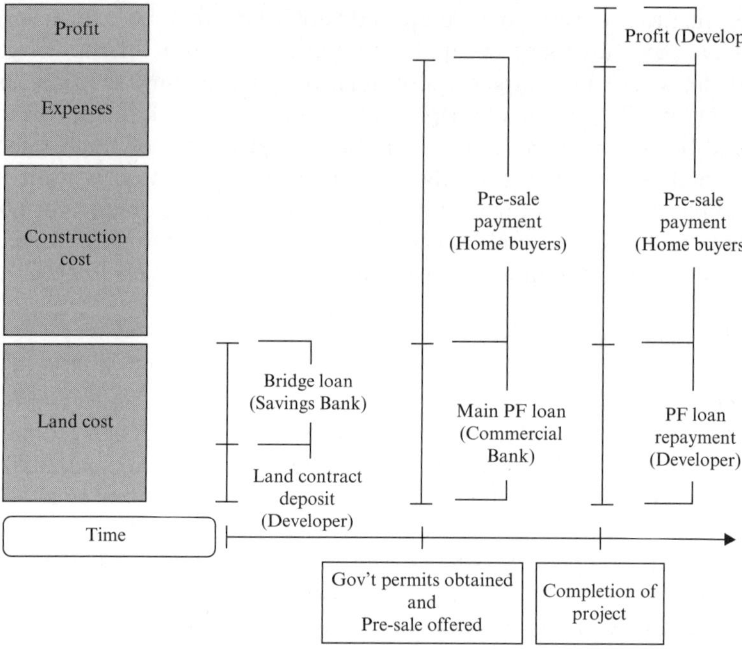

Source: Kim et al. (2012), modified by author.

Figure 9.2 Schematic representation of K-PF development project

and oversees the construction process and move-in of residents. Two or more of the above stages may overlap depending on individual site characteristics. The most critical stage of the entire development process is the pre-sale offering. If a sufficient number of buyers sign up for the home purchase, steady flow of cash is secured and the whole process will proceed smoothly until the end. All participants will be handsomely rewarded, but the developer's profit is huge considering their meager equity input and low risk taking ability.

In the early half of the 2000s, the supply and demand situation almost guaranteed success of most housing development projects, and many upstart developers made a great fortune. The number of would-be developers increased dramatically in the mid-2000s, thanks to a low entry barrier to the profession. Since potential profits from any development project were immensely greater than the potential loss, they sought to launch a project by any means, in many cases based on unrealistic optimism. Many projects launched in this period eventually failed, damaging all three participants, i.e., the developer, the contractor, and the lender, tied in the project.

Contractor

One may wonder why the contractor would agree to provide the triple-guarantees, effectively assuming almost all the risks involved in the development project. Fierce competition among contractors and construction cost mark-up were commonly cited reasons. Also, they usually secured means to control the project more aggressively than in the normal developer-contractor relationship.

Was the construction cost mark-up large enough compensation for their risk taking? We asked the question to experienced workers in the construction companies as well as in the development companies. The survey question was "In a K-PF project, how much is the construction cost marked up in return for contractor's credit enhancement?" The results are shown in Table 9.2. It is interesting that the perceived mark-up in general was greater for developers (13 to 25%) than for contractors (8 to 14%). Among contractors, the smaller firms seemed to charge more than the larger firms. It may reflect that these smaller firms took up more risky projects, after larger firms picked less risky ones first. Among developers, the smaller firms had to pay more since their reliance on contractors' credit enhancement was greater. From the tables, one can conclude that the contractors were paid about 10 to 15% of the construction cost in return for their extra risk taking. This pricing may have been flawed, judging from the mass bankruptcy of contractors since the mid-2000s.

Table 9.2 Survey result for construction cost mark-up in return for credit enhancement by contractor(%)

(1) Contractor response						
Contractor size rank	1–10	11–30	31–50	50–100	101 or lower	All
No. of responses	22	25	16	7	19	92
Average	8.6	8.4	13.4	13.2	13.9	11.0
St. Dev.	5.7	4.5	6.0	6.6	14.5	8.4
(2) Developer response						
Firm size (amount of equity capital)	Below 300 mil. won	300–500 mil. won	500–1000 mil. won	1000–5000 mil. won	Above 5000 mil. won	All
No. of responses	8	12	20	17	18	77
Average	25.0	13.1	19.4	14.1	13.1	17.0
Std. Dev.	14.9	8.7	12.9	7.3	4.4	11.2

Lender

Savings banks, regionally licensed small banks, provided the so-called bridge loan for land purchase. The loan was made in the most risky stage of the development process: land owners may demand unreasonably high prices or not sell at any price, development permits may not be obtained from the local government, contractors may not provide credit enhancement, and commercial banks may not give main-PF to retire the bridge loan.

In return for assuming high risk, the savings bank charged various fees in addition to high interest rates. In retrospect, this high price of the bridge loan may not have been high enough, considering the failure of so many savings banks in the late 2000s after the housing boom ended.

Roles of the savings banks and commercial banks, which are large national banks, were not clearly separated, since commercial banks sometimes lent for land purchase while savings banks sometimes continued to lend until the end of the project. However, commercial banks usually provided the so-called main-PF loan after the land purchase was complete and government permits were secured.

Since the pre-sale payments by the consumers finance most of construction costs, the main-PF is used to retire the bridge loan and covers minor expenses not paid by the pre-sale. Also, the main-PF loan is made only after a creditworthy contractor provides triple-guarantees. The main-PF thus is a low-risk low-cost loan relative to the bridge loan. Commercial banks rely so heavily on the contractor's credit enhancement that they do not seriously scrutinize the viability of the actual project. The PF loan is more of a corporate loan made to the contractor, but the interest rate charged for the K-PF loans is higher than normal corporate loans to the same company. Our survey of lenders reveals that the interest rate was on average 2.4%p. higher for the PF loans than the corporate loans to the same company (Table 9.3).

Both the savings bank and the commercial bank began to finance development projects only after the financial deregulation around 2000. They lacked capacity or experience to evaluate the project feasibility. Collateral security and credit enhancement by the contractor were supposed to substitute for such shortcomings. However, mass default of K-PF loans and

Table 9.3 Survey result for interest rate difference between K-PF loan and corporate loan to the same contractor (%p.)

	No. of responses	Average	Sta. Dev.	Min.	Max.
Difference	82	2.4	1.1	0.5	5.0

subsequent bankruptcy of many savings banks reveals that the presumption was not correct.

3. TREND OF K-PF AND ITS PROBLEMS

3.1 Trend

As shown in Table 9.4, total K-PF loans doubled in 2006 and increased by 50% in 2007. This explosion of PF loans reflects the construction boom at the time. Total PF debt peaked in 2009 at 84 trillion won. However, the housing market had already been hit hard by the global financial crisis in 2008 and was heading toward a recession. Table 9.5 shows that problem of unsold houses was concentrated outside the Capital region before the global financial crisis. However, after the crisis, the problem persists in the Capital region housing market while conditions outside the Capital region are improving.

If the developer fails to sell a sufficient number of houses in the pre-sale offering, the project cannot proceed as planned. The project is stalled until the market condition improves or the participants agree on the share of losses each would absorb.

If a project is proved to be a failure and if a contractor has signed for the triple-guarantees, the contractor has to assume the loan and pay the lender. However, many such contractors actually did not have the ability to pay back the loan, and filed for bankruptcy. As of September 2012, 25 of the 100 largest construction companies went under because of the PF guarantee.

If a failed project was still in the early stages without contractor guarantees (or if the contractor could not fulfill its guarantee), the lender, usually the savings bank which made the bridge loan, had to take over the collateral, i.e., project site. However, since the market prospect had already turned sour, it was usually difficult to find a buyer for the collateral land. The price would go down dramatically, turning the PF loan into an unrecoverable loss (Table 9.5).

Table 9.6 shows that the PF problem is on-going. Default rates of commercial bank K-PF loans have not peaked yet, although the rate is within a manageable range. The default rate for savings banks is above 20%, even after turning the worst of bad loans over to the bad bank set up by the Korea Asset Management Corporation on several occasions; such interventions lowered the default rates for only about six months, and then the mounting bad loans again reached the crisis level. In 2011 alone, 16 saving banks were forced to be sold or closed. Altogether 20 savings banks

Table 9.4 Trend of K-PF loans outstanding (trillion won)

	2005.12	2006.12	2007.12	2008.6	2008.12	2009.6	2009.12	2010.6	2010.12	2011.3
Total	24.8	49.2	69.7	78.9	83.0	84.0	81.5	74.2	66.5	58.6
Commercial banks	14	26	42	48	52.5	54.1	51.0	44.9	38.7	36.5
Savings banks	6.3	11.6	12.1	12.2	11.5	11.0	11.8	11.8	12.2	7.0
Insurance	–	–	–	5.3	5.5	5.5	5.7	5.4	4.9	5.1
Security firms	–	–	–	3.0	2.9	2.8	2.7	2.5	2.2	1.8

Source: Financial Supervisory Service.

Table 9.5 Number of houses offered in pre-sale but not sold

	Nation	Capital Region	Outside Capital Region
2000	58,550	19,785	38,765
2001	31,512	9,360	22,152
2002	24,923	1,387	23,536
2003	38,261	7,370	30,891
2004	69,133	15,458	53,675
2005	57,215	12,242	44,973
2006	73,772	4,724	69,048
2007	112,254	14,624	97,630
2008	165,599	26,928	138,671
2009	123,297	25,667	97,630
2010	88,706	29,412	59,294
2011	69,807	27,881	41,926
2012.3	62,949	26,961	35,988

Source: Ministry of Land, Transportation, and Maritime Affairs.

Table 9.6 Default rates of K-PF loans(%)

Lender	2008.6	2008.12	2009.6	2009.12	2010.6	2010.12	2011.3
Total	3.6	4.4	5.9	6.4	7.3	12.9	12.3
Commercial banks	0.7	1.1	2.6	1.7	2.9	4.3	5.3
Savings banks	14.3	13.0	9.6	10.6	8.7	25.1	22.8
Insurance	2.4	2.4	4.1	4.6	7.9	8.3	–
Security firms	6.6	13.9	24.5	30.3	29.5	29.8	26.6

Source: Financial Supervisory Service.

went bankrupt, but the stability of the remaining 93 savings banks is not assured.

3.2 Structural Flaws of the K-PF Loan

In a development project, the developer, the contractor, and the lender are tied up by the K-PF loan. In a booming market, all participants profit handsomely. The contractor is paid more than in ordinary construction projects, the lender is paid higher interests than corporate loans and other fees. The developer's return is enormous considering scanty equity input.

However, when the market goes downward into recession, such a rosy prospect turns into a nightmare. The developer's capacity to absorb loss is negligible, and it is almost irrelevant in salvaging a failed project. As for the contractor, it will find itself burdened with guarantees which it cannot fulfill, with the possible exception of the largest construction companies. Failure of a development project has a spill-over effect. Bankruptcy of a contractor will result in problems in other projects the contractor is involved in. As for the lenders, depending on the stage at which the project stopped, various lenders will now have bad loans which negatively affect their financial stability.

Nationwide, it is roughly estimated more than 500 development projects have been stalled in recent years in various stages of the development for diverse reasons. With so many failed K-PF projects, we were curious about which of many risk factors were mainly responsible for the failure. In our survey, we asked respondents to evaluate relative importance of risk factors presented in pairwise fashion. Our list of risk factors as shown in Table 9.7 contains four primary factors and sixteen sub-factors. After excluding inconsistent ones, the responses were analyzed with the Analytical Hierarchy Process (hereafter, AHP) method.[1]

It was surprising that respondents in all three professions (i.e., developer, contractor, and lender) agreed on the relative importance among primary

Table 9.7 Development risk factors

Primary risk factors	Sub-factors
Market Risk (risk posed by the overall economic conditions)	(1) Macroeconomic condition (2) Real estate policies (3) Local development prospects (4) Competing projects in the vicinity
Project Risk (risk of project not proceeding as planned)	(1) Land acquisition delay or cost overrun (2) Development permit delayed or not obtained (3) Cost control problems (4) Funding problems
Cash-flow Risk (risk of planned cash-flow not being realized)	(1) Pre-sale offering failure (2) Price or rent of completed structure (3) Size of PF loans (4) Delay of planned cash-inflow
Counterparty Risk (risk arising from the other parties in the PF structure)	(1) Developer risk (2) Contractor risk (3) Lender risk (4) Others including local government

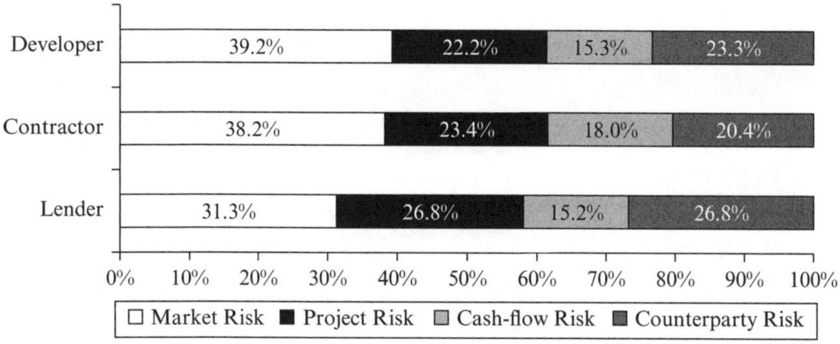

Figure 9.3 Relative importance of primary risk factors

risk factors (Figure 9.3). The market risk was pointed out as the most important among the primary factors. Respondents thought that changes of macroeconomic environment, real estate market conditions, government policies and regulations, and competing projects in the vicinity would determine the success or failure of development projects. Next, respondents from all three professions ranked the project risk and the counterparty risk almost equally important. Cash-flow risk was considered the least important among the primary risk factors.

Among four sub-factors under the market risk category, contractors identified the macroeconomic condition as the most important (Figure 9.4). They seemed to think that success of a development project depends on the macroeconomic environment of the project rather than project-specific details. If the economy is booming and consumers are optimistic about the future of house investment at the time of the pre-sale

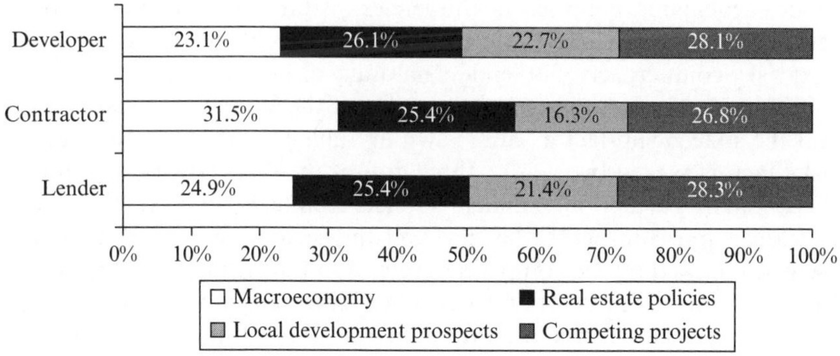

Figure 9.4 Relative importance of sub-factors of the market risk category

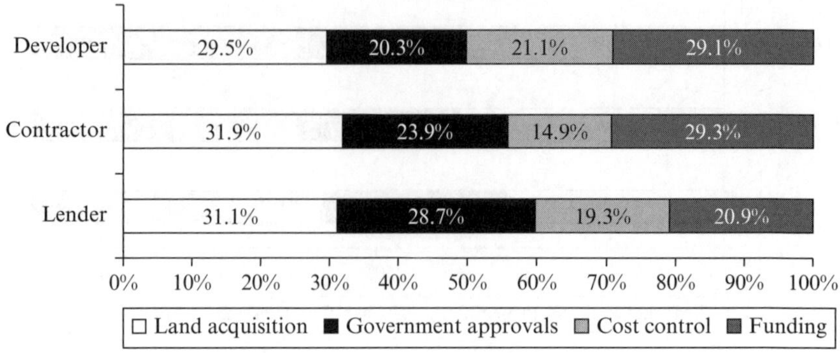

Figure 9.5 Relative importance of sub-factors of the project risk category

offering, then success of the project is assured. Minute features of the projects seem to count less. Other participants weighted the four sub-factors similarly.

Under the project risk category, we listed four sub-factors: land acquisition, development permit and other government approvals, cost control, and funding arrangement (Figure 9.5). All three groups of respondents agreed that land acquisition is the most important risk factor. Developers and contractors ranked securing funding arrangement as the second, but lenders thought that securing necessary permits and government approval was more important. However, they all agreed that the cost control is a minor factor.

As expected, success of the pre-sale offering was considered the most important factor under the cash-flow risk category, followed by the sale price or rent (Figure 9.6). Among sub-factors of the counterparty risk category, even developers pointed out that the developer is the weak link in K-PF projects (Figure 9.7). Of course the degree of riskiness perceived by other participants, contractors and lenders, is far higher than developers' self-evaluation. Developers and contractors thought that lenders are the next risky counterparty, but lenders naturally disagreed.

The result of combining relative weights of the four primary risk factors and the sixteen sub-factors are shown in Table 9.8. The four top ranked risky factors picked by each of three groups of K-PF participants reveal the different perception. Lenders ranked counterparty risk, both from developer and contractor, the first and the second most important risk factors, followed by the competing projects in the vicinity, and the acquisition of land. Contractors on the other hand ranked three of the sub-factors of the market risk and the counterparty risk from the developer as the most important four risk factors. Developers' top four risk factors are all sub-factors of the market risk.

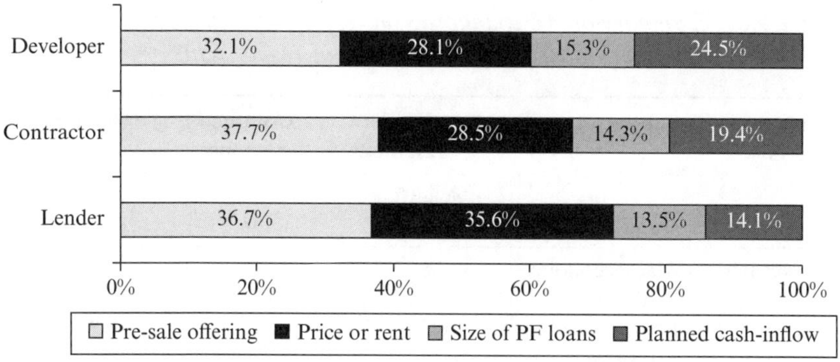

Figure 9.6 Relative importance of sub-factors of the cash-flow risk category

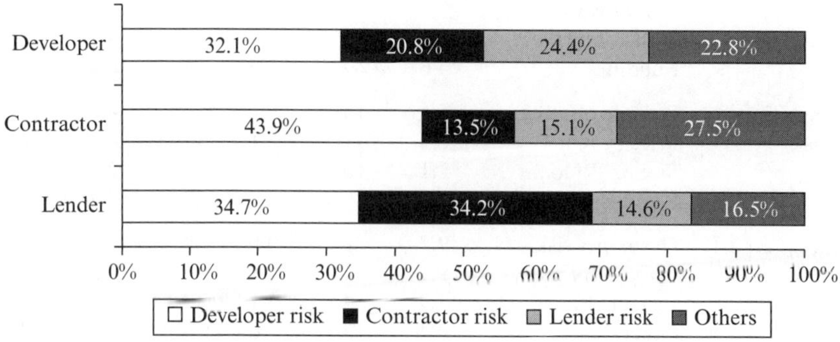

Figure 9.7 Relative importance of sub-factors of the counterparty risk category

Our analysis reveals that:

- Lenders rely more on credit worthiness of developers and contractors for repayment of the loan than on the project characteristics. They probably look into the most basic aspects of the project such as land acquisition and local competition but not much more, indicating that lenders are unwilling or unable to thoroughly evaluate proposed projects.
- Contractors and developers are concerned mostly with the market risks which reflect the short-term economic conditions and affect investment psychology. This is because the pre-sale offering determines the project's success or failure.
- The developer is the weak link in the K-PF structure. Most of them

Table 9.8 Summary of AHP analyses on relative importance of development risk factors by group of respondents

Primary risk factors	Sub-factors	Lender responses		Contractor responses		Developer responses	
		weight (%)	rank	weight (%)	rank	weight (%)	rank
Market Risk	Macroeconomy	7.8	6	**12.0**	**1**	**9.1**	**3**
	Real estate policies	7.9	5	**9.7**	**3**	**10.2**	**2**
	Local development prospects	6.7	8	6.2	8	**8.9**	**4**
	Competing projects	**8.9**	**3**	**10.2**	**2**	**11.0**	**1**
Project Risk	Land acquisition	**8.3**	**4**	7.4	5	6.6	6
	Government approvals	7.7	7	5.6	10	4.5	13
	Cost control	5.2	12	3.5	13	4.7	12
	Funding	5.6	9	6.9	6	6.5	7
Cash-flow Risk	Pre-sale offering	5.6	10	6.8	7	4.9	10
	Price or rent	5.4	11	5.1	11	4.3	14
	Size of PF loans	2.1	16	2.6	16	2.3	16
	Planned cash-inflow	2.1	15	3.5	12	3.7	15
Counterparty Risk	Developer risk	**9.3**	**1**	**9.0**	**4**	7.5	5
	Contractor risk	**9.1**	**2**	2.8	15	4.8	11
	Lender risk	3.9	14	3.1	14	5.7	8
	Others	4.4	13	5.6	9	5.3	9

have capital only slightly more than the land contract deposit, and cannot cope with any unexpected difficulties arising along the development process.

4. REDESIGNING THE DEVELOPMENT FINANCE SYSTEM

Conventional K-PF is a flawed financial instrument which can last only while the development market is booming. Recession has awakened market participants as well as the government to the problem, and proposals for improvement have been put forward by market participants and researchers. Common elements of such proposals are the following.

Minimum capital requirement for developers

Most developers have capital just enough for the contract deposit for land purchase. If the project fails, they lose that amount of money. If the project succeeds, however, the profit is tremendous compared to their equity input. This asymmetry drives them to be overly zealous in any potential projects. They persuade contractors and lenders into the project presenting unrealistically optimistic forecasts of the project outcome. Sometimes unlawful transactions are made between them.

In addition to being a main factor in launching bad projects, developers' low capitalization increases debt financing requirements. Needless to say, heavy dependence on debt finance makes a project more vulnerable to unexpected delays, cost increases, and other external shocks. Also, sufficient amount of skilled manpower can be assembled only with sufficient capital.

For these reasons it is better for developers to have larger capital, but should the government intervene in the development market and impose a regulation on the minimum capital requirement?

Several strong arguments for regulation have been raised in related discussions. Firstly, the government has to clean up the aftermath of K-PF failures, especially bankrupt savings banks, with tax payers' money. It is reasonable for the government to intervene in advance to prevent such a failure. Secondly, the pre-sale offering of houses is backed by a government guarantee that the houses will eventually be built or the money be returned when the developer or the contractor cannot perform contractual duties. Although the developer pays a modest fee for the guarantee, pre-sale of houses is essentially a loan from the general public to the developer. It is proper for the government to regulate such a financial mechanism that affects a large number of consumers.

If the government requires minimum capital for the developer, how high should the requirement be? Our survey includes a related question. Respondents from both the developer and the contractor firms agreed that the equity of the developer should be raised, but their answer for the adequate requirement differed with contractors setting a far higher requirement than developers. Contractors thought that the developer equity should be on average between 30% and 37% of the land cost depending on the project size. This response implies that the equity input by developers should be at least three times the current input. In comparison, developers answered that the requirement should be on average between 15% and 22%. Even developers agree that the equity input should be at least 50% higher than in current K-PF structure.

Equity participation of lenders and improving project evaluation

It is now certain that the developer and the contractor are not capable of absorbing risks of real estate development. The lender is better positioned to properly price risks and arrange a financial structure which can take over the risks. Korean financial institutions were beginning to build up investment banking divisions in the 2000s, but the effort has been mostly abandoned due to the global financial crisis.

In the current K-PF structure, lenders prefer to make straight loans with high interest rates and costly fees, making development projects vulnerable to unexpected negative events. If lenders take equity position in any form, it will lower cash outflow requirements and thus the total risks of the project, and reduce the risks taken up by other participants.

Should the government be involved in expanding the role of the lender? One of the reasons why the lenders are conservative is that the institutions as well as individual loan officers are tightly supervised by regulators. This regulatory system does not encourage experimenting with new financial structures in which the lender takes up more risks than in conventional loans. The government should instead support new innovation in development finance.

Also, the government can help build social infrastructure for assessing risks related to real estate development. Currently, the lender lacks expertise to assess and manage development risks. Accumulation of such expertise is a prerequisite both for continuation of K-PF loans, albeit in altered form, and for any new financial devices with which the lender takes up equity position. Evaluation of development projects requires costly data assembly, model building, and tests. In the past ten years, K-PF participants were reluctant to pay the related costs, and private sector researchers have not come up with any standard evaluation tools. It is time to admit that such evaluation tools are more of a public good, and the government research institutions should develop standard evaluation tools, and build and provide the necessary database.

Currently, conventional K-PF loans are almost dried up except for the largest contractors or for projects with a third party guarantee. In one form, the third party insurer guarantees that in case a large number of houses remain unsold, they will take those houses as collateral and make necessary loans to complete the project. Another form of the guarantee provided by the public sector insurer is to repay PF loans in case the project fails. These third party guarantees are given selectively depending on credit worthiness of the contractor and a basic project evaluation. However, without employing more sophisticated project evaluation, proliferation of the third party guarantees may generate new problems in the future.

Experimenting with new financial instruments

In addition to efforts to salvage the K-PF structure, various new financial instruments have been tried. One supposedly promising device was the specialized development real estate investment trust (REIT). With this, a developer would sponsor establishment of a self-managed REIT, raise capital from the public market, and start a development project. Although establishment of a REIT and IPO of its shares required substantial capital and various permits and approvals, the development REIT was enthusiastically welcomed by developers as the ultimate solution for development finance.

One of the early development REITs succeeded in an IPO in August 2010, and its share price rose steadily, reflecting positive reception from investors. However, it was soon revealed that the firm's initial capital was in fact borrowed fund against the regulation, and the money raised in the IPO was plundered by the firm's officers. The REIT was expelled from the stock exchange in June 2011, setting a record for the earliest expulsion.

This scandal halted the effort to deregulate operation of REIT in general, and establishment and IPO of the development REIT in particular. In retrospect, it was imprudent to allow a new start-up company to raise funds in the public market, exposing the uninformed investors to risks of real estate development. Due to subsequent tightening of REIT regulation and IPO requirements, the development REIT is no longer an easy financing mechanism.

Another alternative to K-PF is a financing device referred to as land trust or development trust offered by the real estate trust companies. With the land trust, a land owner commissions a real estate trust company to develop his or her land by entrusting the land to the company. The trust company then raises funds, usually by corporate loans, and proceeds with the project on a fee base. The land trust was popular in the mid-1980s when other development finance was almost non-existent. However, the Asian economic crisis in the late 1990s resulted in mass failure of the land trust projects, and most real estate trust companies operating at that time went bankrupt. Newly licensed real estate trust companies after the Asian economic crisis are currently divided in their business strategy. Some real estate trust companies still stay away from land trust projects while others are enjoying surging business opportunities generated by the decline of K-PF loans. Real estate trust companies are now much more sophisticated than those in the 1980s, but they are exposed to risks which may prove to be too large when unexpected negative events happen.

Introducing a new corporate structure

Revision of the commercial law in April 2012 introduced a new corporate structure which is similar to the limited partnership in the US. Applied to real estate development, the developer would be the general partner who manages the project and takes up unlimited liability, and investors or land owners would be the limited partners whose loss is limited to the invested capital.

The limited partnership is well suited to real estate development in several aspects. Firstly, the structure ensures stable management of successive projects by the skilled developer. In a corporation the developer may lose control of the company as the company grows and investors' control increases. Secondly, the partners may agree to differentiate compensation among them, appreciating and rewarding the general partner's expertise. Thirdly, since the partnership is a form of cooperative, corporate tax is not imposed on the partnership, avoiding double taxation.

The partnership introduced in Korea's commercial law was originally designed for high tech start-ups which need a large infusion of capital but must retain control of the firm. The real estate developer shares essential features of high tech firms; the founder's expertise is essential for firms' continued operation, but a large amount of outside capital is required. One difference may be that in a real estate development, some investors may want to invest land, not cash, in the project. Such investors will receive partnership units in return. In the US partnership structure, such an exchange does not trigger taxation on the capital gain accrued to that point. Taxation is deferred until the investor sells partnership units or exchanges them with REIT shares. However, under the Korean tax code, investment in the form of land is subject to the capital gains tax. Until this provision is changed, application of the partnership will be severely restricted.

5. CONCLUSION

We have reviewed achievements and failures of the Korean version of project finance, and introduced ideas proposed for its improvement. Our discussion can be summed up by the following lessons obtained mostly from K-PF's failures.

1. Real estate development is a truly risky business, and every participant should be aware of how much risk he or she is taking and whether the risk is manageable. When the market is booming, however, this principle is hard to follow. Aggressive players prosper and crowd out prudent ones. Few market participants can resist following "the leaders". Far too many Korean savings banks and construction companies failed for this reason. Lenders as well as contractors must have strong internal project evaluation and risk management procedures.

2. Project evaluation and risk management is important to prevent mass-failure of development finance. Some assert that the government should introduce a scoring system to evaluate every individual development project. This proposal seems to be radical and impractical, but it reflects a wide agreement on the need for industry-standard project evaluation tools. We suggested that the government researchers should provide standard evaluation tools and necessary data to participants of development projects, since the private sector has failed to come up with any in the past ten years. Such an evaluation method is also necessary for emergence of related insurance instruments.
3. The developer initiating a project which is not feasible, the contractor providing guarantees which it cannot keep, and the lender making loans without meaningful assessment all exhibit the moral hazard problem. These behaviors explain why so many development projects failed simultaneously in Korea recently. Instead of intervening afterwards to stabilize the financial system, the government should establish safeguards to prevent such events. Introducing the minimum capital requirement for developers seems to be a good start. Contractors should not be allowed to provide guarantees that they cannot honor. Also more strict supervision of financial institutions is necessary to maintain financial stability.
4. The developer and the contractor alone cannot absorb risks involved in real estate development. The lender should also take up a share of risks, with corresponding rewards, which implies that they take equity position in some form. The lenders should accumulate expertise and experience to build an investment banking division which would assess related risks and arrange a financial structure to take them on.
5. New financing vehicles and/or supplementary arrangements such as REIT, partnership, land trust, and third party insurance etc. respectively have some features which can be usefully applied to real estate development finance. However, some have already failed and some need regulatory changes to be applied. More detailed studies and policy changes remain to be done.

NOTES

* This paper was written as part of Konkuk University's research support program for its faculty, on sabbatical leave in 2012.

1. See Saaty and Kearns (1985) for AHP method. Our survey was conducted between

December 2011 and February 2012 on professionals from development companies, construction companies, and financial institutions who had at least five years of experience with PF projects. We got back 83 completed questionnaires from developers, 98 from contractors, and 108 from lenders.

REFERENCES

Kim, W.J., J.R. Son, J.H. Kim, and S.R. Kim (2012), "Korean Real Estate Development Finance: State and Prospects", Hana Financial Information No. 5, Hana Financial Management Institute (in Korean).

Lee, J.H. and S.H. Cho (1995), "Economic Effects of House Pre-sale", Housing Finance, Korea Housing Bank, May (in Korean).

Saaty, T.L. and K. Kearns (1985), Analytical Planning: the Organization of Systems, Oxford.

PART IV

Policy responses

10. Mortgage defaults and risk-based capital: post-global financial crisis development and implications for emerging markets

Tyler T. Yang and Jessie Y. Zhang

1. INTRODUCTION

The housing finance institutions have a significant impact on the growth of the housing market. Various capital requirements are established by the U.S. government to ensure the financial safety and soundness of these institutions. However, the recent subprime crisis reminded us that even the seemingly most sophisticated housing finance system in the world can suddenly collapse. Since then, governments and think tanks around the world have devoted substantial effort to exploring the cause of the collapse. Many new policies and regulations with regard to capital requirements are introduced and implemented by the U.S. government in order to mitigate possible future impact of the Global Financial Crisis (GFC) to the overall economy to date. Among all the regulatory principles, some new regulation trends arise:

Risk retention The Dodd-Frank report of 2010 mandates a risk-retention requirement of 5% capital reserve for all newly originated loans, except for the safest Qualified Residential Mortgages (QRM). This and similar regulations are intended to increase the responsibility of mortgage underwriters and encourage sound quality control behaviors.

Counter-cyclical policies toward more stable housing and housing finance markets Previous static capital regulations tend to induce pro-cyclical market consequences. That is, banks have excess capital when the economy is good. As a result, a more relaxed mortgage underwriting process is adopted, triggering more supply for housing finance capital and further enhancing the housing boom. On the other hand, when the housing market contracts, lenders need to set aside more loss reserves and have less capital available to fund new mortgages. In response, they tend to tighten their underwriting rule, which leads to reduced housing finance resources and further depresses the housing market. New risk capital rules, such as the Basel III, are geared toward a counter-cyclical principle.

Risk sharing Over years, new products, institutions and regulators have been created in the housing finance industry that lead to the risk sharing among lenders, borrowers and government. Proper risk management and risk sharing among these market participants have also been key issues that are currently being explored to ensure a healthy and sustainable housing finance system.

Based on these new regulatory trends, we analyze the new policies introduced after the GFC and consider their expected effectiveness in mitigating the severity of the GFC.

Following a review of the U.S. experience from the GFC, we establish lessons that can be leveraged by emerging markets in establishing and managing robust housing finance systems. Some of the most important lessons include: (1) responsible underwriting standards focusing on borrowers' ability to sustain mortgage repayment through an uncertain future economy; (2) ability to accurately measure mortgage credit risks embedded in various mortgage product types, multiclass securities, and derivatives; (3) integrated capital rules that can stabilize housing markets; (4) clear definition of the government's roles by balancing the goals of affordable housing and financial soundness.

2. RISK RETENTION AND QUALIFIED RESIDENTIAL MORTGAGE

2.1 Regulatory Background

Intended to prevent potential future financial crisis, the Dodd-Frank Wall Street Reform and Consumer Protection Act (the Act) was signed into law by the U.S. President on July 21, 2010. In response to the agency problem of mortgage underwriting created by the massive structured securitization of mortgage products, the Act intended to increase lenders' "skin in the game". Specifically, companies that issue products like collateralized mortgage obligations (CMOs) or collateralized debt obligations (CDOs)[1] will be required to retain at least 5% of the credit risk unless the underlying loans meet certain standards, i.e. they are Qualified Residential

Mortgages (QRMs).[2] The standards for QRMs will be based on loans that are perceived to be of low risk according to their historical performance. Under the new regulation, the cost of securitizing non-QRM loans will be significantly higher than QRM loans. Therefore, the definition of QRMs is a critical factor in the effectiveness of this new risk retention regulation.

On March 29, 2011, FDIC published a Notice of Proposed Rulemaking (NPR) with five other federal regulatory agencies regarding risk retention with details about the QRM definition. Public comments were collected by August 1, 2011. There has not yet been a schedule for the release of the final rules.

The proposed QRM standards include the following features:[3]

- The proposed QRM would have an 80% maximum allowed LTV, which implies a 20 percent down payment requirement.
- The proposed rule would limit the mortgage payment to not exceed 28% of the borrower's gross income and all debt payment to not exceed 36% of the gross income.
- No credit score requirement is specified, but a mortgage loan would qualify as a QRM only if the borrower is not currently in 30 or more days delinquent on any debt obligation within the preceding 24 months.
- The borrower cannot have, within the preceding 36 months, been through bankruptcy, been foreclosed on, engaged in a short sale or deed-in-lieu of foreclosure, or been subject to a Federal or State judgment for collection of any unpaid debt.
- Only fully amortized loans are allowed. Negative-amortization, interest-only, and balloon-payment loans are not eligible.

QRMs defined in the NPR have a lower thus more restrictive debt ratio requirement than that of most loans prior to the GFC. However, the market is more concerned with the LTV requirement in the NPR, which we will discuss in detail next. Various institutions and many researchers argued that the proposed QRM standards can do more harm than good to the housing finance system if they are too restrictive.

2.2 Impact of Proposed QRM Standards

There is no question that the proposed QRM rules are well intentioned. In theory, the purpose of establishing standards for loans with low risk and allowing financial institutions to retain less of their capital for these qualified loans is to promote responsible lending, reduce total mortgage credit risk originated, and restore investors' confidence in securitization.

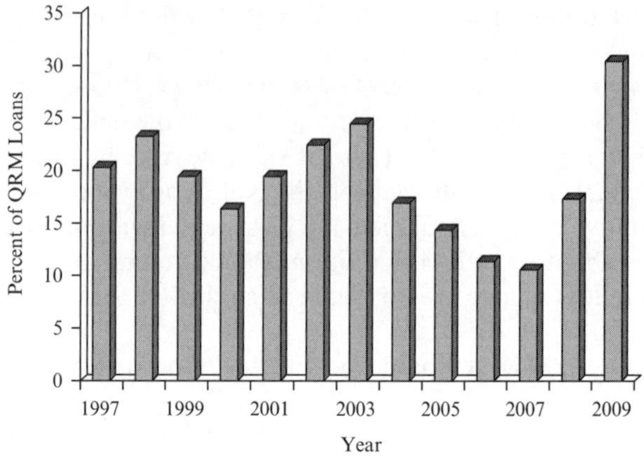

Source: FHFA, 2011. Mortgage Market Note 2011–02.

Figure 10.1 Percent of all mortgages that would have met all requirements under the proposed QRM standards, by year of origination

Nevertheless, an inadequately designed regulation could lead to negative consequences and defeat the original intention. There are three main reasons for concern:

Reason 1: Over-restrictive standards of QRM can increase the cost of housing finance for both consumers and lenders, preventing numerous borrowers from accessing the credit, while the benefit of reducing default may be limited

Statistics show that most of the existing loans do not meet the proposed QRM standards. For example, a study conducted by FHFA on Fannie Mae and Freddie Mac's portfolio shows that only 19.8% of all loans originated between 1997 and 2009 would have met the proposed QRM standards.[4] Figure 10.1 displays the trend of the percentage of loans satisfying QRM rules by year of origination.

Under the current market structure, Fannie and Freddie's portfolio is considered as QRMs. However, there has been a proposal to gradually wind down the GSEs, whose current market share is more than 50% of the existing loans. This implies an increase of non-QRM loans by around 40% in the future. Moreover, because requirements imposed by the GSEs tend to be more stringent than non-GSE loans, the percentage of QRMs among all mortgage loans is likely to be even lower than 20%.

An article published by the Coalition for Sensible Housing Policy suggests that even with only the new requirement on LTV, lots of loans will be disqualified as QRMs.[5] The study finds that, from year 2004 to 2008, around 19% of loans would be disqualified if we increase the down payment requirement from 5% to 20%. Since a significant barrier for homeownership is the wealth level required for the down payment, many families will have to save for a long time to purchase a house. For a typical American family, a 20% down payment generally requires more than 15 years' saving.

As a result of the highly restrictive QRM standards, lenders will have to increase the mortgage interest rate on non-QRM loans to compensate for the increased risk retained in their portfolio and the higher cost of capital. Some researches show that the increase of mortgage interest rate will be much more substantial than what is suggested by regulators.[6] For example, an analysis conducted by Moody's Analytics suggests that a typical non-QRM borrower could see mortgage rates rise by between 75 and 100 basis points, which consists of (1) QRM eligibility, which adds 30 to 50 basis points to non-QRM loans; (2) the premium capture rule (explained later), which will add 10 to 15 basis points; and (3) the lack of direct government backing and reduced liquidity in the non-QRM mortgage market, which will add approximately 35 basis points.[7]Another study by National Association of Realtors (NAR) suggests that the increase of interest rate will be 80 to 185 basis points.[8] The estimated interest rate increase compositions in that study are shown in Figure 10.2.

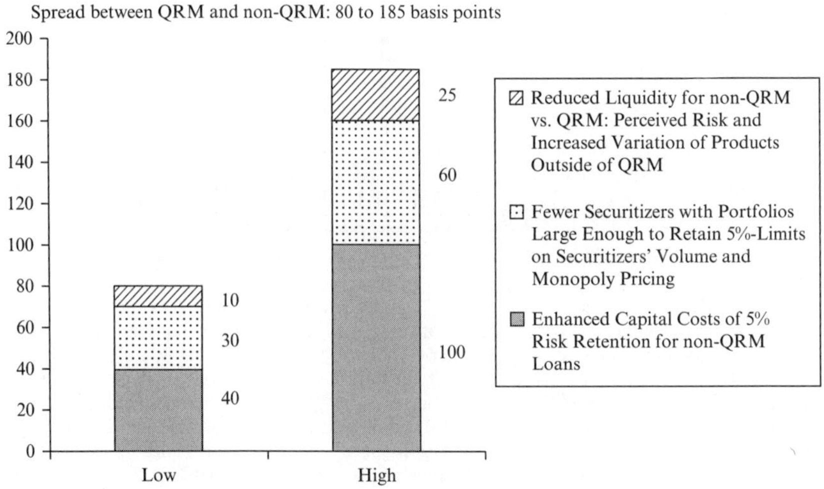

Source: NAR (http://economistsoutlook.blogs.realtor.org/2011/06/17/qrm-higher-mortgage-rates-on-the-horizon/).

Figure 10.2 Interest rate spread between QRM and non-QRMs

While aiming at ensuring borrowers' ability to repay their loan, the NPR can deny many borrowers access to credit, even if the elasticity of homeownership rate to interest rate has been found to be rather flat.[9] For example, by increasing a 30-year FRM rate from 4% to 5% on a $200,000 loan, the monthly payment will increase from $955 to $1,073 making the loan less affordable.

In order to justify the welfare loss accompanied by a restrictive QRM standard, one needs to also examine the policy benefit: the effectiveness on reducing default risk. Ideally, default rate on QRMs should be significantly lower than non-QRM loans to best serve this objective. However, a study by the Coalition for Sensible Housing Policy suggests the reduction on default risk of QRMs to be negligible.[10]

Through Figure 10.3, the Coalition for Sensible Housing Policy illustrates the impact of LTV requirement on the probability of default for

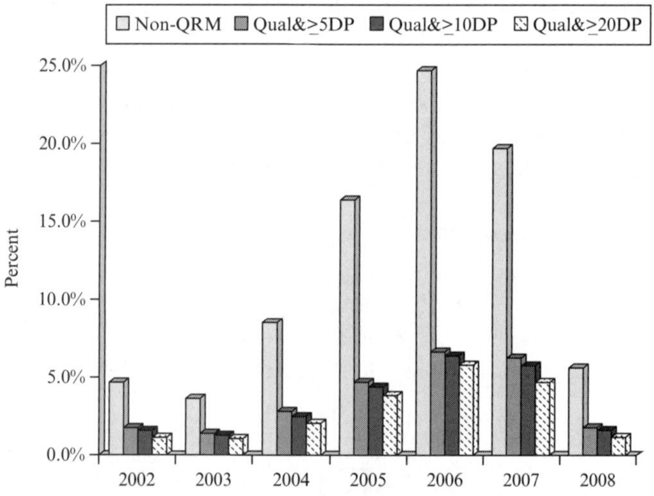

Note: a. The statistics come from Vertical Capital Solutions of New York, an independent valuation and advisory firm that conducted this analysis using loan performance data maintained by First American CoreLogic, Inc. on over 30 million mortgages originated between 2002 and 2008. Default rates are by origination year, through the end of 2010. The sample QRM in this analysis is based on fully documented income and assets; fixed-rate or 7-year or greater ARMs; no negative amortization; no interest only loans; no balloon payments; 41% total debt-to-income ratio; mortgage insurance on loans with 80% or greater LTV ratios; and maturities no greater than 30 years.

Source: Coalition for Sensible Housing Policy[a].

Figure 10.3 Impact of increasing minimum downpayment on default rates for loans that meet sample QRM standards

loans that meet all other QRM standards. Historical loans are divided into four groups: non-QRM loans, loans that meet all other QRM standards and with a 5% down payment, loans that meet all other QRM standards and with a 10% down payment, and loans that meet all QRM standards including the 20% down payment. Figure 10.3 indicates that after controlling all other characteristics of mortgage products, the improvement of loan performance obtained through a prohibitive down payment requirement is quite small. For example, by increasing down payment from 5% to 20% the default rate only decreases from 1.8% to 1.2% for loans originated in 2008.

It is also shown in Figure 10.3 that for loans originated during the massive expansion time of mortgage securitization (year 2004–07), mortgage performance for non-QRM loans is much worse than QRM loans even with only 5% down payment. In the peak of housing market growth (year 2006), non-qualified loans have a default rate of 24.7%, while the qualified loans with 5% down payment have a default rate of 6.6%. The enlargement of default rate gap between qualified and non-qualified loans coincides with the market share expansion of non-conventional mortgage products such as sub-prime and Alt-A (typically with reduced or no documentation verification requirement) loans that carry higher risk. The default rate gap is much lower for loans originated in 2008 as the subprime market disappeared. Compared with conventional loans, subprime mortgage loans tend to have less income documentation and borrowers tend to have a lower credit score, but not necessarily a higher LTV. This again suggests that once the quality of loan is properly controlled through a rigorous underwriting process, for example by validating borrowers' ability to repay their loans, there is limited marginal improvement on the credit risk from further requiring a 20% down payment.

Creditworthy borrowers with limited resource to meet proposed QRM standards will be punished by a higher mortgage interest rate. The new QRM standards, therefore, can restrict credit from being accessible to creditworthy new borrowers and prolong the duration for the market to absorb the huge inventory of foreclosed properties.

The down payment requirement would also deny borrowers' chance to refinance as they do not own enough equity in the property. This is, in spirit, working against the many foreclosure-prevention programs instituted by the Treasury and the HUD that try to help "under-water" homeowners to refinance into lower interest rate loans. The proposed strict QRM standards would increase the cost to these borrowers or exclude them from refinancing.

Reason 2: The proposed QRM standards are against housing finance system reform which is trying to reduce government's involvement in the housing market and encourage private investors' participation

Because of the exemption of FHA, VA and government-backed loans from the QRM requirements, these loans are viewed more favorable by the investors. Therefore, if the QRM standard is too restrictive, the market may continue to depend on the government's support which could delay the recovery of the private mortgage industry.

There is another complicated issue with regard to the risk retention of non-QRM loans. To prevent the interest rate on non-QRMs from rising too much, regulators have introduced a premium capture rule. The rule requires a securitizer to establish a cash reserve account composed of the premium received by the securitizer at issuance. The account is in true first loss position and must remain in place for the entire term of the transaction. Its investment opportunities are highly limited. As a result, lenders may come up with new ways to charge borrowers in cash up-front, or an even higher interest rate, or find other creative ways of mortgage product innovation to circumvent the new rule and compensate themselves for the higher cost. This complication of mortgage securities may increase the difficulties of risk assessment and result in increased reliance of investors on safer and lower cost products, most likely products backed by government. Consequently, the premium capture rule may not be able to prevent the interest rate of non-QRMs from increasing, and it can also further extend the market's dependence on government's support.

Reason 3: An alternative measure can be used to better control loan qualities rather than requiring a low LTV

As shown above, LTV ratio by itself may not have a significant impact on mortgage performance, after controlling for other risk factors. Among all factors related to loan quality, a borrower's credit report has been proven to be one of the most effective measures of loan performance, but is excluded from the QRM standards.

Current market standard for credit reporting is the Three Bureau[11] Merge Report (TBM). Together with automated underwriting processes, the duration for loan approval decreases from days to minutes, and the cost is reduced as well. Before TBM, a more comprehensive method was used in the mortgage industry; the Residential Mortgage Credit Report (RMCR). According to research conducted by the National Credit Reporting Association (NCRA), the RMCR method is more time-consuming but more accurate than TBM.[12] In RMCR, big mortgage institutions reconciled their specific credit guidelines to reach a standard and uniform format across all entities for residential mortgage loans. Procedures in the

RMCR but not in the TBM include removal of all duplicate account listings and addition of any accounts listed in the loan application but not found in the national bureau records. Lack of these extra steps in TBM to treat duplicate and missing records creates significant problems on data accuracy and completeness as concluded by NCRA's study.

Comparing TBM with RMCR, some important issues NCRA find include:

- 30% of the consumer accounts completely missed by the TBM had accounts in RMCRs;
- 35% of the total estimation error rate in the TBM could have been corrected with an RMCR.

Besides the accuracy problem embedded in the TBM method, conflict of interests between lenders and the credit reporting company also raises concern. As lenders profit from higher mortgage interest rates imposed on borrowers, a conflict of interest exists if a credit reporting company is owned by a lender, and generates the credit report for a borrower whose loan is originated by the same lender.

The conflict of interest problem can be solved by prohibiting lenders from owning or investing in a credit report company. But improving the accuracy of credit reporting requires a balance among quality, efficiency and cost. Without sacrificing much efficiency or increasing the cost too much, it is suggested in NCRA's report that a hybrid of TBM and RMCR can be used.[13]

2.3 Lessons for the Emerging Market

As emerging markets are starting to expand mortgage securitization business, it is critical to ensure that lenders have adequate incentive to implement proper loan quality control. Since securitization shifts risk of mortgage portfolios to private investors, future loan performance will have little impact on banks and other originators' profitability, unless originators are required to buy back problematic loans in case of defaults. Predatory lending that lures borrowers into riskier products may arise when originators or their agents try to chase higher returns. Therefore, risk retention and exemption of QRM can be useful to keep lenders' "skin in the game". However, specific measures require great caution. Due to the cultural and legal environment differences, measures that work effectively in one country may be harmful in another country.

In emerging markets, the combined policy of risk retention and proposed QRM standards may not be as tight as it appears in the U.S. For example, the 20% down payment requirement that raised many concerns in the U.S. may not be considered restrictive at all in some emerging markets. Currently, China requires at least 30% down payment for the first house, and 60% for the second. Korea just reduced the LTV ratio of home purchase mortgages in Seoul and other urban areas from 60% to 50% in July 2011, which means a 50% down payment. The regulatory debt ratio in emerging markets may also already be more confining than what is proposed in the U.S. standards. However, further reduction of LTV and debt ratio can still be used to increase the cost of housing finance and reduce demand for housing. This method combined with risk retention rules can be helpful when the housing market becomes over-heated.

As indicated in the literature, there are alternative credit risk indicators that may work more effectively than the LTV ratio. One approach is to improve the credit reporting system. A well-developed credit reporting system requires years of market performance data and sensible statistics for building an accurate credit report. For emerging markets where the data is not readily available, verification of borrowers' income and/or verification of employment for multiple years, similar to some of the practice adopted in the RMCR method, enable more accurate measurement of credit risk. Tax record, balances in bank account and bill payment history of a borrower are also indicators of creditworthiness. In the U.S., some of these data have been adopted for underwriting a borrower with not enough credit history to generate credit scores. Property value must be verified to ensure the adequacy of the collateral. As a standard procedure in emerging markets, recourse clauses can also be included as a way of containing the default risk.

Another lesson we learn from the U.S. experience is that it is very easy for a well-intended policy to result in negative consequences. A combination of many individually plausible rules may end up with an unrealistic or unenforceable policy. Regulatory changes need to be carefully examined and analyzed through fire-drill impact studies to avoid undesired side-effects. The public comment period provided by regulators is a useful mechanism to collect input and insight from as many different points of view as possible.

3. COUNTERCYCLICAL BUFFER

3.1 Concept

Currently the common market practice of static capital regulations is pro-cyclical in nature. When the market is booming, banks tend to have fewer defaults and require lower loss reserve. The reduction in loss reserve account feeds into more available capital, which leads to higher lending capacity. When many banks compete to gain business to utilize the excess capital, they tend to lower underwriting criteria or expand into non-traditional borrower markets. For example, during the housing market boom period between 2003 and 2007, the static capital regulation encouraged lenders to step into subprime lending and relaxed the underwriting verification process. The U.S. government took a passive position in regulation and expected the private market to self-discipline to balance the tradeoff between risk and return. However, what we observed is that the growth of the market continued to accelerate and fueled the build-up of the housing bubble until it finally broke at the end of 2007.

On the other hand, when the market is in recession, an increased number of delinquent loans would require lenders to move capital into loss reserve accounts. This reduces the bank's lending capacity. As the target loan volume decreases, banks can be more selective in borrowers. Thus, banks raise the underwriting standard, making loans harder to obtain. The reduced credit availability and higher underwriting standard cut housing demand, and further compound the decline in market house prices. The GFC brought such an embedded pro-cyclical feature in existing capital regulation to the attention of global financial regulators and started the initiative of moving toward a counter-cyclical framework.

To take into account the macro-financial environment in which banks operate, new risk-based capital rules under design are geared toward a counter-cyclical capital regulation. The new "Basel III: A Global Regulatory Framework for More Resilient Banks and Banking System" has set a general tone for the market. The countercyclical buffer regime of Basel III consists of the following elements:[14]

> National authorities will monitor credit growth and other indicators that may signal a build-up of system-wide risk and make assessments of whether credit growth is excessive and is leading to the build-up of system-wide risk. Based on this assessment they will put in place a countercyclical buffer requirement when circumstances warrant. This requirement will be released when system-wide risk crystallizes or dissipates.
>
> Internationally active banks will look at the geographic location of their private sector credit exposures and calculate their bank specific countercyclical capital buffer requirement as a weighted average of the requirements that are being applied in jurisdictions to which they have credit exposures.
>
> The countercyclical buffer requirement to which a bank is subject will extend the size of the capital conservation buffer. Banks will be subject to restrictions on distributions if they do not meet the requirement.

According to Basel III, each Basel Committee member jurisdiction will identify an authority with the responsibility to make decisions on the size and timing of the countercyclical buffer. Depending on the build-up of the system risk, the size of the buffer can vary between 0 and 2.5% of risk weighted assets. A jurisdiction is required to pre-announce its decision to raise the level of countercyclical buffer up to 12 months, and the decision to decrease the level of buffer will take effect immediately. Basel III also adds a capital conservation buffer of 2.5% to ensure that banks build up capital buffers outside periods of stress which can be drawn down as losses incur.

This buffer regime is countercyclical in that, during the market booming period, internationally active banks will be required to hold extra capital reserves to protect the system from potential future losses due to the build-up of system-risk. The increase of capital ratio also reduces financing resources and slows down the speed of market growth. When the market goes into recession, the extra capital reserve requirement is removed and the extra reserve from the conservation buffer and the countercyclical buffer can be used to cover the loss and improve market liquidity, thus helping the economy to recover.

Table 10.1 illustrates the capital conservation ratios a bank must meet at different levels of the Common Equity Tier 1 capital ratio[15] with both capital reservation buffer and countercyclical buffer. Banks will face further restrictions, by subjecting to a higher capital conservation ratio, if they fall short of the requirement.

The countercyclical regime is scheduled to be phased in with the capital conservation buffer between January 1, 2016 and year end of 2018, and becomes fully effective on January 1, 2019.

Table 10.1 Individual bank minimum capital conservation standards (%)

Common Equity Tier 1 Ratio[a]	Minimum Capital Conservation Ratios
4.5–5.75	100
>5.75–7.0	80
>7.0–8.25	60
>8.25–9.5	40
>9.5	0

Note: a. The common equity tier 1 ratio in this context includes amounts used to meet the 4.5% minimum Common Equity Tier 1 requirement, but excludes any additional Common Equity Tier 1 needed to meet the 6% Tier 1 and 8% Total Capital requirements.

Source: Basel III. A capital reservation buffer of 2.5% and a counter-cyclical buffer of 2.5% are used for the calculation.

3.2 Implementation

The difficulty of implementing a countercyclical capital buffer relates to the determination of market cycle, specifically, how to determine if the market is growing too fast and when credit expansion is excessive so as to trigger a countercyclical buffer. Similarly, how to decide when the market has returned to equilibrium and when the level of countercyclical buffer should be relieved? The timing of these actions is critical to the effectiveness of the countercyclical buffer policy.

A common reference guide based on the aggregate private sector credit-to-GDP gap is proposed in "Guidance for National Authorities Operating the Countercyclical Capital Buffer" (the Guide) by Basel Committee. There are three steps in calculating the jurisdiction specific guide:

Step 1: Calculate the aggregate private sector credit-to-GDP ratio
The definition of credit suggested in the Guide includes all credit extended to households and other non-financial private entities in an economy independent of its form and the identity of the supplier of funds.

The credit-to-GDP ratio in time period t for each country is calculated as:

$$\text{Ratio}_t = \text{Credit}_t \,/\, \text{GDP}_t \times 100\%$$

where GDP_t is domestic GDP and Credit_t is a broad measure of credit to the private, non-financial sector in period t in nominal terms.

Step 2: Calculate the credit-to-GDP gap

$$\text{Gap}_t = \text{Ratio}_t - \text{Trend}_t$$

where Trend_t is an approximation of credit-to-GDP that is believed to be sustainable based on historical experience. The Guide suggested a Hodrick-Prescott filter, which is a common practice in macroeconomics.[16]

Step 3: Transform the credit-to-GDP gap into the guide buffer add-on
Two thresholds (L and H) need to be determined so that when Gap_t is below L, the buffer add-on is set to zero, and when Gap_t is above H, then the buffer is set to the maximum level, denoted by VB. Between L and H, the buffer add-on varies linearly between 0% and VB. The challenge here is to set the thresholds properly. The Guide recommends L=2 and H=10.[17]

U.S. and Korea from the Guide have been selected to show the implied buffer add-on based on the above methods using historical data in Figure 10.4. The credit-to-GDP approach appears to fit reasonably well to

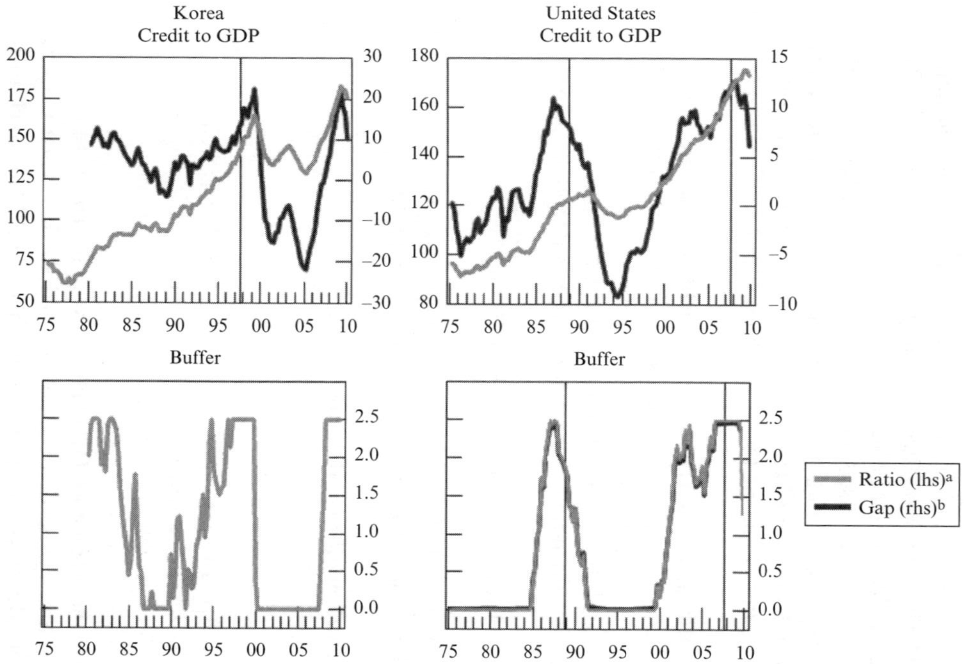

Notes:
1.Broad credit to GDP, in percent.
2. Deviations of the credit-to-GDP ratio from its long term trend, calculated by a one-sided HP filter using a smoothing factor l=400,000, in percentage points.

Source: Guidance for National Authorities Operating the Countercyclical Capital Buffer.

Figure 10.4 Historical performance of the guide

market cycles according to its historical performance. If the countercyclical buffer had been applied, the capital requirement add-on would start to build up from the year 2000 and reach the maximum in year 2007 for the U.S. Thus, the capital requirement would have increased during market boom. The buffer would have started to decrease in 2009 to facilitate market recovery. For Korea, the countercyclical buffer calculation captures the market expansion in the 1990s, and the next episode of market expansion did not happen until 2008 based on the credit-to-GDP criteria. The buffer add-on should have been moved to its maximum level in 2008 according to the credit-to-GDP standard. This is consistent with the tightening policies that Korea has been adopting in recent years.

It is not likely that the Guide would work well in all jurisdictions at all times. Therefore, it is important that no matter what criterion is used to trigger the countercyclical buffer, the essential objective should be met, i.e., to protect the banking system against potential future losses caused by excess credit growth and system-wide risk increase. Specific rules of setting the buffer add-on can be determined by individual jurisdictions, but the decisions need to be explained and the criteria need to be consistent with the build-up of system risk.

3.3 Cyclical Regulatory Practice in the U.S. after the GFC

Authorities in the U.S. have made various regulatory changes to minimize the losses from the housing market crash and prevent the system from creating another market failure in the future. Some of the measures are consistent with the countercyclical concept, while others are still pro-cyclical.

Lenders have been tightening their underwriting standards since the housing bubble burst. While improving the loan quality itself is a key component of establishing a sustainable and healthy housing market, to start tightening the credit market during the recession may not be the right timing. Housing demand has fallen to a historically low level since many borrowers are already in distress because of unemployment or other reasons, and may have lost most wealth in their previously purchased housing. Imposing a tighter underwriting standard during this period would further restrict borrowers' access to credit and hurt housing demand, thus further amplifying the magnitude of the housing recession. Likewise, the over-restrictive QRM standards proposed by regulators also stand in the way of market recovery as explained in the previous section.

Various actions taken by the HUD are also perceived to be pro-cyclical. Despite the fact that housing market recovery is slow and the U.S. economy is facing a potential "double-dip" recession, the U.S. housing regulators took several initiatives to tighten the FHA program.

For example, following the private mortgage insurance companies and the GSEs, FHA has imposed a minimum credit score requirement of 500 on loans originated on or after October 2010.[18] Borrowers with a decision credit score between 500 and 579 are limited to 90% LTV. FHA also increased the annual insurance premium for the first time in 40 years from 50 basis points to 85 basis points on mortgages with more than 5% down payments originated on or after October 4, 2010.[19] The annual insurance premium was adjusted upward again to 110 basis points for loans originated after April 2011.[20] The most recent development on the FHA insurance portfolio is the termination of temporary maximum loan limit increase introduced in 2008.[21] The new "ceiling" loan limit for higher cost areas is reduced from $729,750 to $625,500 for one-unit properties[22] These pro-cyclical rules aimed at improving FHA's capital condition to avoid potential risk. However, these tightening policies may destabilize the already weakened housing market if the private market is not ready to serve the market in full capacity.

The Federal Reserve Bank Board of the United States (the Fed), however, is geared toward a countercyclical policy rule. Several credit and liquidity programs were used to provide liquidity directly to borrowers and investors in key credit markets. As market condition improved, some programs were wound down, such as the Term Auction Facility and the Asset Backed Commercial Paper Money Market Mutual Fund Liquidity Facility. Other programs such as Term Asset-backed Securities Loan Facility (TALF) and Term Deposit Facility are still active. Under these facility programs, the Fed lends to holders of qualified securities on a non-recourse basis, using qualified assets as collateral. Borrowers who use these facility programs will be under more strict oversight. The purpose of the Fed liquidity facility programs is to spur consumer credit lending when financial institutions are tied up by the bad assets in their portfolio due to the decreased value of the asset-backed securities and other high credit risk securities issued prior to the GFC. By increasing credit availability and supporting economic activities, the Fed expects financial institutions to pay back their loans when the economy recovers.

A similar policy instrument was used by the U.S. Treasury starting from year 2008—the Troubled Asset Relief Program (TARP). "Troubled Assets" defined in TARP cover a wider range than qualified assets defined by the Fed. They include mortgage, mortgage backed securities and any instruments the purchase of which can promote market stability. TARP expired in October 2010. According to "TARP: Three Year Anniversary Report", of the $413 billion disbursed, $314 billion has been paid back as of August 31, 2011, which represents more than 75% of the investment. The government is expected to recover more funds at a faster speed as shown in the report.[23]

In 2011, the Fed rolled out a new plan to reduce borrowing cost as the market became a little immune to its quantitative easing policy. The new policy announced after the September 2011 Board Meeting is for the Fed to invest in long-term Treasury securities using the money raised from selling the short-term federal debts. The so-called "Twist Policy" tries to stimulate long term investment. Yields of long term bonds as well as the mortgage rate decreased after the policy announcement.

3.4 Other International Regulatory Practice

In September 2011, the Financial Stability Board announced a list of 28 banks that are considered as global systematically important financial institutions (G-SIFI), and will require additional loss absorbency capacity for these G-SIFIs according to the "bucket" they are assigned to.[24]

The list of G-SIFIs is constructed based on a score calculated on five categories of systemic importance: cross-jurisdictional activity, size, interconnectedness, substitutability, and complexity. Each category is normalized to a score of 1 so that the maximum possible total score is 5. The cut-off point for a G-SIFI is set between the 27th and 28th banks in 2011 based on the clustering of the indicator scores. One bank is added in due to supervisory judgment. G-SIFIs are allocated to five buckets based on the score. The proposed buckets are equal sized to ensure the consistency of standards over time. The magnitude of additional loss absorbency depends on a G-SIFI's bucket as illustrated in Table 10.2. For example, a bank whose score is between C and D will be required to hold an extra 2.5% capital reserve. The loss-absorbing capital will be effective in 2016.

Even though this new capital rule is a more general regulation to

Table 10.2 Bucketing approach

Bucket	Score range*	Minimum additional loss absorbency (common equity as a percentage of risk-weighted assets) (%)
5 (empty)	D	3.5
4	C–D	2.5
3	B–C	2.0
2	A–B	1.5
1	Cut-off point –A	1.0

Note: *Scores equal to one of the boundaries are assigned to the higher bucket.

Source: Basel Committee "Global Systemically Important Banks: Assessment Methodology and the Additional Loss Absorbency Requirement".

address the systemic and moral hazard risks associated with G-SIFIs, it is still related to the countercyclical capital buffer stated in Basel III. The cross-jurisdictional activity, size, and complexity of a financial institution depend on its own expansion as well as the economic condition. When a specific country is experiencing rapid market growth, more financial institutions from that country may be considered as G-SIFI and subject to the extra capital reserve ratio.

3.5 Implications for the Emerging Markets

So far we have discussed different countercyclical policies that may be implemented to stabilize the financial system. The capital buffer rule of Basel III requires a careful judgment from the regulator on when to pull the policy trigger and when to call it off. Given the long effect lag of monetary policy and the time needed for banks to raise extra capital, it is necessary for regulators' action to lead the cycle. Otherwise, the policy will be "fighting the last battle". The suggested criteria of credit-to-GDP ratio may not work well for all circumstances. Therefore emerging markets need to determine their own standards and justify the rationale behind their choices.

There are other methods that can tighten the financial system when the market growth is over-heated and relax constraint when the market is in recession. Liquidity provided by the U.S. government and the Fed during the recession helped to stimulate credit lending, facilitate spending and clear housing market faster. The FHA's losing market share during the subprime period and gaining market share after the GFC obviously provided a counter-cyclical balance in the U.S. housing market. Risk retention and tight QRM standards would also be more useful if applied before the build-up of the housing bubble, but they may lead to negative effects during a recession when the market needs more impetus. Korea has been using LTV ratio actively as a countercyclical instrument since 2002. The Korean financial supervisory authority reduced LTV ratio in 2002, 2006 and 2009 to prevent mortgage lending from getting over-heated. It also raised LTV ratio in 2008 to provide relief to home buyers. China has also used LTV ratio together with other policies to tame its housing market. Property price started to decline in August 2011 among major cities in China, and continued to do so for September and October.

Regardless of which specific measure each country adopts, the principle is to establish a financial system that is stable and resilient so that growth can be sustainable.

4. MARKET RISK SHARING

Over the years, new products, institutions and regulators have been created in the housing industry that lead to different risk sharing among lenders, borrowers and government. Proper risk management and risk sharing among these market participants is also a key issue that is being explored to ensure a healthy and sustainable housing finance system.

4.1 Risk Sharing in the Private Sector

Risk sharing of mortgage risk among participants in the private sector involves lenders, borrowers, private investors and private mortgage insurance companies.

Lenders share mortgage risks with borrowers by offering products with various payment schemes. Differently from most other countries, the dominant form of mortgage product in the U.S. is the 30-year fixed rate loan (FRM). Banks suffered tremendously during the late 1970s and early 1980s when interest rates skyrocketed. During the fast rising interest rate period, banks' cost of finance increased but the interest income from FRM loans remained low. A matured financial system and innovation of financial derivatives allowed banks to control their interest rate risk through hedging with interest rate derivatives such as interest rate futures, swaps, and swaptions. But for a less developed fixed income market, especially the emerging market, there was no such option. Due to the difficulty of managing interest rate risk, banks in those markets tend to transfer interest rate risk to the borrowers in the form of adjustable rate mortgages (ARMs). Currently, ARMs remain the dominant mortgage product in many countries such as Australia and Korea as shown in Figure 10.5.

By allowing lenders to readjust the mortgage rate on a periodical schedule, the risk of loss incurred by future interest rate increase is transferred to borrowers. On the other hand, the decrease of interest risk is accompanied by the increase of credit risk. Future interest rate changes introduce payment shocks to borrowers as the monthly payments increase with the mortgage rate. Therefore ARM loans require even more scrutiny during the underwriting process. Lenders must evaluate the capacity of borrowers' future income to afford potential mortgage rate increase. More restrictive payment to income (PTI) or debt to income (DTI) ratios may be used to reduce credit risk. Other mortgage product innovations producing similar effects of risk sharing between lenders and borrowers are essentially an allocation of risk to the party that is most capable of absorbing or managing the specific risk elements as well.

Lenders also share the risk of mortgage with private investors through

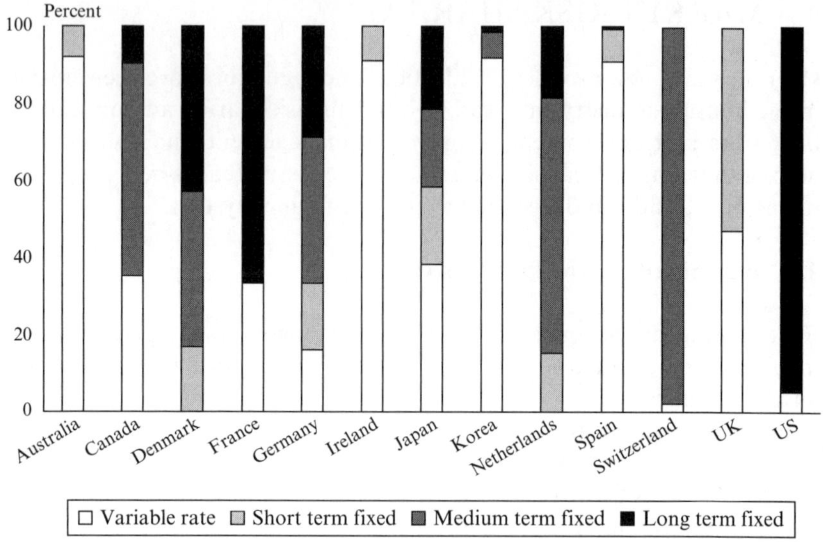

Note: Market shares by interest rate type for selected countries as of 2009.

Source: Michael Lea (2010).

Figure 10.5 Mortgage product by interest rate variability

securitization in the secondary market. In the extreme case where a lender sells all its mortgages to the secondary market, it becomes a pure loan originator. Its profit depends on the mortgage origination process but not on the subsequent performance of the loan. Thus securitization gives rise to the agency problem. As discussed in Section 2, risk retention aligns lender's incentive with the eventual investor and helps assure the quality of mortgage underwriting. The creation of the Office of Credit Rating under the U.S. SEC targets at solving problems with the credit reporting rating industry. For emerging markets, a more demanding regulation may be needed to ensure accuracy and efficiency in credit scoring and reporting. High-quality mortgages help build investors' confidence in the housing market and reduce the borrowing cost.

Lenders use mortgage insurance to transfer credit risks to insurance companies as well. Insurance companies can be either private or public. They usually cover a certain percentage of loss in the event of loan default. In exchange, lenders need to pay an up-front premium as well as annual premiums. Mortgage insurance helps lenders manage credit risks, but also complicates the risk measurement. It is important to understand that mortgage with an insurance is not risk free for the lender. First, insurance only covers part of the loss. If the loss given default exceeds the amount covered by the insurance policy, the lender will have to bear the remaining loss. Second, insurance companies, especially private ones, may not be able to fulfill their obligation if the economic condition deteriorates too much. Therefore, credit risk management requires sophisticated modeling to properly measure the true level of protection from mortgage insurance.

4.2 Risk Sharing between Private Sector and the Government

Government housing agencies around the world that were originally created to provide inexpensive credit to low and moderate income borrowers have evolved to be much more powerful in housing finance systems. For example, during the subprime expanding years, FHA's market share of home purchase activity shrunk from a historical average of 10–15% to less than 4% in 2006. After the GFC, its market share jumped to nearly 20% by the end of year 2010, as a result of the drying up of the private market during the credit crunch and the temporary increase of FHA's loan size limit.[25] The GSEs are central players of securitization of mortgage products in the U.S. They enjoy a favorable capital reserve requirement, which gives them an advantage in lowering financing cost over private investors. Moreover, loans guaranteed by GSEs have been set as the benchmark for QRMs, and thus are exempted from the risk retention rule stated in the Dodd-Frank Act. Canada Mortgage and Housing Corporation (CMHC) and Korea Housing Finance Corporation (KHFC) are hybrid versions of FHA and GSEs in Canada and Korea. KHFC started with the loan insurance function but has gradually expanded into the securitization business. Both entities have significant influence in their housing finance industries.

The increasing involvement of government agencies introduced the possibility of risk sharing between the private sector and the government. The insurance premium paid to the government entitles lenders to file claims in the event of mortgage default, and shifts credit risk from lenders to the government. As a government expands the range of loans it insures or guarantees, more risk will be transferred from lenders to the government. Securitization by government agencies and holding of MBS in their own portfolio also generates the risk sharing between lenders and government. Agency problems arise among private sector participants as a result of risk shifting. Moreover, too much government support for housing finance could hurt the development of a robust private market.

Nevertheless, a successful reform takes more than winding down GSEs and other government support to the housing market. A report to Congress by the U.S. Department of HUD lists several steps to reform the U.S. housing market.[26] The first preparation includes reducing GSEs' role in the market in a responsible timeline, returning FHA to its traditional role of promoting affordable mortgages, and ensuring support for small and medium-sized financial institutions. Currently, HUD is weighing a risk-sharing proposal to sell part of GSE's MBS holdings to the private market. The new plan works by trenching a pool of securities into different risk categories. The trenches sold to the private market will no longer carry a government guarantee but may have a higher expected yield. The objective is to allow government and private partnership and allocate different layers of credit risk to the party most suitable to take them.

Another key part of the proposal is to restore trust and integrity in the broader housing market. To help borrowers avoid predatory lending practice and make fully informed decisions, the Bureau of Consumer Financial Protection (CFPB) was created by the Dodd-Frank Act. Lenders are prohibited from abusive practices that lure borrowers to high-cost loans. Clear and consistent rules will be proposed by CFPB to promote choice and clarity, and lenders will be required to improve underwriting procedure and verify borrowers' ability to repay.

Risk retention and QRM are used to increase the accountability of securitization. Meanwhile, SEC is in the process of setting stricter disclosure and reporting requirements for the transparency of information. An Office of Credit Ratings will be established by SEC to strengthen rating agencies' reliability. Regulatory oversight will be strengthened together with the mortgage servicing and foreclosure operational risk management requirements.

In short, a responsible and responsive regulatory environment is necessary to restore investors' confidence in the housing market. Usually, this can only be achieved by strong support from the government.

As emerging markets are shaping the structure of their housing finance systems, it is important to ensure that the private sector, particularly the risk underwriters, retains enough risk to align the incentive of assuring loan quality. It is equally important that regulatory agencies establish a healthy private market with enough support from the government to promote affordable housing finance to qualified households otherwise unable to access credit. The balance of risk sharing between lenders and the government would allow the government to make the most impact and serve the most borrowers with limited resources.

In conclusion, risk sharing is quite pervasive in housing finance. The chain of mortgage origination, insurance and securitization links lenders, borrowers, government and investors together. After the GFC, numerous regulatory changes have been made in the U.S. to restore the system and re-establish each party's role in the risk-sharing chain. However, most of these new regulations/policies are still in their early implementation stage.

The eventual effectiveness is yet to be scrutinized. Emerging market governments should conduct careful due diligence studies of their own market conditions before adopting any of these regulations.

5. CONCLUSIONS AND IMPLICATIONS

Four years after the housing market crash that almost brought down the entire world economy, countries are still struggling to recover from the damage. Countless efforts have been made to improve and restructure the housing finance system by developed markets, but problems still exist. As the current GFC is still on going, it is difficult to conclude which policy has worked and which has not. However, the impact to date of these various policies does shed light for emerging markets with respect to some principles in establishing or assuring a robust housing finance market. Based on worldwide housing finance experience, especially the GFC, several lessons have direct implications for emerging markets.

5.1 Sustainability is as Important as Affordability and Home Ownership Rate

Claiming to help households to afford mortgages and become home owners, the subprime mortgage industry relaxed or voided one or more of the underwriting limits that control for loan quality. However, as the traditional credit risk measurements projected, default rates of these loans skyrocketed after the housing bubble burst. Deviation away from the wisdom of credit risk underwriting process has caused great losses in the GFC to all participants in housing related markets including lenders, private investors, the government, and borrowers. Therefore, governments who try to promote homeownership need to work out policies that balance both affordability and sustainability of housing. If loans are originated to increase homeownership in the short run but borrowers' repayment ability is not guaranteed, borrowers' welfare will be hurt in the long run when they have to default on their loans.

However, the best credit risk measurement system is only as good as the quality of data fed into the system. It is extremely important to enforce solid quality control processes during loan underwriting. A robust quality control process can ensure that the borrower indeed has a stable income and wealth to pay back the loan as presented in the application. The lesson we learnt from GFC is that precariously speeding up the loan approval process just to gain efficiency or reduce cost can motivate both moral hazards and agency problems in the lending industry.

Emerging markets without a developed credit reporting system should still try to establish a standard and uniform format across all entities for residential mortgage loans. The old "character" method of the "3 Cs" standards should still be used, until credit and payment history databases in emerging markets have enough observations to construct credit scores that summarize borrowers' previous relationship with lenders and reflect borrowers' creditworthiness. Lenders in emerging markets need to make more effort than those in developed markets to validate borrowers' income, wealth and collateral value. Prior payment history should be collected as much as possible to verify a borrower's credit or willingness to pay. Emerging markets must be careful in adopting an automated underwriting system and should wait until their credit-reporting system is mature.

The U.S. experience showed that without the assurance of sustainability, mortgages can cause substantial loss to the households, the lenders, the capital market, and the government. It is extremely important to consider the potential downside risk prior to initiating any programs to promote housing affordability or to increase home ownership rate.

5.2 Accurate Understanding and Segment of Credit Risk is Crucial to a Stable Housing Finance System

One of the major elements that led to the GFC is the market failure to properly measure credit risks associated with mortgage backed securities. Over the years, as MBS structures became increasingly more complicated and their information more opaque, market participants, including some large institutions and private investors, formed a reliance on rating agencies to understand credit risks. This led to a substantial concentration of systematic risk. When rating agencies underestimated risks of MBS products, the world economy went down together when the housing bubble burst. The lesson we learned is that over-reliance on rating agencies can create great risk to the financial system since mistakes made by one institution will affect a vast majority of entities in the capital market. It is critical for any market players to clearly understand the assumptions and rationales used by individual rating agencies in deriving their rating opinions. Without such clear understanding, the rating opinion may be misinterpreted to support important investment or risk management decisions.

For emerging markets that are designing new mortgage products and MBS, regulators need to promote clarity and transparency of product disclosure, so that market participants can truly understand the risks they are taking. Not only should borrowers understand the mortgage product they use, lenders also need to realize the tradeoff of interest rate risk and credit risk as they use more ARMs or ARM like mortgages. Risk sharing and credit tranching in structured CMO and REMICs can dramatically change the risk profile. It is inadequate to exclusively depend on the opinions of other parties such as the rating agencies, especially when there is a lack of clear understanding of the assumptions and limitations of those opinions.

It is also important to understand that even with a proper rating system and a well-developed mortgage insurance industry, market participants can still bear certain risks. For example, as we discussed earlier, in the U.S. all private mortgage insurance companies are required to have a credit rating of AA or above. For insurance companies with an AA credit rating, the maximum level of stress these companies can sustain is an AA stress scenario. Insurance companies will not be able to meet their commitment under a more stressful economic condition. As a result, investors protected by the mortgage insurance policy of an AA rated insurance company should expect to recover only part of the coverage when facing the most difficult market environment. This gives rise to the need to consider "haircuts" in the capital substitution when using private mortgage insurances.

Moreover, as the highest credit rating is an AAA rating, which denotes the lowest expectation of default risk, it still implies a certain degree of risk, no matter how small it is. No private institution will be able to undertake the risk beyond an AAA stress scenario. Therefore, the government is the only entity capable to take on credit risk above an AAA stress test scenario.

To summarize, for emerging markets to build a risk resilient housing finance system, market investors need to understand credit risks related to structured MBS and conduct their own credit risk analysis, including PD, LGD and the risk drivers, instead of completely relying on rating agencies. Investors should also realize that a certain degree of risk remains even with the presence of a mortgage insurance company behind the underlying mortgages. The government is the eventual risk protection to the system in case the worst economic condition occurs. On the other hand, private institutions may be more efficient in taking and managing risks during the normal economic environment.

5.3 Responsive Capital Regulations can Improve Sustainability of Market Growth

Responsive capital regulations need to be able to accurately reflect the level of credit risk in an institution's portfolio holding to ensure its solvency. The newest development of the risk-based capital rules put a high priority on the counter-cyclical feature intended to offset the systematic risk induced by economic cycle.

Under the newly proposed rules, when a market is expanding and systematic risk is building up, an extra capital buffer needs to be set aside to contain a bank's lending activities. This action would put a brake on the economic expansion and slow down the build-up of the housing bubble. The extra capital buffer also builds a cushion for potential future loss in case of bubble burst.

Not all measures taken by developed countries after the GFC are geared toward a countercyclical policy rule, such as those used by the GSEs and the FHA that tighten underwriting requirements and increase mortgage insurance premiums. As these policies impose more constraint on housing finance during a weak market recovery, demand would be further depressed. With the backlog of foreclosed property piling up, it will take longer for the housing market to clear off. These pro-cyclical policies are natural consequences of the traditional capital regulations and pressure from Congress to reduce the magnitude of the government bailout. Alternatively, the government could consider providing certain relief programs similar to those used by the Fed to give the market more impetus to recover. Of course, the market easing policies must not be taken too far as they may lead to inflation and create other moral hazard problems. The countercyclical LTV rule adopted by Korea and the capital standard imposed by China appear to be consistent with the new trend. When used in combination with a countercyclical capital buffer, they can be effective in reducing the volatility of economic cycles.

Another aspect of responsive capital rules is related to credit risk assessment. Supervisory authorities among different industries need to be consistent and integrated to avoid cross industry capital arbitrage. Capital arbitrage can occur as a result of inconsistent capital requirements with regard to the same mortgage product when the credit risk is held by entities in different industries or with different credit ratings.

We can use the U.S. example to illustrate this problem. According to the Notice of Proposed Rule Implementing the Basel II Standardized Risk-Based Capital Framework, special provisions are required for residential mortgage with PMI coverage to reflect the risk mitigating effects. A bank can reduce the loan exposure up to the amount covered by loan-level PMI, and therefore is allowed to hold less capital. The rule does not differentiate between mortgage insurance companies with AA or AAA rating. However, as we discussed earlier, mortgage insurance companies can only protect credit loss up to a level that is consistent with their rating. In a catastrophic event, insurance companies will not be able to fulfill their commitments. If mortgages are insured by an AA rating insurance company, the protection is up to AA rating stress level. Because Basel II targets 99.9th percentile protection, which is more restrictive than the AA rating standard, the deductibility of insured loan exposure takes a heavier haircut to reflect the embedded counterparty risk.

Another more general form of capital arbitrage pervasive in the mortgage industry arises from the difference of capital requirement among industries including banks, GSEs, private mortgage insurance companies, and government agencies. Under traditional Basel I, banks have a required capital ratio of 8%. For QRMs, this ratio is reduced to 4%. The requirement is further reduced to 1.6% if the holding is in the form of QRM based-MBS. GSEs' minimal capital requirement imposed by Congress is 2.5% for whole loans and 0.45% for guarantees. Private mortgage insurance companies are regulated by individual states and face a different set of capital requirement rules. Due to the different standards imposed by supervisors among different industries, participants in the mortgage industry tend to push the risk into the particular entities with the lowest capital requirement. For example, if a bank swaps a pool of QRM qualified whole loans with a GSE in exchange for MBS, the combined required capital reserve on this pool of mortgage products will be 0.45% by the GSE and 1.6% by the bank. These required capital ratios are much lower than the 4% capital requirement when the bank holds these whole loans in portfolio. The bank can also sell these mortgages to the GSE without receiving MBS. Under such a scenario these loans will be protected by the GSE's 2.5% capital requirement. To avoid such inter-industry capital arbitrage, regulators among different industries must coordinate their capital regulations to ensure their consistency. Otherwise, capital arbitrage would lead the total capital reserved for the particular risk to be lower than every regulator's expectation and increase the risk for government bailout when extreme conditions occur in the future.

5.4 Clear Policy Goals Need to be Set by the Government

After the GFC, we observe multiple new policies introduced by the U.S. government. Some of these policies may provide different, sometimes conflicting, effects. For example, FHA's initial role was to provide housing finance to low and moderate income families and help first time homebuyers to achieve homeownership. As a social welfare program, one would expect the FHA program to incur cost to the government. After the GFC, the government's role gradually expanded into higher value housing markets by raising its loan size limit, with the intention of providing loss mitigation solutions to more distressed mortgages on the market. Later on, when FHA's capital reserve fell below the Congress mandate, the government shifted its focus to quickly rebuild FHA's capital to reach the long term target level. This shift of focus led to various pro-cyclical policies, including tightening underwriting rules and increasing insurance premiums. These actions result in lower housing finance supplied by the FHA during the most severe housing recession since the Great Depression. If the FHA successfully restores the capital back to the targeted 2% level, then it implies that FHA is making profit even during an AAA equivalent stress environment, while all private mortgage lenders/insurers are losing money. This is equivalent to saying that the FHA program may be making more profit than the private market entities. In essence, it may no longer be a subsidy program.

As emerging markets consider the establishment of their own housing finance agencies, they need to set clear and consistent policy goals. For example, whether they want to provide public subsidy or whether they want to pursue financial profits. Once the policy goals are established, the government needs to ensure the goals do not change with respect to short term situations. Although it may sometimes cause financial difficulties to the government in the short run, maintaining credible and consistent policy goals can provide the market confidence and ensure market stability in the long run.

NOTES

1. CMOs and CDOs are the most popular forms of credit tranched mortgage backed securities.
2. Dodd-Frank Act Sec 941.
3. http://www.fdic.gov/news/board/29Marchno2.pdf
4. FHFA "Mortgage Market Note 11–02", http://www.fhfa.gov/webfiles/20686/QRM_FINAL_ALL_R41111.pdf
5. "Proposed Qualified Residential Mortgage Definition Harms Creditworthy Borrowers While Frustrating Housing Recovery", Coalition for Sensible Housing Policy, August, 2011.
6. For example, a study published by the United States Government Accountability Office claims that "interest rates on the non-QRM loans would likely be only moderately higher than those for QRMs". (http://www.gao.gov/new.items/d11656.pdf)
7. "Reworking Risk Retention", Mark Zandi and Cristian deRitis.
8. "QRM: Higher Mortgage Rates on the Horizon", Ken Fears. 2011.
9. Glaeser and Shapiro 2002.
10. The Coalition for Sensible Housing Policy is a broad alliance including realtors, mortgage lenders, civil rights groups, consumer advocates and others formed to campaign for changes to the proposed rules. The study can be found at http://www.sensiblehousingpolicy.org/White_Paper.html
11. TransUnion, Equifax and Exprian.
12. "The Impact of the Qualified Residential Mortgage Requirements on the Housing Industry and an Alternative Approach for Quality Lending Standards", National Credit Reporting Association, Inc. 2011.
13. The new method uses TBM as a starting point. If the report generates a score that qualifies a borrower for the best interest rate, then the lender proceeds with the automated underwriting process. If not, the lender should compare this borrower's credit scores from three credit bureaus. If the difference of credit scores is smaller than a certain number, for example 25 points, then the lender proceeds with the automated underwriting process. However, if scores differ by more than 25 points, then the lender should require additional credit analysis similar to the RMCR procedure prior to approval.

14. "Basel III: A Global Regulatory Framework for More Resilient Banks and Banking System", Basel Committee on Banking Supervision.
15. The common equity tier 1 ratio is a measurement of a bank's core equity capital compared with its risk-based assets. The common equity tier 1 includes: common shares issued by the bank that meet certain criteria, stock surplus, retained earnings accumulated, other comprehensive income and other disclosed reserves, and common shares issued by consolidated subsidiaries.
16. Hodrick and Prescott (1997).
17. The Section 2. c) of the Guide provides a discussion of analysis regarding the level of L and H.
18. Mortgagee Letter 10–29, HUD.
19. Mortgagee Letter 10–28, HUD.
20. Mortgagee Letter 11–10, HUD.
21. Mortgagee Letter 11–29, HUD.
22. In November 2011, Congress increased the ceiling on size of mortgages that can be guaranteed by FHA back to $729,750. The limits for GSEs were not restored.
23. "Troubled Asset Relief Program: Three Year Anniversary Report", U.S. Department of Treasury, Office of Financial Stability, 2011.
24. Global Systemically Important Banks: Assessment Methodology and the Additional Loss Absorbency Requirement, Basel Committee 2011.
25. Statistics are from http://portal.hud.gov/hudportal/documents/huddoc?id=fhamkt0611.pdf.
26. "Reforming America's Housing Finance Market" 2011, U.S. Department of Treasury and HUD.

BIBLIOGRAPHY

Ambrose, Brent W., and Charles A. Capone, Jr. 2000. The hazard rates of first and second default. *The Journal of Real Estate Finance and Economics* 20 (3): 275–293.

Ambrose, Brent W., and Michael LaCour-Little. 2001. Prepayment risk in adjustable rate mortgages subject to initial year discounts: some new evidence. *Real Estate Economics* 29 (2): 305–328.

Ambrose, Brent W., Richard J. Buttimer, Jr., and Charles A. Capone. 1997. Pricing mortgage default and foreclosure delay. *Journal of Money, Credit and Banking* 29 (3): 314–325.

Ambrose, Brent, Henry Cassidy and Tyler T. Yang. 2007. The Measurement and Management of Mortgage Credit Risk in the United States: Implications for Emerging Mortgage Markets. HUD USER Economic Development Publications Series #39147

Basel Committee on Banking Supervision. 2006. International Convergence of Capital Measurement and Capital Standards.

Basel Committee on Banking Supervision. 2011. Basel III: A Global Regulatory Framework for More Resilient Banks and Banking System.

Basel Committee on Banking Supervision. 2011. Guidance for National Authorities Operating the Countercyclical Capital Buffer.

Calem, P.S., LaCour-Little, M., 2004. Risk-based capital requirements for mortgage loans. *J. Banking Finance* 28(3): 647–672.

Capone Jr., C.A. 2000. Credit risk, capital, and Federal Housing Administration mortgage insurance. *Journal of Housing Research* 11(2): 373–401.

Clapp, John M., Yongheng Deng, and Xudong An. 2006. Unobserved heterogeneity in models of competing mortgage termination risk. *Real Estate Economics* 34 (2): 243–274.

Coalition for Sensible Housing Policy. 2011. Proposed Qualified Residential Mortgage Definition Harms Creditworthy Borrowers While Frustrating Housing Recovery. http://www.sensiblehousingpolicy. org/White_Paper.html

Deng, Yongheng. 1996. Mortgage Default and Low Downpayment loans: The costs of public subsidy. *Regional Science and Urban Economics* 26: 263–285.

Deng, Yongheng. 1997. Mortgage termination: An empirical hazard model with a stochastic term structure. *Journal of Real Estate Finance and Economics* 14 (3): 310–331.

Deng, Yongheng, John Quigley, and Robert Van Order. 2000. Mortgage terminations, heterogeneity and the exercise of mortgage options. *Econometrica* 68 (2): 275–307.

Dodd-Frank Wall Street Reform and Consumer Protection Act. 2010.

Elmer, Peter, and Steve Seelip. 1999. Insolvency, trigger events, and consumer risk posture in the theory of single-family mortgage default. *Journal of Housing Research* 10 (1): 1–25.

Fears, Ken. 2011. QRM: Higher Mortgage Rates on the Horizon.

Federal Housing Finance Agency. 2011. Mortgage Market Note 11–02. Qualified Residential Mortgage http://www.fhfa.gov/webfiles/20686/QRM_FINAL_ALL_R41111.pdf

Glaeser, Edward and Jesse Shapiro. 2002. The Benefits of the Home Mortgage Interest Deduction. NBER Working Paper No. 9284.

Government Accountability Office. 2011. *Mortgage Reform: Potential Impacts of Provisions in the Dodd-Frank Act on Homebuyers and the Mortgage Market*. Report to Congressional Committees, July (GAO-11–656).

Green, Jerry, and John B. Shoven. 1986. The effects of interest rates on mortgage prepayments. *Journal of Money, Credit, and Banking* 18(1): 41–50.

Hancock, D., A. Lehnert, W. Passmore, and S.M. Sherlund. An Analysis of the Potential Competitive Impacts of Basel II Capital Standards on US Mortgage Rates and Mortgage Securitization. Board of Governors of the Federal Reserve System working paper. (http://www.federalreserve.gov/ generalinfo/Basel2/docs 2005/potentialimpact.pdf).

Hodrick, Robert, and Edward Prescott. 1997. Postwar U.S. Business Cycles: An Empirical Investigation. *Journal of Money, Credit, and Banking* 29(1): 1–16.

Integrated Financial Engineering. 2011. Actuarial Review of the Federal Housing Administration Mutual Mortgage Insurance Fund Forward Loans for Fiscal Year 2011.

Lea, Michael. 2010. International Comparison of Mortgage Product Offerings.

Mortgage Insurance Companies of America (MICA), *Letter dated November 3, 2003 to the Board of Governors of the Federal Reserve System regarding Docket No. 03–14, Risk-Based Capital Guidelines; Implementation of New Basel Capital Accord* (http://www.federalreserve.gov/SECRS/2003/November/20031105/R-1154/R-1154_18_1.pdf)

National Credit Reporting Association, Inc. 2011. The Impact of the Qualified Residential Mortgage Requirements on the Housing Industry and an Alternative Approach for Quality Lending Standards. http://www.sec.gov/comments/s7-14-11/s71411-255.pdf

Notice of Proposed Rulemaking to Implement Section 941 of the Dodd-Frank

Wall Street Reform and Consumer Protection Act (Credit Risk Retention). 2011. (http://www.fdic.gov/regulations/ laws/federal/2011/11proposedAD74.pdf)

OFHEO Regulations (February 2003) Part 1750 – Capital (http://www.ofheo.gov/Media/ pdf/mincap.pdf)

Pennington-Cross, Anthony. 2003. Credit History and the Performance of Prime and Nonprime Mortgages, *Journal of Real Estate Finance and Economics* 27(3) 279–302.

Pennington-Cross, Anthony and Michelle Danis. 2005. A Dynamic Look at Subprime Loan Performance, with Michelle Danis. *Journal of Fixed Income*, 15(1) 28–39.

U.S. Department of Housing and Urban Development (9/1/2010). Mortgagee Letter 2010–28. Changes to FHA Mortgage Insurance Premiums. Washington, D.C.

U.S. Department of Housing and Urban Development (9/3/2010). Mortgagee Letter 2010–29. Minimum Credit Scores and Loan-to-Value Ratios. Washington, D.C.

U.S. Department of Housing and Urban Development (2/14/2011). Mortgagee Letter 2011–10. Annual Mortgage Insurance Premium Changes and Guidance on Case Numbers. Washington, D.C.

U.S. Department of Housing and Urban Development (8/19/2011). Mortgagee Letter 2011–29. Federal Housing Administration's (FHA) Maximum Loan Limits Effective October 1, 2011 through December 31, 2011. Washington, D.C.

U.S. Department of Treasury. 2011. Troubled Asset Relief Program: Three Year Anniversary Report.

U.S. Department of Treasury, and U.S. Department of Housing and Urban Development. 2011. Reforming America's Housing Finance Market. A Report to Congress.

Weicher, J.C. 1992. FHA reform: Balance public purpose and financial soundness. *Journal of Real Estate Finance and Economics* 5(2): 133–150.

Yang, T. Tyler, Henry Buist, and Isaac F. Megbolugbe. 1998. An analysis of the ex ante probabilities of mortgage prepayment and default. *Real Estate Economics* 26 (4): 651–676.

Yang, T. Tyler, Che-Chun Lin, and Man Cho. 2011. Collateral Risks in Residential Mortgage Defaults. *Journal of Real Estate Finance and Economics* 42(2): 115–142.

Zandi, Mark and Cristian deRitis. 2011. Reworking Risk Retention. http://www.economy.com/mark-zandi/documents/Reworking-Risk-Retention-062011.pdf.

11. Housing and macroeconomy, Korea: the role of housing loan-to-value*

Inho Song

1. INTRODUCTION

Korean housing has become a hot issue in current macroeconomic movements since the global finance crisis in 2008. In fact, since then, the Korean economy has been affected by shocks to globally weakening demand. In particular, the linkage between housing and macroeconomic activity has been recently explored by several branches of the macroeconomic literature through various channels: (1) consumption channel through the wealth effect (Goodhart and Hofmann 2007); (2) financial market channel through the collateral effect from credit in balance sheet (Mishkin 2007); and (3) construction investment channel contributing to GDP (Muellbauer 2011).

As shown in Figure 11.1, housing and macroeconomic activity is mutually and circularly dependent. The shocks to both demand and supply in a housing sector have an impact on consumption, investment, and financial credit markets, which eventually lead to changes in GDP. These changes in GDP affect the housing sector in a circular process.

The linkage between housing and the macroeconomic activity is a key element of macro prudential policy, since housing plays an important role in the Korean macroeconomy in several points. For example, housing consists of 1.5 times of the gross domestic product (GDP) (Table 11.1) and 76 percent of household assets as of 2010. The construction investment contributed to 17 percent of GDP in 2011, while private consumption comprises 53 percent of GDP. Since the ratio of consumption to GDP is relatively small compared to other advanced countries, the importance of housing policy in macroeconomic activity may be focused on the financial market, and residential and nonresidential investment.

In order to understand the role of housing in the macroeconomic activity, the unique features of housing should be understood. As a matter of

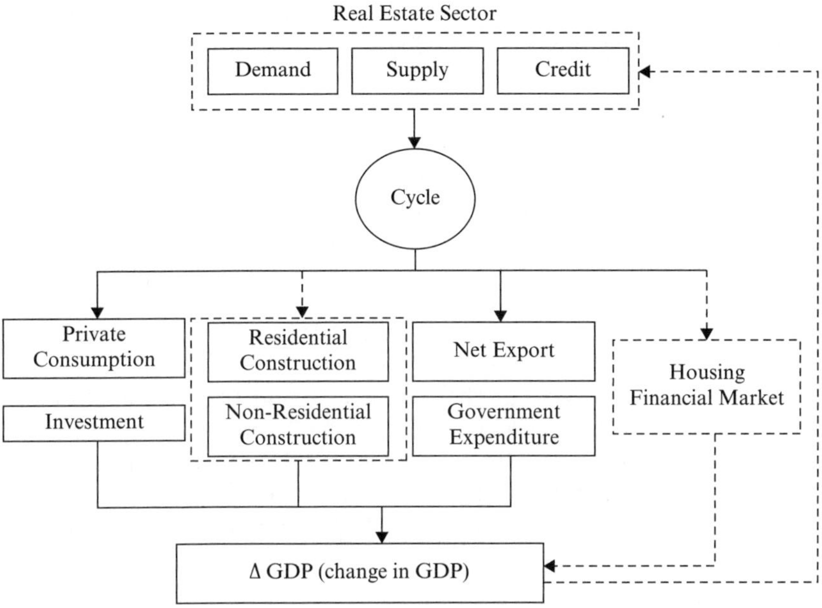

Source: Real estate trends of Q2 2012 by KDI Real Estate Research Team.

Figure 11.1 Link between housing and macroeconomy

Table 11.1 Korean housing to GDP ratio (%)

2001	2002	2003	2004	2005	2006	2007	2008	2009	2010p)
124.89	125.33	132.89	137.18	142.49	145.73	151.93	158.95	162.50	154.51

Source: Bank of Korea, National Korean Wealth Statistics. Song (2012) recite.

fact, housing is different from other durable goods in several important respects. First, changes in housing stocks incur substantial transaction costs proportional to existing house values. Second, the average housing depreciation rate is very small compared to the depreciation rates of other durable goods. Housing is associated with both land and building construction, through which housing services can be provided over time. Typically land is characterized as an immovable asset and depreciates marginally, in which it differs from other durable goods. Third, with a required down payment, houses are highly leveraged. Housing is generally used as collateral for the financial banking system. Since the collateral value is essential to the balance sheet credit, house prices are consistently monitored for their financial soundness. Housing provides a connection between the financial market stability and household housing services. Fourth, house values are three times larger than all other durable good stocks. Fifth, houses perform a dual role; they are both an investment asset and housing service consumption.

Capturing these housing features, I construct a DSGE model in which the economy consists of heterogeneous households, entrepreneurs, retailers, and the central bank. I assume that there are shocks to the monetary policy, which is common across heterogeneous households. The different levels of loan-to-value (LTV) restrictions are set to be 50 percent and 70 percent, respectively, so that the response simulations of both house prices and consumption may be obtained. I find that tightening monetary policy further decreases consumption and housing prices facing the higher LTV ratio. Moreover, the responses of constrained households' consumption become more sensitive to the tightening monetary policy shock. To put it another way, house prices and consumption become volatile with LTV.

1.1 Implications from the Model

The housing price in the model is affected by housing demand shocks, housing transaction costs, loan-to-values, discount factors across lenders and borrowers, and the ratio of consumption to housing. With the presence of a positive shock to housing demand, housing prices further increase as the house loan-to-value ratio increases, and housing transaction costs decrease. When transaction costs are equal to zero, housing prices are determined by the discount factors of lenders and borrowers, and the ratio of consumption to housing. From the budget constraints, net worth is used to finance the difference of new debt and the next unit of new housing. Selling one's existing house affects net worth, which is used to purchase a new house. The difference between the price of a new house and net worth is the household's debt.

Figure 11.2 shows the housing price mechanism in the DSGE model. A rise in housing prices increases borrowing capacity and net worth. Housing and consumption are boosted because of heightened collateral values and net worth. In turn, higher housing demand further increases housing prices. The change in housing net worth is associated with a high leverage effect, measured in the loan-to-value (LTV), which makes net worth much higher relative to a required down payment. Indeed, LTV representing leverage plays an amplifying role in net worth. This is consistent with Kiyotaki and Moore's (1997) observation that "The usual notion

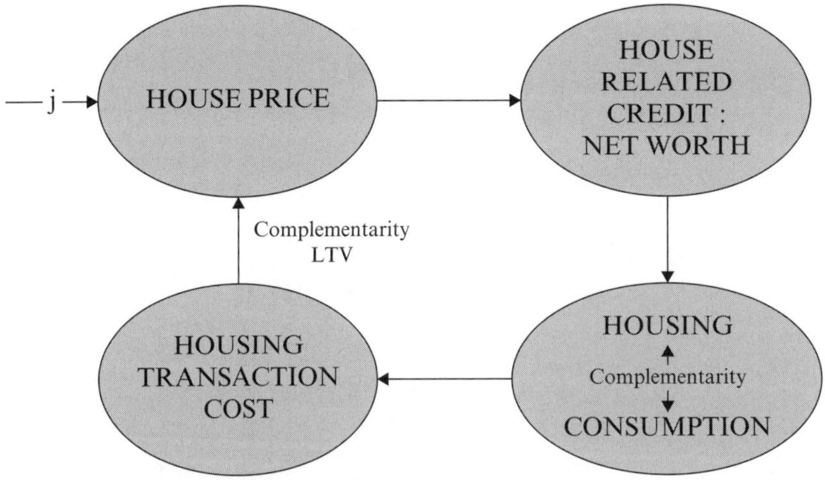

Figure 11.2 Housing price mechanism

that a higher land price reduces the farmers' demand is more than offset by the facts that (i) they can borrow more when next period housing price is higher, and (ii) their net worth increases as housing prices rise". The converse holds when there is a decline in housing prices. As the leverage ratio rises, it reduces net worth. Housing and consumption can shrink because of tighter borrowing constraints, as a fall in collateral values and net worth further depresses housing and consumption, so that changes in housing prices may amplify a plunge in macroeconomic variables.

Consistent with the above housing price mechanism, Figure 11.3 demonstrates the co-movements between mortgage growth and housing price growth. It shows whether the rise in housing prices contributes to the expansion in credit supply caused by the housing collateral. According to this figure, it turns out that the relationship between the growth rates of housing loans and housing prices are headed in a positive direction. In other words, the growth of housing loans and housing prices show interactional, coordinated movements in general. The growth rate of loans appears to be slightly lagging behind housing prices, meaning that a rise or fall in housing prices causes a rise or fall in loan growth.

1.2 Literature Review

Goodhart and Hofmann (2007) outlined impacts of housing prices on economic activities through various channels. They particularly emphasized that the interaction between housing prices and credit is

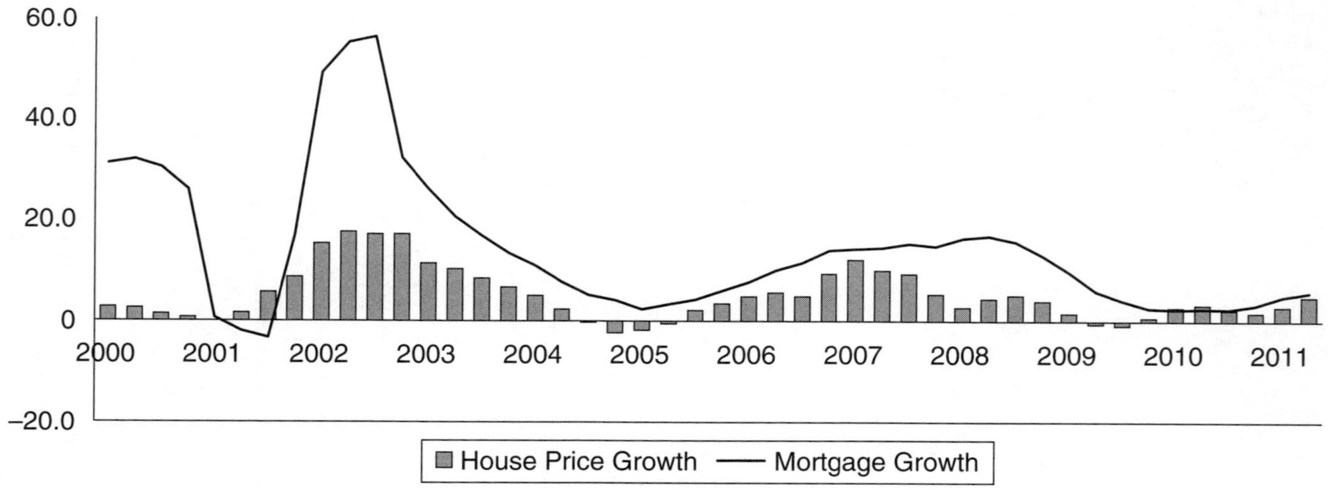

Source: Kookmin Bank and Bank of Korea.

Figure 11.3 Korean mortgage and housing price (YOY)

a useful indicator to detect a bubble in housing and credit markets. Bernanke and Gertler (1985), Kiyotaki and Moore (1997), Iacoviello (2005), and Bernanke et al. (1999) analyzed that the role of housing mortgage can theoretically account for changes in consumption as it is connected to mortgage capability and lending cost. Duca, Muellbauer and Murphy (2010) empirically analyzed how the loosened credit standards (deregulation) – loosened enough to cause a housing bubble – could render the role of housing as collateral and thereby could affect the U.S. mortgage market and consumption. They also conducted an empirical analysis of the wealth effect of assets, and, based on the results, they concluded that the wealth effect continues to change and become larger with time. Mishkin (2007) argued that in order to analyze the effectiveness of monetary policy, it is necessary to understand the role of housing under the monetary transmission mechanism. He also explained that in this mechanism, a significant role is played by user costs of capital, current and expected future housing prices, house supply, the wealth effect of housing prices and the relationship among credit channels, consumption and housing ownership. Ko and Yoon (2008) are devoted to the analysis of the effect of debt-to-income (DTI) on housing consumption using the Korean consumption data. Their empirical results show that constrained households are more responsive to the negative shock. In addition, several branches of the macroeconomic literature examine the amplification effect with financial constraints in business cycles. Kiyotaki and Moore (1997), Campbell and Cocco (2006), Carlstrom and Fuerst (1997), and Bernanke et al. (1999) integrate firm based financial constraints with a macroeconomic model.

Unlike these related studies, my model is constructed based on the financial constraints on both heterogeneous households and firms along with the housing adjustment costs. Then I investigate the responsiveness of heterogeneous households' consumption and housing prices with respect to different levels of LTV, following a rise in the interest rate.

1.3 The Structure

This chapter consists of five sections: I construct a DSGE model with financial constraints in section 2. In section 3, I calibrate my model and estimate the structural parameter governing the consumption-housing elasticity using a minimum distance method that minimizes the difference between impulse responses from the model versus the data. Then, policy simulations are presented in section 4, and section 5 concludes.

2. A DYNAMIC STOCHASTIC GENERAL EQUILIBRIUM (DSGE) MODEL

The economy in the model is populated by unconstrained households, constrained households, entrepreneurs, retailers and the central bank, as in Iacoviello (2005). Households are heterogeneous in that unconstrained households are not affected by their collateral, provide loans to constrained households, and receive lump sum profits from the ownership of retail firms.[2] Constrained households are affected by house collateral, receive loans from unconstrained households and are relatively impatient in comparison to unconstrained households. Since proportional transaction costs come from moving costs and real estate brokerage fees, I assume that constrained households and entrepreneurs have to pay transaction costs to unconstrained households (realtors), whenever there are housing transactions. Entrepreneurs produce intermediate goods using labor, houses and capital as inputs. Retailers, who buy intermediate goods from entrepreneurs and sell final consumption goods to heterogeneous households, are monopolistically competitive and have infrequent opportunities to adjust prices. The central bank takes the nominal interest rate as a policy instrument. Monetary policy is assumed to follow a Taylor rule responding to past inflation and past output. This model economy is described as in Figure 11.4.

2.1 Unconstrained Households

Unconstrained households receive utility from consumption and housing services, and disutility from labor. Their utility is represented by a constant elasticity of substitution (CES) between consumption and housing. Unconstrained households maximize the following objective function:

$$\max_{\{b_{1,t},C_{1,t},H_{1,t},N_{1,t}\}_{t=0}^{\infty}} E_0\sum_{t=0}^{\infty}\beta_1^t\left\{\frac{1}{1-\varsigma}\left[\left(C_{1,t}^{\frac{\varepsilon-1}{\varepsilon}}+j_tH_{1,t}^{\frac{\varepsilon-1}{\varepsilon}}\right)^{\frac{\varepsilon}{\varepsilon-1}}\right]^{1-\varsigma}-\frac{N_{1,t}^{\eta_2}}{\eta_1}\right\},\ \varsigma=\frac{1}{\sigma} \tag{11.1}$$

where E_0 denotes the expectation operator.[3] The parameter ς can be interpreted as the households' coefficient of relative risk aversion. $C_{1,t}$ denotes non-housing consumption. $H_{1,t}$[4] denotes the stock of housing. $N_{1,t}$[5] denotes labor hours. The discount factor β for unconstrained households is assumed to be greater than that of constrained households, or $0<\beta_2<\beta_1<1$. The parameter ε is the elasticity of intra-temporal substitution between housing and (non-housing) consumption. As long

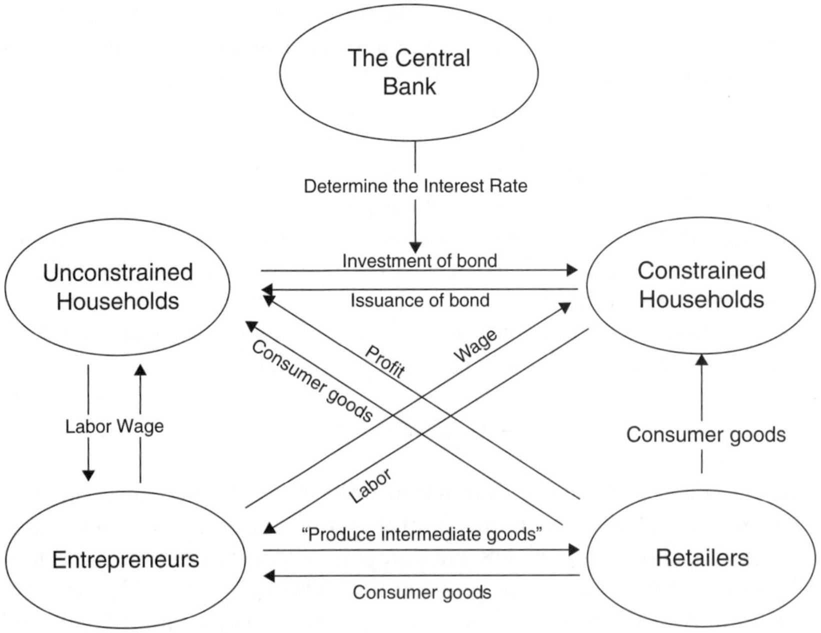

Figure 11.4 The model economy

as ε is less than one, housing and consumption are complements. The parameter ς can be interpreted as the households' coefficient of relative risk aversion.

I assume that the housing demand shock follows the stochastic process:

$$\ln j_t = (1-\rho_j)\ln \bar{j} + \rho_j \ln j_{t-1} + \varepsilon_{j,t},\ \varepsilon_{j,t}: iid \sim N(0;\sigma_j^2) \tag{11.2}$$

where $\bar{j} > 0$, $\rho_j \in (-1,1)$ measures the persistence of the shock, and $\varepsilon_{j,t}$ is independent and identically distributed *i.i.d.* with mean zero and variance σ_j^2. Each period unconstrained households choose a level of consumption, houses and work hours, given the period budget constraint:

$$C_{1,t} + (H_{1,t} - H_{1,t-1})q_t + \frac{R_{t-1}}{\pi_t} b_{1,t-1} = w_{1,t}N_{1,t} + b_{1,t} + f_t + fee_t \tag{11.3}$$

where $w_{1,t}$ is the real wage from their labor supply, q_t is the real house price, $b_{1,t}$ is the real debt[6], $f_{t,}$ is the real lump sum profits from retailers, and π_t denotes inflation, or $\pi_t = \frac{P_t}{P_{t-1}}$. Since the non-separable utility function is associated with housing transaction costs, the curvature parameter, ς, can be greater than, equal to or less than the inverse of the marginal rate of inter-temporal elasticity of substitution. I define the curvature of the utility function as $\varsigma = \frac{1}{\sigma}$. When ε is equal to σ, the utility function becomes separable. When the limit is taken as ε goes to one, the utility function becomes the Cobb-Douglas specification. I assume that housing transaction costs are proportional to the sale price of houses, which are introduced into the budget constraints of both households and entrepreneurs. Housing transaction costs capture an important fact. New house purchases mainly depend on the sale of existing housing. Housing transaction costs include time costs, moving costs, tax, and realtor fees. I assume that constrained households and entrepreneurs have to pay these housing transactions to unconstrained households whenever there are housing transactions, which can be represented by

$$fee_t = \varphi \cdot q_t(H_{e,t-1} + H_{2,t-1}) \tag{11.4}$$

where φ denotes housing transaction costs for entrepreneurs and constrained households. As a result, transaction costs across constrained households and entrepreneurs can dampen movements in housing prices. The household optimization problem is to choose b_{1t}, C_{1t}, H_{1t}, and N_{1t} to maximize Equation (11.1), subject to constraints Equation (11.2) and Equation (11.3). From the unconstrained household problem, the following two optimality conditions are derived:

$$1 = E_t\left(\frac{U_{C_{1,t+1}}}{U_{C_{1,t}}} \frac{\beta_1 R_t}{\pi_{t+1}}\right), \tag{11.5}$$

where

$$U_{C_{1,t}} = \left\{C_{1,t}^{\frac{\varepsilon-1}{\varepsilon}} + j_t(H_{1,t})^{\frac{\varepsilon-1}{\varepsilon}}\right\}^{\frac{\sigma-\varepsilon}{\sigma(\varepsilon-1)}} C_{1,t}^{\frac{-1}{\varepsilon}}, \tag{11.6}$$

and

$$\frac{U_{H_{1,t}}}{U_{C1,t}} = q_t(1 + \varphi_1) - \left(\frac{\pi_{t+1}}{R_t}\right)q_{t+1}, \tag{11.7}$$

where

$$U_{H_{1,t}} = \left\{C_{1,t}^{\frac{\varepsilon-1}{\varepsilon}} + j_t(H_{1,t})^{\frac{\varepsilon-1}{\varepsilon}}\right\}^{\frac{\sigma-\varepsilon}{\sigma(\varepsilon-1)}} (H_{1,t})^{\frac{-1}{\varepsilon}} j_t.$$

Equation (11.5) is the standard Euler equation requiring that the household expected discounted real marginal utility return from saving one unit is equal to the current marginal utility cost of giving up a unit of consumption. Equation (11.7) determines the marginal rate of substitution between housing and consumption. These two equations can be combined into

$$\frac{U_{H_{1,t}}}{U_{C1,t}} = \frac{(H_{1,t})^{\frac{-1}{\varepsilon}} j_t}{C_{1,t}^{\frac{-1}{\varepsilon}}} = \left(\frac{C_{1,t}}{H_{1,t}}\right)^{\frac{1}{\varepsilon}} j_t \tag{11.8}$$

Equation (11.8) gives the optimal ratio of consumption to housing, which is related to house prices, transaction costs, housing demand shocks and the nominal interest rate.[7] The higher the interest rate is, the higher is consumption relative to housing, because the demand for housing is more sensitive to the interest rate. The higher the positive housing demand shock is, the lower is the ratio of consumption to housing, because housing is more valuable.

2.2 Constrained Households

The optimization problem for constrained households is

$$\max_{\{b_{2,t}, C_{2,t}, H_{2,t}, N_{2,t}\}_{t=0}^{\infty}} E_0 \sum_{t=0}^{\infty} (\beta_2)^t \frac{1}{1-\varsigma}\left[\left\{C_{2,t}^{\frac{\varepsilon-1}{\varepsilon}} + j_t (H_{2,t})^{\frac{\varepsilon-1}{\varepsilon}}\right\}^{\frac{\varepsilon}{\varepsilon-1}}\right]^{1-\varsigma} - \frac{N_{2,t}^{\eta}}{\eta_2}, \tag{11.9}$$

subject to

$$C_{2,t} + (H_{2t} - H_{2t-1})q_t + \varphi_2 q_t H_{2t-1} + \frac{R_{t-1}}{\pi_t} b_{2,t-1} \leq w_{2,t} N_{2,t} + b_{2,t}, \tag{11.10}$$

where

$$R_t b_{2t} \leq m_2 E_t (q_{t+1} \pi_{t+1} H_{2t}). \tag{11.11}$$

For constrained households, housing transactions incur realtor fees, $\varphi_2 q_t H_{2t-1}$. The transaction costs are proportional to the value of house sales and are paid to unconstrained households. Equation (11.11) represents the financial constraint, which binds. As in Kiyotaki and Moore (1997), when debtors default on obligations, creditors repossess houses by paying $(1 - m_2)\beta q_{t+1} \pi_{t+1} H_{2,t}$. Hence, $(1-m_2)$ can be interpreted as a down-payment ratio. The loan-to-value ratio is denoted as m_2, where $0 \leq m_2 \leq 1$. Liquidation, however, takes time and bears costs. The collateral constraint implies that mortgages cannot exceed the house value. I assume that the housing demand shock, j_t, for constrained households is the same as that for unconstrained households described above.

The first order conditions imply the following Euler equation and housing price equation:

$$U_{C_{2,t}} = R_t \lambda^m_{2,t} + U_{C_{2,t+1}} \frac{R_t}{\pi_{t+1}} \beta_2, \tag{11.12}$$

$$q_t = \frac{U_{H_{2,t}}}{(1+\varphi_2)U_{C_{2,t}}} + \frac{\beta_2(1-\delta_{h2})}{(1+\varphi_2)} \left(\% \frac{U_{C_{2,t+1}}}{U_{C_{2,t}}} \right) q_{t+1} + \frac{\lambda_{m2t}}{U_{C_{2,t}}} \frac{m_{2t} E_t q_{t+1} \pi_{t+1}}{(1+\varphi\%_2)} \tag{11.13}$$

where

$$U_{C_{2,t}} = \left\{ C_{2,t}^{\frac{\varepsilon-1}{\varepsilon}} + j_t (H_{2,t})^{\frac{\varepsilon-1}{\varepsilon}} \right\}^{\frac{1-\sigma\varepsilon}{\varepsilon-1}} C_{2,t}^{\frac{-1}{\varepsilon}},$$

and

$$U_{H_{2,t}} = \left\{ C_{2,t}^{\frac{\varepsilon-1}{\varepsilon}} + j_t (H_{2,t})^{\frac{\varepsilon-1}{\varepsilon}} \right\}^{\frac{1-\varepsilon\sigma}{\varepsilon-1}} (H_{2,t})^{\frac{-1}{\varepsilon}} j_t.\ \lambda^m_{2,t}$$

is the Lagrange multiplier associated with the borrowing constraint. House prices depend on ε, σ, and housing demand preferences. The realtor fee rate, φ_2, affects house prices negatively. When ε rises relative to σ, households are more willing to substitute housing services and housing consumption within a period than they are to substitute overall consumption between the periods. When ε is equal to σ, house prices are fully determined by composition risk and consumption risk. House prices in the steady state satisfy

$$q = \frac{\bar{j}}{(1+\varphi_2) - \beta_2 - (\beta_1 - \beta_2)m_2} \left(\frac{C_2}{H_2} \right)^{\frac{1}{\varepsilon}}. \tag{11.14}$$

The house price depends on the housing demand shock, transaction costs, loan-to-values, and the ratio of consumption to house. The degree of intra-temporal substitutability, ε, is also an important element in determining asset prices. House prices increase when the house loan-to-value ratio, m_2, increases and when transaction costs φ_2 decrease, ceteris paribus. When transaction costs are equal to zero, house prices are determined by the discount factors of lenders and borrowers, the ratio of consumption to housing for constrained households. From the budget constraint, net worth is used to finance the difference of new debt and the next unit of housing. Selling one's existing house affects net worth, which is used to purchase a new house. The difference between the price of a new house and net worth is the households' new debt. Hence, houses for constrained households satisfy,

$$H_{2,t} = \frac{1}{E_t\left(q_t - \frac{m_2 q_{t+1}\pi_{t+1}}{R_t}\right)}\left(q_t H_{2,t-1} - \frac{R_t b_{2,t-1}\%}{\pi_t}\right). \quad (11.15)$$

This equation is consistent with the result of Kiyotaki and Moore (1997). As the loan-to-value, m_2, rises, house prices increase. This occurs because a higher loan-to-value results in higher housing demand. As house prices rise from both date t and $t+1$, the current net worth, $q_t H_{2,t-1} - \frac{R_t b_{2,t-1}}{\pi_t}$, and the collateral value, $\frac{q_{t+1}\pi_{t+1}}{R_t}$, increase, which induces an increase in housing demand. The extent to which houses can be used as collateral determines the extent to which the conventional law of demand is overturned. In fact, an increase in house prices induces a rise in housing demand through the collateral effect. From Equation (11.15), we see there is a transmission mechanism that connects house prices to macroeconomic fluctuations. Suppose house prices rise. Overall, a rise in house prices increases borrowing capacity and net worth. Housing and consumption are boosted because of heightened collateral values and net worth. In turn, higher housing demand further increases house prices. The change in housing net worth is associated with a high leverage effect, measured in the loan-to-value, which makes net worth much higher relative to a required down payment. Indeed, leverage plays an amplifying role in net worth. The converse holds when there is a decline in housing prices. As the leverage ratio rises, it reduces net worth. Housing and consumption can shrink because of tighter borrowing constraints, as a fall in collateral values and net worth further depresses housing and consumption. Therefore, changes in house prices may amplify fluctuations in macroeconomic variables.

2.3 Entrepreneurs

Entrepreneurs derive utility only from consumption. They produce intermediate goods according to the following constant return to scale Cobb-Douglas production function with labor, housing and capital as inputs:

$$Y_t = Z_t(K_{t-1}^{\nu} H_{t-1}^{1-\nu})^{\mu}(N_{1,t}^{\alpha} N_{2,t}^{(1-\alpha)})^{(1-\mu)}, \quad (11.16)$$

where Y_t denotes output and Z_t represents productivity in period t. K_{t-1} and H_{t-1} denote capital and housing in period $t-1$, respectively. The shock to Z_t follows the stochastic process:

$$\ln Z_t = (1 - \rho_z) \ln \overline{Z} + \rho_z \ln Z_{t-1} + \varepsilon_{Z,t}, \quad (11.17)$$

where $\overline{Z} > 0, \rho_Z \in (-1, 1)$ measures the persistence of the shock and $\varepsilon_{Z,t}$ is a white noise process with mean zero and variance σ_Z^2. Capital accumulation follows

$$K_t = (1 - \delta)K_{t-1} + I_{Kt} - \frac{\xi}{2}\frac{(K_t - K_{t-1})^2}{K_{t-1}},$$

where I_{Kt} denotes investment in capital, and adjustments to the capital stock incur quadratic costs parameterized by ξ. Capital depreciates at the rate δ.

Housing accumulation follows

$$H_{et} = H_{et-1} + I_{Het} - \varphi_e H_{et-1},$$

where I_{Het} denotes investment in houses. Housing transactions are associated with transaction costs like, $\varphi_e q_t H_{et-1}$, which are paid to unconstrained households.

The utility maximization problem for entrepreneurs may be written as follows:

$$\max_{\{C_{et}, b_{et}, I_t, K_t, H_t, N_{1,t}, N_{2,t}\}_{t=0}^{\infty}} E_0 \sum_{t=0}^{\infty} \gamma^t \ln C_{et}, \quad (11.18)$$

subject to

$$\frac{Y_t}{X_t} + b_{et} \geq C_{et} + \frac{R_{t-1}}{\pi_t} b_{et-1} + w_{1,t}N_{1,t} + w_{2,t}N_{2,t} + I_{kt} + I_{Het} + \xi_{Kt} + \xi_{Het}, \quad (11.19)$$

where

$$I_{Kt} = K_t - (1 - \delta)K_{t-1}, \xi_{Kt} = \frac{\psi_K}{2\delta}\left(\frac{I_{Kt}}{K_{t-1}} - \delta\right)^2 K_{t-1},$$

$$I_{Het} = \{H_{et} - H_{et-1}\} q_t, \ \xi_{Het} = \varphi_e q_t H_{et-1},$$

and

$$R_t b_{et} \leq m_e E_t(q_{t+1}\pi_{t+1}H_{et}). \tag{11.20}$$

Equation (11.20) represents the collateral constraint facing entrepreneurs, with the constant parameter m_e reflecting their loan-to-value ratio.

2.4 Retailers

Retailers in this model face precisely the same problems as in Iacoviello (2005) and Bernanke et al. (1999). They produce a continuum of differentiated final goods indexed along the unit interval. They supply their goods in monopolistically competitive markets, and their profits are paid to unconstrained households. The retailers' supply curve implies a Phillips curve, determined by an optimal pricing equation. Retail prices are sticky,[8] and the probability of any retailer being able to adjust its nominal price is $1 - \theta$. Retailers purchase intermediate goods from entrepreneurs at price P_t^I and sell final goods to households at price, $P_t(g)$. Final goods are

$$Y_t = \left(\int_0^1 Y_t(g)^{(\xi-1)/\xi} dg \right)^{\frac{\xi}{\xi-1}} \text{ with } \xi > 1.$$

The solution to the firms' cost minimization problem gives a demand function for intermediate goods and a price index,

$$P_t = \left(\int_0^1 P_t^I(g)^{1-\xi} dg \right)^{\frac{1}{1-\xi}}.$$

Profit maximization by each retail firm implies that the optimal price of retail goods, $P_t^*(g)$ satisfies

$$\sum_{i=0}^{\infty} \theta^i E_t\left(\beta \frac{C_{1,t}}{C_{1,t+i}} \left(\frac{P_t^*(g)}{P_{t+i}} - \frac{X_t}{X_{t+i}} \right) Y_{t+i}(g) \right) = 0,$$

where X_t is the markup. P_t^* makes discounted marginal revenue be equal to expected discounted marginal cost. The aggregate price index is

$$P_t = (\theta P_{t-1}^{\xi} + (1 - \theta)\% P_t^{*(1-\xi)})^{\frac{1}{1-\xi}}.$$

From the optimization of retailers, the log-linearized aggregate supply curve can be derived as $\hat{\pi}_t = \beta\hat{\pi}_{t+1} - k\hat{X}_t + \hat{\varepsilon}_{u,t}$, where

$$k = \frac{(1 - \theta)(1 - \beta\theta)}{\theta}.$$

2.5 The Central Bank

The central bank is assumed to follow a Taylor rule taking the nominal interest rate as the instrument for monetary policy:

$$R_t = (R_{t-1})^{\gamma_R}\left(\pi_{t-1}^{1+\gamma_\pi}\left(\frac{Y_{t-1}}{\overline{Y}}\right)^{\gamma_y}\overline{rr}\right)^{1-\gamma_R} e_{R,t} \qquad (11.21)$$

2.6 Equilibrium

Given initial conditions $H_{e,0}$, $H_{1,0}$, $H_{2,0}$, $b_{e,0}$, $b_{1,0}$, and $b_{2,0}$, the dynamic stochastic equilibrium is a sequence of allocations,

$$\left\{\begin{matrix} Y_t, C_{e,t}, C_{1,t}, C_{2,t}, H_{e,t}, H_{1,t}, \\ H_{2,t}, b_{e,t}, b_{1t}, b_{2t}, N_{1,t}, N_{2,t} \end{matrix}\right\}_{t=0}^{\infty}$$

and a sequence of prices,

$$\{w_{1t}, w_{2t}, R_t, q_t, P_t, \%P_t^*, \lambda_t\}_{t=0}^{\infty},$$

at which all agents satisfy their budget constraints, borrowing constraints and first order conditions, and all market clear in each date. For the markets to clear, the bond market for b_t, goods market for Y_t and the house market for H_{et}, H_{1t} and H_{2t} should meet the following conditions:

(a) $N_{1t} = N_{2t}$
(b) $H_{e,t} + H_{1,t} + H_{2,t} = 1$,
(c) $C_{e,t} + C_{1,t} + C_{2,t} + I_t = Y_t$,
(d) $I_t = I_{Kt} + I_{Het} + I_{H1t} + I_{H2t}$,
(e) $fee_t = \varphi_e q_t H_{et-1} + \varphi_1 q_t H_{1t-1} + \varphi_2 q_t H_{2t-1}$,
(f) $b_t + b_{1t} + b_{2t} = 0$

Wages are different across households and based on their productivity. In the steady state, unconstrained households receive wage bills of $w_1N_1 = \alpha(1 - \mu - v)Y$, while constrained households receive a wage bill of $w_2N_2 = (1 - \alpha)(1 - \mu - v)Y$.

3. CALIBRATION AND ESTIMATION

3.1 Calibration

Table 11.2 shows the calibration of the DSGE model. The subjected discount factors for unconstrained households β_1, constrained households β_2, and entrepreneurs γ are 0.99 (Kim and Yang 2004), 0.95 (Kang 2006), and 0.98 (Iacoviello 2005), respectively. The parameter value 0.21 for housing demand shock, j, is calibrated to match the ratio of housing values to GDP. The capital elasticity to GDP, μ, is 0.3 (Kim and Yang 2004). The loan-to-value (LTV) ratio, m, and housing transaction costs, φ, are the first moment of the data from the Korean Housing Surveys. The capital depreciation rate, δ, the inverse of labor supply, η, and the housing elasticity to GDP, ν, are adopted following the values of Iacoviello (2005).

For the parameters of monetary policy (Table 11.3), I assume that policy follows a Taylor rule responding to past inflation and output as in

Table 11.2 Calibration

Parameter	Value	Parameter	Value
β_1 Subjective Discount for Unconstrained Households	0.99	β_2 Subjective Discount for Constrained Households	0.95
γ Subjective Discount for Entrepreneurs	0.98	δ_K Capital Depreciation Rate	0.03
j Housing Demand Shock	0.21	X Markup	1.05
μ Elasticity of GDP to Capital	0.3	v Elasticity of GDP to Real Estate	0.03
η Inverse of Labor Supply	1.01	φ Housing Transaction Costs	0.03
m_e Loan to Value Ratio for Entrepreneurs	0.5	m_2 Loan to Value Ratio for Constrained Households	0.5

Source: Song (2012) recite.

Table 11.3 Monetary policy parameters

Parameter	Value	Standard Deviation
Persistency of Interest: α_R	0.89	0.034
Inflation coefficient: α_π	0.15	0.039
Output gap coefficient: α_Y	0.04	0.007

Source: Song (2012) recite.

Table 11.4 Estimation

Parameter	Value	Standard Deviation
Elasticity of Substitution ε	0.398	0.009
Curvature ζ	2.027	0.2999
Share of Wage α	0.512	0.035
Autoregressive Rate for Inflation ρ_π	0.01	0.139
Autoregressive Rate for House Price ρ_q	0.89	0.023
Autoregressive Rate for Technology ρ_z	0.01	0.211

Source: Song (2012) recite.

Equation (11.21). I log-linearized Equation (11.21) and then regress inflation and output on the interest rate. I used macro data from 1991 Q1 to 2011 Q4 including the call rate, inflation (GDP deflator), and real GDP. This regression is depicted as following:

$$\hat{R}_t = 0.89\hat{R}_{t-1} + 0.15\hat{\pi}_{t-1} + 0.04\hat{y}_{t-1},$$

which can be represented by interest smoothing policy:

$$\hat{R}_t = 0.89\hat{R}_{t-1} + 0.11(1.36\hat{\pi}_{t-1} + 0.345\hat{y}_{t-1}).$$

3.2 Estimation

Estimation is conducted by the minimum distance method. For this method, the VAR impulse responses from the data (see Appendix I) are used to derive the differences between the DSGE model and the data. The distance function is *f(b)=model responses(b)-data responses(b)*, where *b* is the vector of parameters to be estimated. The solution to minimize the differences is summarized as in Table 11.4.

4. POLICY SIMULATIONS

4.1 Housing Transmission Mechanism in the Economy

Figure 11.5 shows that the housing market crisis contracts housing demand and the housing financial market. The housing values are deteriorating in the circular process as the credit market and housing financial market operates, resulting in an economic recession. On the one hand, the decline in housing demand causes housing prices to fall at a faster pace,

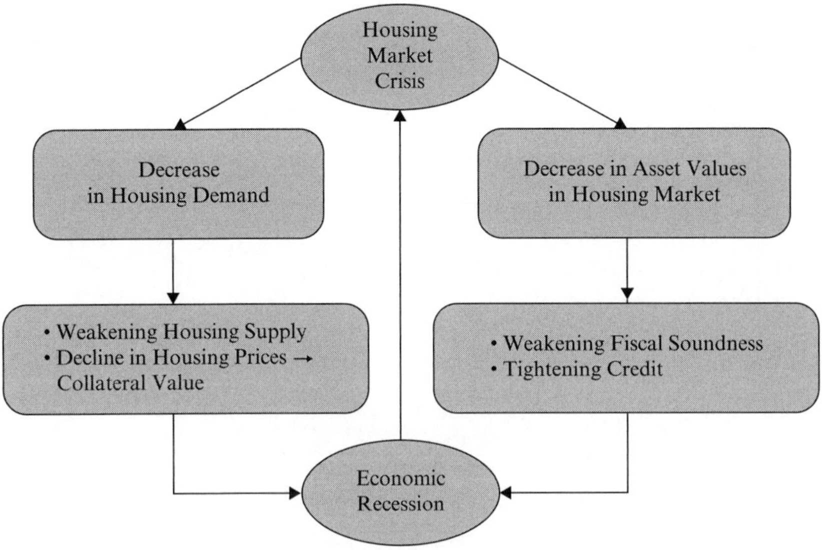

Source: The figure is modified based upon Muellbauer (2011).

Figure 11.5 Housing and macroeconomy

contracting housing supply. A decrease in housing prices is deteriorating the housing collateral value, and this, in turn, leads to a recession. On the other hand, the contraction of the housing financial market is triggered by a fall in asset values, resulting in a recession. Such a cycle represents the amplifying process through the volatility of housing prices.

4.2 Simulation 1: A Rise in Housing Prices Increases Consumption

According to Figure 11.6 as a simulation result, the rise in housing prices serves as a stimulus of consumption. In the economic structure with higher LTV ratio, in particular, the rise in housing prices turns out to bring significant positive impacts on consumption. In the case of 50% of the LTV ratio (the triangle line), a 1% increase in housing prices causes the consumption to rise by 0.03%, and in the case of 70% (the circle line), the same degree of increase in housing prices causes a 0.2% increase in consumption.[9] This simulation is consistent with the empirical analysis by Young Il Kim (2010). Kim (2010) estimated the short-term elasticity of consumption to housing prices to be between 0.08 and 0.26. In the DSGE model, such an effect of housing prices can be interpreted as follows: The rise in housing prices enlarges the asset values of households, generating the wealth effect. At the

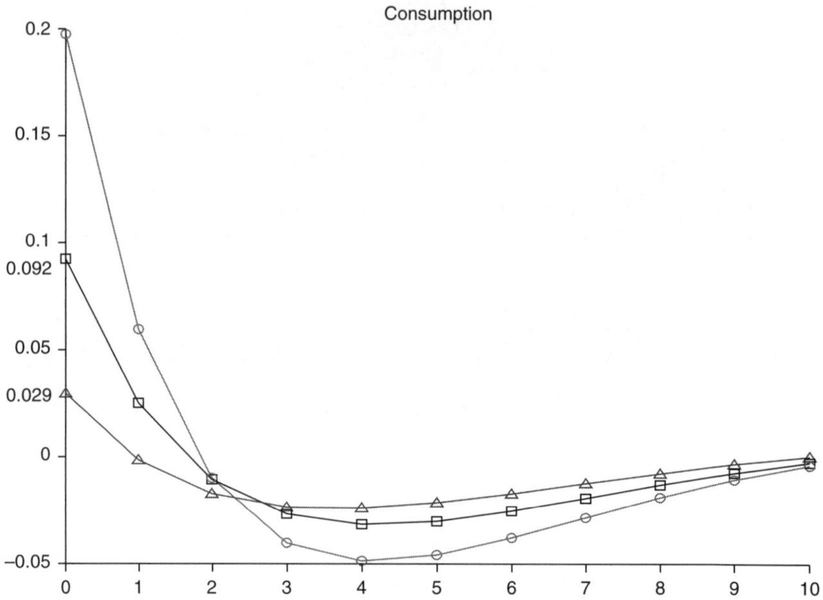

Source: Song (2012) recite.

Figure 11.6 Housing and consumption

same time, according to the first-order condition for optimal household choices, the rise in housing prices would lead to the rise in net worth, and then to the increase in both housing and consumption, eventually causing the co-movements of housing and consumption. This phenomenon serves to raise housing prices again, playing the role as an accelerator. As the LTV ratio becomes higher alongside a rise in housing prices, the collateral effect becomes stronger and serves to enhance household credit, contributing to further boosting consumption.

4.3 Simulation 2: Constrained Households are More Responsive to a Rise in Housing Prices

Households are heterogeneous. Simulation 1 is focusing on the overall responses across all households. In Figure 11.7, I investigate the consumption responsiveness of credit constrained households facing a rise in housing prices. Figure 11.7 shows that the rise in housing prices tends to encourage credit constrained households to consume more. This can be seen as a leverage effect brought by the collateral value. Compared to

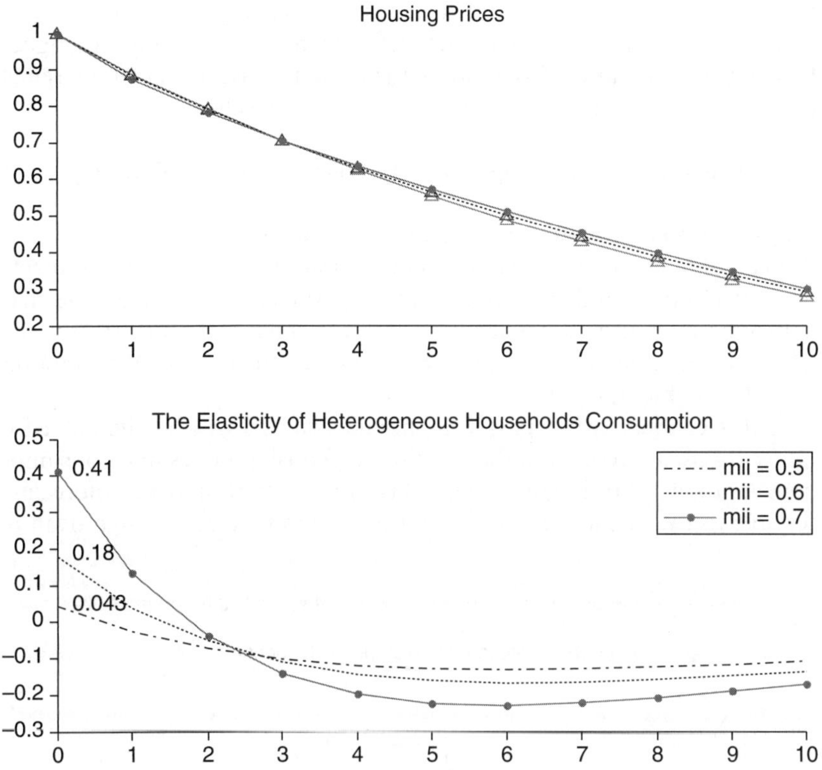

Source: Song (2012) recite.

Figure 11.7 The consumption response of constrained households

unconstrained households, constrained households who use houses as collateral are more encouraged to use heightened housing credit, because a rise in housing prices enhances the consumption capacity of constrained households more than that of unconstrained households. In other words, the increase in housing prices causes the collateral value of houses to rise and this in turn causes the increase in consumption capacity through credit expansion. In the economic structure with 50% of LTV, a 1% increase in housing prices results in a 0.043% increase in consumption of constrained households, and this is much higher than 0.02% of the aggregate consumption as in Figure 11.6.[10] To put it another way, the consumption of constrained households is much more responsive to a rise in housing prices than that of unconstrained households. This phenomenon is particularly evident in the economic structure with 70% LTV ratio, meaning that the increase in housing prices causes the consumption of constrained households to rise by 0.41%. In fact, in the economic structure with higher LTV ratio, constrained households turn out to have a higher marginal propensity to consume out of increases in housing values.

4.4 Simulation 3: Tightening Monetary Policy and the LTV Ratio

4.4.1 A rise in the interest rate decreases consumption

With a tightening monetary policy, interest rates produce negative impacts on consumption, and this appears to be particularly true, meaning that tightening monetary policy tends to contract consumption further as the LTV ratio gets higher. Figure 11.8 shows the changes in consumption caused by tightening policy.

In this chapter, two types of economic structures with different LTV ratios are used to compare the volatility of housing prices and consumption. As the LTV ratio got higher, households turned out to be more susceptible to the impact of a 1% increase in interest rates and significantly

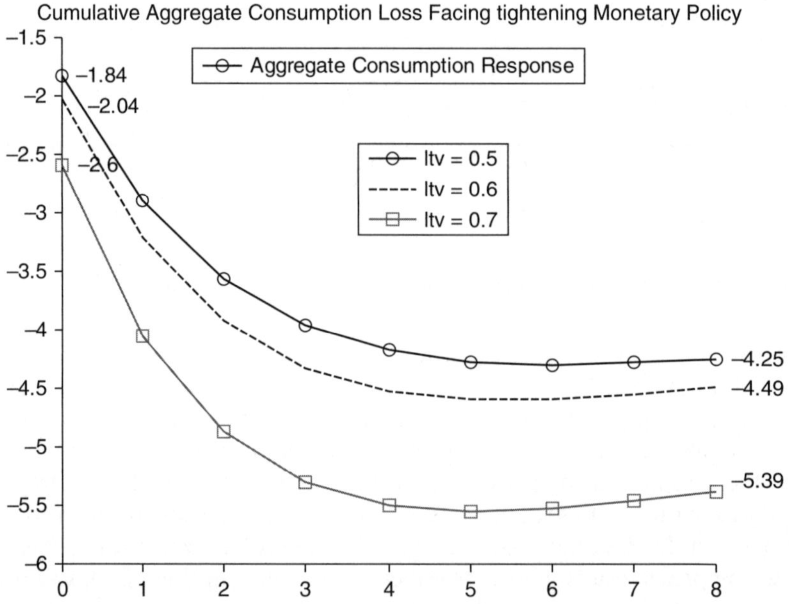

Source: Song (2012) recite.

Figure 11.8 Tightening monetary policy, the loan-to-value ratios, and consumption

reduced their consumption. For a household with a 50% LTV ratio, a 1% rise in interest rates caused their consumption to decrease by only 1.84%, whereas for those with a 70% LTV ratio, the same degree of increase in interest rates caused their consumption to further decrease by 2.6%. This simulation can be accounted for by the housing price mechanism. The increase in interest rates causes housing prices to fall, leading to reducing the capacity for mortgage lending, to contracting the credit and then to eventually affecting consumption to fall further. As the collateral effect with a higher LTV is larger, a fall in housing prices would amplify the leverage-driven decline in net worth. The next section explains this mechanism by showing the degree to which house prices are affected by tightening monetary policy.

4.4.2 A rise in the interest rate decreases housing prices

Figure 11.9 shows that the increase in interest rates causes housing prices to fall, which leads to the decrease in housing and consumption demand. The fall in housing prices means the decline in asset value, which is linked to the fall in the collateral value, resulting in the contraction in credit and eventually leading to the decline in demand of both housing and consumption. This can be viewed to signify that, as the LTV ratio gets higher, the fall in collateral value contributes to amplifying the negative leverage effect, and thereby susceptibility to the fall in interest rates.

It is found that in the economic structure with a higher LTV ratio and hence large amount of housing loans, responses of housing prices turned out to be more susceptible to interest rates. For the economy with a 50% LTV ratio, a 1% increase in interest rate causes housing prices to drop by 2.8%, whereas with a 70% LTV ratio, the same increase further causes a 3.1% fall in housing prices. Housing prices in the economic structure with the high LTV ratio turned out to be more volatile.[11]

5. CONCLUSION

In my model, the credit channel is assumed to be driven by the LTV system through the housing prices. The housing collateral value is quantified by the LTV ratio, and the focus of credit channels is to make this value operate as a supply resource of credit markets. The DSGE simulations show that the loan-to-value ratios not only affect the financial market, but they also influence the real economy. As a matter of fact, consumption falls in response to tightening monetary policy. The drop speed in consumption is also faster as loan-to-value ratio becomes higher. In the case of a higher LTV ratio, key macroeconomic variables including private consumption

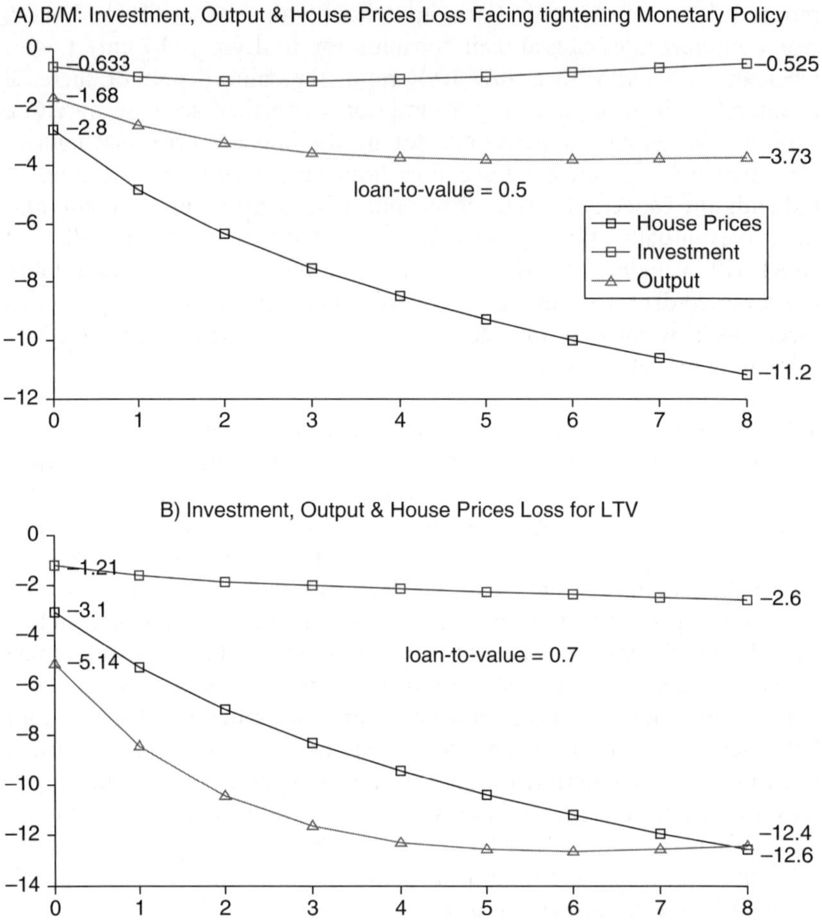

Source: Song (2012) recite.

Figure 11.9 Tightening monetary policy, the loan-to-value ratios, and housing prices

turn out to become increasingly volatile. When the economy is constructed by higher loan-to-values, policy makers should be cautious whether monetary policy is tightening or easing, since the interest rate decelerates the real economy under the high loan-to-values.

In the opposite case, as the LTV ratio is lower, the leverage becomes smaller, thereby leading to reducing the volatility of housing prices. This implies that a lower LTV ratio may be helpful to stabilizing the housing market in the financial system. As the LTV control is set to be lower, however, housing affordability is sacrificed, generating a tradeoff between financial market stabilization through the LTV system and housing services affordability. Future studies may be needed, to study the maximization process of social welfare triggered by this tradeoff. It would also be necessary to estimate an appropriate LTV ratio for the Korean economy and analyze the LTV effects in relation to the DTI effects.

NOTES

* This paper is based upon on the KDI policy research paper from Song (2012).

1. The economy is based on Song (2012) and the method to solve the household problem is borrowed from Uhlig (1999) and Miranda and Fackler (2002). The relationship between housing and consumption is studied in Piazzesi et al. (2007).
2. Throughout the chapter, the subscripts *1,2*, and *e* refer to unconstrained households, constrained households, and entrepreneurs, respectively.
3. Housing services are assumed to be proportional to the stock of housing.
4. Households allocate their time between labor hours, $N_{1,t}$ and leisure, $L_{1,t}$. Their endowment of time is one, hence $N_{1,t} + L_{1,t}=1$.
5. Since unconstrained households provide loans to constrained households in this model, the real debt $b_{1,t}$ is negative term.
6. Equation (11.8) can be rearranged with respect to the ratio of consumption to housing:

$$\frac{C_1}{H_1} = (q_t)^{\varepsilon}\left(\frac{(1+\varphi_1)}{j_t} - \frac{\pi_{t+1}}{j_t R_t}\frac{q_{t+1}}{q_t}\right)^{\varepsilon}$$

7. I borrowed the sticky price idea from Calvo (1983).
8. The squared black line represents the economy with 60 percent of the LTV ratio.
9. The aggregate consumption is a consumption sum of constrained households, unconstrained households, and entrepreneurs.
10. The rise in interest rates tends to shrink investment, and this is particularly severe in an economic structure with a high LTV ratio. In an economic structure with a 50% LTV ratio, a 1% rise in interest rates causes investment to fall by 0.63%, whereas with a 70% LTV ratio, the same increase causes a 1.21% fall in investment.

REFERENCES

Bernanke, B.S. and M. Gertler (1995). Inside the black box: Credit channel of monetary policy transmission. Journal of Economic Perspectives 9 (4), 27–48.

Bernanke, B.S., M. Gertler, and S. Gilchrist (1999). The financial accelerator in a quantitative business cycle framework. Handbook of Macroeconomics.

Calvo, G. (1983) Staggered prices in a utility maximizing framework. Journal of Monetary Economics 12.

Campbell, J.Y. and J.F. Cocco (2006). How do house prices affect consumption? Evidence from micro data. Journal of Monetary Economics.

Carlstrom, C.T. and T.S. Fuerst (1997). Agency costs, net worth, and business fluctuations: A computable general equilibrium analysis. American Economic Review 87 (5), 893–910.
Duca, John V., John Muellbauer and Anthony Murphy (2010), Housing markets and the financial crisis of 2007–2009: Lessons for the future. Journal of Financial Stability 6 (4), 203–217.
Goodhart C. and B. Hofmann (2007), House Prices and the Macro-economy: Implications for Banking and Price Stability. Oxford University Press.
Iacoviello, Matteo (2005), House prices, borrowing constraints and monetary policy in the business cycle. American Economic Review.
Kiyotaki, N. and J. Moore (1997). Credit cycles. Journal of Political Economy 105, 211–248.
Miranda, M., and Fackler, P. (2002), Applied Computational Economics and Finance. MIT Press.
Mishkin, Frederic S. (2007), Housing and the monetary transmission mechanism. Finance and Economics Discussion Series Divisions of Research & Statistics and Monetary Affairs, Federal Reserve Board, Washington, D.C. 2007–40.
Muellbauer, J. (2011), Housing markets and the macroeconomy. The International Encyclopedia of Housing and Home. Elsevier.
Piazzesi, M., M. Schneider, and T. Selale (2007), Housing, consumption and asset pricing. Journal of Financial Economics 83.
Song, I.H. (2011), House prices and consumption. Ph.D. dissertation, The Ohio State University.
Uhlig, H. (1999), A Toolkit for Analyzing Nonlinear Dynamic Stochastic Models Easily. Oxford University Press.

Korean Publications

Kang, Hidon (2006), Changes in housing prices and monetary policy responses. Working paper, Bank of Korea.
Kim, Youngil (2010), Dynamic responses of changes in asset prices and consumption. KDI Research, 32–4.
Kim, Taehwan and Yang Junmo (2004), Taylor Rule Effect in the presences of tightening credit on the real economy. Applied Economics, 6–3, Korean Applied Economic Association.
Ko, Sungsu, and Yoon, Yeosun (2008), The effect of housing financing regulations on housing services with different income levels. Journal of Korea Real Estate Analysis Association 14 (2), 57–74.
Song, Inho (2012), "An anlaysis on linkages between housing financial sectors and macroeconomy through credit channel" A New Paradigm in Housing Policy after Global Financial Crisis, KDI Policy research, 2012–01, 258–297.

APPENDIX I

VAR using the Data from Interest, Inflation, Housing Prices and GDP

The Vector Autoregression (VAR) model in this analysis uses call rate, housing price index (provided by Kookmin Bank), CPI-based inflation and GDP. In particular, in order to secure the stationarity of housing prices and GDP, the Hodrick-Prescott (HP) filter was used to remove trends. The output gap of GDP was calculated from the difference between the trend and log-linear aggregate production extracted by the HP filter. In general, output gap is calculated from the difference between GDP and potential output, but since the VAR in this study extracted output gap from the HP filter, it may be fair to say that the notion of the output gap here may be different from that in a general-use definition.

The Cholesky decomposition was set in the order of the call rate, housing prices, inflation and GDP, and the trend in housing prices and GDP was removed by the HP filter as in Table 11A.1.

Unlike the VAR which orthogonalizes respective error terms in order to structure each shock, the Cholesky decomposition, defined as a lower triangular matrix in this chapter, is to produce significant results in which the decomposition order of each variable represents mutual correlation. Variables are generally arrayed in the order of a strong to weak heterogeneousness, and the magnitude of heterogeneousness could be identified by the Granger Causality. However, this study found no meaningful significance to define an explicit causal relationship. Therefore, the study used

Table 11A.1 Criteria for appropriate time lag

Time Lag	LR	FPE	AIC	SC	HQ
0	NA	1425.07	18.61	18.73	18.66
1	414.3	4.99	12.95	13.58*	13.20
2	54.3*	3.32*	12.54*	13.67	12.99*
3	23.62	3.51	12.59	14.22	13.24
4	9.60	4.67	12.85	14.99	13.24
5	14.89	5.62	13.01	15.64	14.06

Notes:
* Time lag selected based on threshold value.
Akaike information criteria: AIC, Schwartz Bayesian criteria: SC, Hannan-Quinn information criteria: HQ, Final prediction error: FPE,sequential modified LR test statistic:LR.

Source: Song (2012) recite.

several different orders instead to examine the changes in responses of variables to VAR shocks and found that the change in shock-evoked responses caused no significant impacts on the outcome. Based on this, this chapter adopted the order of the call rate, housing prices, inflation and GDP. Table 11A.1 shows the result of the time lag test and in this chapter, lag 2 was chosen as an appropriate time lag. The VAR Lag Order Selection Criteria was applied to determine which time lag is most appropriate, according to the Akaike information criteria (AIC).

Figure 11A.1 shows the shock-evoked responses, representing internal correlation between variables through the VAR model. The first row shows the responses of housing prices, inflation and aggregate output to the shock of the rise in interest rates, and as initially expected, both housing prices and aggregate output show negative movement. In the second row showing the responses of interest rates and GDP to the shock of the rise in housing prices, GDP turns out to move in a positive direction. In the last row, interest rates and housing prices rise in a positive direction to the shock of the rise in GDP. Such correlation observed between housing prices and macroeconomy is to be explained by the DSGE model.

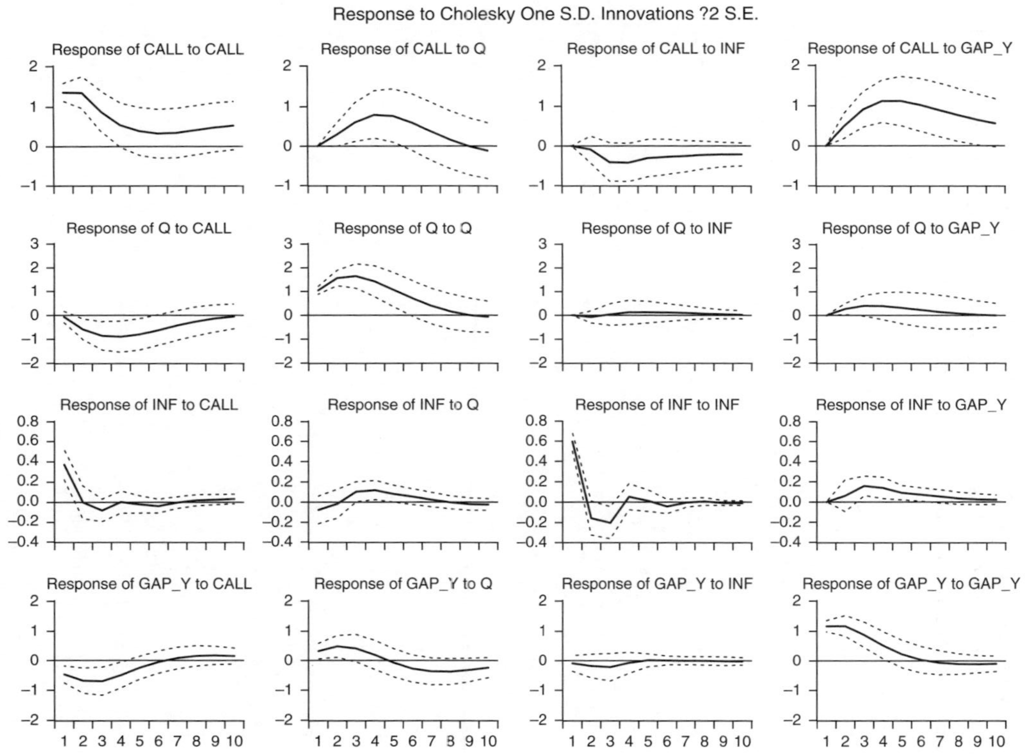

Source: Song (2012) recite.

Figure 11A.1 VAR with respect to interest, inflation, housing prices, and output

APPENDIX II

Spread and House Price Growth

Figure 11A.2 shows that house prices rise as the spread (the difference between the CD rate and mortgage rate) goes down in the period of 2005 and 2006. In the period of 2008 and 2009, house prices fall as the spread (the difference between the CD rate and mortgage rate) goes up.

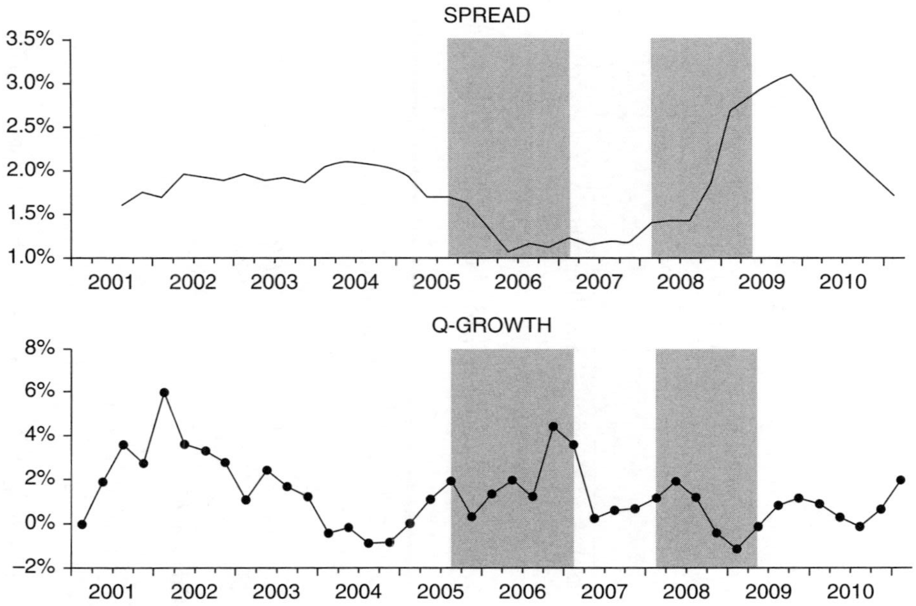

Source: Song (2012) recite.

Figure 11A.2 The spread and house prices

APPENDIX IIIA: STEADY STATE

Intermediate Good Producers

$$K = \frac{\gamma\mu Y}{(1 - \gamma(1 - \delta_k)X)} = \varsigma_1 Y$$

$$I_{Kt} = K_t - (1 - \delta)K_{t-1} \rightarrow I_K = \delta K = \delta\zeta_1 Y$$

$$w_{1,t}N_{1,t} = \frac{\alpha(1 - \mu - v)Y_t}{X_t}$$

$$w_{2,t}N_{2,t} = \frac{(1 - \alpha)(1 - \mu - v)Y_t}{X_t}$$

$$q = \frac{\gamma v}{((1 + \varphi_{he}) - \gamma(1 - \delta_{he}) - xm_e(\beta - \gamma))X}\left(\frac{Y}{H_e}\right) = \varsigma_2\left(\frac{Y}{H_e}\right)$$

$$C_e = \frac{Y}{X} - w_1N_1 - w_2N_2 - \delta K - \left((\delta + \varphi_e) - \left(1 - \frac{1}{\beta}\right)\beta m_e x\right)\varsigma_2$$

$$b_2 = \frac{xm_e(q\pi H_e)}{R} = \beta xm_2 q\pi H_e = \beta xm_e\varsigma_2$$

$$\lambda_e R = \frac{1}{C_e}(1 - R\gamma) = \frac{1}{C_e}R(\beta - \gamma)$$

Unconstrained Households

$C_1 = (1 - R)b_1 + w_1N_1 + F + Fee,$
where $b_1 = -(b_e + b_2)$

$$C_1 = (1 - \beta)x(m_e\zeta_2 + m_2\zeta_4C_2) + w_1N_1 + F + \zeta_2\varphi_e + \zeta_4C_2\varphi_2$$

$$q = \frac{j}{1 - \beta_1}\left(\frac{C_1}{H_1}\right)^{\frac{1}{\varepsilon}} = \varsigma_3\left(\frac{C_1}{H_1}\right)^{\frac{1}{\varepsilon}}$$

$$R = \frac{1}{\beta_1}$$

$$\frac{C_1}{H_1} = (q_t)^{\varepsilon}\left(\frac{(1+\varphi_1)}{j_t} - \frac{\pi_{t+1}q_{t+1}}{j_t R_t \; q_t}\right)^{\varepsilon}$$

Constrained Households

$$q = \frac{j}{(1+\varphi_2) - \beta_2(1-\delta_{h2}) - (\beta-\beta_2)m_2 x}\left(\frac{C_2}{H_2}\right)^{\frac{1}{\varepsilon}} = \varsigma_4\left(\frac{C_2}{H_2}\right)^{\frac{1}{\varepsilon}}$$

$$C_2 = \frac{1}{(1+(1-\beta)xm_2\varsigma_4+\varphi_2\varsigma_4)}w_2 N_2$$

$$\lambda_\mu = \lambda_2(\beta - \beta_2)$$

APPENDIX IIIB: FIRST ORDER CONDITIONS

Entrepreneurs

$$q_t/q = E_t\frac{C_{et}}{(1+\varphi_{he})}\left(\frac{\gamma}{C_{et+1}}\left(v\frac{Y_{t+1}}{X_{t+1}H_{et}} + (1-\delta_{he})q_{t+1}\right) + \lambda_{mt}x_t m_{et} q_{t+1}\pi_{t+1}\right)/q$$

Constrained Households: Housing Price

$$q_t/q = \left(\frac{U_{H_{2t}}}{U_{C_{iit}}} + \beta_2(1-\delta_{h2})\frac{U_{c_{mx+1}}}{U_{C_{mx}}}q_{t+1} + \frac{\lambda_{iit}}{U_{C_{mx}}}m_{2t}x_t E_t q_{t+1}\pi_{t+1}\right)/(1+\varphi_2)q$$

Unconstrained Households: Housing Price

$$(1+\varphi_{h1})\frac{q_t}{q} = \left(\frac{U_{H_{2t}}}{U_{C_{2t}}} + (\beta_1\psi_t)(1-\delta_{h1})\frac{U_{C_{2t+1}}}{U_{C_{2t}}}q_{t+1}\right)/q$$

Euler Equation for Entrepreneurs

$$\left(1+\frac{\psi}{\delta}\left(\frac{I_t}{K_{t-1}} - \delta\right)\right) = \gamma\frac{C_{et}}{C_{et+1}}E_t\left(\frac{\mu Y_{t+1}}{K_t X_{t+1}} + 1 + \frac{\psi}{\delta}\left(\frac{I_{t+1}}{K_t} - \delta\right)\left(\frac{1}{2}\left(\frac{I_{t+1}}{K_t} + \delta\right) + 1\right)\right)$$

$$1 = R_t C_{et}\left(E_t\left(\frac{\gamma}{\pi_{t+1}}\frac{1}{C_{et+1}}\right)\lambda_{et}\right)$$

Euler Equation for Constrained Households

$$R_t\lambda_{m2t} = U_{ciit} - U_{C_2,t+1}\frac{1}{\pi_{t+1}}\beta_2$$

Euler Equation for Unconstrained Households

$$1 = \beta_t E_t\left(\frac{\lambda_{1,t+1}}{\lambda_{1,t}}\frac{R_t}{\pi_{t+1}}\right)$$

Borrowing Constraint for Entrepreneurs

$$R_t/R = \frac{m_e}{R}\varsigma_t E_t(q_{t+1}\pi_{t+1}H_{et})/b_{et}$$

Borrowing Constraint for Constrained Households

$$R_t/R = \frac{m_2}{R}\varsigma_t E_t(q_{t+1}\pi_{t+1}H_{et})/b_{2t}$$

Labor for unconstrained households

$$N_{1,t}^{\eta} = U_{cit}\alpha(1-\mu-v)\frac{Y_t}{X_t}$$

Flow of Funds

$$b_{et} = C_{et} + \frac{R_{t-1}}{\pi_t}b_{et-1} - (\mu+v)\frac{Y_t}{X_t} + q_t(H_{et} - (1-\delta)H_{et-1}) + I_t + \psi_{K,t} + \varphi_e H_{et}q_t$$

$$C_{2,t} + q_t(H_{2,t} - H_{2,t-1}) + \varphi_2 q_t H_{2t} + \frac{R_{t-1}}{\pi_t} = w_{2,t}L_{2,t} + b_{2,t}$$

APPENDIX IIIC: LOGLINEARIZATION

Housing Market

$$0 = H\hat{H}_t + H_1\hat{H}_{1,t} + H_2\hat{H}_{2,t}$$

Production Function

$$Y_t = \hat{Z}_t + v\hat{H}_{t-1} + \mu\hat{K}_{t-1} + \alpha(1-\mu-v)\hat{N}_{1,t} + (1-\alpha)(1-\mu-v)\hat{N}_{2,t}$$

Phillips Curve

$$\hat{\pi}_t = \beta\pi_{t+1} + k\hat{X}_t + \hat{u}_t$$

12. Rental housing system and housing market volatility: monthly rent-based vs. asset-based systems

Kyung-Hwan Kim, Chang-Moo Lee and Young-Man Lee

1. INTRODUCTION

The importance of a well-functioning private rental housing sector is appreciated more than ever in recent years. This reflects the increasing pressure on government budgets in many industrialized nations which makes it difficult to maintain a large public rental sector, and the recognition that pushing homeownership too far in the U.S. was a contributor to the subprime mortgage crisis. There is a growing interest in finding sustainable rental housing in the aftermath of the global financial crisis (Oxley et al. 2010, Scanlon and Kochan 2011 for U.K.; Quigley and Rafael 2004, Gramlich 2007, Glaeser and Gyourko 2008 for the U.S.). On the other hand, Sinai (2011) argues that volatility is not the same thing as risk and that both renting and owning entail multi-dimensional risks of their own. But he is also in favor of providing an even playing field for renting by either reducing subsidies to homeownership or improving support to rental housing.

The choice between ownership and renting by individuals and the consequent homeownership rate are determined by economic variables as well as government policies and institutions which vary across countries. International comparative studies of tenure decisions reveal that there is no strong correlation between per capita income and homeownership rate, and that some government policies to encourage homeownership such as tax breaks and low-cost mortgage financing do matter (Proxenos 2002, Fisher and Jaffe 2003, Gwin and Ong 2004, Englund et al. 2005, Andrews and Sanchez 2011).

The impact of tenure composition on financial stability is indirect as it works through the mortgage system. Since rents are determined mainly by market fundamentals affecting demand and supply while demand for owner-occupancy is driven by expectations in addition to economic and policy variables, rents tend to be less volatile than housing prices. To the extent that changes in housing prices affect private consumption through a wealth effect and new housing investment, a larger owner-occupied sector might imply larger fluctuations in aggregate demand and hence output, other things being equal. Also to the extent that supply of new mortgage loans tends to move in the same direction as housing price, mortgage lending tends to increase rapidly during a period of housing price run-up which exposes the lenders to a potential loss in the event of a collapse of housing price.[1] All things considered, one can argue that promoting a well-functioning rental housing market might contribute to the stability of the financial sector and the macroeconomy.

This chapter explores the role of the private rental sector in promoting financial stability. For this purpose, the chapter conducts an international comparison of the pattern of the volatility of housing price and rents paying attention to the differences in institutions and policies. We also present the case of chonsei, an asset-based rental system that has dominated the Korean rental sector for many years. We try to draw some policy implications for promoting a sustainable rental housing sector. Following this introduction, section 2 describes the changing tenure composition in selected countries during the recent global housing price boom-bust cycle. Section 3 explains the key features and the housing outcomes of the chonsei system in Korea. Section 4 presents an analysis of volatility in housing price and rents in the housing markets in selected countries, and examines whether the asset-based rental system, chonsei, behaves differently from a typical monthly rental system in this respect.

Section 5 raises policy issues and concludes the chapter.

2. GLOBAL HOUSING PRICE CYCLE, HOMEOWNERSHIP, AND THE RENTAL HOUSING SECTOR

2.1 Global Housing Price Boom-Bust and Homeownership Rate

The latest housing price boom that started in the late 1990s and lasted until 2006–07 was the first global cycle that simultaneously affected many industrialized countries. The synchronized housing boom to which Germany, Japan and Switzerland were exceptions, was driven by the record low interest rates, rapid expansion of mortgage lending, relaxation of lending criteria, as well as optimistic expectations (Kim and Renaud 2009, Duca et al. 2011, Case et al. 2012).

Table 12.1 Mortgage debt outstanding to GDP ratio and housing prices in selected countries (%)

Country	MDO/GDP				Change in real house price		
	1995	2000	2006	2011	1995–2000	2000–2006	2006–2011
Belgium	20.8	27.7	35.9	47.2	15.5	47.1	7.3
Denmark	65.9	67.7	89.1	100.9	33.7	57.6	−26.3
France	20.1	21.2	32.1	42.4	15.7	77.0	0
Germany	45.1	53.2	51.2	45.3	−8.7	−8.2	−2.4
Ireland	23.5	31.0	69.5	83.5	110.0	54.0	−47.2
Italy	8.1	8.3	16.7	22.9	−2.7	43.5	−12.7
Japan	34.4	36.6	36.1	37.0	−13.4	−23	−12.1
Korea	11.0	13.0	35.7	30.5	−27.2	33.3	0
Netherlands	47.9	68.2	96.7	106.2	72.5	18.5	−12.3
Spain	16.6	29.9	58.1	62.1	22.8	63.0	−23.5
Sweden	56.2	44.6	63.8	78.1	46.2	49.7	8.6
U.K.	53.2	55.8	82.2	83.7	48.6	90.3	−18
U.S.	46.4	58.9	81.3	76.1	19.7	49.1	−39.7

Table 12.1 shows the trend of the ratio between mortgage debt outstanding (MDO) and GDP and the change in real house price in selected countries since 1995. The pace of real house price increase accelerated during the period 2000–06 in most countries that experienced the house price boom. Although more diverse across countries than the price trend, the MDO/GDP ratio increased substantially between 1995 and 2006, and more rapidly between 2000 and 2006 in many countries.

In general, the homeownership rate of a country evolves slowly over time (Figure 12.1). An exception is the U.K. where the homeownership rate jumped from 56.6 per cent to 67 per cent during the 1980s thanks to the "right to buy policy" of the Thatcher government, which encouraged the tenants of council housing to buy their homes at a discount. Rapid expansion of mortgage lending and housing price hikes in the late 1990s and 2000s have affected homeownership rates in different countries in different ways. For example, relaxation of underwriting criteria and the introduction of innovative loan products led the U.S. homeownership rate to a record high level of 69.4% in 2004 before it fell back to 68.5% in 2006 and eventually to 65.4% by 2011. On the other hand, the U.K. homeownership rate did not increase during the housing price boom despite the expansion of mortgage lending, and later dropped to 64% by 2011, the lowest since 1987. This is attributed to the tightening of lending standards by lenders in the wake of the Global Financial Crisis. A similar pattern is found in

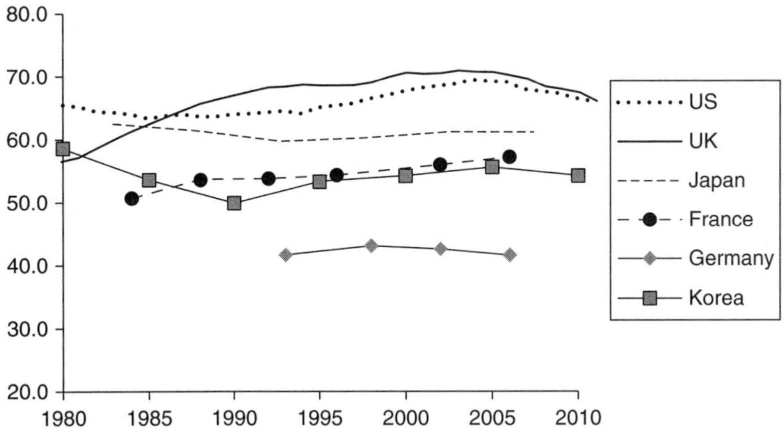

Figure 12.1 The trends in homeownership rate in selected countries

Korea where mortgage lending expanded sharply since 2000 but there was no noticeable gain in homeownership rate. Finally, in Japan, the increase in mortgage lending was moderate and the homeownership rate stood still at 61%.

2.2 Evolution of the Rental Housing Sector

The size and the structure of the rental housing sector vary across countries. The rental housing sector typically consists of public rental housing (social housing) and private rental housing, but the composition of the two differs greatly from country to country. For example, social housing is of a negligible size in the U.S. but it dominates the rental sector in Hong Kong, Netherlands and Austria. Some countries have broad based social housing systems with no income limit whereas other countries have targeted systems with income limits.[2] Private rental housing is provided mostly by individual landlords in the U.S. and many European countries.[3] The stock of private rental housing, especially that owned by individuals, is fluid as a house can be occupied by its owner or leased out to a tenant at a given point in time and the status of occupation could change over time. Therefore, it is somewhat difficult to define the private rented stock if it refers to the units that are rented out on a long-term basis if not permanently.

Table 12.2 presents the share of social housing, private rental housing as well as owner-occupied dwellings in selected countries. It should be noted that the exact definition of tenure breakdown is not identical across

Table 12.2 Owner-occupiers, social renters and private renters in selected countries (%)

	Owner occupiers	Social renters	Private renters	Others	All tenures
U.K.					
2000	69.8	20.3	9.9		100.0
2005	69.3	18.2	12.5		100.0
2010	65.2	17.5	17.4		100.0
U.S.					
2000	67.4	1.2	31.4		100.0
2009	67.4	1.0	31.6		100.0
France					
2002	56.0	17.3	20.7	6.1	100.0
2006	57.2	17.1	20.4	5.3	100.0
Japan					
2001	60.3	11.3	27.4		100.0
2006	61.2	12.0	26.8		100.0
2011	61.1	12.0	26.9		100.0
Korea					
2000	54.2	1.9	41.1	2.8	100.0
2005	55.6 (60.3)	2.3	39.0	3.1	100.0
2010	54.2 (61.3)	4.6	38.5	2.7	100.0
Hong Kong					
2002	48.8	31.1	19.1	1.0	100.0
2007	50.9	30.3	18.1	0.7	100.0
2012	53.2	29.1	17.1	0.6	100.0

countries and this can make international comparison difficult. When the exact data on the share of households living in private rental housing (public rental housing) is not available, we impute the figure by subtracting the owner-occupation rate and that of public (private) rental housing residency from 100%.[4]

Some countries have gone through a noticeable change in the size of the rental sector and/or the composition of the rental sector between social housing and private rental subsectors. For example, in U.K., the percentage of households living in rental housing remained virtually constant around 32 per cent between 1991 and 2001, but the share of social housing fell from 23 per cent to 19 per cent while that of private renting rose from 9 per cent to 12 per cent. As the homeownership rate fell between 2001 and 2011, the share of the rental sector increased to 36 per cent, of which social housing and the private rental sector accounted for 18 per cent each. In the case of Korea, the homeownership rate[5] remained stable since 1995, but the share of monthly rental leases increased whereas the asset-based chonsei rental leases decreased. This will be further elaborated in the next section.

3. ASSET-BASED RENTAL HOUSING: THE CASE OF KOREA

3.1 The Mechanism of Chonsei Contracts

A typical rental housing lease entails a small security deposit (equivalent to the rent for a month or two) and monthly rents. However, Korea has a unique asset-based, and wealth-based, rental contract type known as chonsei, which emerged as a natural response to a severe housing shortage and lack of savings opportunities in financial markets during the early stage of economic development.

Under a chonsei contract the tenant makes a lump sum deposit up front to the landlord at the signing of the lease and pays no monthly rents during the lease period. The deposit is refunded in full to the tenant at the end of the lease. The landlord invests the deposit in such a way as to recoup a return comparable to a monthly rent or higher. Although it is on a declining path, chonsei remains the most important type of rental tenure, accounting for 21.7% of all types of housing tenure in 2010. At the same time, monthly rental contracts with varying amounts of deposit are increasing in some markets in recent years, comprising 20.1% of all tenure types in 2010.

Chonsei is not a pure rental contract. In fact, it is also an informal housing loan made by the tenant to the landlord at the interest payable to the tenant in the form of the right to the flow of housing services that originates from a house. The landlord (who owns another unit for her own residence) can combine the deposit with her own equity and possibly a bank loan to purchase the house, and rent it out to the tenant. Chonsei is an example of antichresis lease which involves giving a credit against the use of a property (Navarro and Turnbull 2010, p. 34). The estimated size of the chonsei market in 2010 measured as the total claims on deposits was larger than the outstanding balance of housing loans by commercial banks in Korea.

Since the chonsei deposit is a sizable amount, mobilizing the initial deposit or the subsequent increase to the existing contract deposit can be a challenge for the tenant. The asset-based nature of chonsei puts younger households with no or little equity at a disadvantage. The ratio between chonsei deposit and the value of the house varies across markets and property types as well as over housing price cycles. The current level of deposit is about 50% of the asset price for apartments (condominiums in the US terminology) in Seoul and 60% for the whole country.

3.2 The Linkages Between Chonsei Deposit and House Price

The two key determinants of the deposit-price ratio are the interest rate and the expected capital gain on housing. Suppose that a household chooses between chonsei and buying a house with a mortgage loan. In equilibrium, the costs of the two types of tenure should be equated. If we further assume that the opportunity cost of capital tied up in a chonsei deposit (or the required rate of return on deposit) made by a tenant is equal to the opportunity cost of (or the required rate of return on) own equity of a home buyer, and that property tax and maintenance cost on owner-occupied housing remain stable, then the chonsei deposit to house price ratio is determined by the interest rate and expected capital gain. As the interest rate rises, the user cost of homeownership increases relative to chonsei and more households would opt for chonsei instead of buying. As expected capital gain increases, more households would prefer home purchase to renting on chonsei. These results can be demonstrated as follows.

The user cost of chonsei tenancy, i.e. the economic cost borne by the chonsei tenant of leaving the deposit to the landlord, is given by

$$U_c = i_c C \tag{12.1}$$

where i_c is the opportunity cost of a chonsei deposit C

The user cost of homeownership financed through a combination of chonsei deposit (C) made by the tenant and a mortgage loan (the difference between the price of the house P and the deposit C) can be expressed as

$$U_0 = i_0 C + i_m (P - C) + tP - a_e P \tag{12.2}$$

where i_m is the mortgage interest rate, t is the maintenance and property tax rate, i_0 is the opportunity cost of equity invested in housing, and α_e is expected rate of housing price appreciation.

In equilibrium, user cost of chonsei should equal that of homeownership.[6]

$$U_c = U_O \tag{12.3}$$

This requires that

$$kC = (k - i_m) C + (i_m + t - a_e) P, \text{ if } i_c = i_0 = k^7 \tag{12.4}$$

From this, we can derive an expression for the ratio between chonsei deposit and the asset price of housing as follows

$$\frac{C}{P} = 1 + \frac{t - a_e}{i_m} \tag{12.5}$$

The chonsei to price ratio is a function of two variables, i_m and a_e

$$C/P = f(i_m, a_e) \tag{12.6}$$

where

$$\frac{\partial f}{\partial i_m} = -\frac{t - a_e}{i_m^2} > 0 \text{ and } \frac{\partial f}{\partial a_e} = -\frac{1}{i_m} < 0^{8}$$

4. THE RENTAL HOUSING SECTOR AND HOUSING MARKET VOLATILITY

4.1 Some Background

A major argument for promoting rental housing is that excessive volatility in housing price can create a systemic risk. A boom-bust cycle of housing price and procyclical mortgage lending can push homeowners with large mortgage debt into financial hardship and expose lenders to a larger credit risk[9]. The magnitude of such risk would depend on the size of the mortgage market and the values of the key parameters in mortgage lending such as loan-to-value ratio and debt-service-to–income ratio. A stable rental housing market can help avoid such risk. Renters are less exposed to housing market volatility because landlords bear the risk of housing price downfall.

Historical data for the U.S. and U.K. suggest that rents are much more stable than housing prices (Gallin 2008, Stephens 2011). In this section, we conduct an empirical analysis of the volatility of housing price and rents using some international data. In so doing, we examine whether the asset-based rental system, chonsei, behaves differently from a typical monthly rental system in terms of the relative volatility of housing price and rents.

Before we look at the data, it should be noted that the chonsei deposit might be more volatile than housing price. It can be shown that the variance of the rate of change in chonsei deposit equals the sum of the variance of the rate of change in housing price and the covariance between the rate of change in housing price and the change in the ratio of expected capital gain to the interest rate. This means that the chonsei deposit can be more volatile or less volatile than the asset price of housing depending on the magnitude of the covariance term. This can be demonstrated as follows.

Equation (12.5) above can be rewritten as

$$C = \left(1 + \frac{t - a_e}{i_m}\right)P \tag{12.7}$$

Let $y = d\ln C$, $q = d\ln P$, and $s = d\left(\frac{t - a_e}{i_m}\right)$

Then $Var(y) = Var(q) + Var(s) + 2\,Cov(q, s)$.
Therefore, $Var(y) \ < or > \ Var(q)$

4.2 An Empirical Analysis of Volatility of Housing Price and Rents

We now turn to look at the behavior of house price and rents in six countries for which we were able to gather data. It is well known that internationally comparable housing price data is difficult to come by, but finding matching data on rents is even more difficult. Even in countries such as the U.S. and U.K., where multiple indexes of housing price exist, rent index is not available for the same sample of houses. Empirical literature on the behavior of rent to price ratio in the U.S. points out the problem associated with using the rent component of the consumer price index together with a housing price index (Kim 2008). The data we used are as follows: U.K.: Residential Property Prices, Private Sector (Halifax, BIS data) and Private Registered Provider Rents (DCLG); U.S.: Residential Property Prices, Existing dwellings (CORELOGIC, BIS data) and Rent of CPI (Bureau of Labor Statistics); Canada: Residential Property Price, New Houses (Statistics Canada, BIS data) and Rent of CPI (Statistics Canada); Germany: Residential Property Price, Existing (Deutsche Bundesbank, BIS data) and Net rent of CPI (Statistisches Bundesamt): Hong Kong: Private Domestic Price Indices (Rating and Valuation Department) and Private Domestic Rental Indices (Rating and Valuation Department); Korea: Housing Price Index (Kokmin Bank) and Chonsei Index (Kokmin Bank).

Table 12.3 presents mean and standard deviation of housing price index and rent index in these six countries. The frequency of the data and the time span covered by the data differ across countries.

The figures in the table show that the rate of change in housing price exhibits a larger variance than that of rents in Canada, U.S., Germany, U.K., and Hong Kong. On the other hand, the Korean data suggest that the variance of housing price and that of rents measured in chonsei deposit

Table 12.3 Mean and standard deviation of housing price and rent in selected countries (%)

	Frequency	Time period	Housing price		Rents	
			Average	Std. Dev.	Average	Std. Dev.
Canada	Annual	1981–2012	2.82	4.73	2.58	1.99
U.S.	Quarterly	1976:1–2012:4	5.48	7.39	4.13	1.99
Germany	Annual	1995–2012	0.19	0.29	1.33	0.61
U.K.	Annual	1997–2011	6.75	9.33	3.76	1.85
Hong Kong	Monthly	1993.1–2013.4	6.44	19.33	2.97	12.37
Korea	Monthly	1986.1–2012.12	6.18	9.73	8.22	9.63

are about the same.[10] This result can be attributed to the very nature of the chonsei system whereby fluctuations of chonsei deposit are driven by the changes in interest rates and expected capital gains on housing as well as factors affecting demand and supply in a typical rental market.

We also analyzed the time-varying pattern of the volatility of housing price and rents using a conditional heteroscedasticity model for four countries excepting U.K. and Germany for which the available annual time series is considered too short. We computed the first difference of logarithm of housing price index and that of rent index, and estimated a GARCH model. Figure 12.2 presents the conditional variance of the two series for the time period for which data are available.

The graphs in Figure 12.2 reveal some interesting points. First, it appears that housing prices in Canada, the U.S. and Korea were highly volatile in the late 1980s, became less volatile in the 1990s and more volatile again around the 2008 Global Financial Crisis. Hong Kong housing price exhibits a pattern of increasing and decreasing volatility in a more frequent manner. Secondly, the time pattern of variability in rents is more diverse among the four countries than that of housing price. In the case of the U.S. and Canada, variability of rent has decreased since the 1980s and did not increase around the Global Financial Crisis. Hong Kong's rent index has been volatile throughout the entire period. The time pattern of the Korean data is more complex. The variability of chonsei deposit increased in the late 1980s, decreased in the 1990s, increased again in the early 2000s and decreased again in the late 2000s.

One needs to be cautious in interpreting these findings from an analysis of a small number of countries. But it seems that rents are less volatile than housing price in countries with a monthly-rent based rental market than in Korea with an asset-based rental market. This makes sense because rents

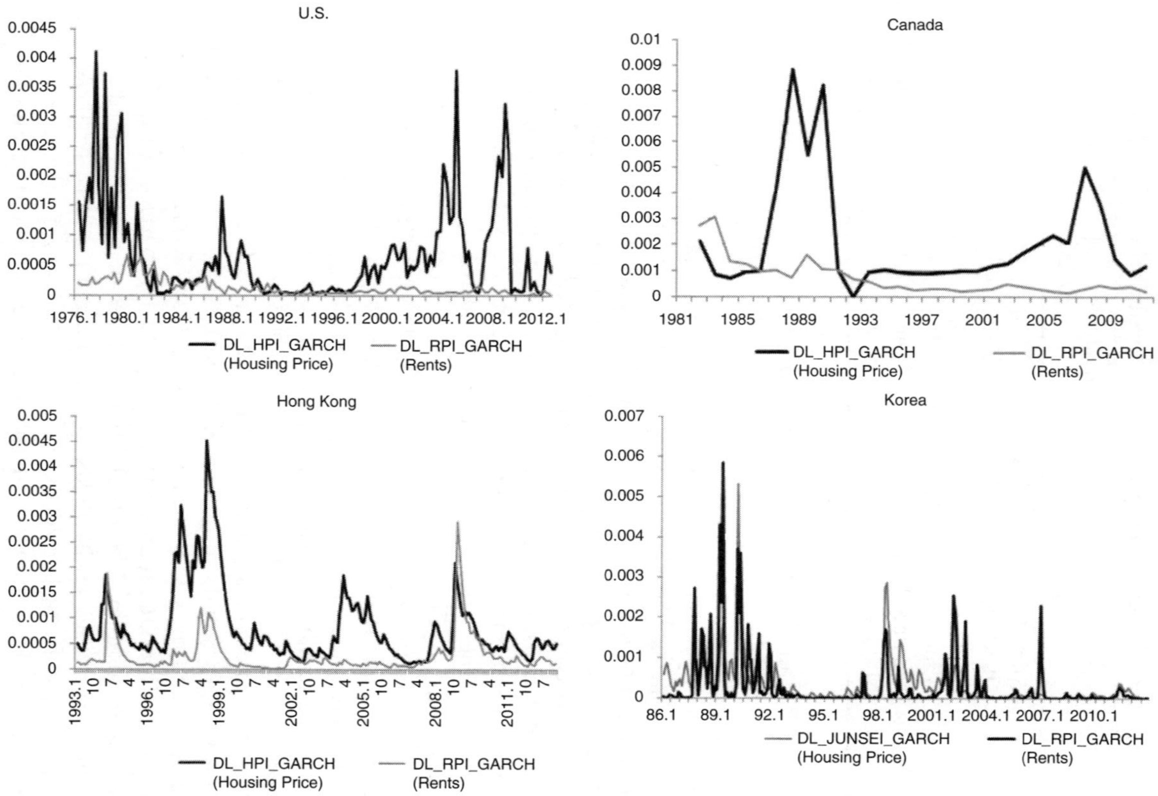

Figure 12.2 Conditional variance of housing price and rents in Canada, U.S., Hong Kong and Korea

in countries other than Korea are not affected by expected capital gains unlike the chonsei deposit in Korea. The case of Hong Kong is also interesting in that both housing price and rents in the private sector are highly volatile despite a very large public rental sector.

5. SOME POLICY ISSUES

There is a growing interest in affordable and sustainable rental housing in many countries for various reasons. One is the concern about the ramifications, for financial stability, of pushing homeownership too far. A well-functioning rental housing sector is essential since it offers a viable alternative to owning a house, especially for those who cannot afford to buy homes due to inadequate savings or those who choose not to be homeowners due to high mobility or personal preferences. In this final section, we discuss some policy issues towards the rental housing sector.

Rental housing policy instruments include direct production/provision of rental housing by the public sector (public rental) or by non-profit providers (social housing), tax and financial incentives to the private developers of rental housing (supply-side subsidies), subsidies to qualifying tenants (demand-side subsidies), and regulations of rental leases (rent regulations and tenant protection). The exact combination of these instruments varies across countries depending on the history of housing markets, public perception about the role of government, government budget constraint and other factors. Therefore, what is deemed an ideal combination for one country may not be relevant for another country, and what was once accepted as the best package may lose its value with the passage of time. With this in mind, we posit some generic issues in exploring ways to promote affordable and sustainable rental housing.

The first question concerns the division of responsibilities between the government and the private sector in the provision of rental housing. A specific issue is about how large a public (social) rental sector to purse in light of a wide spectrum of systems. At the one extreme is the U.S. where public housing is a legacy of the past and constitutes just about 1% of total housing stock. At the other extreme, there are several European countries such as the Netherlands and Austria[11] as well as Hong Kong where public rental housing dominates the rental sector.[12] It is argued that a significantly large stock of public rental housing is essential for housing welfare. But the right size for a specific country should be determined in conjunction with other instruments of rental housing policy available as well as market conditions and budget implications from a long run perspective. The examples of other countries may not be a relevant benchmark.

As was mentioned earlier, small individual landlords are the predominant suppliers of private rental housing in most countries, whereas the role of institutional providers is much more limited. A major reason for the weak presence of institutions in private rental housing is that the share of rental properties represents a small portion of their total portfolio. A comparative study of 15 European countries shows that the average share of rental property holdings is 15% but it varies greatly from zero (Belgium, Ireland, Spain, Italy and Portugal) or negligible (U.K. and Norway) to 40–50% (The Netherlands and Switzerland[13]) (Alakeson 2011).

The private rental housing sector is responsive to the institutional arrangements and government policies on financing, taxation and regulations that affect the profitability of rental housing business. Various incentives are provided to private rental housing suppliers including accelerated depreciation allowance or deduction of the capital cost from taxable income (Germany and France), capital gains tax exemption for qualifying rental housing operators (Germany), Low Income Housing Tax Credit (LIHTC, the U.S.) and negative gearing, or offsetting losses from rental business against other income (Germany, France, and Australia). These incentives go with some requirements on the type of housing, rents and lease terms, tenant selection, and holding period of housing asset. Demand subsidies deserve more serious consideration as an instrument of enhancing affordability of rental housing to targeted tenants (Quigley 2008). However, demand subsidies will be effective only in the presence of adequate supply of rental housing in the right price range. Increasing demand subsidies against inelastic rental housing supply would simply raise rents.

As for regulations, many countries and cities have some form of rent regulation and/or tenant protection. These regulations have become more flexible over the years, but their negative impact on the private rental housing market is quite clear. An empirical study of the determinants of homeownership rates in OECD countries found that stricter rent controls and higher security of tenure are associated with lower probability of homeownership, and thereby create a large pressure on the rental sector (Andrews and Sanchez 2011). Montezuma (2006) reports a survey result that rent regulations and tenant protection laws are a major constraint for attracting institutional investors to rental housing. Nevertheless, these regulations remain popular and difficult to remove once introduced.

We conclude the chapter with a discussion of some policy issues specific to Korea. Korea is experiencing a decrease in demand for homeownership in recent years, partly driven by the negative prospects for capital gains, and this spills over to the rental market and thereby increases the demand for rental housing. Therefore, there is a strong case for increasing the supply of rental housing. Public rental housing stock has been increasing and it now comprises 5% of the total housing stock and is expected to rise in the future. However, there is a limit on government budget and supply side constraints on increasing public rental housing, which makes it imperative to promote the private rental sector. However, institutional investors are not likely to put their money into the Korean rental market because the private rental housing business does not generate a competitive return, and the asset-based chonsei system fails to generate a steady cash flow. This makes the private individual owners the most logical candidates for investors in and suppliers of rental housing. In this regard, Korea needs to rethink the validity of the policy of pursuing the ideal of one owner-occupied house for each household and of penalizing owners of more than one house as speculators. The latest government proposal to abolish punitive capital gains tax on these individuals is a step forward. Other incentives might be needed to ensure a steady inflow of funds into the private rented sector such as tax credit and negative gearing, assuming that rental income will be taxed properly. A pass-through vehicle pooling funds from individual investors in rental housing and having a property management company operate and manage the rental property for a fee might also be considered.

A final question concerns the future of the chonsei system. Since chonsei emerged naturally from a combination of urban housing shortages, underdeveloped mortgage market, and inadequate financial investment opportunities, it has been expected to phase out as these constraints loosen over time. In fact, the market share of this unique asset-based rental tenure has declined in recent years due to decreases in expected capital gains and declining interest rates. However, chonsei continues to be more attractive than monthly rents (with a small deposit) for the tenants who can mobilize the initial deposit and its increment from family sources or through bank loans. This is mainly because the implicit interest rate used to convert deposit to rents remains substantially higher than the cost of funds. In addition, government policy favors chonsei over monthly rents through tax treatment and financing. This might reflect government concern over an abrupt structural change in the rental market. Although managing the transition is important, policies should be made neutral between chonsei and monthly rental options by improving taxation of landlords on income from chonsei and allowing for deduction of monthly rents paid by tenants from taxable income. The case for neutral policy can be further strengthened if one considers the equity consequences of chonsei contracts which work to the disadvantage of younger households with little equity to make a sizeable deposit up front and mobilize a lump sum increment at renewal.

NOTES

1. There is also the controversial Oswald hypothesis that there exists a positive correlation between homeownership and unemployment rate (Oswald 1996, Green and Hendershott 2001, Rouwendal and Nijkamp, 2007, Blanchflower and Oswald 2013).
2. See Andrews et al. 2011 for details.
3. An international comparative study of the private rented sector in 15 advanced economies reveals that the share of the private rented sector dwellings owned by individuals (or couples) exceeds 60 % in all countries except the Netherlands (44%), Denmark (8%), Austria (very few) and Sweden (very few) (Scanlon and Kochan 2011, p. 23).
4. Scanlon and Kochan (2011) provide a range of the share of private rental housing for the same reason.
5. There are two measures of tenure breakdown, the owner-occupancy rate expressed in terms of the composition of housing stock and the homeownership rate expressed in terms of the composition of households by tenure. The difference between the two is small in most countries, but it is substantial in Korea as more than 20% of the renters own houses somewhere else.
6. Here we consider the chonsei lease that requires an up-front deposit only. In practice, there is a continuum of rental contracts that combine a deposit and a monthly rent payment. This makes the analysis much more complicated. See Lee and Chung (2010) for details.
7. When a household with equity C decides whether to rent a house on a chonsei lease or buy a house, the opportunity cost on the equity should be the same. However, chonsei tenancy and homeownership entail different risks, and therefore i_c might not be the same as i_m We assume that the two interest rates are equal to simplify the model.
8. Historically, C/P has been less than 1. Therefore, $\frac{C}{P} - 1 = \frac{t - a_e}{i_m} < 0$, and $(t - a_e) < 0$. This gives $\frac{\partial f}{\partial i_m} = -\frac{t - a_e}{i_m^2} > 0$
9. Investors in rental housing who leveraged housing purchase with a mortgage and chonsei deposit might also face the risk of not being able to return the deposit to the tenant.
10. It turns out that the chonsei deposit index was less volatile than the housing price index until the 1997 Asian Financial Crisis, but the trend was reversed after that.
11. See CECODHAS for data on European countries.
12. Singapore is an example where the public sector plays a dominant role in the provision of owner-occupied housing.
13. Institutions in Switzerland are required by law to hold real estate, and rental housing is an important part of property holdings (Scanlon and Kochan 2011).

REFERENCES

Alakeson, Vidhya, 2011, "Making Rented House a Home: Housing Solutions for 'Generation Rent'", Resolution Foundation.

Andrews, Dan and Aida Caldera Sanchez, 2011, "Drivers of homeownership rates in selected OECD countries", ECO-WKP(2011) 18.

Andrews, Dan, Aida Caldera Sanchez, and Asa Johansson, 2011, "Housing Markets and Structural Policies in OECD Countries", OECD Economics Department Working Papers No. 836.

Blanchflower, David G., and Andrew J. Oswald, 2013, "Does High Home-Ownership Impair the Labor Market?", mimeo.

Case, Karl E., Robert J. Shiller, and Anne Thompson, 2012, "What Have They

Been Thinking? Home Buyer Behavior in Hot and Cold Markets", NBER Working Paper 18400.

CECODHAS Housing Europe's Observatory, 2011, "Housing Europe Review 2012", Brussels

Duca, John, John Muellbauer, and Anthony Murphy, 2011, "House Prices and Credit Constraints: Making Sense of the U.S. Experience", *Economic Journal*, 121, 533–551.

Englund, Peter, Kyung-Hwan Kim, Stephen Malpezzi and Bengt Turner, 2005, "Housing Tenure Across Countries: The Effects of Regulations and Institutions", mimeo.

Fisher, Lynn M., and Austin J. Jaffe, 2003, "Determinants of International Home Ownership Rates", *Housing Finance International*, September, 34–42.

Gallin, J., 2008, "The long-run relationship between house prices and rents", *Real Estate Economics*, 36(4), 635–658.

Glaeser, E.L. and J. Gyourko, 2008, *Rethinking Federal Housing Policy: How to Make Housing Plentiful and Affordable*, American Enterprise Institute Press.

Gramlich, Edward, 2007, *Subprime Mortgages: America's Latest Boom and Bust*, Brookings Institution.

Green, Richard K., 2011, "Thoughts on Rental Housing and Rental Housing Assistance", *Cityscape, A Journal of Policy Development and Research*, 13(2), 39–55.

Green, Richard K. and Patric H. Hendershott, 2001, "Home-ownership and Unemployment in the US", *Urban Studies*, 38, 1509–1520.

Gwin, Carl R., and Seow-Eng Ong, 2004, "Do We Really Understand Home Ownership Rates? An International Study", Hankamer School of Business Working Paper 2004–053-ECO, Baylor University.

Kim, Kyung-Hwan and Bertrand Renaud, 2009, "The Global House Price Boom and its Unwinding: An Analysis and a Commentary", *Housing Studies*, 24(1), 7–24.

Kim, Yong, 2008, "Rent-price Ratios and the Earnings Yield on Housing", mimeo, University of Southern California.

Lee, C.-M. and E.-C. Chung, 2010, "Monthly rent with variable deposit: A new form of rental contract in Korea", *Journal of Housing Economics*, 19, 315–323.

Malpezzi, Stephen, 2012, "Rental Housing Policies in U.S.A.", prepared for the Ministry of Land and Transport, Korea.

Montezuma, J., 2006, "A Survey of Institutional Investors' Attitudes and Perceptions of Residential Property: The Swiss, Dutch, and Swedish Cases", *Housing Studies*, 21(6), 883–908.

Navarro, I. and G.K. Turnbull, 2010, "Antichresis leases: Theory and empirical evidence from the Bolivian experience", *Regional Science and Urban Economics*, 40, 33–44.

Oswald, A., 1996, "A Conjecture on the Explanation of High Unemployment in Industrialized Nations: Part I", mimeo, Department of Economics, University of Warwick.

Oxley, M., M. Haffner, R. Lishman, J. Hoekstra, and T. Brown, 2010, "Promoting Investment in Private Rented Housing Supply: International Policy Comparisons", UK: Department of Communities and Local Government.

Peppercorn, Ira Gary and Claude Taffin, 2012, *Rental Housing: Lessons from International Experience and Policies for Emerging Markets*, World Bank.

Proxenos, Soula, 2002, "Homeownership rates: A global perspective", Housing Finance International, 17(2), 3–7.
Quigley, John M., 2008, "Just Suppose: Housing Subsidies for Low-Income Renters", in N. Retsinas and E. Belsky (eds), *Revisiting Rental Housing: Policies, Programs and Priorities*, Brookings Institution, pp. 299–316.
Quigley, John M. and Steven Rafael, 2004, "Is Housing Unaffordable? Why Isn't It More Affordable?" *Journal of Economic Perspectives*, 18(1), 191–214.
Rouwendal, Jan and Peter Nijkamp, 2007, "Homeownership and Labour Market Behaviour: Interpreting the Evidence", TI 2007–047/3 Tinbergen Institute Discussion Paper.
Scanlon, K. and B. Kochan (eds), 2011, "Towards a Sustainable Private Rented Sector: The Lessons from Other Countries", London School of Economics and Political Science.
Sinai, Todd, 2011, "Understanding and Mitigating Rental Risk", *Cityscape, A Journal of Policy Development and Research*, 13(2), 105–125.
Stephens, Mark, 2011, *Tackling Housing Market Volatility in the U.K.*, Joseph Rowntree Foundation.
Taffin, Claude, 2012, "Rental Housing Policies in France.", prepared for the Ministry of Land and Transport, Korea.
Whitehead, Christine M., 2012, "Rental Housing and Policies in England and the U.K.", prepared for the Ministry of Land and Transport, Korea.

13. Dealing with real estate booms*

Giovanni Dell'Ariccia and Deniz Igan

1. INTRODUCTION

Until the global financial crisis, the main policy tenet in dealing with a real estate boom was one of "benign neglect" (Bernanke, 2002). The widespread consensus was that it was better to wait for the bust and pick up the pieces than to attempt to prevent the boom. This was based on two assumptions. First, the belief that it is extremely difficult to identify unsustainable real estate booms, or "bubbles", in real time. Second, the notion that the distortions associated with preventing a boom outweigh the costs of cleaning up after a bust.

The crisis has challenged this view. Post-bust policy intervention was of limited effectiveness and, thus, the costs associated with this particular bust were daunting. While early intervention may engender its own distortions, it may be best to undertake policy action on the basis of a judgment call (as with inflation) if there is a real risk that inaction could result in catastrophe.

Yet, a call for a more preventive policy action raises more questions than it provides answers. What kind of indicators should trigger policy intervention to stop a real estate boom? If policymakers were fairly certain that interventions were warranted, what would be the policy tools at their disposal? What are their impacts? What are their negative side effects and limitations? What practical issues would limit their use? What are the optimal institutional arrangements for their control? This chapter explores these questions taking the characteristics of housing cycles and the linkages between housing and mortgage markets and business cycles into consideration.

It should be recognized at the onset that there is no silver bullet. A more proactive policy stance can help reduce the risks associated with real estate booms, but will inevitably entail costs and distortions, and its effectiveness will be limited by loopholes and implementation problems. With this in mind, we reach the following conclusions. Policy efforts should focus on booms that are financed through credit and when leveraged institutions are directly involved, as the following busts tend to be more costly. In that context, monetary policy is too blunt and costly a tool to deal with the vulnerabilities associated with increased leverage, unless the boom occurs as a result of or at the same time as broader economic overheating. Fiscal tools may be, in principle, effective. But, in practice, they would likely create distortions and are difficult to use in a cyclical fashion. Macroprudential tools (such as limits on loan-to-value ratios) are the best candidates to deal with the dangers associated with real estate booms as they can be aimed directly at curbing leverage and strengthening the financial sector. But their careful design is crucial to minimize circumvention and regulatory arbitrage. Further, they will entail a cost to the extent that some agents find themselves rationed out of credit markets.

In what follows, we first give a summary of how real estate boom-bust cycles are linked to the broader economy and may threaten financial and macroeconomic stability. We discuss the case for policy action, and then look at different policy options to reduce the risks associated with real estate booms, drawing upon several country experiences (a more detailed analysis of country cases is in Crowe et al., 2011). We conclude with a brief discussion of the tradeoffs involved in designing a macroprudential regulator.

2. THE STATE OF KNOWLEDGE ON REAL ESTATE MARKETS AND LINKAGES TO THE ECONOMY

Real estate markets have come to the fore of economic policy discussions in the aftermath of the global financial crisis. What do we know about real estate cycles, especially in residential markets? What do we know about linkages between housing, credit, and business cycles? How can we improve our knowledge? These are the questions to which this section aims to provide some answers.

Cycles, sometimes rather pronounced, are a common feature of real estate markets. Several features could explain this fact, for example, the delay in demand and supply responses given the time to build and the physical constraints on the supply side (i.e., land is in limited supply and zoning restrictions put additional limits on new construction). From a global perspective, the cyclical movements are evident in Figure 13.1, which shows the average real house price index across countries since the 1970s. There have been three episodes during which prices increased at a particularly rapid pace: first, in the early 1970s; second, in the mid-1980s; and third, in

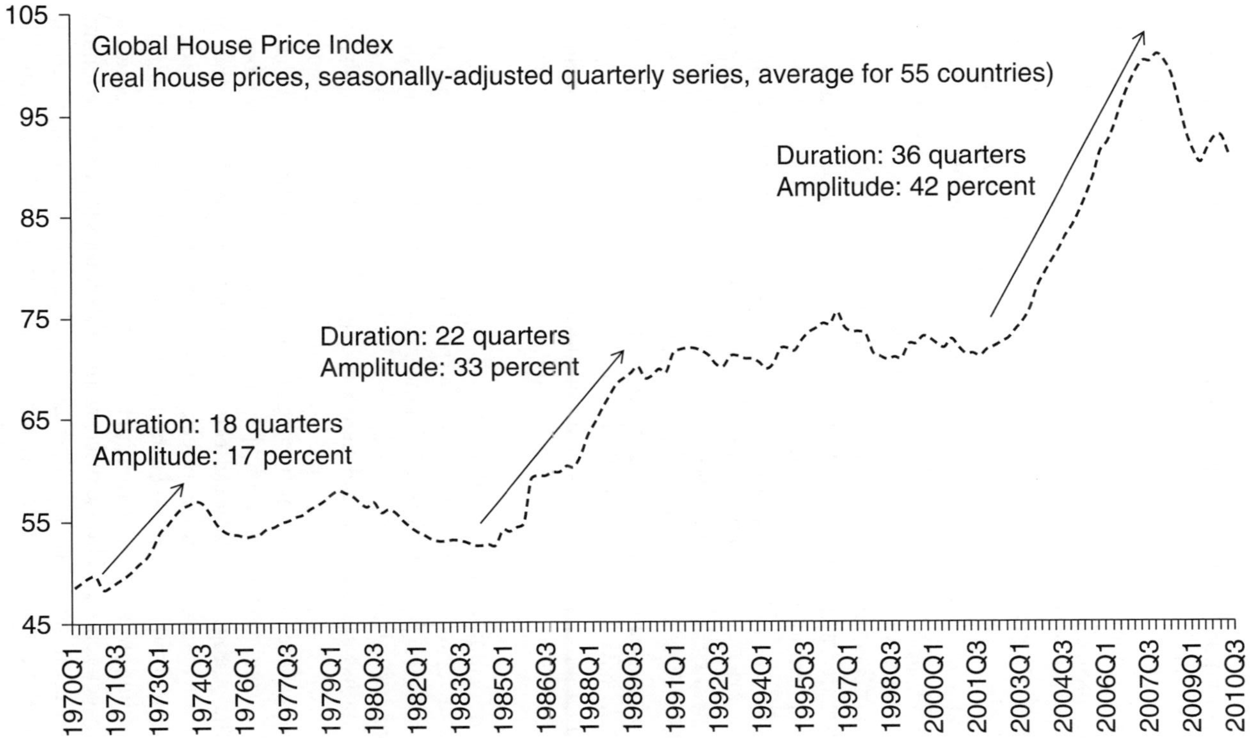

Sources: OECD, BIS, Global Property Guide, national sources; authors' calculations.

Figure 13.1 Global house price cycles

the early 2000s. The last upturn, however, has been much larger and longer than the first two.

The fact that the last upturn has been larger and longer has implications for the downturn phase. Stylized facts on the duration and amplitude of house price cycles suggest that, the longer and higher prices go up, the more they will come down (Igan and Loungani, 2011). The average upturn during the past cycles in a sample of OECD countries lasted 20 quarters and prices rose by 48 percent while the downturn lasted 18 quarters and prices fell by 23 percent. In the present cycle, the upturn was 38 quarters and prices increased by a mind-blowing 126 percent. The downturn has so far spanned 20 quarters with the price fall reaching about 20 percent. This comparison suggests that real house prices at a global scale may still continue their path downward for a couple more years.

What matters even more for policymakers is the fact that housing cycles are closely intertwined with credit and business cycles (these linkages and the reasons behind them will be discussed more in the next section on the case for policy action in response to housing cycles). In general, credit and house prices cycles tend to be slightly more protracted on average than business cycles but the peaks and the troughs are not too far from each other across cycles in different markets. Credit and housing (both in terms of price and quantity – proxied by residential investment) cycles also tend to have larger swings than real activity cycles. Housing cycles lead credit and business cycles over the long run, reflecting housing's feature as an asset whose value is ultimately driven by "fundamentals" in the long run.

It is important to note that there are significant differences across countries in terms of these general patterns. In particular, the legal and institutional structure of housing finance systems (often emerging as a product of historical events), the degree of government intervention, and supply responsiveness are crucial elements determining the characteristics of housing cycles and the degree of spillover to the rest of the economy. For example, the presence of mortgage equity withdrawal, prevalence of variable-rate mortgages, typical loan-to-value ratios, etc. have bearings on the strength of wealth effects on consumption that may emerge as a result of a surge in house prices. Similarly, housing credit provision by government-owned and government-sponsored entities, rent controls, social housing initiatives, tax treatment of housing, etc. may introduce a wedge between rents and house prices with implications for housing tenure choice and economic activity. Geographical conditions as well as urban planning policies can amplify cycles and affect how cyclical movements in house prices and construction activity spill over to the other parts of the economy. As a result, the estimated impact of a decline in house prices on

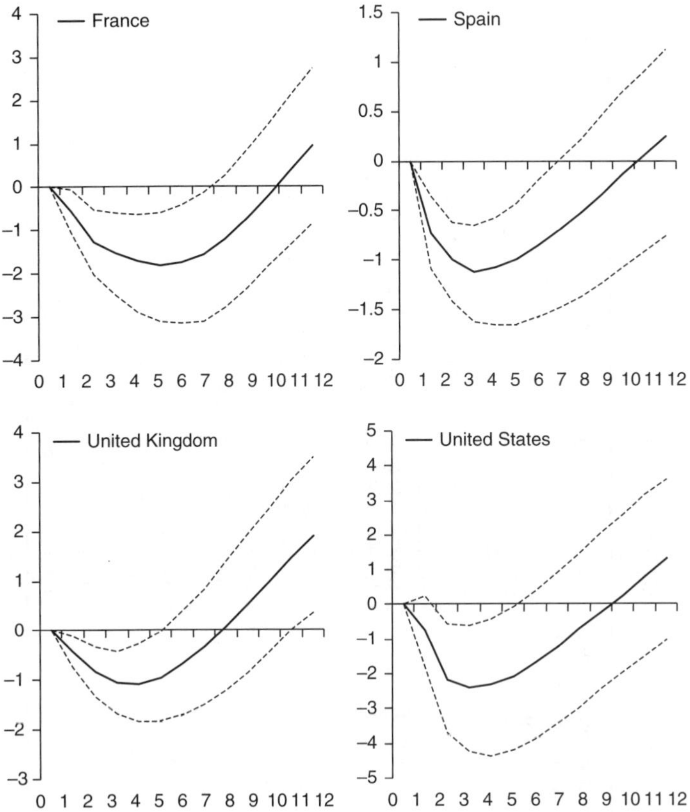

Figure 13.2 Economic impact of house price declines

real GDP varies considerably across countries (Figure 13.2). Some of these differences can be traced back, for instance, to the features of the mortgage markets (Table 13.1).

At a cross-sectional perspective, it is interesting to observe that country cycles are largely driven by global factors whose role has increased over time, especially for credit and business cycles, and that U.S. cycles tend to lead other countries' respective cycles (Igan et al., 2009).

What does such a state of knowledge imply for conduct of macroeconomic policy in relation to real estate markets? There appear to be two broad lessons. First, a uniform policy prescription of taking into account asset prices in monetary policy making is probably not the wisest direction. Statistical properties of housing cycles vary across countries. In addition, some shocks to house price inflation appear to be persistent, suggesting

Table 13.1 Mortgage market characteristics and economic impact of house price declines

	Average estimated impact on GDP by VAR analysis (in percent)	Countries included in the calculation of average impact
Penalty-fee prepayment and refinancing		
available	−2.77	Australia, Denmark, Japan, United Kingdom, United States
not available	−1.71	Austria, Belgium, Canada, Finland, France, Germany, Greece, Italy, Netherlands, Norway, Spain, Sweden
Option to withdraw mortgage equity		
available	−2.27	Australia, Canada, Denmark, Finland, Greece, Ireland, Japan, Netherlands, Norway, Sweden, United Kingdom, United States
not available	−1.61	Austria, Belgium, France, Germany, Italy, Spain
Typical loan-to-value ratio at origination		
less than or equal to 60 percent	−0.06	Austria, Italy
between 60 and 79 percent	−1.67	Canada, Finland, France, Germany, Norway, Spain, United Kingdom
more than or equal to 80 percent	−2.21	Australia, Belgium, Denmark, Ireland, Japan, Netherlands, Sweden, United States

that monetary policy should not react to such a shock at all. Second, domestically-focused policies may not be enough. The role of global factors has increased even for the ultimate nontradable good (i.e., real estate) and the room for policy coordination across borders has potentially grown.

Before we move on to discussing the case for policy intervention and the available policy options in detail, a word on challenges facing the researchers focusing on the nexus of macroeconomics and real estate markets is warranted. Availability of reliable data continues to be a major issue. After the global financial crisis, there have been several initiatives to fill the information gap on this front. Badly-needed improvement in construction of harmonized time series of real estate prices and information gathering on other indicators such as transactions, construction, mortgages as well as legal and structural characteristics are in progress. Meanwhile, initiatives to improve provision of data at the micro level (e.g., households, loans, banks regarding their real-estate-related activities) should also be a part of the agenda. These initiatives would help with a more in-depth analysis of real estate market characteristics and policy effectiveness, our understanding of which is still in its infancy, as is discussed in more detail below.

3. THE CASE FOR POLICY ACTION ON REAL ESTATE BOOMS

3.1 Leverage and the Link to Crises

From a macroeconomic stability perspective, what matters may be not the boom in itself, but how it is funded. Busts tend to be more costly when booms are financed through credit and leveraged institutions are directly involved. This is because the balance sheets of borrowers (and lenders) deteriorate sharply when asset prices fall. When banks are involved, this can lead to a credit crunch with negative consequences for real economic activity. In contrast, booms with limited leverage and bank involvement tend to deflate without major economic disruptions. For example, the burst of the dot-com bubble was followed by a relatively mild recession, reflecting the minor role played by leverage and bank credit in funding the boom.

Real estate markets are special along both these dimensions. The vast majority of home purchases and commercial real estate transactions in advanced economies involve borrowing. And banks and other levered players are actively involved in the financing. Moreover, homebuyers are allowed leverage ratios orders of magnitude higher than for any other investment activity. A typical mortgage loan carries a loan-to-value ratio of 71 percent on average across a global sample of countries. In contrast, stock market participation by individuals hardly ever relies on borrowed funds. And when it does, loans are subject to margin calls that prevent the buildup of highly leveraged positions.

During the recent crisis, highly leveraged housing markets had a prominent role, but this pattern is not limited to the United States, nor is it new to this crisis. The amplitude of house price upturns prior to 2007 is statistically associated with the severity of the crisis across countries (Claessens et al., 2010). Put differently, the U.S. market may have been the initial trigger, but the countries that experienced the most severe downturns were those with real estate booms of their own. And, historically, many major banking distress episodes have been associated with boom-bust cycles in property prices (Reinhart and Rogoff, 2008). A distinguishing feature of "bad" real estate boom-bust episodes seems to be coincidence between the boom and the rapid increase in leverage and exposure of households and financial intermediaries. In the most recent episode, almost all the countries with "twin booms" in real estate and credit markets (21 out of 23) ended up suffering from either a financial crisis or a severe drop in GDP growth rate. Eleven of these countries actually suffered from both damage to the financial sector and a sharp drop in economic activity. In contrast, of the seven countries that experienced a real estate boom but not a credit boom, only two went through a systemic crisis and they, on average, had relatively mild recessions.

3.2 Wealth and Supply-side Effects

Real estate is an important, if not the most important, storage of wealth in the economy. Additionally, the majority of households tend to hold wealth in their homes rather than in equities. Typically, in advanced economies less than half of households own stock (directly or indirectly) while homeownership rates hover around 65 percent. In addition, the supply-side effects can be substantial. In most advanced economies, house price cycles tend to lead credit and business cycles (Igan et al., 2009). This suggests that fluctuations in house prices create ripples in the economy through their impact on residential investment, consumption, and credit while the reverse effect is not as prominent, implying that the housing sector can be a *source* of shocks. Recessions that coincide with a house price bust tend to be deeper and last longer than those that do not, and their cumulative losses are three times the damage done during recessions without busts. Again, by contrast, recessions that occur around equity price busts are not significantly more severe or persistent than those that do not (Claessens et al., 2008).

3.3 Illiquidity, Opacity, and Network Effects

Boom-bust cycles are an intrinsic feature of real estate markets. This reflects delays in supply response to demand shocks and the slow pace of price discovery due to opaque and infrequent trades as well as illiquidity owing to high transaction costs and the virtual impossibility of short sales. In other words, real estate prices and construction activity can be expected to display large swings over long periods, even absent the distortions due to institutional features of real estate finance and policy actions. Network externalities also complicate the picture. Homeowners in financial distress have diminished incentives to maintain their properties and do not internalize the effects of this behavior on their neighbors. Similarly, foreclosures reduce the value of neighboring properties beyond their effect through fire sales. The double role of real estate as investment and consumption good may reduce mobility and increase structural unemployment, as households in negative equity may be reluctant or unable to sell and take advantage of job opportunities elsewhere. Hence, a housing bust may weaken the positive association between employment growth and mobility.

4. POLICY OPTIONS

The crisis has lent some support to the camp favoring early intervention in real estate boom-bust cycles. If we accept that intervention may be warranted although it is difficult to separate good from bad booms, the question arises as to which policy lever is best suited to reining in the latter. The main risks from real estate boom-bust cycles come from increased leverage in both the real (in particular, households) and financial sectors. Then, policies should, whenever possible, aim at containing these risks rather than price increases. In that context, policies should target two main objectives (not to be taken as a mutually exclusive categorization): (i) preventing real estate booms and the associated leverage buildup altogether, (ii) increasing the resilience of the financial system to a real estate bust. Table 13.2 gives a summary of policy measures available towards these objectives along with their pros and cons.

What follows are explorations. The narrative focuses on residential real estate but several (although not all) of the measures discussed would easily apply to commercial real estate booms as well. We examine the potential role of monetary, fiscal, and macroprudential policies. We discuss the

Table 13.2 Pros and cons of policy options to deal with real estate booms

	Potential impact	Side effects	Practical issues
Macroeconomic Policy			
Monetary measures			
Interest rates / Reserve requirements } responding to property prices and/or real estate loan growth	potential to prevent booms, less so to stop one that is already in progress	inflict damage to economic activity and welfare	identifying 'doomed' booms and reacting in time; constraints imposed by monetary regime
Fiscal measures			
Transaction / Capital gains taxes linked to real estate cycles	automatically dampen the boom phase	impair already slow price discovery process	incentive to avoid by misreporting, barter, folding the tax into the mortgage amount
Property taxes charged on market value	(could) limit price increase and volatility	–	little room for cyclical implementation
Abolition of mortgage interest deductibility	reduce incentives for household leverage and house price appreciation	(potentially) inflict damage on the real estate sector by taking away a sectoral advantage	little room for cyclical implementation

Regulatory Policy			
Macro-prudential measures			
Differentiated capital requirements for real estate loans Higher risk weights on real estate loans	increase cost of real estate borrowing while building buffer to cope with the downturn	costs associated with potential credit rationing	may get too complicated to enforce, especially in a cyclical context; effectiveness also limited when capital ratios are already high
Dynamic provisioning for loans collateralized by real estate	increase cost of real estate borrowing while building buffer to cope with the downturn	earnings management	data requirements and calibration
Limits on mortgage credit growth	(could) limit household leverage and house price appreciation	loss of benefits from financial deepening	move lending outside the regulatory periphery
Limits on exposure to real estate sector	(could) limit leverage and price appreciation as well as sensitivity of banks to certain shocks	costs associated with limiting benefits from specialization	shift lending to newcomers for whom exposure limits do not yet bind or outside the regulatory periphery
Limits on loan-to-value ratio Limits on debt-to-income ratio	(could) limit household leverage and house price appreciation while decreasing probability of default	costs associated with potential credit rationing	calibration is difficult, circumvention is easy

benefits and challenges associated with the various policy options, using case studies of countries with experience in the use of particular measures and, where possible, cross-country evidence.

4.1 Monetary Policy

Can monetary tightening stop or contain a real estate boom? An increase in the policy rate makes borrowing more expensive and reduces the demand for loans. Besides, higher interest payments lower affordability and shrink the number of borrowers that qualify for a loan of a certain amount. Indirectly, to the extent that monetary tightening reduces leverage in the financial sector, it may alleviate the financial consequences of a bust even if it does not stop the boom (De Nicolo et al., 2010).

Yet, monetary policy is a blunt instrument for this task. First, it affects the entire economy and is likely to entail substantial costs if the boom is limited to the real estate market. Put differently, a reduction in the risk of a real estate boom-bust cycle may come at the cost of a larger output gap and the associated higher unemployment rate (and possibly an inflation rate below the desired target range). Obviously, these concerns are diminished when the boom occurs in the context (or as a consequence) of general macroeconomic overheating.

A second concern is that, during booms, the expected return on real estate can be much higher than what can be affected by a marginal change in the policy rate. It follows that monetary tightening may not directly affect the speculative component of demand. If that is the case, it may have the perverse effect of leading borrowers towards more dangerous forms of loans. For instance, in the Czech Republic, Hungary, and Poland, monetary tightening led to decreased domestic currency lending but accelerated foreign-currency-denominated loans (Brzoza-Brzezina et al., 2007). Moreover, under free capital mobility, the effectiveness of monetary policy may be limited, especially for not-fully-flexible exchange rate regimes. Finally, the structure of the mortgage market also matters: in systems where mortgage rates depend primarily on long-term rates, the effectiveness of monetary policy will depend on the relationship between long and short rates.

To a large extent, empirical evidence supports these concerns, leading to the bottom line that monetary policy could in principle stop a boom, but at a very high cost. Policymakers would have to "lean against the wind" dramatically to have a meaningful impact on real estate prices and credit, with large effects on output and inflation. This is confirmed by a panel vector autoregression, which suggests that, at a 5-year horizon, a 100 basis point hike in the policy rate would reduce house price appreciation by only

1 percentage point, compared to a historical average of 5 percent increase per year (see Crowe et al., 2011, for details). But it would also lead to a decline in GDP growth of 0.3 percentage points.

4.2 Fiscal Tools

A variety of fiscal measures (transaction taxes, property taxes, deductibility of interest payments) bears on the decision to invest in real estate. The result is often a socially driven favorable treatment of homeownership (and sometimes housing-related debt). In theory, some of these fiscal tools could be adjusted cyclically to influence house price volatility, while preserving the favorable treatment of homeownership on average over the cycle.

Yet, if the net present value of all future taxes are capitalized in property prices, adjusting taxes countercyclically around the same expected mean would not affect the prices. Also, the evidence on the relationship between the tax treatment of residential property and real estate cycles is inconclusive: during the most recent global house price boom, real house prices increased significantly in some countries with tax systems that are highly favorable to housing (such as Sweden) as well as in countries with relatively unfavorable tax rules (such as France). Similarly, appreciation was muted in countries with both favorable systems (e.g., Portugal) and unfavorable ones (e.g., Japan). Overall, taxation was not the main driver of house price developments during the recent global housing boom (Keen et al., 2010).

Technical and political economy problems may further complicate implementation of cyclically adjusted fiscal measures. In most countries, tax policy is separated from monetary and financial regulation policies, making it extremely hard to implement changes in tax policies as part of a cyclical response with financial stability as the main objective. Instead, local governments may use lower property or transaction taxes to attract residents during good times if the burden in the case of a bust is shared with other jurisdictions. The ability of cyclical transaction taxes to contain exuberant behavior may be further compromised if homebuyers do not respond to these taxes fully, because they consider them to be an acceptable cost for an investment with high returns and consumption value. Also, during a boom phase, the incentives to "ride the bubble" may increase efforts to circumvent the measure by misreporting property values or folding the tax into the overall mortgage amount. Finally, as with most tax measures, the distortions created by a cyclical transaction tax may make it more difficult to evaluate a property, which already tends to be a hard task, and may also affect the mobility of households, with potential implications for the labor market.

4.3 Macroprudential Regulation

At least in theory, macroprudential measures such as higher capital requirements or limits on various aspects of mortgage credit could be designed to target narrow objectives (for instance, household or bank leverage) and tackle the risks associated with real estate booms more directly and at a lower cost than with monetary or fiscal policy.

Against the benefit of a lower cost, these measures are likely to present two shortcomings. First, they may be easier to circumvent as they target a specific type of contracts or group of agents. When this happens, these measures can be counterproductive, as they may lead to liability structures that are more difficult to resolve/renegotiate in busts. Second, they may be more difficult to implement from a political economy standpoint since their use could be considered an unnecessary intrusion into the functioning of markets and since winners and losers would be more evident than in the case of macro policies.

We focus our analysis on three specific sets of measures: (1) capital requirements or risk weights that change with the real estate cycle, (2) dynamic provisioning (the practice of increasing banks' loan loss provisions during the upswing phase of the cycle), (3) cyclical tightening/easing of eligibility criteria for real estate loans through loan-to-value (LTV) and debt-to-income (DTI) ratios. These tools may be able to achieve both objectives: (i) reducing the likelihood and/or magnitude of a real estate boom (for instance, by imposing measures to limit household leverage), and (ii) strengthening the financial system against the effects of a real estate bust (for example, by urging banks to save in good times for rainy days).

A major limitation in assessing the effectiveness of macroprudential tools stems from the fact that macroprudential policy frameworks are still in their infancy, and only a handful of countries have actively used them. And these measures have been typically used in combination with macroeconomic policy and direct interventions to the supply side of housing markets (such as in Singapore), further complicating the challenge to attribute outcomes to specific tools.

Yet, much can be learned from case studies. Following the Asian crisis, some countries in the region took a more heavy-handed approach to deal with risks posed by real estate booms. Countries in Central and Eastern Europe experimented with various measures to control the rapid growth in bank credit to the private sector in the 2000s. Others put in place a dynamic provisioning framework. On the whole, success stories appear to be few, perhaps to some extent reflecting the learning curve in expanding the policy toolkit, improving the design of specific tools, and sorting out implementation challenges. But, when policy succeeded in slowing down a boom and avoiding a systemic crisis in a bust, it almost always involved some macroprudential measures (a detailed account of these cases is in Crowe et al., 2011).

4.3.1 Higher capital requirements/risk weights

Capital regulation has a procyclical effect on the supply of credit. During upswings, better fundamentals reduce the riskiness of a given loan portfolio, improving a bank's capital adequacy ratio and its ability to expand its assets. In a downturn, the opposite happens. Procyclical capital requirements could help reduce this bias. Further, by forcing banks to hold more capital in good times, it would help build buffers for future losses.

For real estate loans, the procyclical element of capital regulation is largely absent. In most countries, existing rules do not take collateral values into consideration or reflect the heterogeneity among loans backed by real estate, other than the commercial-residential distinction. Under Basel II's standard approach, risk weights for property loans are fixed (50 percent for residential mortgages and 100 percent for commercial property loans). As a result, mortgage loans with predictably different default probabilities (for instance, because of different LTV ratios or exposure to different aggregate shocks) are often bundled in the same risk category and no adjustment is made over time to account for the real estate cycle. In this context, capital requirements or risk weights linked to real estate price dynamics could help limit the consequences of boom-bust cycles. By forcing banks to hold more capital against real estate loans during booms, these measures could build a buffer against the losses during busts. And, by increasing the cost of credit, they might reduce demand and contain real estate prices themselves. Finally, weights could be fine-tuned to target regional booms.

A few caveats are in order. First, absent more risk-sensitive weights, an across-the-board increase in risk weights (or capital requirements) carries the danger of pushing lenders in the direction of riskier loans. Thus, the introduction of procyclical risk weights for real estate loans should be accompanied by the implementation of a finer cross-sectional risk classification as well. Second, as with any other measure increasing the cost of bank credit (when credit is in high demand), procyclical risk weights may be circumvented through recourse to nonbank intermediaries, foreign banks, and off-balance-sheet activities. Third, these measures will lose effectiveness when actual bank capital ratios are well in excess of regulatory minima (as often happens during booms). Fourth, while improving the resilience of the banking system to busts, tighter requirements are unlikely to have a major effect on credit availability and prices. Put differently, they are unlikely to reduce vulnerabilities in the real (household) sector. Finally, regulators may be reluctant to allow banks to reduce risk weights during a bust (when borrowers become less creditworthy).

The empirical evidence on the effectiveness of these measures is mixed. In an effort to contain the rapid growth in bank credit to the private sector and the associated boom in asset markets, several countries have raised capital requirements and/or risk weights on particular groups of real estate loans. Some attempts (such as the cases of Bulgaria, Croatia, Estonia, and Ukraine) failed to stop the boom; others (such as the case of Poland) were at least a partial success. Yet, it is not easy to say why measures taken in one country may have been more effective than those taken elsewhere or how much other developments account for the observed changes. Furthermore, even in countries where tighter capital requirements appeared to produce some results on controlling the growth of particular groups of loans, real estate price appreciation and the overall credit growth remained strong.

4.3.2 Dynamic provisioning

Dynamic provisioning (the practice of mandating higher loan loss provisions during upswings and one of the elements in Basel III) can help limit credit cycles. The mechanics and benefits are similar to those of procyclical capital requirements. By forcing banks to build (in good times) an extra buffer of provisions, it can help cope with the potential losses that come when the cycle turns (see, for example, the case of Spain). It is, however, unlikely to cause a major increase in the cost of credit, and thus to stop a boom. That said, one advantage over cyclical capital requirements is that dynamic provisioning would not be subject to minima as capital requirements are, so it can be used when capital ratios maintained by banks are already high. Provisioning for property loans could be made a specific function of house price dynamics. In periods of booming prices, banks would be forced to increase provisioning, which they would be allowed to wind down during busts. As in the case of risk weights, provisioning requirements could depend on the geographical allocation of a bank's real estate portfolio.

This measure is primarily targeted at protecting the banking system from the consequences of a bust rather than having a significant impact on credit and containing other vulnerabilities, such as increases in debt and leverage in the household sector. In addition, practical issues and unintended effects such as calibration of rules with rather demanding data requirements and earnings management (which may raise issues with tax authorities and securities markets regulators) should be discussed in each country's context to design a framework that best fits the country's circumstances. There are also other shortcomings, similar to those of procyclical risk weights (being primarily targeted at commercial banks, dynamic provisioning may be circumvented by intermediaries outside of the regulatory perimeter). Lastly, application of the measure only to domestically regulated banks may hurt their competitiveness and shift lending to banks abroad, raising cross-border supervision issues.

The experience with these measures suggests that they are effective in strengthening a banking system against the effects of a bust, but do little to stop the boom itself. Spain led the countries that have adopted countercyclical provisioning and constitutes an interesting case study for a preliminary assessment of its effectiveness. Starting in 2000 and with a major revision in 2004, the Bank of Spain required banks to accumulate additional provisions based on the "latent loss" in their loan portfolios (for more details on the Spanish dynamic provisioning framework, see Saurina, 2009). Dynamic provisions forced banks to set aside, on average, the equivalent of 10 percent of their net operating income. Yet, household leverage grew by a still-high 62 percent in Spain. At the end of 2007, just when the real estate bust started, total accumulated provisions covered 1.3 percent of total consolidated assets, in addition to the 5.8 percent covered by capital and reserves (for some perspective, the value of the housing stock has, so far, decreased by roughly 15 percent in real terms). Hence, Spanish banks had an important buffer that strengthened their balance sheets when real estate prices started to decline and the economy slipped into recession.

4.3.3 Limits on loan-to-value and debt-to-income ratios

A limit on LTV can help prevent the buildup of vulnerabilities on the borrower side. The lower the leverage, the greater the drop in prices needed to put a borrower into negative equity. This will likely reduce defaults when the bust comes as more borrowers unable to keep up with their mortgages will be able to sell their houses. In addition, in case of default, lenders will be able to obtain higher recovery ratios. On the macro front, a limit on LTV will reduce the risk that a large sector of the real economy ends up with a severe debt overhang. In addition, it will reduce the pool of borrowers that can obtain funding (for a given price) and thus will reduce demand pressures and contain the boom.

Similar to limits on LTV, DTI limits will rein in the purchase power of individuals, reducing the pressure on real estate prices. In particular, they will be effective in containing speculative demand (they will screen out borrowers that would qualify for a mortgage only on the assumption the house would be quickly turned around). They will also reduce vulnerabilities, as borrowers will have an "affordability" buffer and will be more resilient to a decline in their income or temporary unemployment.

Careful design of these measures is key to limit circumvention. For instance, in Korea, lower LTV limits for loans with less than three years of maturity spurred a boom in loans originated with maturity of three years *and* one day. In the United States, during the housing boom, the practice of combining two or more loans to avoid mortgage insurance (which kicked in when LTV exceeded 80 percent) became common. Similarly, an obvious way to get around a DTI limit would be to extend sequential loans and report the ratios separately. In Hong Kong SAR, where regulators impose maximum limits on the debt service ratio (which takes into account the payments the borrower has to make on non-mortgage loans as well), supervisors often encounter cases where lenders do not report all outstanding debt obligations. Circumvention may entail significant costs, as it may result in liability structures that can complicate debt resolution during busts (for example, in the United States, it is often second-lien holders that object to restructuring). In addition, circumvention may also involve shifting of risks not only across mortgage loan products, but also outside the regulatory perimeter, through expansion of credit by nonbank, less-regulated financial institutions and/or by foreign banks (which may result in increased currency mismatches as the proportion of foreign-currency-denominated loans rises).

The narrow target nature of these measures may increase political economy obstacles (as happened in the case of Israel), particularly since the groups more impacted by LTV and DTI limits tend to be those more in need of credit (poorer and younger individuals). In addition, unlike with more "macro" measures, the consequences of these limits are immediate and transparent. Beyond these political economy considerations, LTV and DTI limits, by rationing sensitive groups out of credit markets, will entail a cost in terms of diminished intertemporal consumption smoothing and lower investment efficiency.

The scant existing empirical evidence suggests that these are promising measures. For example, in a simple cross-section of 21 (mostly) developed countries, maximum LTV limits are positively related to house price appreciation between 2000 and 2007 (Figure 13.3). And back-of-the-envelope calculations suggest that a 10 percentage point increase in maximum LTV allowed by regulations is associated with a 13 percent increase in nominal house prices (see also Duca et al., 2010).

Experiences of countries that experimented with changing mandatory LTV limits in response to real estate market developments also suggest that doing so can be quite effective. When the Korean authorities introduced LTV limits in September 2002, month-on-month change in house prices decreased by 3 percentage points immediately and remained low until April 2003. A similar pattern applies to DTI limits, with month-on-month change dropping by 2 percentage points in August 2005 with the introduction of the measure. Interestingly, the measures had a much

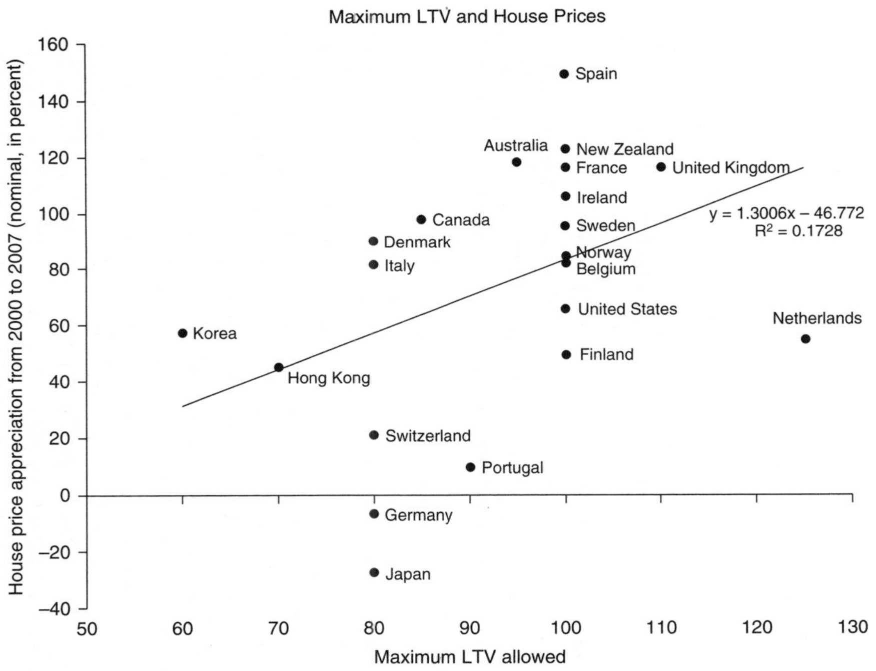

Notes: Maximum LTV allowed refer to new mortgage loans and, in most cases, shows the limits over which additional requirements such as mortgage insurance would apply.

Sources: BIS, OECD, UNECE, ECLAC, IDB, European Mortgage Federation, International Union for Housing Finance, International Union of Tenants, National statistics, and central bank statistics.

Figure 13.3 House price appreciation and loan-to-value ratio smaller (or no) impact on prices in "non-speculative" areas where the limits were untouched. The impact on year-on-year changes, however, has been smaller, since prices tend to start increasing at a faster pace again after the first immediate reaction. In Hong Kong SAR, prudent lending practices guided by LTV and DTI limits have been credited with pausing the house price boom briefly in 1994 and guarding the system against the fallout from the crash in 1997 (Wong et al., 2004; also see Wong et al., 2011).

5. WHO SHOULD CONTROL THE MACROPRUDENTIAL LEVER?

If, as suggested in the analysis above, macroprudential tools are to play an important role in how authorities deal with real-estate booms and busts, the question arises of who should be in charge of macroprudential policy. Economists and policy makers are still far from reaching a consensus on this question. What follows are preliminary explorations.

Several issues bear on the question of who should control the macroprudential lever, and, in particular, on whether it would be better to centralize monetary and macroprudential policies under one roof or to keep them under separate agencies. First, as in other policy contexts, there exists a trade-off between policy coordination and credibility. Second, there is the issue of information sharing (the debacle in dealing with the Northern Rock crisis highlighted the problems associated with agency coordination). Third, since expertise is path dependent, there is the issue of how to best exploit the experience and talent already accumulated in existing agencies. This is especially critical in small countries in which there may be a shortage of human resources. This section focuses primarily on the game-theoretical problems associated with the first issue.

Start with separate agencies with different mandates. Think about a central bank (pretty much like those we have now) in charge of monetary policy and tasked with price and output stability. It is obviously not indifferent to bank risk taking and financial stability, but puts greater weight and priority on its traditional mandate: low inflation and output gap. Think about a financial authority in charge of macroprudential policy and tasked with macro-financial stability. It does care about inflation and growth, but not for themselves, only to the extent that they affect the stability of balance sheets. It focuses on things like credit growth, leverage, and debt overhang, that more directly affect financial stability.

In principle, this is a simple problem. We have two instruments (the policy rate and macroprudential policy) and two objectives (some combination of output/price-stability and financial stability). The complication is that each instrument affects both objectives. Interest rates will affect behavior in financial markets and macroprudential policy will, through its effects on the cost of credit, affect aggregate demand. This means that policy action by one regulator entails an externality for the objectives of the other. Absent other issues, the obvious solution to solve an externality is consolidation: put everything under one roof. A centralized authority will always be able to replicate what independent regulators would do. However, separate agencies playing Nash may not end up coordinating on the first-best centralized solution.

The example of the relationship between fiscal and monetary authorities may be useful. Relative to the coordinated solution, the Treasury will push for greater output (a larger deficit) anticipating that the central bank will increase interest rates in reaction. The CB will keep interest rates higher as it will assume that the Treasury will run a larger deficit. The result will be an equilibrium where the deficit and the policy rate are both higher than optimal (implying more crowding out).

One can imagine a similar game between the central bank and the macroprudential regulator. For example, in a recession, the central bank may cut the policy rate aggressively to stimulate demand. Worried about the effects of a relaxed monetary stance on risk taking, the financial authority reacts by tightening macroprudential regulation. Anticipating this response and its contractionary effect on demand, the central banks cut rates even more aggressively. And so on. The outcome is a policy mix with too low interest rates and too tight macroprudential measures relative to what a coordinated solution would deliver.

The problem is that there is a second complication: Policy effectiveness (especially on the monetary policy front) depends critically on the credibility of institutions. And this will be inevitably undermined when an institution is tasked with potentially conflicting objectives.

Again, the example of fiscal and monetary policy is useful. It was concluded long ago that central bank independence from the Treasury is critical to preserve price stability. Absent independence, the credibility of the central bank will be challenged by concerns about its willingness to act against inflation, as it may be too concerned about output and the effects of an increase in interest rates on public deficits (see Barro and Gordon, 1983).

A similar argument can be made for separation between monetary and macroprudential policymaking. Take the case of an economy with rising inflation, but too little risk taking that has resulted in stagnant credit (for example after some shock has raised risk aversion). A joint regulatory authority will have a harder time convincing the public that it will fight inflation (and thus anchor expectations), when this conflicts with the other objective. This, in turn, will worsen the sacrifice ratio (as for the fiscal/monetary policy case). Then, a Nash game between two separate independent regulators may dominate the coordinated solution.

The key tradeoff is, then, between coordination and credibility. In the absence of credibility issues, a joint regulator will always be preferable (although in the absence of conflicts, coordination can help in reducing the shortcomings of separate agencies). But if credibility is central and conflicts between the two objectives are likely, the preferable solution will entail separate and independent authorities.

The optimal structure may depend on the relative weight of these concerns and needs to figure in the remaining aspects that were mentioned at the outset. In that context, when the policymakers are closely aligned institutionally, as under the new arrangements in the United Kingdom and the EU (ECB, ESRB), separate accountability arrangements for monetary and macroprudential policy may help address credibility concerns (see IMF, 2011).

6. CONCLUDING REMARKS

The correct policy response to real estate booms is, like many other policymaking decisions, an art more than a science. Macroprudential measures seem to be the best option to achieve the objective of curbing real estate prices and leverage because they attack the problem at its source, adapt to specific circumstances in different locations at different times, and give the added benefit of increasing the resilience of the banking system.

Ultimately, policy recommendations depend on the characteristics of the real estate boom in question (Figure 13.4). If property prices are out of sync with income and rent, *and* leverage is increasing rapidly, taking action is advisable. In deciding which policy option to choose, policymakers should adopt a wider view of the economy and complement targeted measures with broader macroeconomic tightening if the boom is a part or reflection of general overheating in the economy.

Looking ahead, should a more proactive use of macroprudential tools become the norm, the question arises of who should be in control of these levers. In particular, the close interaction with monetary policy raises the question of whether the central bank should be charged with both price and financial stability. In that context, a trade-off emerges between policy credibility/accountability and the efficiencies stemming from coordination. When the former is paramount, separate agencies are preferable. When the latter prevails, a centralized solution would dominate.

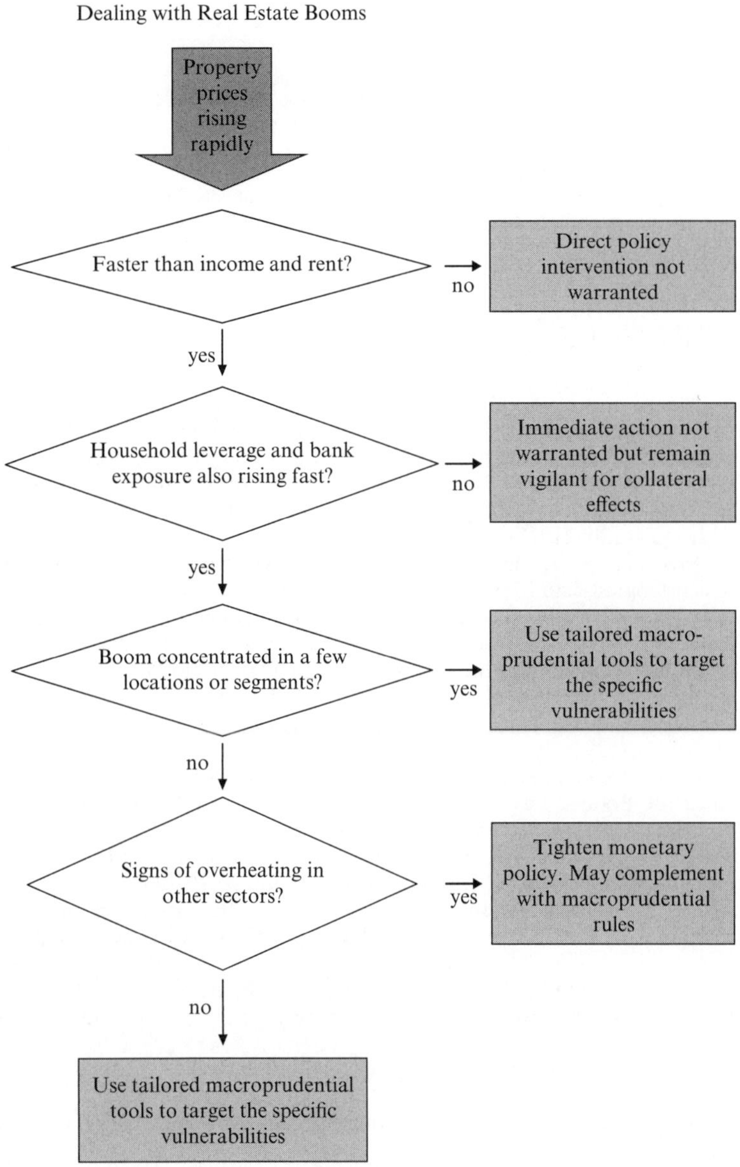

Figure 13.4 Policy recommendations to deal with real estate booms

NOTE

* This chapter derives from "Policies for Macrofinancial Stability: Options to Deal with Real Estate Booms," available as IMF Staff Discussion Note No. 11/02 and co-authored with Christopher Crowe and Pau Rabanal as well as "How to Deal with Real Estate Booms: Lessons from Country Experiences,"*Journal of Financial Stability*, volume 9 (3), pages 300–319. The authors thank the participants at the BOK-IMF Workshop on Managing Real Estate Booms and Busts for useful comments. The views expressed here are those of the authors and do not necessarily represent those of the IMF, its Executive Board, or its Management.

REFERENCES

Barro, Robert, and David Gordon, 1983, "Rules, discretion and reputation in a model of monetary policy", Journal of Monetary Economics, 12 (1).

Bernanke, B.S., 2002, "Asset Price Bubbles and Monetary Policy," Remarks before the New York Chapter of the National Association for Business Economics, New York, NY, Oct. 15 (available at http://www.federalreserve.gov/boarddocs/speeches/2002/20021015/).

Brzoza-Brzezina, M., T. Chmielewski, and J. Niedzwiedzinska, 2007, "Substitution between Domestic and Foreign Currency Loans in Central Europe: Do Central Banks Matter?" National Bank of Poland Working Paper.

Claessens, S., M.A. Kose, and M.E. Terrones, 2008, "What Happens During Recessions, Crunches and Busts?" IMF Working Paper No. 08/274.

Claessens, S., G. Dell'Ariccia, D. Igan, and L. Laeven, 2010, "Cross-Country Experiences and Policy Implications from the Global Financial Crisis," *Economic Policy* 25, 267–293.

Crowe, C., G. Dell'Ariccia, D. Igan, and P. Rabanal, 2011, "How to Deal with Real Estate Booms: Lessons from Country Experiences," IMF Working Paper No. 11/91; and *Journal of Financial Stability*, 9 (3), pages 300–319.

De Nicolo, G., G. Dell'Ariccia, L. Laeven, and F. Valencia, 2010, "Monetary Policy and Risk Taking," IMF Staff Position Note No. 2010/09.

Duca, J.V., J. Muellbauer, and A. Murphy, 2010, "House Prices and Credit Constraints: Making Sense of the U.S. Experience," Oxford University Working Paper.

Igan, D., A.N. Kabundi, F. Nadal-De Simone, M. Pinheiro, and N.T. Tamirisa, 2009, "Three Cycles: Housing, Credit, and Real Activity," IMF Working Paper No. 09/231.

Igan, D., and P. Loungani, 2011, "Global Housing Cycles," forthcoming IMF Working Paper.

IMF, 2011, "Institutional Models for Macroprudential Policy," Staff Discussion Note No. 11/18.

Keen, M., A. Klemm, and V. Perry, 2010, "Tax and the Crisis," *Fiscal Studies* 31 (1), 43–79.

Reinhart, C.M., and K.S. Rogoff, 2008, "This Time Is Different: A Panoramic View of Eight Centuries of Financial Crises," unpublished manuscript.

Saurina, J., 2009, "Dynamic Provisioning: The Experience of Spain," Crisis Response Note 7, The World Bank Group.

Wong, J., L. Fung, T. Fong, and A. Sze, 2004, "Residential Mortgage Default Risk in Hong Kong," Hong Kong Monetary Authority Working Paper.

Wong, E., T. Fong, K. Li, and H. Choi, 2011, "Loan-to-Value Ratio as a Macroprudential Tool: Hong Kong's Experience and Cross-Country Evidence," Hong Kong Monetary Authority Working Paper No. 01/2011.

Index